641.3372 Heiss, Mary Lou.
HEI
        The story of tea.

$29.95

THE STORY OF TEA

THE STORY OF TEA

A Cultural History and Drinking Guide

MARY LOU HEISS AND ROBERT J. HEISS

TEN SPEED PRESS
Berkeley | Toronto

Ten Speed Press
PO Box 7123
Berkeley, California 94707
www.tenspeed.com

Distributed in Australia by Simon and Schuster Australia, in Canada by Ten Speed Press
Canada, in New Zealand by Southern Publishers Group, in South Africa by Real Books,
and in the United Kingdom and Europe by Publishers Group UK.

Book design by Toni Tajima
All location photography by Mary Lou Heiss and Robert J. Heiss, except as noted in the
   captions.
Studio photography by Angie Cao, with styling by Bergren Rameson and photo assistance
   by Cody Pickens, on the front cover jacket and pages iii, 138, 189, 193, 194, 245, 255–73,
   275, 295, 299–301, 304, 306, 309, 313, 318–20, 322, 324, 330, 334–36, 342, 343,
   348, and 396.
Maps on pages 5 and 30 by Scott Lowry.

Library of Congress Cataloging-in-Publication Data
Heiss, Mary Lou.
   The story of tea : a cultural history and drinking guide / Mary Lou Heiss
and Robert J. Heiss.
      p. cm.
   Includes bibliographical references and index.
   ISBN-13: 978-1-58008-745-2
   ISBN-10: 1-58008-745-0
   1. Tea—History. 2. Cookery (Tea) I. Heiss, Robert J. II. Title.
   TX415.H44 2007
   641.3'372—dc22

                              2007007188

First printing, 2007
Printed in Korea

1 2 3 4 5 6 7 8 9 10 — 11 10 09 08 07

To William H. Ukers

You blazed the trail and in your footsteps we all follow.

CONTENTS

PREFACE

AS TEA MERCHANTS, we are drawn to teas that possess a distinctive style, teas that hold the feeling of the place where they were made in the folds and creases of their tiny leaves. We are captivated by the influence of what the French call *terroir*—that distinction of flavor akin to a cultural stamp of identity that undeniably pinpoints a product to its origin.

Terroir is determined by the physical realities of soil, altitude, climate, and geography, and also by the more evanescent and less apparent threads of history, cultural preferences, and tradition. All of these determinants consort to yield what author Fred Plotkin has referred to as "somewhereness." Think about a glass of chilled, effervescent Champagne or a mug of spicy, rich hot chocolate embellished with a touch of ground chile and cinnamon, and you are envisioning two great examples of "somewhereness." Each beverage is unique and specific to its "somewhere"; each is completely foreign in spirit to the other place.

Terroir exists for all foods, but the effects of terroir are most easily understood and tasted in such examples as coffee, cheese, olives and olive oil, rice, spirits, water, wine, and tea. Viewed in concert with these other food products, tea perhaps seems to be the simplest of the group—a humble green leaf that is plucked from a bush, then dried and brewed. In fact, the experienced Chinese farmer who has a few tea bushes growing by his back door can simply pick and parch a few tea leaves in a hot wok over a charcoal fire pan for his own tea-drinking enjoyment.

But along its more than two-thousand-year journey to today, tea has developed into something much more complicated and place specific. Time has allowed for the creation of tens of thousands of different teas, each of which are produced by people who till the soil in a multitude of tea gardens large and small. The net result is a staggering amount of tea produced annually—not just tea, but different teas, unique teas, teas that are made nowhere else. Six classes of tea (each with several subclasses) have developed into an industry that ranges from vital to emergent in approximately fifty countries.

Statistics for worldwide tea consumption pegs tea as second only to water as the most commonly drunk liquid in the world.

In tea-producing countries, tea is as important to life as is food. Tea is consumed both as a thinking person's beverage and as an everyman's delight. Tea drinking is a tactile, sensory activity that provides both intellectual stimulation and aesthetic inspiration during times of social gathering or solitary contemplation. In the East tea is more highly regarded for these transcendental qualities than it is for its caffeine content or healthful benefits. The pleasurable ritual of tea drinking is deeply encoded in these cultures and religions, and tea permeates and sustains life in ways that those of us in the West simply fail to comprehend.

Our search for fine tea draws us back time and again to Asia, for tea that is carefully crafted in small villages by master tea processors who have learned their skills from previous tea masters. These tea processors will in turn pass their skills on to younger workers and to the new generation graduating from agricultural universities with degrees in tea management.

In some countries tea production is still very much hands-on work. Tea production is a combination of science and cooperation from nature along with the experienced senses of tea workers who can see, feel, and hear the elusive changes occurring in the transformation of the fresh leaf into finished tea. From hand-plucking to hand-sorting, to hand-processing to hand-sorting again, and finally to hand-packing, we are fascinated by tea that is made by human hands that have developed the necessary sense of touch and feel that we call "knowing." This human factor conveys—in hand movements, glances, and the concentration etched on the tea workers' faces— indefinable but almost tangible connections to the wisdom of the sages and the tea masters who came before.

From China to India to Sri Lanka these tea workers all share a common connection with the land and a keen awareness of the way their tea should be. Perhaps most important and most difficult to define is an appreciation for the way that the *leaf wants to be*. Experienced tea workers know to work *with* the leaf and the calendar, not against either. To pluck the right size leaf at the right time of the season, and leave the rest alone until its proper time, is a decision that can only be made from knowledge and experience. The same goes for knowing when to prune and when to let a plant rest. No calendar can tell a tea master when the precise moment is right to pluck the first tender tea sprouts that emerge in the earliest days of frost-laden spring.

Determining how long to let the tea wither, how long to roll it, to oxidize it, to fluff it, or how long to let it sit over the charcoal embers to dry is an art. The timing must be impeccable or the tea will be less than spectacular or ruined. An experienced tea master must pay attention not only to the progress of the leaf's transformation but also to the weather—the dryness, the humidity, the lack or abundance of rain.

When we visit tea-producing countries, we become the students to these masters. We are always humbled by the depths of their knowledge, their experience, and their willingness (despite the language pitfalls) to educate us so that we may in turn educate our customers and readers. For the past thirty years tea has played an important role in our Northampton, Massachusetts, shop Cooks Shop Here. Since those early days, tea became our passion. This book is our attempt to transmit the information and knowledge that we have garnered trekking along the tea trail to our interested readers. We hope to cut through the sometimes confusing prattle about tea by providing in-depth information and understanding about processes that many people have written about but few have actually witnessed.

Explaining to someone how something is made is always a tricky balance of deciding what information is important and to whom that information is relevant. Because we answer questions about tea every day in our shop (and have had hundreds of tea discussions with customers over the years), we have attempted to provide in this book material that appeals to beginning tea enthusiasts as well as to seasoned tea professionals. Our goal is to give readers the behind-the-scenes information about the life rhythms and work cycles in a tea village or factory. We also offer our sensibilities regarding the complexity and intrigue of an ancient beverage in today's fast-paced, modern world. If along the way we convert new enthusiasts into the ranks of regular tea drinkers, or if we pique readers' interests to branch out and try new teas, we will have been successful.

ACKNOWLEDGMENTS

AT THE BEGINNING OF THIS PROJECT, we hoped we would do justice to how extraordinarily fascinating and colorful the world of tea is. Thankfully, during our travels, research, and writing both in the United States and abroad, we found many kindred spirits who provided us with information, explanations, photographs, meals, travel guidance, language translation, delicious cups of rare and distinguished tea, compassion, and understanding, as well as friendship and congenial hospitality. Without them this book would not be possible, and with them we have succeeded in our task.

None of us in the tea industry would have a job were it not for the hard work and dedication of the tea pluckers, tea factory managers, and tea processors worldwide who continue to maintain high standards of excellence despite ever-increasing difficulties. To all of you, we bow in awe and gratitude.

Our understanding of the patterns of life in the tea gardens would all be academic rhetoric were it not for the men and women who welcomed us into their tea gardens, tea factories, tea research facilities, and university classrooms. Their efforts to educate us enabled us to observe and document the continuation of a time-honored, traditional craft. To all of you who are part of the success and the vigor of today's tea industry, we thank you from our hearts and wish you a thousand blessings.

Our literary agent, Lisa Ekus, steered us brilliantly and with great foresight to Ten Speed Press for this project. The trust and support we have found from Philip Wood, Lorena Jones, and Aaron Wehner at Ten Speed Press have allowed us to tell the story of tea from our insider's point of view. Our editor, Brie Mazurek, showed courage and forbearance in handling the onslaught of text and images, wrangling a sleek book with strong voice out of a mountain of information. Copyeditor Amy Smith Bell is to be commended for her fine, sensitive hand and dagger pencil. Studio photographer Angie Cao and stylist Bergren Rameson brought our collection of teawares to life in the studio.

And designer Toni Tajima created a visually stunning book that compliments the colorfulness and the humanity of the tea industry.

We wish to specifically thank the following colleagues and friends who helped us fill in the information gaps, understand the minutia of tea manufacturing techniques, and grasp the transitory nature of time, weather, and change over the course of a season in a tea garden in lands so far away.

For generosity without equal, we are grateful to Joel Schapira, who was there in the beginning and from whom we learned what matters, and Stephen Chao and Lydia Kung, who gave us undreamed-of opportunity and experiences. Words of thanks seem inadequate, so we will express our feelings by asking, "What's next?"

To our colleagues in Japan, who gave freely and generously of their time and energies to make our tea trip to Japan a full and extraordinary experience: Elizabeth Andoh; Den Shirakata and everyone at Shirakata-Denshiro Shoten; Dr. Kiyoshi Hayakawa and the Fukujuen Cha Research Center; Suichi Kawano, Kenji Tatsumi, and Hideaki Tokuda, at Kyoto Industrial Support Organization 21; Kono Maso, Haruhide Morita, Masashi Yamamoto, and Takahiro Yamamoto; Jun Yasunaga and members of Kyoohoo; Kotobuki Trading Co.; the Japan External Trade Organization; and the Eishunnji Temple.

For graciously unlocking the mysteries of Chinese tea for us, we express sincere appreciation to the Tea Boards of Anhui, Jiangxi, and Zhejiang Provinces, as well as the following individuals: *In Anhui:* Li Nian Hua, Jiang Ren Hua, Chen Lu, and Gao Man Li. *In Fujian:* Peter Wu, Wei Yue De, Wang Wu He, Jiang Yuanxun, Wang Gui Qing, and Lin Jing Qing. *In Jiangxi:* Hong Peng, Yu Guang Zhong, Yu Jing Hong, Yu Xin Chun, and Xu Yaojin. *In Sichuan:* Tang Xiaojun, Pan Guicheng, Chen Shuqiong, Professor Mu Jihong, Professor Liao Mingan, Professor Yao Jide, Wan Zhonglin, and Zeng Ying Hui. *In Yunnan:* Zheng Yue, Luo Nai Xin, Chen Guo Feng, and Dane Xuhe. *In Zhejiang:* Jianming Wu, Hairong Xu, He Bao Zhang, Wang Ya Tao, Wang Jia Yang, Mao Zhi Fang, Jin Zhong Ming, Yan Yuan Du, Li Jun, and Wei Cui Lan.

We also thank the numerous colleagues who donated their time and provided us with information beyond our experiences: Brother Anthony of Taizé in South Korea; Donald J. Baer and Beverly Clevidence, PhD, at Beltsville Human Nutrition Research Center, Agricultural Research Service, U.S. Department of Agriculture; Douglas A. Balantine; Saunam Bhattacharjee, at Tfactor Specialty Teas; Chinese Academy of Agricultural Sciences in Hangzhou, Zhejiang; Carl Chu; Richard Enticott, at Plantextrakt; Dilhan C. Fernando at Dilhma

Tea; Charlotte Gardner, at Nepal Himalayan Tea; Darra Goldstein, at *Gastro-nomica*; Christina Green, at the Gardiner Museum of Ceramic Art; William B. Hall, at the Charleston Tea Plantation; Mimi Hellman, Assistant Professor of Art and Art History at Skidmore College; Jim Herron Sr., at Simpson and Vail; Q Li Holmes; Sharon Hudgins; Elliott Johnson, at Mark Wendell Tea; Yeonok Kim, at Hankook Tea; Amanda Lange, Ned Lazaro, and Penny Leveritt, at Historic Deerfield; Eileen and Dechen Latshang; William McMelville; Wanja Michuki, at Highland Tea Company; Titus Gerard Pinto, at Chamraj Estates; Victoria Abbott Riccardi; Bob Rifkin; Galina Rothstein; Milton Schiffenbauer; Robert B. Sheeks and Robert H. Sheeks; Joseph. P. Simrany, President of the Tea Association of the U.S.A; Tea Research Institute and Yunnan Academy of Agricultural Sciences, Yaan, Sichuan; Larry Sokyo Tiscornia; the Urasenke Foundation in San Francisco; Srimathie Weerasuriya, at the Sri Lanka Tea Board; Tea Research Institute in Hangzhou, Zhejiang; Zhan Tian Buddhist Temple; and Chongbin Zheng, at Red & Green Company.

We especially wish to thank those who graciously allowed us to reproduce their images and photographs: Eliot Jordan, Historic Deerfield, Saunam Bhattacharjee, and Sonam Zoksang.

With great affection and respect, we send a wink to Tom Lisicki and Eliot Jordan, whose companionship along the tea trail makes the bumpy roads, the endless hours on the bus, and the precipitous drives seem all the less daunting.

We are ever grateful for the dedication of our courageous associates Beth Grubert and Michael Labenz, who flawlessly manned our store while we headed to Asia in search of tea.

And lastly, we want to thank all dedicated tea drinkers. Please know that your support of artisan tea supports the health and vitality of tea makers around the world and gives them hope for a bright future.

INTRODUCTION

TEA HAS A LONG AND TURBULENT HISTORY, filled with intrigue, adventure, fortune gained and lost, embargoes, drugs, taxation, smugglers, war, revolution, religious aestheticism, artistic expression, and social change. Tea's association with colorful, far-off lands fabled for richly textured fabrics, aromatic spices, and delicate porcelain tableware helps to explain how a humble commodity from China came to both fire the imagination and stimulate the palate of upper-class Europeans in the early seventeenth century. Eventually this commodity would capture the attention of the entire Western world. This sweeping history, contained in a single cup of tea, is a riveting narrative that belies the gentle and relaxing nature of this mild-mannered beverage. Around the planet millions of people in all walks of life begin their day with a brisk cup of hot tea. They rely on the soothing, relaxing nature of tea in the afternoon to smooth away the rough edges of the day.

The days when tall, sleek clipper ships raced full-throttle across the seas to deliver another cargo of precious tea leaf have long been replaced by a new era. Today tea enthusiasts need do nothing more than visit the local teashop to select an aromatic tea that catches our fancy. Although times have changed, the centuries-old relationship between the hands-on work of the tea growers and pickers, the environment and the land, and the natural cycle of the harvests still flows according to the traditional rhythms of the seasons in remote tea gardens. A monumental volume of tea is produced annually, especially in the exceptional crop year, when weather cooperates and generously rewards the strenuous efforts and dedication of tea farmers. Working in harmony with nature and by maintaining a keen understanding of the end product desired, tea farmers, pickers, managers, processors, and researchers work in unison to bring a wealth of tea-leaf styles to market each year. Tea is a balancing act between flavor and aroma that carries in its essence the singular stamp of the culture that produced it.

All tea leaf is plucked from the same species of tea plant, known as *Camellia sinensis*, which is grown from one of three primary origin-specific varietal bushes—China bush, Assam bush, and Java bush. *Camellia sinensis* is a sturdy evergreen bush that features dark green, glossy, serrated leaves. Tea is cultivated by every tea-producing country from numerous local hybrids that have been developed for vigor, disease resistance, and weather tolerance. But when we taste a selection of teas, we can clearly see that Chinese tea differs from Indian tea, and neither tastes like Ceylon tea. China is famous for fresh-tasting, sweet, and delicate green tea, while India leads the world in the production of aromatic, flavorful, and bracing black tea—yet, interestingly, both teas originate from the same plant. Japan is known for carefully tended, fresh, and astringent green teas that differ greatly in style and flavor from Chinese green teas.

So if all teas are harvested from the same species of tea bush, what accounts for the great differences between the seemingly endless varieties of tea? The most clearly visible answer is in the method of manufacture the leaf

A tea plucker gathers leaves that will be processed and rolled into Gunpowder tea at the local tea factory in the hills surrounding Shengxian (Zhejiang Province, China).

is given. In other words the process of turning fresh tea leaf into green tea differs from that used to make a black tea or an oolong or a white tea, because theoretically any fresh leaf can be made into any style of tea.

But that is the simple answer, which does not do justice to the intricacies and complexities of the world of tea. Many other invisible influences come into play that are not as easy to see. When we take a wide-angle look at the differences between tea leaves, we are only able to discern the obvious distinctions between black tea, green, oolong, and white teas. If we move in for a closer look at a selection of green teas or black teas, however, we can begin to see that culture and heritage are reflected in the various leaf styles. Tea-producing countries work within the boundaries of their established traditions, preserving much and changing little. These strong cultural factors bring character and individuality to the manufacturing techniques, resulting in teas that are as unique as a fingerprint.

When we zoom in even closer, we discover that tea production for any single country is actually a composite of a multitude of place-specific teas produced in various regions within that country. For example, whether tea is harvested in the north or south, central or coastal areas, each regional tea contributes a leaf of unique character and style to that region's roster of specialties. In each region all the variables of tea production—the soil, the growing conditions, the habit and pruning of the bushes, the timing of the picking, the leaf style being picked, the skill of the tea pickers, the weather during the harvest, and the experience of the tea processors—must be considered. It is here, within the different interpretations of these variables, that tradition, culture, and *terroir* combine to create the great teas of the world.

It's no wonder that a simple cup of tea is far from a simple matter, and that tea enthusiasts' attraction to this exhilarating beverage was responsible for changing the course of history for more than one country. So journey with us to the exotic lands where tea gardens cloak the hillsides in blankets of soft emerald green and a warm welcome always awaits in the hand of a stranger extending a humble cup of hot, fragrant tea.

CHAPTER 1

A BRIEF HISTORY OF TEA

IN THE VEILED DAWN OF PREHISTORY, tea was consumed in the vast nexus of Assam (in northeastern India), the Yunnan Province (in southwestern China), along the northern borders of neighboring Burma (known today as Myanmar), Laos (officially Lao People's Democratic Republic), Vietnam, and Thailand. Tea's origins and ascendancy began in China, long considered to be the source of indigenous tea bushes and, later, the birthplace of the first cultivated tea gardens. Along Yunnan's southern edge its borders with Myanmar and Laos meet to form a rugged, mountainous area that is easily defined on paper but difficult to separate in reality. Here a thick covering of forest jungle melds this place into one lush, tropical expanse. Anthropologists now know that tea trees existed and still exist today in large swaths of remote, forested land that straddled the border areas of these countries.

For centuries this region has supported populations of ethnic minorities for whom the borders have provided porous access through the jungle—and the tea bushes and trees therein have provided fresh leaf for indigenous styles of tea and tea-drinking customs.

Awareness of tea spread first from Yunnan, throughout China, then to the rest of Asia, and finally to the West. In Yunnan indigenous wild tea trees are still found in the old-growth forests of Xishuangbanna, an agricultural region nourished by the rich and fertile watershed of the Mekong River. The tea trees are located across seven tea mountains, many of which are calculated to be five hundred to a thousand years old. These ancient trees are a living patrimony for local populations of Dai and Bulang minorities, who revere the trees as a precious, living inheritance from their ancestors. From the beginning, China found the tea bush to be useful, and the people eventually embraced tea drinking with a deep-rooted passion that captivated the

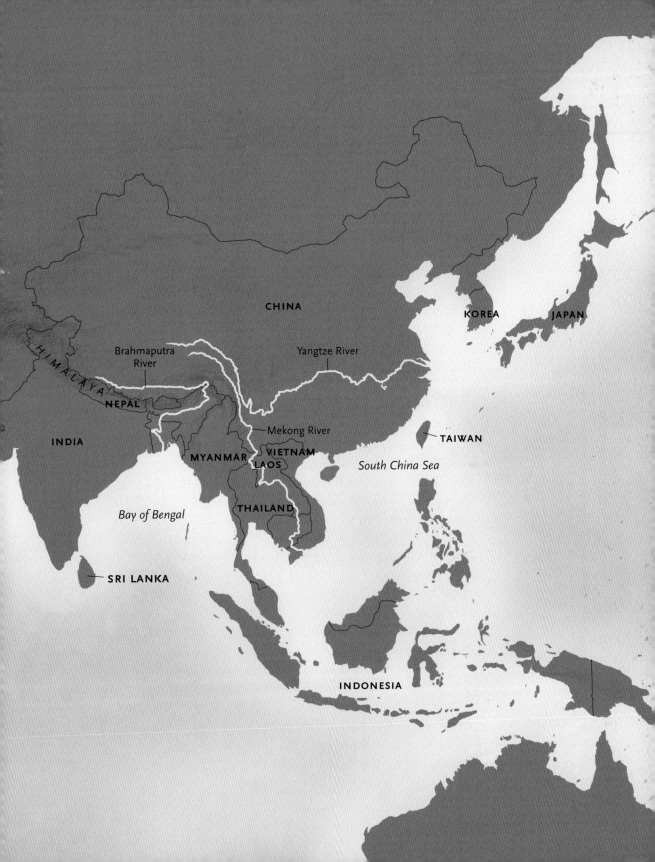

CHINA

KOREA

JAPAN

HIMALAYA

Brahmaputra
River

Yangtze River

NEPAL

INDIA

Mekong River

TAIWAN

MYANMAR

VIETNAM

LAOS

South China Sea

Bay of Bengal

THAILAND

SRI LANKA

INDONESIA

rest of the world. Researchers of Chinese history have reconstructed a time-line tracing the development of tea drinking in China, noting that the use of tea changed and evolved with the advent of each successive dynasty. Thus tea was brewed in various ways, depending on the fashion of the day and the whims of the emperor.

At one time tea leaves were used to concoct a medicinal brew. Later, tea was viewed more as a healthful tonic and was compressed into hard little cakes, then scraped, roasted, and boiled with salt into a bitter brew. Eventually, tea leaves were ground into a fine powder and then whipped with a delicate bamboo whisk into a light green froth, resulting in a beverage that came yet one step closer to what we associate today as a cup of tea. As tea usage in China changed, the culture of tea drinking developed into a highly stylized and sophisticated social etiquette, with established manners, status, and rank that in turn encouraged an appreciation for art, poetry, and songs.

From Food to Medicine: Early Uses for Tea

Anthropologists speculate that prehistoric humans (the species *Homo erectus*) discovered indigenous tea trees growing wild in the forests of Yunnan. The quest to discover edibles in the environment would have eventually tempted these early inhabitants to chew on the leaves of the tea trees, perhaps stimulated by their own curiosity or from watching the actions of forest-dwelling animals. They would have discovered these leaves to be a source of invigorating energy that might sustain them on their daily rounds of foraging for food.

Once these prehistoric humans learned the skills of fire building, they gained warmth and protection from the elements, and soon they acquired the ability to cook meat and boil water. Surrounded by an abundance of wild-growing tea trees, they felled these trees to use for fuel. Most likely along the way they experimented with adding tea leaves and other forest barks and leaves to boiling water, which was then stewed into various strong, bitter, and invigorating concoctions.

By the time of the Shang dynasty (1766–1050 BC), tea was being consumed in Yunnan Province for its medicinal properties. For any given ailment, tea leaves were boiled with a host of other forest plants, seeds, barks, and leaves to concoct healing herbal remedies. Wisdom gleaned from the trial and error of using these herbal concoctions laid the groundwork for the great herbal-healing traditions for which China would later become famous. Early on, tea was thus among the growing pharmacopoeia in China of ingredients considered useful and necessary for maintaining one's health.

By the end of the Zhou dynasty (1122–256 BC), indigenous tea trees were also found growing wild in Sichuan Province, Yunnan's neighbor to the northeast. It is believed that here, for the first time, people began to boil tea leaves for consumption into a concentrated liquid *without* the addition of other leaves or herbs, thereby using tea as a bitter yet stimulating drink, rather than a medicinal concoction.

Tea and China's Great Religions

China's three great philosophy religions—Buddhism, Confucianism, and Daoism—sprouted toward the middle of the Zhou dynasty. Each of these religions embraced tea for its healthful virtues and powers of rejuvenation. Monks and priests who were introduced to tea found that this beverage would help them stay awake during long meditations. To these holy men, tea represented a virtuous and necessary tonic, which they declared to be the "elixir of life" that should be consumed daily by all people. As the popularity of Buddhism, Confucianism, and Daoism spread throughout China, so did an awareness of life-enhancing tea.

A monk (Gyantse, Tibet).

It was under the rule of Qin Shihuangdi, the first Qin emperor (r. 221–210 BC), however, that the greatest number of Chinese citizens came to hear of this beneficial tonic. During his reign China became a unified country; a collection of previously warring states thus turned into a single empire with a centralized administration. The emperor was responsible for monumental building projects the region had not yet witnessed. Under Qin Shihuangdi's rule isolated segments of fortification walls that had been built in earlier times were linked together to create one strong defensive wall that would define his empire. This became the first stage of the Great Wall of China. The emperor ordered the construction of a multitude of grand and elaborate imperial palaces as well as the creation of his own tomb, which he outfitted with thousands of the now famous terracotta warriors. These projects brought massive numbers of workers from across China to live in compulsory labor camps. As workers shared information and praised the wonders of their homelands, their customs and special foods, those from the western provinces spoke of the invigorating qualities of tea. As word of this beneficial tonic spread across the empire, tea became a much sought-after commodity—everyone who heard of tea wanted to try it. Around 53 BC a holy man named Wu LiZhen is credited with planting a cultivated tea garden in an isolated spot atop Mengding Mountain in Sichuan Province. His tea plants, today referred to as the Seven Tea Trees, established a tea garden that yielded tea of such purity and delicacy that it would become one of the exclusive Tribute Tea Gardens reserved for use only by the emperor. Wu LiZhen is thus called the forefather of tea cultivation, as it was from this first garden that the seeds of Sichuan's extensive tea gardens came (see chapter 4).

Tea's destiny changed course during the Han dynasty (206 BC–220 AD). Former western barbarian territories, including Sichuan and Yunnan, and all of the southern provinces were brought into the fold of the Chinese Celestial Empire. This geographic change made it easier for common people to obtain tea from the western provinces. Government control over the Sichuan and Yunnan tea regions meant that tea could be traded more easily, and later, under the Tang dynasty (618–907) these vast regions would be developed into prime tea gardens.

But despite its growing popularity, the way tea was still prepared by many produced a bitter-tasting drink. In the latter part of the Three Kingdoms Period warring factions split the north and south regions, and the Period of Disunity (220–589 AD) brought an unsettled time to China. Refinements in tea drinking continued to progress, however. During this time the method of how fresh tea leaves were processed and brewed changed. Tea leaves, formerly dried and charred, were now steamed to make them pliant. After steaming, the leaves were dried but not charred, then pounded and compressed into small, solid cakes of tea. The cakes were then baked, which hardened them and kept the tea from spoiling. In this state bits of tea could be chipped or scraped off and finally boiled. These changes in the process were reported to have eliminated the bitterness of the leaf, transforming it into a sweet-tasting drink. Although this tea was no doubt still crude and astringent by today's standards, this modification began the final transformation of tea from a bitter tonic to a pleasure beverage. Zhong Zi, a writer of this time, is credited with producing the first document that described tea production and tea drinking in his day. He records a method of tea preparation that involved adding onions, ginger, and orange along with the broken-up bits of tea in the boiling water.

The Tang Dynasty's Refinements in Tea

The celebrated and classic Tang dynasty (618–907 AD) brought a refinement and sophistication to tea drinking. This was a time of high art and culture, and luxurious materials were sought after in furnishings and objects. Tea drinking became an engaging, relaxing pursuit, and it was the Tang who first enjoyed formal tea gatherings that were designed to find delight in this pleasure beverage. Manners and social order were emphasized during the Tang era, and to ensure that rare and costly teas were prepared properly, the role of tea master was created to guarantee that every proper social convention was executed carefully and with great style. Every family of social ranking employed a knowledgeable tea master, as did government officials and of course the emperor.

As tea lost its popular association as a crude, bitter brew, the ritual of tea drinking became a cultured social rite during the Tang era. Tea was now regarded as a healthful tonic that would impart peace, harmony, and well-being. Spiritually, tea was believed to be an "elixir of immortality," an exaggerated ideal that suggested its transcendent nature. Many styles of teaware were created, which was subject to change with every successive emperor, who had his own idea of fashion, glaze color, style, and whether to use incised or applied designs.

During this time Lu Yu—a scholar, recluse, and member of the literati who is often called China's Father of Tea—codified the rituals that he deemed necessary for brewing a proper pot of tea. Besides the goal of yielding a pleasant-tasting tea, Lu Yu preached that inner harmony could be attained through the expression of careful, attentive tea preparation. In his book *The Classic of Tea*, which is still highly regarded today, Lu Yu explained the mindful execution of the rituals of tea preparation. Underlying his practice are many of the philosophical beliefs that took hold in China during his lifetime. He utilized both Confucian and Daoist principles to synthesize the philosophical with the practical.

This statue of Lu Yu resides in the courtyard garden of a tea factory (Jiangxi Province, China).

Tea drinkers were encouraged to develop a spiritual appreciation for the everyday moments in life as they performed the rituals of tea preparation. Lu Yu emphasized that all moments in life be attended by beauty—a concept that was to become central to the pleasure of tea drinking. Under Lu Yu's guidance the Tang introduced utensils that were exclusively designed for preparing, serving, and drinking tea. Before this era no formal utensils existed for tea drinking. As the methodology of tea drinking became more sophisticated, so did the selection of ceramic tea bowls, tea cups, teapots, and water-pouring ewers. With such concepts about tea as "Its liquor is like the sweetest dew of Heaven," Lu Yu instilled in tea drinkers an appreciation for tea that included consideration of the materials used to make tea bowls. During his time low-sided ceramic bowls were favored for their ease in delicately sipping tea. As for the material of the bowls, he favored white Hsing Chou ware and greenish-hued Yueh ware, which was described as having the "verdure of a thousand mountain peaks" and which he found desirable for "enhancing the true color of the tea."

The Tang preferred whole-leaf tea that was flavored with fruit pastes to counter the bitterness of the tea. As it was in the previous dynasty, tea was compressed into small decorative cakes that would keep indefinitely. The cakes were heated until they softened and became, in Lu Yu's words, "as tender as a baby's arm." When cooled, the tea was scraped or broken off into bits and put into a pot and boiled.

Tea was consumed differently by the various members of the social classes in the Tang dynasty. Many tea drinkers favored adding onion, ginger, orange peel, cloves, and peppermint to their tea. Mixing salt into the tea became a popular choice in the western provinces. Ladies of the court sipped tea that was mixed with the delicate extracts of fruits and flowers.

In contrast to the convention of his day, Lu Yu shunned these additions to tea—he believed that tea should be drunk plain. He addressed the topic thusly: "Sometimes such items as onion, ginger, jujube fruit, orange peel, dogwood berries, or peppermint are boiled along with the tea. Drinks like that are no more than the swill of gutters and ditches; still, alas, it is a common practice to make tea that way."

The Tang established a vast government-controlled network of tea gardens in southern and western China, which would ultimately bring China to the pinnacle of tea production. The western border populations of Tibetans and the northern border populations of Mongols and Tartars also found tea a welcome and necessary addition to their meager diets. The Tang government set up a system of trading tea for horses with these border populations, and a method of taxation on tea that would be implemented for centuries.

Tibetans first learned of tea in 641 AD, when the Tang princess Wen Cheng married the Tibetan king Songtsan Gambo and brought tea from Sichuan with her to Tibet. An exchange of trading between Tibetans and the Tang court resulted in a trading relationship that lasted well into the Yuan dynasty (1271–1368). The Tang traded tea for strong, healthy horses, which they needed for their warriors. For the Tibetans tea was indispensable for enhancing the nutrition of their spartan, vegetable-less diet. To expedite trading with groups far from China, horse caravan routes were developed for the long, difficult, round-trip trek across inhospitable terrain and through punishing weather conditions. This created the first of such routes known historically as the Tea Horse Routes, which stretched from Sichuan and Yunnan to Tibet over the rugged Himalaya.

For trading purposes, the Tang devised compressed bricks of dark, coarse, low-quality "border tea" (comprised mainly of tea twigs and leftover bits from the manufacture of the Tang's more select and fine tea cakes) as a practical way to send as much tea as possible to Tibet on each caravan. Eventually, several distinct tea-trading routes developed from western China—the southern routes to Tibet and a western route from Sichuan across Central Asia to Mongolia and Siberia.

At approximately this same time Japan was being introduced to tea through contact between Zen priests and Chinese Buddhist monks. It is believed that the priest Saichō returned to Japan in 815 after living in China for many years and served boiled tea cake to Emperor Saga. Thereafter, Saichō planted tea seeds for the emperor, who served tea from his tea bushes to court officials and important personages. Interest in tea in Japan stayed centered around the emperor's court and nearby temple gardens. But tea would not gain a strong foothold in Japan until several centuries later.

Tea Drinking during the Song Dynasty

During the Song dynasty (960–1279) tea continued to be consumed as a gracious ritual activity and refined leisure beverage. Tea manners and social courtesies initiated under the Tang reached a new level of complexity and formality for members of the Song's elite class. Rules of hospitality extended to guests and strangers and was forged into a fine art, creating a link among tea, courtesy, and cordiality that still endures.

Under Song control tea cultivation also surpassed that of the Tang, and systems were established for grading leaf tea and determining quality. The emperor controlled production of all tea in China, and in the Song dynasty only members of a particular class could drink certain teas. As with tea plucked from Mengding Mountain the most precious "tribute grade" teas were gathered from revered mountains and reserved exclusively for the emperor. The first commissioner of tea, Ts'An Hsiang, was appointed to personally supervise the collection and labeling of the tribute teas in the early weeks of spring. Following this, the next picking of tender young leaves from spring teas were reserved for the upper class and the elite, while the larger, coarser leaves from summer pickings became the daily brew of the working class.

Tea drinking continued to evolve. Tea cakes, to which plum juice was added for sweetness, remained the favorite form of tea for the Song, but finely powdered tea started to replace the coarse leaves in the cakes, which added a refinement of style to the method of preparation. This change heralded the era when tea cake was scraped directly into the bowl and whipped into a lovely green froth. Large-mouthed earthenware ewers (vase-shaped pitchers or jugs) were designed to pour boiled water into a tea bowl in a ritualized motion.

To complement this new powdered tea, Song emperor Huizong (r. 1101–1125) commanded the royal pottery works to create new tea-drinking cups. Known for his aesthetic tastes, he ushered in the creation of luxurious porcelains characterized by refined elegance, underglaze decorations, subtle etched designs, and sensuous glazes. Song porcelains were mostly monochromatic and the most popular type—Qingbai porcelain—had a bluish-white glaze. These cups not only increased tea-drinking pleasure, but they also encouraged awareness and admiration of the tea liquor itself. It was during this point in the development of tea culture that teawares began

Huxin Ting Tea House in the Yu Yuan Garden (Shanghai, China).

to be viewed as objects of desire and value and not just as functional tools. At one time Huizong favored deep chocolate-brown, almost black glazed teacups, streaked with fine, thin tan lines. Known as "rabbit hair glaze," this style became very popular as it was said that the black glaze pleasingly offset the color of the froth of the whisked tea. These dark glazed cups were favorites in Song tea competitions. In these contests, the winner would be the person who could whip a cup of tea that was the greenest in color and the frothiest in style. These dark cups added to the presentation and showed off the tea to an advantage. At one point Song tea drinkers used a *zhan*, a shallow saucerlike bowl that accentuated the color of the whipped tea by barely containing the precious liquid. This imperial desire for strong but thin vessels that could endure near-boiling liquid was the beginning of the Chinese porcelain trade that would, centuries later, influence the course of ceramics manufacturing throughout Japan and Europe.

Teahouses sprang up during this time, providing regular citizens the opportunity to drink tea in public rather than in the seclusion of their own circle of family and friends. Selections of tea were accompanied by light snacks, and teahouses quickly became important places to socialize, conduct business, play board games, listen to poetry and stories, flaunt oneself, and gossip. For the eloquent Song people life had little concern but for pleasurable moments. Toward the end of their reign, the Song began experimenting with drinking tea brewed from loose leaves. Although most people did not give up their cake tea entirely, this new way of drinking tea offered an easier way to measure the tea, but the trade-off was an unsatisfactory flavor.

Tea Arrives in Japan

At the midpoint of the Tang dynasty and into the middle of the Song dynasty in China, Japan was in its Heian era (794–1185), a period when Chinese influence was at its height and the samurai class was beginning to rise to power. Arts and intellectual pursuits flourished in Japan, and of particular note was the introduction of tea drinking to Emperor Saga. During this time many Japanese monks traveled to China for study in the great Buddhist monasteries and temples. Tea drinking was among the intellectual Chinese pursuits that the monks observed and came to enjoy themselves.

Around 1191 a Zen priest named Myoan Eisai (the founder of the Rinsai sect of Zen Buddhism) brought tea seeds and bushes back to Japan from China and planted some of them on the southernmost island of Kyushu. He shared seeds with a friend, who in turn planted them in the Uji hills outside of modern-day Kyoto, an area that is still revered today for its high-quality and expensive tea. Eisai is credited with popularizing tea drinking in Japan during the Kamakura period (1185–1333). After many visits to China he used his experiences growing and drinking tea in China to write the book *Kissa Yōjōki* in 1214 (roughly translated as "Drinking Tea for Health"). Eisai is to Japan what Lu Yu is to China in terms of advocating tea. While Lu Yu proposed rules for proper tea cultivation, brewing, and drinking, Eisai weaved medicinal and healthful benefits with religious ideology without much concern for aesthetics.

The Japanese monk Kūkai (774–835) was the first to return from China and write of his experience drinking tea. Many Japanese poets lauded the ethereal character of tea and connected it with the importance of seasonality and the changing natural landscape. The sages and scholars found meaning and clarity in the experience of drinking tea. Both Tang and Song tea-drinking rituals were revered by the Japanese, who adapted them into elevated and studied composed forms of beauty and high art. The Japanese court and the aristocratic class grasped the same meaning from tea drinking that the Tang and Song poets and literati had earlier: it allowed them to remove themselves from the details of daily life and experience a pure and untainted sagelike experience of otherworldly peace.

Tea Drinking during China's Yuan and Ming Dynasties

As the Song concentrated on perfecting the art of whipped tea and contemplated how to incorporate loose-leaf tea into their tea rituals, storm clouds gathered over their glorious court. Fierce Mongol hordes, long held at bay in their harsh lands outside of China's borders, swept down into the more temperate and lush lands of the Chinese empire. For the next eighty-eight years Kublai Khan's Yuan dynasty (1271–1368) controlled the Middle Kingdom. Tea drinking was reduced to a functional act and was no longer cultivated in court as an aesthetic pleasure. The Mongol rulers, reared on dark and pungent brick tea that was laced with fermented mare's milk, found the Song's loose-leaf tea somewhat satisfactory but had no liking for the frothy whipped tea.

Intrigued by the leaf tea, the Yuan Mongols developed a new technique for drying and roasting fresh tea leaves. Called *chaoqing*, this process resulted in leaves that were less parched and burned, perhaps taking a step closer to discovering the techniques for making green tea. But it would not be until the Ming dynasty (some 275 years later) that tea-leaf manufacture would advance beyond these first steps taken by the Mongols. Thus the elaborate tea rituals of the Song dynasty came to a swift and unfortunate halt at the very moment when the accomplishments of China's tea culture were cresting.

Aesthetic tea pursuits were thus terminated under Mongol rule. Had the Song stayed in power, or had the coarse Mongols not been their predecessors, China most likely would have seen their evolving tea culture culminate into a glorious, formal, stylized tea ceremony. Instead, the Japanese pursued the development of tea culture when the Chinese no longer could. By this time the Japanese had left behind their adoration and imitation of Chinese arts and culture, and they were able to imbue the rituals of the tea ceremony with

In a traditional Chinese teahouse, tea may be served in a gaiwan along with a small snack such as hard-boiled quail eggs (Shanghai, China).

purely Japanese aesthetics, Japanese utensils, and a precise, practiced formality based on Japanese principles.

In time the rise of the Ming dynasty (1368–1644) ushered the Mongol rulers out and back to their harsh, barren lands to the north. Zhu Yuanzhang, a rebel leader who had protested Mongol rule, became the first Ming emperor, and adopted the name Hongwu, which meant Vast Military Power. He reestablished China's former imperial customs and traditions to their former glory, including elaborate Han tea customs from the Song era. Under Hongwu's reign many topics and policies regarding tea cultivation, production, grading, storage, and transportation were established and codified, providing a framework for China's tea industry that is still in use today.

During this time the secrets of oxidation (the process by which fresh tea leaf is turned into black tea) were discovered. This was not a style of tea preferred by the Chinese, who perceived black tea as something only fit for the barbarian foreigners. But they recognized the importance of the discovery and the potential value that oxidization had for improving the condition of tea that would be traveling long distances over land and sea. Now, brick tea exported to the border regions of Tibet and Mongolia could be sent as black tea, which would allow the tea to arrive at its final destination in better shape. Previously, crude green tea bricks suffered from overheating and near freezing in the changing weather conditions and often developed mold when exposed to rain and damp environments.

Ming emperors continued the tradition of commissioning fine tableware. The porcelain kilns at Jingdezhen switched from producing Qingbai wares and pure white Shufu wares to producing underglaze blue and white wares. Known as *mei-ping*, these blue and white wares gained the title of China's porcelain. The Jingdezhen kilns became famous for creating sophisticated and delicate porcelain tableware items. European traders would later marvel at these splendid objects, which at the time had no equal in Europe. Small, handle-less porcelain teacups acquired a lid and a deep saucer for the cup to fit down into. Called a *gaiwan*, this new design helped to prevent spills from this style of cup, which was too hot to hold, and provided the drinker with an easy way to push aside the tea leaves floating in the cup. Practical and elegantly designed gaiwan are still the cup of choice today in Chinese teahouses.

The first porcelain teapots also appeared under Ming rule. Tea was still costly, so these teapots were intentionally made small. This allowed the tea leaves in the teapot to be reinfused several times by successively adding more water, a method of tea brewing still followed in China for green and oolong tea. Small *zisha* clay teapots also began to appear at this time, and they became the favorites of the tea literati (see "Artistic Yixing Teapots in chapter 4).

The Ming also developed an obsession for flowers and aromatic blossoms, and their love of richly perfumed fragrances resulted in their perfecting the art of scenting tea with fresh flower petals. The creation of flower-scented teas such as jasmine, osmanthus, and rose is considered to be the Song's most significant contribution to China's tea culture, even more important than their eventual switch from cake to powdered tea. The Tang dynasty had added sweetness and aroma to tea with the addition of plum juice, fruits, and spices, but the development of splendid flower-scented teas was an achievement that would forever forward belong to China alone.

An assortment of Yixing tasting pots is often used for sampling tea (Fujian Province, China).

Chanoyu: Japan's Way of Tea

While the Ming perfected their culture of the steeped tea leaf, Japanese priests and monks continued to embrace the whipped, powdered tea of the Song dynasty. Zen Buddhist monks incorporated powdered tea drinking into their rituals of prayer and meditation, and they entwined tea drinking with religious and philosophical ideals. By the sixteenth century the ultimate artistic exercise in tea drinking was born in Chanoyu, or "the way of tea." Chanoyu was distilled from all of the previous approaches to tea drinking, and it is an artful practice that embodies harmony, respect, tranquility, humility, purity, mystery, beauty, artful appreciation, symmetry, and total attention to the art of tea brewing. Chanoyu is based on Zen qualities that are different from but not in opposition to the Song's more temporal concepts of connoisseurship and tea appreciation.

Tea master Sen Rikyu (1521–1591) revised the rules of Chanoyu, focusing more on the philosophical virtues of harmony, reverence, purity, and calm rather than on religious principles. Sen Rikyu gravitated away from the smooth, shiny Tenmoku tea bowls that were made in eastern China and had become popular in Japan among tea drinkers. Sen Rikyu ushered in a new style of Japanese stoneware tea bowl that was based on the fifteenth-century Ido-style earthenwares of Korea. These simple bowls introduced a natural, somewhat imperfect and humble appearance that reflected his preference for naturalistic, earth-toned teawares, imperfect in shape but pleasing in appearance and possessing a confident, tactile touch in the user's hand.

Tea Drinking during the Qing Dynasty

Yet another change was in the wind for the Celestial Empire. With the death of the last Ming emperor, tribal banners fluttered over China as Manchu tribesmen claimed power and announced the beginning of their Qing dynasty (1644–1911), also known as the Manchu dynasty. The non-Chinese Manchu rulers, like the Mongol rulers before them, drank coarse dark tea made from black tea and added fermented mare's milk to it. They brought this style of tea drinking with them to the imperial court, but the Han Chinese never converted to drinking tea with milk nor developed a taste for black tea. Tea was important to the Manchus, and they declared that it was as important to people as "salt, rice, vinegar, soy sauce, oil, and firewood" were. At the Qing imperial palace, located in the Forbidden City, the imperial kitchen operated two tea kitchens—one for the preparation of Manchu milk tea and another for Han green or "clear" tea.

The first Manchu emperor, Kangxi (1661–1722), forged a peace treaty with Russia that quelled Tartar rumblings on China's northern border with Siberia. The treaty reinstated an exchange of goods and materials that flowed between China, Siberia, and Mongolia by camel caravan. Border tea,

China's major export to these other regions of the Far East, was still being compressed into a dense tea brick of poor quality leaf and twigs, which could also be scored and broken for use as currency by these outsiders. These long and arduous treks across Central Asia took as long as eighteen months to reach their destination, and consisted of two hundred to three hundred animals traveling across the desert, each carrying approximately six hundred pounds of tea.

The West Comes in Search of China's Teas

The Manchus were in power when trade with Europe turned China into the most important trading country in the world. Although the Portuguese were the first traders to enter the Far East, and the first to bring tea, spices, and porcelains back to Portugal, it was Dutch traders who first created the habit of drinking tea in the West in the early seventeenth century. The Dutch established a trading center at Batavia (known today as Jakarta) on the island of Java and from there consolidated their purchases from Indonesia and China for the long trip home. Chinese tea men faced the challenge of producing tea for the Dutch that would endure the long voyage back to Holland without rotting or spoiling in the damp conditions aboard the ships. In their trial and error, the Chinese hit on the notion that for this purpose tea needed to be allowed to darken, then fired and bake-dried in a way that green tea was not.

Over time the Chinese refined and perfected the production of black tea, and for many years these teas were produced in the Wuyi mountains of northern Fujian Province. From here, the tea was sent downriver to the trading port of Canton. In 1610 the first shipment of Chinese tea reached The Hague, and wealthy patrons were dazzled by it. The Dutch embraced tea with a fervent passion, and they laced it heavily with milk based on reports from Dutch traders that this was how the Chinese emperor took his tea. Because the emperor at the time was the Manchu emperor, these reports were based on information that was only true for him; Han Chinese emperors never did nor never would add milk to their tea. Nevertheless, Dutch physicians lauded tea as a curative and necessary medicine.

The Dutch also purchased such fine and delicate Chinese goods as lacquer objects, porcelains, spices, and silks, while continuing to send home greater quantities of tea. Soon they had enough tea to ship quantities of this invigorating beverage from Holland to their colony of New Amsterdam (New York) in North America. The first record of Dutch tea in the Massachusetts colony appeared in 1670, when Benjamin Harris and Daniel Vernon advertised the availability of black tea. In 1674 New Amsterdam passed from Dutch hands to English rule and was renamed New York. By 1682 tea had been introduced to the city of Philadelphia by the Quaker William Penn.

After the Dutch adopted the tea habit, members of the French upper class began to drink tea as well. In Paris the Marquise de Sevigné, a cultured woman of letters, extolled the way that her friend Mme. de la Sablière drank "tea à la Chinoise" (or tea with milk). Tea reached Germany about 1650, and was first mentioned to have appeared in Scandinavia in 1723. But it was not until 1658 that the first public sale of Dutch-traded Chinese tea commenced in London at Garraway's Coffee House. Like their fellow explorers, the English went mad for tea, which was touted as a healthful curative. Tea became fashionable in the coffeehouses, and the drink joined coffee and hot chocolate as one of the new temperance beverages that appealed to the privileged class of professional men and "literati."

When in 1662 Charles II wed Princess Catherine of Braganza, a Portuguese princess and tea drinker, tea became the fashionable beverage for English ladies. This opened the way for the rapid rise of the social traditions of "teatime." Like the Dutch, the English added milk to their tea. They also added lumps of sugar, which England imported in vast quantities from the West Indies. Sugar added another boost to the energizing effects of tea, and a cup of black tea with cream and sugar defined the English style of twice-daily tea drinking.

With trade opening in the Far East, the English desired trading rights there as well. Dutch seafaring dominance barred the English from establishing a territory in any place other than India, however. Admitting defeat to the Dutch monopoly, England set up trading stations in India, the country that would later, under the hand of the English, become the largest and most powerful tea-producing country in the world. By 1669, England granted a group of merchants a monopoly on English trade in the Far East. These men had made large sums of money with a company called the Levant Group, which had organized an overland trade route with India. This newly formed company was known as the John Company and was established as the lawful English East India Company.

The John Company sent regularly scheduled shipments of Chinese tea to England from their base in India. But this tea was still being purchased from Dutch traders in India and was brought to England aboard company ships. The English were desperate for cheaper prices and more direct purchasing, but it was not until 1684 that the first English East India Company ships arrived at the port of Whampoa, downriver from the Chinese port of Canton, and gained official clearance from the Chinese to purchase tea directly. Although the Europeans continued to arrive in China in ever-increasing numbers, the Chinese remained wary of the "barbarian outsiders" and would not allow them entry onto Chinese soil. The port of Canton was off-limits to foreigners, who were made to stop their ships at the anchorage of Whampoa, some sixty miles down the Pearl River from Canton. Here, the Hong merchants would greet each arriving vessel and escort only the captain upriver to Canton to conduct business.

For the next 150 years the English East India Company had exclusive import rights to bring Chinese tea to England and set the prices of tea sold to the Crown. But other adventurous traders and merchants, anxious to join this race to the riches, protested the monopoly. In 1834 the Crown broke the monopoly, and almost instantly dozens of independent traders sprang up in London. A frenzied race across the seas to the port of Canton began, with the sole intent of purchasing as much tea as possible, as cheaply as possible. With the trade monopoly ended, the English East India Company was desperate to find a place where it could grow tea and control all aspects of production. Their problem was thus: trade with China was no longer exclusive, and the Dutch controlled Indonesia. What remained was India, which, while solidly under English rule, had no established tea industry. The English, wishing for a better solution, had to settle for what it had—India.

The Boston Tea Party

On December 16, 1773, a band of sixty American patriots known as the Sons of Liberty dressed as Mohawk Indians and under cover of night boarded three sailing ships that were docked in Boston Harbor. These ships—the *Dartmouth*, the *Eleanor*, and the *Beaver*—had arrived in Boston with cargoes of precious tea from the British tea merchant Davison, Newman, & Co. for the colonists.

ORIGINS AND DERIVATIONS OF WORDS FOR TEA

Tea is historically recorded as being originally sourced from and shipped to the rest of the world from China. There were two major points of exit for Chinese tea in the mid-1600s, and local dialects provided the origins of the two main spellings and pronunciations for the words used to transliterate the Chinese character for tea. In Chinese there is only one written character for tea; however, there are several ways that this character is pronounced.

The history of the words used around the world for tea all trace back to one of two sources: either the eastern China port of Amoy (now known as Xiamen) or the southern China ports of Canton (now known as Guangzhou) and, to a lesser degree, Hong Kong. In the Min-Nan dialect (also referred to as the Amoy dialect) spoken around Xiamen, the character for tea is pronounced and spelled similarly to *te*. Both the Cantonese dialect spoken by the southern coastal population of China and the Mandarin dialect of the northern Chinese pronounce this character as *cha* or *ch'a*.

With the Dutch and the Portuguese (and later the English) being the early links to the West as far as the tea trade is concerned, one would expect that the use of one or the other of these pronunciations would follow the historical trade routes that became established by these merchant explorers. This may have been true during the late seventeenth century, but it does not follow true after the mid-eighteenth century, for reasons that are not completely clear to linguists.

The two main pronunciation branches follow, with representative examples of their worldwide variations (various accent uses not noted).

te: Catalan, Danish, Hebrew, Italian, Latvian, Malay, Norwegian, Spanish, Swedish

tea: English, Hungarian

tee: Afrikaans, Finnish, German, Korean

the: French, Icelandic, Indonesian, Tamil

thee: Dutch

cha: Greek, Hindi, Japanese, Persian, Portuguese

chai: Russian

chay (caj):   Albanian, Arabic, Bulgarian, Croatian, Czech, Serbian, Turkish

Frustrated and angry over years of taxation imposed on them by England for such items as tea, sugar, glass, paper, coffee, and wine, the colonists rebelled in 1767 by boycotting English goods. The Crown's reason for the taxation was to offset the cost of shipping these goods all the way across the Atlantic to the "colonies." The colonists felt that they did not have a say in matters of the Crown and that they would receive no direct benefit from these tax payments. Colonial merchants also supported this boycott, and they began to smuggle "contraband tea" from Dutch traders. Dutch traders had at one time supplied tea to the colonists before they lost control of sales to the colonies to the English in 1674. The Dutch, who were happy for the boost in business, imposed no tax on the colonists.

The trade in smuggled tea began to cut deeply into the sales of English tea. In an attempt to empty their warehouses of unsold tea, King George III devised a scheme to sell the tea on these three ships to the colonists at a low cost, which would in turn put the Dutch smugglers out of business. But, as the colonists quickly realized, this move was a gambit that would only make them vulnerable once again to "taxation without representation" from England. So the colonists declined the offer and refused acceptance of the tea. For weeks leading up to December 16, meetings were held and the course of action discussed and debated. On November 29 broadsides appeared all over Boston, which read:

> Friends, Bretheren, Countrymen!
> That worst of Plagues, the Detestable Tea ship'd for this Port
> by the East India Company, is now arrived in the harbour;
> the Hour of Destruction or manly Opposition to the
> Machinations of Tryanny stares you in the Face;
> every Friend to his country, to Himself and Posterity
> is now called upon to meet at Faneuil Hall at nine of clock,
> this Day at which time the Bells will begin to Ring to make
> a united and successful Resistence to this last worst and most
> Destructive Measure of Administration.

Finally, on December 16, a group of more than five thousand townspeople gathered at the Old South Meeting House to request that the three ships sitting in the harbor be turned around and returned to England. When the governor of Massachusetts refused this request and demanded that the colonists accept the shipment of tea, the patriots felt they had no choice but to act. Swarms of people filled the streets surrounding Griffins Wharf, where the ships were docked. Someone was recorded as asking "how tea will mix with salt water." Shortly after dusk a group of patriots dressed like Mohawks, and brandishing hatchets and axes, followed Samuel Adams aboard the ships. They seized all 342 chests of tea from British tea merchant Davison, Newman, & Co. They split open the chests and dumped the contents of precious tea one by one overboard into Boston Harbor.

This act of rebellion unleashed smoldering feelings of resentment toward England and served as a starting point for the gathering storm of resistance building in the colony. During the following months, American sentiments against the British ran high; tea arriving via clipper ship from England was boycotted at the docks in Annapolis, Philadelphia, and New York. In Delaware broadsides signed by the Committee for Tarring and Feathering were posted that warned: "A ship is now on her way to this port, being sent out by the ministry for the purpose of enslaving and poisoning all the Americans . . . she cannot be brought to anchor before this city." On March 7, 1774, at a second Boston Tea Party, sixteen chests of tea from British tea merchant Davison, Newman, & Co. were among those once again thrown into Boston Harbor.

England received the message loud and clear that it could no longer control the American colonies. Pressing further in their desire for independence and self-rule, the colonists continued to stand their ground and won their much-desired freedom from England in the bloody Revolutionary War (1775–1783). Such were the passions of the time that tea fell victim to. This miscalculation by England cost the Crown the loss of a fledgling nation that went on to become the largest and most powerful consumer nation in the world, with a great thirst for a different temperance drink: coffee.

The English Explore the Assam Valley of India

From as early as 1815, rumors had spread that local Singpho tribes in the northeast region of the Assam valley near the town of Sibsagar knew of the existence of wild-growing tea in that region. These locals were used to drinking a picked and fermented concoction of tea leaves called *miang* or *letpet*.

Letpet was a preparation of tea leaves that had once been eaten as a vegetable but was now also being consumed as a fermented drink. In 1823 the English explorer and trader Major Robert Bruce found this rumor to be true. Bruce had been dispatched on a trading expedition to this region, known then as Burmese Assam. He found extensive areas of wild-growing tea, which the local tribes had used for centuries as both food and beverage.

Bruce arranged for the local Singpho chief to send him a supply of these tea plants and tea seeds, which on arrival in Calcutta were determined by the English to be of a different and therefore inferior species of tea bush. Consequently, the English did not put much credence into Bruce's discovery. It was not until years later that the English realized that they had simply not recognized this plant for what it was—a different variety of tea bush indigenous to Assam and thus different from the Chinese tea bushes. Bruce died in 1825, but his brother, Major C. A. Bruce, continued efforts to convince government officials that the wild tea plants that thrived in the lush, dense jungle of Burmese Assam had a connection to the tea trees of Yunnan, China. He brought British officials from the India Tea Committee to the Sibsagar region, who ultimately gave their approval to start experimental tea gardens in this area.

England and China: Exchanging One Addiction for Another

By now the English wished that they had listened to earlier advice from Sir Joseph Banks, an English explorer and naturalist. Back in 1788 he had recommended that England pursue the idea of cultivating tea in northeastern India, but at the time the Crown chose to ignore this advice and fixate instead on trying to control the tea trade with China. The English had grown desperately dependent on Chinese tea. With their trade deficit growing, England launched a devious scheme to utilize the one thing they had that the Chinese could be made to want—Indian opium. For many years the English East India Company had operated opium production in Bengal. In 1776 the English intentionally began to create a market in China for opium, simply and ruthlessly exchanging one addiction for another: the Chinese became as hooked on opium as the British were on tea. But the consequences became much more dire for the Chinese.

Money from the sale of opium in China began to flow back into depleted English coffers, offsetting the money that was continually draining out to purchase tea. Despite years of protests for the British to stop dumping opium in China, the Chinese emperor could not stop sales of this popular drug. Failing to ban the drug, the emperor ordered vast quantities of British opium to be destroyed by setting fire to the warehouses. English retaliation against this rebellious Chinese act was the spark that ignited what became known as the Opium Wars of 1839–1842.

By the end of the conflict the Chinese were powerless against the might of the English forces. They were forced to pay the English for both the cost of the opium and the expenses of the war. Perhaps the greatest indignity was their forced cooperation at signing the Treaty of Nanjing, which gave the English ownership of the colony of Hong Kong and free trading rights in all Chinese ports.

Despite these heavy concessions from China, England was still desperate to control tea imports in an even greater way. While continuing to pursue the goal of growing their own tea, England's India Tea Committee argued over where to grow the tea gardens and chose locations out of ignorance where the bushes did not thrive. They also insisted on cultivating Chinese tea bushes, not the indigenous India tea bushes (at this time they did not believe these were tea bushes simply because they had a different appearance and habit). Because of their lack of understanding on these two points, cultivation was not going well in India. The English knew that they needed to learn the process of tea cultivation from the Chinese, the only people who knew these secrets. But fearful of foreigners, the Chinese exercised control over traders and zealously guarded any information about tea production. Foreigners had always been barred access to travel into China's interior. Ever fearful of the possibility of interactions with Western females, China kept Western women even further at bay than were Western men.

In 1848, in a well-crafted plan of espionage and pretense, the English hired the Scottish botanist Robert Fortune to dress as a Chinese businessman and go undercover in Fujian Province with the intent of collecting tea plants and learning the Chinese processes for manufacturing both green and black tea. With the help of Chinese accomplices Fortune's subterfuge was successful. He returned triumphant, with smuggled tea cuttings, technical information, and more than eighty Chinese tea specialists who were ready to put their knowledge to work in India. The subsequent tea bushes

THE GOLDEN AGE OF SAIL:
THE TEA CLIPPERS

Despite the protests against English taxation that led to the Boston Tea Party, New England colonists remained tea drinkers. In fact, the United States began to trade directly with Canton, China, after 1784 for purchases of tea. In the 1840s fast, sleek, streamlined ships called Yankee Clippers became a new force in the highly profitable merchant trade.

The fast-sailing clipper ships were built to bring valuable cargo of tea, silks, and porcelains to port by the fastest means possible. These graceful, three-masted, fully rigged ships ruled the seas for a time. When the Crown decentralized control of imports of tea into England in 1834, the East Indies Tea Company no longer had sole grip on the two-hundred-year monopoly on tea imports. The company was suddenly encountering competition from other English businessmen and entrepreneurs. This was followed by another blow in 1849, when England repealed the Navigation Acts. Now, anyone, including non-English, could bring goods into a British port.

American shipbuilders raced into the game. Competition from America was on in full force in this Age of Sail. England retaliated with a fleet of British-built tea clippers, and the race was on for the fastest delivery of tea from China to England. The tea clippers not only provided the freshest tea, but a boisterous interest in this exciting new twist in tea commerce fed the passions of a committed tea-drinking public. Wagering on which ship would make the journey fastest became a social exercise of the day, and the tea from the winning ship gained a special cachet in social circles and of course commanded the highest price.

The development of steamships in the early part of the 1800s and the opening of the Suez Canal in 1869 put an end to the glorious and romantic era of these sleek clipper ships. Even though the tea clippers such as the *Houqua*, the *Flying Cloud*, the *Taeping*, and the *Rainbow* could make the trip in 107 days, steamships could do it in just under fifty. The only surviving tea clipper, the British *Cutty Sark*, is now kept in a specially created dry dock in Greenwich, England.

SIR THOMAS LIPTON

Perhaps no one has done more to promote tea than the Scottish merchandising whiz Sir Thomas Lipton. After the coffee blight of the mid-1880s decimated the coffee crops in Ceylon, Lipton purchased bankrupt estates in Ceylon and began cultivating tea. He undercut the going selling price for tea and created the slogan "Direct from the Tea Gardens to the Teapot," a selling tactic that brought him great financial success. Lipton emphasized the adventurous nature of his tea enterprise, and played on the exotic, foreign nature of Ceylon to captivate the interest of tea drinkers back home.

Lipton was the first merchant to sell his tea in sealed packets, emphasizing freshness, cleanliness, and honest weight. He became a millionaire and succeeded by capturing the loyalty of tea drinkers in both England and later in America. His efforts to encourage and realize colonial tea expansion in Ceylon added to the British empire's already firmly established control of tea production in India. This expansion brought about the ability of the British to control tea cultivation at the source and to sever trade ties with China for tea forever.

propagated from cuttings and seeds he smuggled out of China numbered more than twenty thousand plants.

Now it seemed that England had the pieces of the puzzle necessary to begin establishing tea gardens in India. Fortune's plants and seeds were sent to the Darjeeling region, where by sheer luck the Chinese plants thrived in the cool, high elevations. But things were moving much more slowly in Assam. Not understanding that China had different varieties of local tea plants that were acclimated to cooler weather and higher elevations, the English planted Chinese tea bushes in the warm, humid, rainy lowland region of Assam. These bushes failed, as did thousands of other plants, cuttings, and seeds that had been brought from China. It was not until 1847 and the arrival of George Williamson in Assam that English understanding of tea cultivation began.

Williamson was appointed manager of Assam, and he began to make a careful study of tea plants and the successes and failures of various tea gardens. He determined that the problem was not with the local Assam bushes but with the English insistence on planting China bushes there. In experimental gardens where Assam bushes had been carefully pruned and cultivated, tea had successfully habituated. Williamson lobbied to remove all China bushes from the tea gardens and replace them with cultivated Assam bushes. From that point on the English tea industry in Assam flourished.

It was not until the English began to hybridize these varieties that they achieved tea bushes that possessed the best virtues of each bush, and the modern "Assam bush" was successfully propagated. Despite their trials and errors, the English had accomplished their goal of controlling tea imports to England in fewer than fifty years. By 1900 India was supplying 154 million pounds of tea to England. Purchases of Chinese tea, which had once constituted 90 percent of all tea purchased, dwindled to a mere 5 percent a year. The Chinese tea industry would falter under this loss, and would not recover from this blow until the end of the twentieth century.

With success under their belt in India, the English were able to use their tea knowledge to propagate tea on their island colony of Ceylon in 1875. This island paradise, the jewel in the English Crown, was well known for extensive coffee farms that had been established nearly a hundred years before. A devastating coffee blight hit the Ceylon coffee farms in 1869, however, and the coffee industry, once booming and highly profitable, was in ruins by 1878. Systematically, the English changed the coffee farms into tea gardens, where the tea bushes luxuriated in Ceylon's rich soil and tropical climate.

The Modern Age and Changes in the World of Tea

In 1878 the success of the English in India led the Dutch to import Assam tea bush cuttings onto the island of Java. After close to forty-five years of only mediocre luck cultivating tea bushes brought from China and Japan, this was the final attempt to establish a thriving tea industry on this Indonesian island. A decade earlier the government of Java had privatized the tea industry, making way for ambitious tea planters to expand facilities, create better roads, and improve the conditions of the existing tea gardens. The Assam bush acclimated easily to the island's weather, and this proved to be the key that opened the door to success.

The English and the Dutch had managed to crumble China's once tightly held dominance in the tea world. The taste preferences of western Europeans for strong, dark tea succeeded in nearly pushing the once beloved Chinese teas completely from their tea tables—Chinese tea imports fell from 100 percent to just under 10 percent, lashing a devastating blow to the Chinese tea industry. To make matters worse for the Chinese, the Russian Revolution in 1917 brought Russia's trading relations with China to a halt.

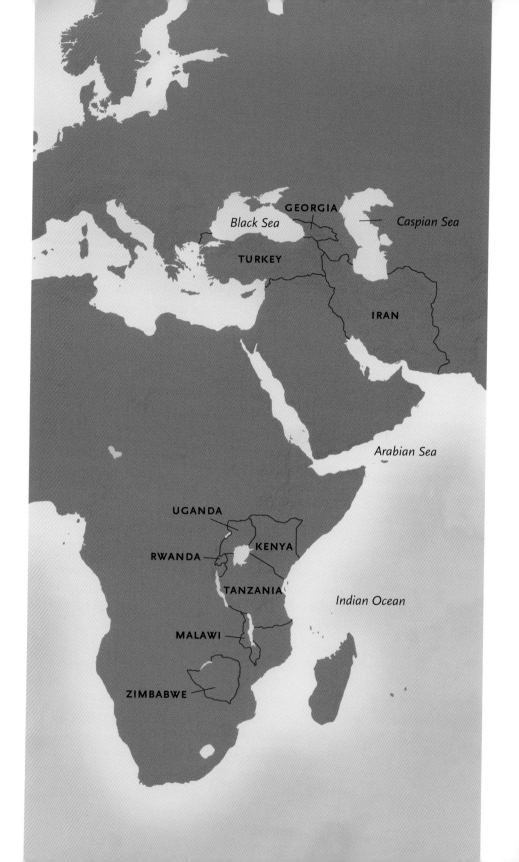

Black Sea

GEORGIA

Caspian Sea

TURKEY

IRAN

Arabian Sea

UGANDA

KENYA

RWANDA

TANZANIA

Indian Ocean

MALAWI

ZIMBABWE

With the dawn of the modern age came other changes in the world of tea. In the early 1900s the camel-driven tea caravans to Mongolia and Siberia ended when the Trans-Siberian Railway was completed. Now this once impossibly long journey could be completed in just seven weeks. And the heavenly "tribute teas," once held in reserve for use by only the celestial Chinese emperors, became classified as "famous teas" and are now for sale to tea connoisseurs worldwide. The bygone era of adventure, mystery, and colorful intrigue once associated with tea evolved into a mature and robust industry through the continued efforts of dedicated tea growers rooted in a proud tradition of producing high-quality tea.

Africa has also become a world player in tea production. The continent's major tea gardens were started just before and after the turn into the twentieth century in the Portuguese, Dutch, and British colonies of East Africa and in the eastern portion of South Africa. Success with experimental tea gardens in Malawi, which were begun in the mid-1880s, led to the pursuit of tea cultivation in other African colonies. In 1903 tea seeds from Assam tea bushes were first planted in Kenya, then in Tanzania in the mid-1930s. The African tea industry was modeled after the flourishing tea industries of India and Ceylon, so without the need for experimentation or the foibles of misjudgments, the gardens developed quickly.

Today—in addition to Africa, China, India, Indonesia, Japan, and Sri Lanka—tea production has spread to more than forty-five countries in the Middle East, South America, the South Pacific, and Southeast Asia. Interest in tea culture and the rediscovery of tea's appealing nature has a new generation of tea drinkers embracing this ancient beverage in record numbers. Across America and Europe, cafés, restaurants, and tea salons offer selections of teas to suit every palate. Classic Asian and English tea service is more popular than ever in upscale hotels and specialty tea salons. The history of the world's oldest beverage continues to be made every day.

CHAPTER 2

THE LIFE OF
A TEA BUSH

EARLY TEA PLANT USAGE PREDATES WRITTEN HISTORY, and Chinese emperors had a tradition of "adjusting" the historical record to take credit for revered aspects of culture (such as tea cultivation as well as brewing and drinking rituals), so the exact origins of the plant that today we know as *Camellia sinensis* will be forever unknown. Experts agree that the two most probable sites, however, are the portion of the Tibetan Plateau in northwestern China that includes the upper reaches of Yunnan Province eastward to Mengding Mountain in northwestern Sichuan Province, and the Brahmaputra valley at the point where India, Myanmar, and Tibet meet. Peoples indigenous to these areas have been consuming the leaves of this plant in various forms for centuries, from the Burmese *letpet* (pickled tea salad) to Tibet's milk tea (a hot beverage brewed from caked tea and then churned with barley meal, salt, and goat or yak butter).

Although no documentation exists for the early peoples of the inner reaches of the Brahmaputra valley, where it rises from the Assam valley to meet the Himalaya, there is evidence that ancient people cultivated tea gardens there that then became overgrown and not reclaimed until long after the British had "discovered" what they assumed were wild indigenous tea plants. Modern-day tea growers and latter-day explorers in the area have encountered roads and well-planned "gardens," indicating that long ago tea was an important crop in the region. Like the area surrounding Angkor, in Cambodia, much of the current access is possible only because of this historical development. This is one of the few remaining untamed places on earth, and not many travelers have ventured into the region. It is ruled by the tribal warlords of the indigenous ethnic minorities, so it is extremely

Jade Mountain (Yunnan Province, China).

unstable politically. But tea bushes thrive there, growing quickly into trees in this, one of the wettest places on earth.

Chinese historians trace the origins of *Thea sinensis* to the valleys and foothills of the lower Tibetan high plateau in northwestern Yunnan Province. This region is close both geographically and topographically to the Brahmaputra valley. Flying from Chengdu to Lhasa on China Airlines in late February 2004, we looked out over this incredible part of the world with appropriate awe.

It is certainly apt that this region would also be the origin of the former Tea Horse Route that brought tea from the lush Sichuan mountains to be traded for the wild horses of the upper plateaus. We believe that the "original" tea grew throughout this area, including Myanmar and south along the Mekong River to the Chinese border with Laos. Selecting one particular spot as *the* origin is not only historically impossible but also expressively unnecessary. Although governments have divided this region in various ways over time, the story of tea throughout this area's history has been a coalescing factor.

Camellia sinensis, the evergreen plant that we call the tea bush, was originally named *Thea sinensis*. In May 1753, in volume 1 of his *Species Plantarum* (the work considered to be the start of modern systematic botany), the Swedish botanist Linnaeus assigned the tea plant to the family (or genus) *Thea*. Unfortunately, in August of the same year he also named the plant as belonging to the family *Camellia*, in volume 2 of the same work. What was he thinking?

For years botanists have argued as to whether these two genera are identical, and if not, to which does the tea plant belong. The consensus seems to be that they are similar, though not identical, suggesting that *Thea* be retained as a separate genus. This confusion is exacerbated by the fact that there are many subvarieties of the tea plant (with different habits) that grow in different places. In 1905, after enduring several name changes (such as the beautiful *Thea borea* and *Thea viridis*) and the addition of many subvariety monikers, the International Code of Botanical Nomenclature determined that the plant would be known as a member of the family *Camellia*. Therefore, we use the term *Camellia* throughout this book.

Growing Habit and Climate Preferences

Two primary genera of *Camellia sinensis* exist, each having been found in one of these two historical locations. Which was known first is unclear, as early explorers familiar with one variety did not recognize the other in the wild until long after *Thea sinensis* had naturally hybridized itself into many subdivisions. This lack of early identification was due to their extremely different growing habits.

Today, the tea plant is a general term for the several genera of *Camellia sinensis*. These include *Camellia sinensis* var. *sinensis* (China bush), *Camellia sinensis* var. *assamica* (Assam bush), and *Camellia sinensis* var. *cambodi* (Java bush), also known as *Camellia assamica* subsp. *lasiocaly*. Each of these genera has many subdivisions. All together, there are more than a thousand subvarieties of the tea bush *Camellia sinensis*!

CAMELLIA SINENSIS VAR. *SINENSIS* (CHINA BUSH)

This tea plant thrives on cool mountainsides with a southern exposure at elevations of 6,500 to 9,800 feet (2,000 to 3,000 meters). Its short growing season generates a small yield of a tender, fine leaf that often has less tannin content than the leaf of its cousin, the Assam bush. Equally evergreen, it may suffer seasonal die-off due to extreme temperature variations or the reduction of oxygen and earth nutrients in its environment, but it tolerates frost 6 inches (15 centimeters) into the ground. China bush grows as a shrub, 3 to 10 feet high (1 to 3 meters), with straight, nearly vertical branches that rise from the base of the plant like a fountain.

Allowed to grow free, it will develop a domed shape, so it is often pruned flat to create a table from which the new growth is plucked. The mature leaves are alternate, deeply green, leathery, and smooth, with serrated margins. Because of the seasonality of the climate, China bush has distinct picking times, with no more than four to five plucks a year. The new growth consists of erect, light green elliptical blades that present the classic profile of two leaves and a bud.

Above: Nature's most perfect leaf configuration.

China bush is grown throughout China, Japan, Taiwan, and some locales in Southeast Asia, as well as the Himalaya (most notably the half-dozen traditional gardens of Darjeeling). This genus, combined with hand-plucking and careful manufacture, is celebrated primarily for the finer, most highly regarded quality leaf for green tea. It is also the plant of choice for producing all the classes of tea in China, particularly the softer-style oolongs of Fujian, the smooth black teas of Yunnan Province, and the winey, brisk, and stylish Keemun tea of Anhui Province in central China.

Ready to be plucked, these tea "tables" in the well-planted Satrupa Garden show the larger leaf and verdant growth of Assam bush (Assam, India). Photo courtesy of Saunam Bhattacharjee.

CAMELLIA SINENSIS VAR. ASSAMICA (ASSAM BUSH)

This tea plant prospers in junglelike conditions. It thrives in rich, loamy soil that is preferably light, well drained, and slightly acidic. High humidity, rainfall of 100 inches (254 centimeters) a year, and an average temperature of 85°F (29°C) guarantee luxuriant growth. When the topography allows for a junglelike environment to ascend a mountain and tea grows there, above 6,500 feet (2,000 meters), conditions can be as ideal as they are in the flat, lower-altitude Assam valley.

Assam bush more closely resembles a small tree, potentially attaining a height of 35 to 50 feet (10 to 15 meters). Supported by a distinct trunk with a ramifying branch system, its leaves are large and glossy with distinct marginal veining. Its leaf is broadly elliptical, 4 to 8 inches long (10 to 20 centimeters) and 1½ to 3 inches wide (4 to 8 centimeters), and resembles the leaf of an orange tree or holly more than the feathery profile of the smaller leaf of its cousin, the China bush. In the subtropical and tropical conditions it prefers, Assam bush can often be picked every ten days, year-round, although for this volume of production, it needs to be fed heavily. Assam bush is the variety preferred for the high-quality black tea production of northeastern India, Sri Lanka, and most of Africa. Assam bush has a natural tendency to grow into a taller, less-rounded plant that is pruned and plucked differently than China bush is.

THE FUKUJUEN TEA RESEARCH CENTER

At the Fukujuen Research Center in Kyoto, we were given a walking tour of a collection of tea bushes planted outside of the facility by Dr. Kiyoshi Hayakawa. The research center has many types of Japanese cultivars growing in a tidy tea garden, as well as plants from China, India, and Sri Lanka. It was a treat to see such a veritable international gathering of the plants. According to Dr. Hayakawa, Japan has successfully cloned close to seventy-five cultivars of *Camellia sinensis*, including *Kanayamidori, Okumidori, Sayamakaori, Yabukita,* and *Yutakamidori.* But growers tend to favor the *Yabukita* variety, which accounts for approximately 80 percent of all the tea cultivars planted. Just as the Chinese are experimenting with the oolong varietal Tieguanyin for manufacture into black tea, the Japanese are cloning Tieguanyin into varietals for use as a new flavor profile in green tea or for future Japanese oolong production.

CAMELLIA SINENSIS VAR. *CAMBODI* (JAVA BUSH)

This is the tea plant of choice for growing areas that are tropical, rugged, and often mountainous. It is a hearty variety, but its yield is less dependable than that of the Assam bush. Its history is one of intrigue and stealth, having been snuck onto the Indonesian archipelago during the days of Dutch control, in an effort to expand the quantity of tea available to Dutch traders.

The Java bush is arguably a close relative of the Assam bush, sharing many similarities; however, biologists have given it subvariety status because of its unique characteristics of habit and flowering. It is the variety on which many hybrids are based, and it provides many of the "mother trees" for the vegetative propagation of modern-day cultivars. Java bush is found in the regions of Southeast Asia, especially Indonesia, where it is used for the higher volume–lower quality tea production needed for local consumption. The Java bush, being a more vigorous but inconsistently productive plant, has a range that is limited to the searing temperatures and humid conditions of the more tropical regions of tea cultivation.

Setting the "Table"

Density of planting is a critical factor, ranging from the traditionally wild-grown Chinese plantings (where bushes develop at random on mountain slopes, often with considerable shade canopy but rarely any crowding), to highly cultivated plantings in full sun in Sri Lanka, Malawi, and India (where there can be three thousand to four thousand bushes per acre), and Japan (where tea bushes are planted in surveyed, well-organized, and meticulously planned gardens).

Tea bushes produce well and are most conducive to being plucked when they are pruned to a manageable height. This varies by growing region. Careful pruning of young *Camellia sinensis* var. *sinensis* plants encourages the formation of a flat top surface of the bush, known as the "plucking table." From this table new growth emerges and is plucked for harvest, and old wood is removed during the annual pruning to maintain shape and airiness. This plucking table is at a maximum height of 3 feet (1 meter), and the bush is shaped to have a diameter of 3 to 4 feet (1 to 1.25 meters). Together these factors stimulate the bush to produce bountiful tender new leaf rather than a woody stem that would transform it into a tree. In Japan this same variety of tea bush is trimmed to a taller height and given a more sculpted, flowingly connected form. This maximizes yield and accommodates the shearing machinery that plucks the leaf. The pruning of *Camellia sinensis* var. *assamica* plants, however, gives shape to the larger, taller, shrublike bushes that are more apt to produce the larger leaf being plucked.

Whichever variety is planted, the goal is to harvest an abundance of fresh leaf appropriate to the style of tea for which the particular region is famous. Although all types of tea can be made anywhere, with leaf plucked from any of the different varieties of bush, it is well proven that certain varieties of the tea plant, grown in a particular location, will thrive and best produce leaf that has the "correct" flavor profile for that place.

Defile not its purity,

For drinking it expunges dust and woe.

The taste of this thing is spiritual,

Taking it from the mountain where naturally it grew,

I planted it in my own garden.

The bushes, to my delight, flourished,

And I could invite my wonderful friends.

—WEI YINGWU, "THE JOY OF GROWING TEA IN MY GARDEN," SONG DYNASTY

The *Terroir* of Tea

So how can it be that thirty-nine countries, producing the six classes of tea with thousands of minor variations of leaf style and shape, all rely on fresh leaf from the same base plant? Black tea from the Tibetan plateau of northern Yunnan Province in southwestern China, made from China bush tea plants, bears resemblance to but is quite different than the black tea from the Darjeeling district of northern India that is also prepared from China bush tea plants. Why is this so?

Both are grown at a similar altitude, longitude, and temperature range. The geographic proximity of these two renowned tea-producing regions, combined with the climatological similarities of their mountainous growing conditions, soil, orientation, and seasons, explains why China bush is the preferred tea plant for these two high-altitude, rugged locations. Historically, traditional tea production in Yunnan yields both exquisite green tea and black tea, while Darjeeling has had considerable difficulty manufacturing a high-quality green tea or oolong to stand beside its elegant black tea. This is particularly so for the gardens that have changed over to growing the hybrid, or clonal, varieties. Through the introduction of some of the characteristics of the Assam bush, these varieties have increased the ruggedness and yield of the harvest but still favor the production of black tea.

TEA FOR BUDDHA

During the Tang dynasty Buddhist monks placed a statue of Buddha in the temple tea gardens. Monks known as tea keepers began the practice of offering sacrificial cups of tea to Buddha.

In the eighteenth century early English tea planters did not understand that all styles of tea—green, black, and later oolong and white—could be manufactured from the same leaf. The Chinese, who had figured this all out, held the secret for a long time. Other tea producers eventually recognized the major factors that would theoretically allow any tea-producing country to manufacture whichever style of tea they desired. Demand has changed, and markets have adjusted to new alliances. Starting in the 1990s, Darjeeling tea producers began to manufacture oolong, green, and white teas that (although not yet as good as the Japanese and Chinese versions) show that it is the variety of the tea plant in its terroir that provides the raw ingredient to which need only be added the learned expertise of manufacture.

China bush tea plants have the flavor that one expects from Chinese tea, especially for the tea styles being processed at high altitude, in rugged terrain, and at a cooler climate. This is also the same base flavor necessary for green, oolong, or white Darjeeling tea. Fundamental experience in manufacture and processing of these styles of tea is vital in turning out high-quality versions of these "new" teas from the Himalaya. In time, the Himalayan tea artisans will master the technical production of oolong, green, and white teas.

But will this newly learned skill produce tea of a quality that matches up to the tea of the same three styles when produced in Japan or China? To date, most Himalayan green tea and oolong has been purchased inexpensively by the Taiwanese and Japanese for their domestic consumption, freeing up more of their homegrown, high-quality tea for export at a higher

The next generation of tea bushes ready for transplant (Darjeeling, India). Photo courtesy of Eliot Jordan.

price than they pay for this imported tea. Economically, this buying low and selling high helps keep the balance of trade in their favor, while contributing to the Himalayan tea producers' cash flow.

Conversely, just to the east of Darjeeling, in the Assam valley, the Assam bush yields some of the finest black tea produced. But the Assam bush has yet to produce a world-class green tea or oolong, in the Assam valley or anywhere else that it has been planted (such as in Indonesia and mainland Southeast Asia). This is a result of the different growth habit, plucking technique, and natural flavor profile of the Assam bush, as well as the inherent difficulty in crafting it into a first-quality oolong, green, or white tea. With the advent of modern hybrids and clonal varieties, the introduction of China bush characteristics into Assam bush plants is expected to yield a hearty new variety that will be able to be crafted into a good-tasting version of the oolong, green, and white teas that are so much in demand. Interestingly, a small amount of excellent quality (and expensive) white tea is now coming from a few Assam gardens, a sign that the science of tea plant–hybrid creation may be combining with traditional manufacture to produce at least one example of a quality "new" tea.

The narrow Straits of Taiwan separate Fujian Province on the Chinese mainland from the island of Taiwan. Both of these world-famous tea regions produce superior oolong teas. This is the result of the combination of planting the time-tested subvarieties of the China bush varietal that yield great-tasting oolong tea, how they are planted (whether or not they are wild-grown), the ter-

The grandfather plants and raises the tea bushes, the father harvests the tea, and the son drinks it.

—CHINESE SAYING

roir, and the skill of the tea maker. Some of the teas from these two regions are quite similar, and some are extremely different; however, the factors that they share exceed those that they do not. The reason that these two regions excel at oolong production is explained in the same way that one can understand how authentic Champagne from France differs from other sparkling wines, and why traditional Roquefort cannot be produced anywhere else but in the limestone caves of the French Auvergne, no matter the effort exerted. Fresh tea leaves from any tea plant can be forced to manufacture into any of the tea styles, but when naturally occurring factors combine to create the definitive version of a type, a certain magic happens.

The Yearly Cycle of a Tea Bush

A tea bush's annual growth cycle is determined by a combination of factors: (1) which subdivision of the *Camellia sinensis* family it is in, and (2) precisely where the plant is being grown. Every tea-growing region has a unique climatological character. Most geographical areas grow a specific variety or two of tea bush. The eventual manufacture of plucked leaf into the desired class of tea may require that a certain pluck from a particular plant be used to create the highest-quality tea of a specific type. This model of terroir bolsters the reputation of such place-specific teas as single-garden Darjeelings, Tieguanyin, Longjing, and Keemun Hao Ya.

Tea that grows wild is superior; garden tea takes second place.

—LU YU, CHINA'S "FATHER OF TEA"

The two major subspecies of the *Camellia sinensis* plant family share some growing-condition preferences, but they tend to favor dissimilar geographic locations. *Camellia sinensis* var. *sinensis*, the China bush, although evergreen, has a distinct growing season. China bush generally thrives in locations near the northern or southern margins of the subtropical zone, at a significant altitude, generally preferring to be between 3,000 and 5,000 feet (900 to 1,500 meters) on mountainsides having a 45- to 60-degree slope. Its cousin, *Camellia sinensis* var. *assamica*, the Assam bush, grows mostly in the subtropics on rolling hills at modest altitude, so it produces new leaf either continuously or with a less-distinct season than China bush does.

All tea bushes require plentiful moisture—100 inches (254 centimeters) minimum of rainfall a year is ideal—and good drainage. A southeast-facing slope that embraces morning humidity in the form of mist, fog, or dew, followed by moderate afternoon sun, provides the ideal orientation for growing tea. Intermittent drying-off periods throughout the year assist with the harvest and processing of the leaf, and a really wet phase or monsoon season ensures replenishment of adequate moisture and nutrients to the soil. Particular regions in the world excel in producing leaf destined to become a certain specific finished tea. These unique areas tend to have a reliably constant climate from year to year.

CHINA BUSH

In general, tea bushes are not pruned immediately before the harvest season. Pruning and fertilizing are done, if at all, after the harvest has ended, as a resolution to the season's production and a preface to the dormant season. Dependent on a resting period during its yearly cycle (during which it tolerates cold temperatures, possibly including minor frost), China bush sends its new growth out in early spring, breaking dormancy. Influenced by orientation, elevation, and landmass or coastal location, this bud break occurs between March and May in the northern hemisphere and September and November in the southern hemisphere. After the bush is picked (or pruned, see "Uniquely Japanese" later in this chapter), in the early spring, new growth appears every several weeks for the duration of the growing season, continuing through late autumn.

The spring bud break is known generally as the "first flush" and signals the start of the growing period for new leaf. As the first flush is almost universally the finest crop of the year's production, it is picked carefully and thoroughly. A tea bush can often be plucked fully as a first flush, because the plant has the entire growing season to regenerate the leaf necessary to maintain its vigor through the dormant period. When leaf is plucked by hand, the selection of budset, bud, or leaf picked through the rest of the season is critical to both the manufacture of the tea being produced at that time and the future vigor of the tea bush. In most tea-growing locations, there is a rainy season that separates the first and second flushes that provides respite and renewal for the plants after the heavy picking done during the first pluck. This period also affords the tea workers time to regroup after their busiest harvest time.

There is also the phenomenon of the monsoon season, which occurs fairly predictably at various times in different regions but generally during the summer months. During a monsoon period it is difficult to pick and process leaf, but when accomplished well it can result in fabulous tea, soft and lush with little astringency. In contrast, drought or a burst of high heat can stimulate an exceptional concentration of flavor. Even when leaf is not plucked during midharvest rainy or hot intervals, there is usually a valuable minor harvest in autumn, when the temperature cools, the air dries, fog and mist abound, and quality leaf reemerges.

In general, to manufacture traditional white tea, fancy green tea, and high-quality tippy or full budset black tea, budsets are plucked primarily in the spring and then to a lesser degree again as they develop throughout the season, depending on the weather and style of tea production in a region. In many locations the autumn harvest is often second to the first flush in quality. The finest oolongs, excellent-to-good-quality whole-leaf green teas, many black teas, and several other "ordinary" tea harvests are plucked in the period between the first flush and dormancy. So subject to location, type of bush being plucked, and the desired finished tea, the season of harvest varies from one tea-producing region to another.

ASSAM BUSH

When cultivating Assam bush, geographical location becomes the dominant factor that dictates quantity and timing of picking. Because the preferred climate for Assam bush allows that the leaf can emerge at any time, it is critical to be aware of and work with the rainy or dry seasons of a particular region. Assam bush will readily tolerate high temperatures and humidity, while still requiring good drainage. Assam bush does not tolerate cold or frost, however. Ideally, Assam tea bushes benefit from plentiful rainfall (even more than for China bush), interspersed with dry intervals and plucking. When this cycle occurs regularly throughout the year, the annual crop will be consistent in volume and quality. Assam and Sri Lanka both enjoy this type of cycle.

If a growing area is particularly either rainy or dry throughout the year, the finished tea produced will tend to be inconsistent but will have "vintages": occasional years of exceptional quality tempered by many years of mediocrity. This explains the common lack of marketable high-quality tea from Southeast Asia, Indonesia, and other more weather-volatile growing regions. Because leaf tea is inexpensive and rarely stores well for years and years, the world tea market overall does not recognize vintage growth. Historically, highs and lows in the quality of leaf teas from Assam bush are more often judged negatively as being inconsistent rather than as a cycle in which a particular harvest might be worthy of individual recognition. In general, China bush leaf generates more interest and has a greater acceptance as being of a generally higher quality than does leaf produced from Assam bush. This is changing, however, as new flavor profiles are being appreciated and unique clonals incorporate the best virtues of each variety.

UNIQUELY JAPANESE

In Japan a different method is used for harvesting the bulk of the tea leaf. Pruning is done both in autumn and again in March, so that the first flush in May or June is unvarying in size and timing throughout the plantings in a garden. Tea-leaf picking in Japan is generally accomplished with mechanical "shears" that fashion an arched shape to their carefully sculpted rows of tea bushes. This unique shape maximizes the surface area available for new growth and is easily maintained.

As the tea season in Japan is late and short, these rows are then fertilized and shorn thoroughly on a regular schedule to produce a consistent, high yield for about four months. The most rare, and therefore costly, highest grades of Japanese tea are plucked by hand, and traditional methodology is followed. This hand-plucking occurs most famously in Uji and Shizuoka prefectures, first in early spring for the Shincha ("first pick") harvest and again later in the season for top-quality gyokuro and the finest sencha.

As Japan produces primarily green tea, there are two distinct seasons, the early growth tea gathered in April and May known as Ichiban Cha ("new tea") and the rest of the season's harvest. Within the Ichiban Cha harvest there is one subdivision called Shincha, the first tea harvest of the year. Celebratory in nature, great fanfare is given to Shincha's release, a salute similar to that given to the Beaujolais nouveau wine and *olio novello* olive oil issues. The amount of Shincha produced is tiny and, until recently, it was only available within the region of production. Today Shincha is available to tea lovers throughout Japan and is air-shipped to tea enthusiasts worldwide.

Tea gardens in Japan are highly organized and trim (Shizuoka, Japan).

In this garden, both old- and new-style covering material is used for tana (Uji, Japan).

Two other distinctly Japanese variations of growing technique occur in the spring. These involve the preparation for the harvest of the leaf used for gyokuro and *tencha* (the leaf that is processed into *matcha*). Twenty to thirty days before harvest the bushes to be plucked for these two styles of Japanese green tea are enclosed with curtains. Known together as *kan-reisha*, there are two styles: *tana* and *jikagise*. A tana covering is a semipermanent greenhouse that resembles the structure used to shield shade tobacco.

The more common tana is a wire-frame construction with woven mesh curtain walls and cover that allows workers to move about beneath its canopy to tend the bushes and harvest the leaf. Sheltering many rows of bushes at once, a tana enclosure is extremely important for a grower with a quantity of leaf tea to harvest. Both the side and top curtains can be adjusted for air circulation during harvest and on cloudy days. The older, more traditional-style tana is made of reed mats tied together as both vertical sidewalls and blinds, creating the structure. We investigated both types of these tana during our recent visit to the gardens of Uji. We found that the reed mat tana fashioned a wonderfully dappled light that was both mysterious and curious. A jikagise is basically a cloche, tied down so that it floats just above the bush, sheltering just one row per section of fabric. It must be rolled down the row to gain access to the bushes that it covers. Much fussier and less practical for covering very many bushes, jikagise are used by small growers and in family gardens.

Do not pick on the day that has seen rain nor when clouds spoil the sky. Pick tea only on a clear day.

—LU YU, CHINA'S "FATHER OF TEA"

The highest-quality gyokuro and tencha plantings are grown beneath tana coverings. Tea bushes grown under cover yield leaf with reduced astringency and chlorophyll, so in the cup the brewed tea tastes sweet and mild, with little bitterness and a lighter color. Conversely, most Japanese green tea is grown in full sun and has a strident, complex flavor that is vegetal and deliciously bitter, with a bright green color.

Table 2.1. The Seasons of Tea, by Country

Country	Season
Argentina	October through November (dormant June through August)
China (except subtropical regions)	March through May (dormant December through mid-February)
India (northern)	March through mid-April and mid-May through June (dormant December through February)
India (southern)	December through February (some year-round)
Japan	May through August (dormant September through April)
Java	July through September (some year-round)
Kenya	Mid-January through February, and July through August (some year-round)
Sri Lanka (Nuwara Eliya)	Year-round
Sri Lanka (eastern districts)	June through October (some year-round)
Sri Lanka (western districts)	December through April (some year-round)
Sri Lanka (Dimbula)	December through April (some year-round)
Taiwan	March through October

Table 2.2. A Year in the Life of a *Camellia sinensis* var. *sinensis* (China Bush) Tea Garden

Season	Activity	Northern Hemisphere	Southern Hemisphere
Spring	Bud break/initial budset pluck aka "first flush"	March	September
Spring	Budset pluck	April	October
Spring	Budset pluck	May	November
Summer	Bud and leaf pluck	June	December
Summer	Bud and leaf pluck	July	January
Summer	Leaf and bud pluck	August	February
Autumn	Leaf and bud pluck	September	March
Autumn	Bud and leaf pluck	October	April
Autumn	Pruning	November	May
Winter	Pruning/dormancy	December	June
Winter	Dormancy	January	July
Winter	Dormancy/bud break	February	August

CHAPTER 3

MANUFACTURE: FROM FRESH LEAVES TO DISTINCTIVE TEA

A S WE BEGIN THIS DISCUSSION OF THE DIFFERENT TYPES, or styles, of tea, let's first establish the fundamentals. It is essential that tea drinkers become familiar with these basics: the names given to the different types of tea, some information about the manufacture of tea and the process of oxidation (often incorrectly called fermentation) and the varying degrees to which it can be realized, and the ability to recognize whether a particular tea has been scented or flavored. It is also helpful if tea aficionados can recognize whether a tea is leaf tea, compressed tea, or handworked tea.

Some tea enthusiasts divide tea into two groups: the oxidized and the nonoxidized, while others separate tea into the so-called major and minor classes of tea. Throughout the 1970s and 1980s we used these popular designations in our own store. We have learned over the years, however, that to identify tea comprehensively, these categorizations are not adequate. We now describe tea with a more straightforward approach, so that casual tea customers can readily understand the principal distinctions, and then we guide interested tea enthusiasts in a more in-depth way.

First, readers should have a basic understanding of the difference between leaf tea and compressed tea. Although compressed tea (formerly known as "caked tea") is historically "older" and can qualify as being a form of manufacture or production (depending on the process used), leaf tea is the manufacture style of most tea purchased today. One enduring form of compressed tea, pu-erh, is discussed more fully later in this chapter.

An experienced picker plucks leaf for Gunpowder tea on the high-plateau border near Fujian Province (Zhejiang Province, China).

The Six Classes of Leaf Manufacture

The foundation of our categorization is the six classes of leaf manufacture. These fundamental methods are augmented throughout this chapter with the historically important and popular styles of tea production (including scented, smoked, flavored, compressed or "bricked," and presentation teas). Finished tea has been given many names over the centuries, but there have always been only six main "classes" of leaf tea manufacture. Most of these have subdivisions or distinctions from region to region, however, so read on!

One of the earliest and most logical systems for tea identification was devised early in the Ming dynasty (1368–1644) in China, where tea experts identified tea by the color of the liquor of the brewed beverage. Thus they used the designations of white, yellow, green, blue, red, and black to differentiate the various classes of tea. Over time a few of these names have changed, but their characteristics have not.

During the twentieth century many tea writers used a tea identification system that included only the most common forms of tea consumed at the time. This led to the creation of the "major/minor" list that is still popular today. This system lists only five teas—the majors being green, oolong, and black, and the minors being scented and bricked. Although this system has some practical simplicity for retailers, we disagree with its lack of completeness and therefore correctness. The system combines disparate tea types and leaves out several important styles of leaf manufacture that are well known today.

Table 3.1 shows the evolution of the organization of the styles of finished tea, from the old system to the new. The table provides a detailed definition of each of the six classes of leaf tea manufacture (including their relative oxidation), based on the historical tea-processing tradition and tempered with consideration for modern improvements. Elsewhere in this chapter we explore the many other tea-production methods, showcasing scented, smoked, flavored, and other styles of tea.

Table 3.1. The Organization of the Styles of Finished Tea

Ancient Chinese System (Ming dynasty 1368–1644; by color)	Twentieth-Century System (William H. Ukers and most other twentieth-century tea writers; major/minor)
White	Green
Yellow	Oolong
Green	Black
Blue	
Red	Scented
Black	Bricked
Our Tea Identification System	**Organized by Level of Oxidation**
Green	None
Yellow	None
White	Very slight (>8 percent)
Oolong	Partial (20–80 percent)
Black	Complete
Pu-erh	Always fermented, not always oxidized

The Eight Elements of Tea Production

All tea processing has eight elements in common: plucking; sorting; cleaning; primary drying/withering; the manufacture specific to the different classes of tea (green, yellow, white, oolong, black, and pu-erh); final firing/drying; sorting; and packing. It is the central process known as the *manufacture* (step five above) that differs, and this midway process determines the class to which the finished tea belongs. The difficulties and challenges of this phase are the subject of endless debate among tea producers. The question of which class is the more difficult to coax from the fresh leaf is unanswerable, as each has intricacies and peculiarities that vary from region to region, from day to day, and from tea to tea. Consistency in leaf tea manufacture is an achievable goal, but identicalness goes against nature and is therefore impossible.

The foundation of artisan tea is the pluck. High-quality leaf, which is required to produce exceptional tea, is plucked from the bush by hand, in most locations. The main exceptions to this are in Japan and in the gardens that process tea by the cut-tear-curl (CTC) method (see "Processing CTC-

Manufactured Black Tea" later in this chapter). The plucking method varies, depending on the style and quality of the tea being produced. We have observed incredibly precise, artisanal plucking for such famous teas as Lu'an Guapian, Huang Shan Mao Feng, and Gunpowder. We have also seen so-called relaxed plucking of "run-of-the-harvest" tea.

In the gardens that specialize in the finer teas, the time-honored and exacting methodologies that have been used for centuries are still followed. Depending on which particular tea the finished product is to be, the choice of leaf may be determined as it is picked, it may be sorted before being sent down the mountain, and it will definitely be sorted and further cleaned at the primary processing facility. These techniques are fascinating to observe, learn about, and ultimately taste in the finished tea. Particularly in China, the process is central to the appreciation of tea. In addition to having a glorious flavor when brewed, the leaf tea in China must have an excellent appearance throughout all the stages of manufacture and brewing; more specifically, it must have the appearance expected of its type. Throughout this chapter we provide several examples of this plucking specificity of individual teas.

In other countries, most notably Japan, the "look" of the leaf is less important. What is paramount to Japanese tea drinkers are the qualities of the brewed tea, which have been developed during the craft of the tea's manufacture.

An artisan tea manufacturer examines the progress of his *aracha* (primary tea) (Shizuoka, Japan).

The mode of transport by which fresh leaf, deposited first in hand-carried pouches or baskets in the garden, is moved from the garden to the processing facility differs by region. Transport may be done by donkey-back, bucket conveyor belt, bicycle, tractor, motorbike, jeep, "pik-tuk" (the pickup version of the famous Asian three-wheeled "tuk-tuk"), aerial tram, boat, and truck. Containment during the early transfer must allow for good air circulation and a minimum of compression from the weight of the leaf. During this quick transport to the initial drying area, the fresh leaf begins to wilt, even though it is kept loosely gathered. It is transferred to progressively larger containers during transport to the processing facility.

The fresh leaf is taken to a processing facility, which will range from being a simple pavilion in the garden itself or in a village at the base of the mountain to a meticulously built regional factory specifically designed

This illustration portrays tea being transported by gondola. It is one in a series of nineteen panels that comprise an album that depicts tea production in China, circa 1790–1820. Image courtesy of Historic Deerfield.

One of the most elemental ferries we have ever seen moving fresh leaf was this wooden "gondola," which we rode back and forth to visit the tea gardens on Da Zhang Mountain (Jiangxi Province, China).

to process huge quantities of tea. These larger facilities typically include all the necessities of the employees: housing, schools, and medical facilities, as well as agricultural and recreational areas. Once at the processing facility, the fresh leaf is allowed to air-dry for a varying amount of time, depending on the class of tea to be manufactured.

During this preliminary phase of tea processing the leaf is sorted and cleaned. Debris, such as pieces of twig, broken leaves, and pebbles, is carefully removed, often by hand. Uniformity is critical to processing leaf into quality tea. The leaf must be processed in batches that are consistent, or the processing will not be even, and

Workers transport primary leaf from the receiving area to the manufacturing facility of a regional artisanal tea factory (Jiangxi Province, China).

Above, left: A young mother sorts tea while her daughter watches (Anhui Province, China).

Above: This modern tea facility in Wuyi presents young women with the opportunity to work in a clean, safe environment while earning a good wage (Fujian Province, China).

Left: This illustration from a Chinese tea production album dated 1790–1820 depicts village tea sorting. Image courtesy of Historic Deerfield.

the resulting tea will not meet the expectations necessary to develop into a high-quality finished product.

From this point the fresh leaf will take different paths on the route that will turn it into its eventual finished product. The variously processed leaf will share commonality again at the point of "finishing," when the final firing or drying occurs and the finished tea is given a final sorting. Finishing is an underestimated aspect of the whole of tea manufacture, but it is perhaps the most critical. Just as an ace finisher cannot create quality tea from poor leaf, if the tea is not finished properly, all the work that has gone before will be for naught.

One of the most disappointing moments of our professional tea life has to be the time many years ago that we opened a new "fresh" sack of what should have been a glorious tribute green tea, only to discover that the tea had the musty, damp-hay smell and off-taste that reveals improper finishing. The correct low-moisture content had not been properly achieved during the final firing, so that batch was ruined.

So now let's take a detailed look at the six great classes of tea. We will clarify how *manufacture*, that middle-phase process of tea production, determines which class of tea fresh leaf becomes.

Green Tea

The manufacture of green tea is all the more fascinating because there are several subcategories of the class. By describing the various styles of green tea, we show how their manufacture differs. We passionately encourage you to taste all of these fine teas and explore their intricacies. Perhaps you will be inspired to investigate the hundreds or even thousands of green teas available in the marketplace. We have been tea merchants for more than thirty years, and we are still as amazed and delighted by these artistic little leaves as we were in the early 1990s, when we first introduced extraordinary Chinese green teas to our customers.

The intrigue of artisan green tea has drawn us to Asia several times, allowing us a firsthand opportunity to source tea for our customers. We have been both to the world's largest tea factory (in Kaihua, Zhejiang Province, China) and to tiny, remote rural villages, where a simple common building serves as the local "factory" during tea season. Among our wonderful tea adventures over the years: We have observed tea being fired in a public park on a weekday afternoon, toured one of the first joint-venture facilities established between a Chinese tea grower and a Japanese tea importer, journeyed to the mountainside shrine that honors the monk who first cultivated tea, spotted tea being dried on the patios of simple village residences, tracked down centuries-old ancient tea trees, crossed a reservoir in the dark on a boat that had no running lights, drunk tea with monks on sacred mountains, and navigated hair-raising switchbacks on steep mountain "roads." We have participated in numerous experiences that have contributed to our knowledge of and fueled our passion for green tea.

There is no limit to the complexity, variety, and uniqueness of green tea. Consumers worldwide are being offered more choices of tea every day, and the best way to learn about green tea is to drink it. Many Americans think that they do not like green tea because too often their first taste is of inferior-quality green tea, brewed at too high a temperature and steeped for too long. To avoid this, follow our simple brewing instructions outlined in chapter 6. Green tea is not necessarily astringent. That being said, however, green tea *can* be astringent, and some varieties *should* be astringent, puckeringly so. Working alongside a reputable tea merchant, select the green teas that fit your taste preference.

Green tea is made by many tea artisans, in so many unique ways, that it is almost folly to attempt to describe it. There are reputed to be more than three thousand types of green tea in China alone, so it rivals wine in diversity. Please keep in mind that the information in this section describes artisan, high-quality, regional, authentically made leaf-style (*not teabag*) green tea.

Tea pickers in Tai Ping village (Anhui Province, China).

Fresh leaf for green tea is usually plucked in the morning and then brought down the mountain in baskets or cloth or fiber pouches. These containers promote air circulation and protect the fresh leaf from damage due to compression by weight.

After a quick, gentle sorting to remove twigs and extraneous matter, this fresh leaf is left to air-dry for a short time.

When processing green tea, this process is known as *primary drying* and is a shorter version of that used in the manufacture of oxidized leaf (for black tea and oolong), in which case it is known as *withering*. Primary drying helps prevent oxidation (the darkening of the leaf), whereas withering sets up the leaf for the rolling process that is so important to the manufacture of oolongs and black teas.

In this first phase of manufacture the picking is generally done by women and young adults. The budset is being picked, so it is essential that the smallest hands with the most slender fingers be employed for this delicate task. During the peak of the season everyone (of all ages) plucks, and those who have larger fingers must be more careful and inevitably pluck more slowly.

Primary leaf waiting to be fired (Anhui Province, China).

The entire community becomes involved and, as is the case with agriculture the world over, the appropriateness of an individual's skills to the tasks needing to be done is the guide that dictates who does which task.

When the leaf arrives at the "factory," the men generally assume responsibility, hauling the leaf around, operating the machinery, and performing the firing. But just as there are always men plucking leaf in the garden, skilled women also participate in these factory processes. Children often watch and learn, but they do not participate in these serious production activities. When we visited a remote tea factory in Jingangshan in southern Jiangzi Province in spring 2006, we learned that almost all the top tea firers in that community are female. The policy for that village is that no one is allowed to actually process leaf until he or she is at least eighteen. Before that, individuals can observe at their mentor's side; this period generally lasts two years.

Once the leaf is within the factory, two to five inches of fresh leaf is spread on mats on the floor to air-dry, which reduces the moisture content by several percentage points. The desired change is from a moisture content of between 75 and 77 percent to one between 65 and 70 percent. After a period of time that may range from a few minutes to well over an hour (depending on the leaf, the time of day, and the ambient air temperature and humidity), the first four standard elements of tea processing are completed. It is now time to initiate the manufacture that will create the particular style of green tea desired.

Artisanal basket-rolled primary leaf (Jingangshan, China).

The purpose of the first step in green tea manufacture is to prevent oxidation and to preserve its appealing green color. The drying process also keeps the soluble solids of the fresh leaf's "juice" intact, inside the leaf structure, where they contribute to the flavor, possible astringency, and overall healthfulness of the tea being manufactured. The fresh leaf that develops into green tea should be dried quickly, thoroughly, and completely. This is a critical factor, as improper drying yields low-quality tea at best and in most cases creates absolute waste. Leaf that remains too wet will mold and be unusable.

An integral component of all high-quality artisan green tea manufacture (other than the sun-drying technique, of which we write about on the next page) is the complex and precise handwork. This manipulation is part learned and part inherited. Without it, green tea can be tasty but not aesthetically beautiful. In many styles the handwork is integral to the firing, and in others it is a corollary step; it contributes to the completeness of the manufacture, is fascinating to observe, and offers tea artisans an opportunity to master an art form and share it with a loyal audience. Quick or slow movements of short or long duration yield varying results, depending on the season and the pluck. Every tea bush varietal and growing region has a tea style that its leaf tends toward; it is the artisan's goal, the *challenge*, to perfect that appearance and subsequent flavor. When fresh tea leaf is dried properly in the manufacture of green tea, particularly using the complex Chinese handwork drying techniques of panning or basket-firing, the result is a beautifully prepared and interesting-to-look-at tea, ready to be brewed into one of the world's most elegant beverages.

Table 3.2. The Primary Styles of Green Tea Manufactured Today

Artisanal Methodologies	Modern Methodologies
Sun-dried: *Saiqing*	Oven-dried: *Hongqing*
Basket-fired / charcoal-fired: *Hongpei* or *yaoqing*	Tumbled: (no Chinese equivalent)
Pan-fired: *Chaoqing*	Steamed: *Zhenqing*

SUN-DRIED GREEN TEA

Starting with artisanal tea-processing methods, the most traditional and basic technique is sun-drying. This method is straightforward, simple, and effective: the tea is laid out on mats in breezy, partial sun or shade and is periodically tossed, flipped, or shaken to change the leaf's orientation so that uniform drying occurs. Sun-drying is essentially controlled, lengthy, primary drying. It works best in those magical locations where the weather is particularly cooperative. The environments of the mountainous provinces of Anhui, Sichuan, or Yunnan in China, or the Darjeeling region of India, with their clear, crisply dry breezes and inherently low humidity, are conducive to this process. The sun-drying technique is not particularly successful when attempted in the humid jungle areas of Java or Myanmar.

Sun-dried tea in Xishuangbanna (Yunnan Province, China).

Once the fresh leaf has shed the necessary amount of moisture (approximately 60 percent), it is finish-fired and sorted. Sun-dried tea is one of the bulkiest teas in volume (similar to white tea), in part because of the lack of pressing or other application of weight during manufacture. Sun-dried tea is traditionally made from mature leaf (frequently using leaf picked from ancient, wild-growing trees), which is larger than the young leaf of a pruned tea bush and which has an inherently lower moisture content that makes sun-drying more feasible.

BASKET-FIRED GREEN TEA

This technique is one of the most remarkable to observe. To accomplish basket-firing, a small amount of fresh tea leaf, no more than 2.2 pounds (1 kilo), is placed in an upright bamboo or reed basket. Shaped like an hourglass, this basket is usually constructed in two parts. The upper portion that literally takes the heat deteriorates after only two or three days and is then replaced. Where bamboo is plentiful, the basket might be one piece, crafted so beautifully as to be a work of art.

Whichever construction is used, a tea-leaf firing basket stands two to four feet tall and consists of a top portion that is shaped like an oversized, smoothly conical hat, with a generous brim around the perimeter. After the primary drying, the leaf is put onto this top portion and the whole basket is placed over a small brazier or pile of charcoal embers. The heat must be gentle, so that the bamboo does not burn. The basket is kept over the charcoal for about a minute, and then the entire basket is lifted off and moved to the side, at which time the tea is "fluffed." The resiliency of the bamboo, combined with the particular shape of the cone, allows the tea masters to gently tap the bamboo, causing the tea to jump up and be tossed.

After this step the basket is placed back over the heat for another minute, before being taken off again. The leaf is fluffed and heated, fluffed and heated repeatedly for about fifteen to twenty minutes. Experienced tea masters stand, one on each side of the basket, and essentially dance their way through these movements, in perfect unison, without a misstep, mirror images of each other. It is a marvelous process to observe. When the leaf has shed the required amount of moisture, it is removed from the basket and piled onto a bamboo mat on the floor, where it rests and continues to air-dry until it is combined with other similarly processed leaf, ready for final firing and sorting. We have observed variations of this type of artisanal firing all over China, and the results are spectacular.

Accomplished basket-firers tend to the drying and shaping of the leaf (Anhui Province, China).

Green tea made using this technique tends to be full-flavored and singularly distinctive. A basket-fired green tea's flavor components can range from grassy and assertive to mineral, to being ever-so-slightly charcoal-finished (an esteemed taste in the western provinces of China). The finished tea is always bulky in volume, slightly twisted into open curls or very thin, quill-like needles. A modern adaptation of this technique employs the use of short, round, vertically mounted metal cylinders with a heat source beneath. This is the method of firing for Green Snail Spring (variously Bi Lo Chun or Pi Lo Chun), a famous green tea from Jiangsu Province. See chapter 5 for several examples of elegantly long, basket-fired teas.

Using this technique, one drum to a bank of several drums can be fired simultaneously using the same air-circulated heat source. Banks of this type of firing drums are used in midsized or large factories producing a quantity of tea. Rather than tossing the leaf, the manufacture of Bi Lo Chun tea requires a unique handwork that dictates the shape of the finished tea. Five motions repeated three times result in the leaf assuming and maintaining the desired classic form of Bi Lo Chun. These motions are a combination of a gentle twist and a roll: envision a slightly opened fiddle-head fern or escargot in miniature. We tried our hand at shaping a batch of this leaf in southern Sichuan Province—it is much harder to do than it looks! This style of firing is known as "baked" tea, even though no enclosure or cover is used. It is air-drying pure and simple. In basket-firing, the basket is moved on and off the heat source. When firing baked tea, however, the firing drum is fixed in place; the hot air must be controlled precisely, so that the heat changes from hot to warm to cool on a rotating basis, allowing the leaf to dry evenly and thoroughly.

Skilled Bi Lo Chun firers (Sichuan Province, China).

In both of these techniques, the goal of the tea-firer is to coax the leaf into a naturally relaxed dried shape as effort-lessly as possible, and then "fix" it at that moment with the finish-firing. When brewed later, the rehydrated tea leaf returns to its natural, fresh-leaf shape with as little effort as possible. This ensures that the energy (chi) of the tea is held in reserve to be released into the brewed tea, rather than hav-ing been needlessly driven out along the way by sloppy manufacture. These two types of tea firing, when accomplished artisanally, exemplify what is known as the tai chi of tea.

PAN-FIRED GREEN TEA

Pan-firing is one of the great methods of green tea manufacture. This method singularly accomplishes many of the tasks involved in the manu-facture of green tea. In just one process it fixes the "juice" within the leaf, drives moisture out of the leaf, seals in the flavor, dries the leaf to the proper moisture content before finish-firing, and adds a special toastiness to the taste. One of China's most well-known, highly regarded teas is the pan-fired Longjing (formerly spelled Lung Ching), also known as Dragon Well. Many tea experts would argue that Longjing, with its smooth appearance and flat, sword shape, is the quintessential pan-fired green tea. Every province in China, and perhaps every green tea–producing region in the world, tries its hand at fabricating a pan-fired green tea in the style and tradition of Longjing. Nowhere else on earth, however, are tea producers able to replicate its flavor. This is because of the unique *terroir* of the coastal region of Zhejiang Province, where this tea is grown.

Throughout eastern China we have observed many different styles of firing pans in use—from simple hammered wok-like pans set over a separate heat source (even the top of a range, as a wok would be for stir-fry), to elaborate built-in units fabricated specifically for the tea trade, and every configuration in between. Two versions common in China are the wood-fired double pan and the electric-fired single pan, which can be transported conveniently and set up outside of teashops in the more touristy parts of Shanghai and Hangzhou.

The primary dried leaf is "measured" into the pan with a bamboo scoop of the appropriate size for a sufficient amount of leaf, proportional to the size of the pan (approximately 2.2 pounds, or 1 kilo, of fresh leaf). This quantity is ultimately reduced by a factor of four or five. Even, gentle heat is necessary for the firing of green tea, so the small electric pan is perfect for the expert manipulation of small amounts of high-quality tea by a single person. The

Below left:
Close-up of a Longjing firing pan (Zhejiang Province, China).

Below right:
Workers in Jingangshan village add loft while drying and shaping the leaf (Jiangxi Province, China).

Above: Wood-fired five-pan firing station in Jingangshan village (Jiangxi Province, China).

temperature is controlled by a thermostat, or controls that are close at hand, built into the housing of the pan. When leaf is fired in a wood-fired pan, two pans are usually installed together in the same housing, and often one pair is partnered with another. Each pan must be worked by an individual tea artisan, and the wood fire must be tended by a third person (see the photograph of Tai Ping Hou Kui later in this chapter).

An experienced fire-tender can easily supervise the fires required for two pans, but supervising the fires for four pans requires quite a bit of focus. If the pans get too hot, the leaf quickly burns into ash, but if they get too cool, the tea won't fire properly. Watching the silent communication between the fire-tender and the pan-firer is hypnotic and peaceful. Like a good grill master or bread baker, much of the technique is instinctive and intuitive. On our most recent trip to rural China we observed five-pan "pods" arranged in a semicircle around a central chimney. The fire-tenders for these pods are able to supervise all five fires at the same time, as each pan has its own firebox, fed from behind the chimney.

This illustration from a Chinese tea production album dated 1790–1820 shows traditional wood-fired pan-firing and bamboo mat rolling. Image courtesy of Historic Deerfield.

One of the little-known secrets of most pan-firing is that a tiny amount of solidified tea-seed oil is used to help the leaf glide around the pan and keep it from burning. This solidified oil is the simple oil expelled from the seeds of tea bushes that are periodically left to grow, flower, and seed (while being rested from leaf production), or from the "mother" bushes used for hybridization and grafts. Tea-seed oil is solid at room temperature, so it can be molded into a stick and encased in a tube reminiscent of an oversized, old-fashioned grease pen (the kind that has a string incorporated into the wrapper). In this way the solidified oil can be exposed gradually and applied as needed. Artisan tea-firers keep a stick of this handy on the edge of the pan and use it to apply the thinnest possible "haze" of oil.

By using solid tea-seed oil, no foreign flavor is introduced to the leaf. The oil leaves a residue on many high-quality pan-fired green teas, so some of them (especially Longjing) have a slight luster to the dried leaf before brewing. This residue imparts a thin slick of oil to the surface of the first cup brewed; you must angle the surface of the brewed tea in the cup to the light, and really look carefully to see this. Part of the distinctive toastiness of many pan-fired green teas is due to the flavor of this oil.

In addition to their signature flavor profile pan-fired green teas are identifiable by their flat appearance. They are rarely "fluffy" in volume; rather, they tend to be compact, flattened by the repeated pressing they must receive in order to maintain contact with the firing pan and its directly applied heat. Pan-fired green teas tend to a soft, matte finish, with a color reminiscent of the petals of a baby artichoke. Budsets are commonly used for pan-firing, producing what are often referred to as "sparrow's tongue" or "lark's tongue" tea. However, "first leaf" tea is also processed as pan-fired green tea, in which case the finished tea resembles folded, flattened envelopes (as with Longjing).

One of the Ten Famous Teas, Tai Ping Hou Kui, from Anhui Province in central China, is most unusual and worth searching out. This tea is unique for many reasons, one of which is that it is one of the few teas that is both pan-fired and basket-fired. Following the standard initial preparation, the exceptionally large leaf Tai Ping Hou Kui is pan-fired in twin wood-fired pans and then set aside. The next step is especially unique: paper from the nearby mills that produce the renowned "rice paper" for calligraphy and Chinese scroll painting is laid on the basket tops, and a small amount of leaf is scattered on the paper. Another sheaf of paper is laid on top of the leaf and the whole is pressed, as a blotter, to remove moisture without removing aromatics.

After this blotting, the leaf is then refired in a traditional one-piece basket over a low ember fire to "fix" the tea. After a resting period, the leaf is finish-fired and the final product is realized: a large, flat, bright green whole-leaf tea, with the distinctive pattern of the paper embedded in its surface. Grown in an isolated region surrounding a protected lake, this world-famous tea was once reserved exclusively for use by the emperor or leaders of China, and as special gifts for dignitaries, diplomats, and visiting heads of state. Today, however, tea enthusiasts can source it from a reliable tea merchant who has connections in Mainland China.

TUMBLE-DRIED GREEN TEA

This resourceful variation of firing places the leaf in a perforated metal drum quite similar to that found in an industrial clothes dryer. Mounted horizontally on a central axis, the drum revolves such that the leaf tumbles inside the drum while being "agitated" by internally mounted fins. Heat from a source either below or behind the unit is fanned into the perforated drum and is then vented out the back or top. Incredibly efficient and ultimately remarkably reminiscent of basket-firing, this method can produce quite drinkable tea using a fraction of the energy and labor required for traditional firing of any type. Although the finished tea from this process lacks the subtlety of traditional basket-firing (and the nuance of flavor that charcoal-firing imparts), this reliable technique yields tea that is fluffed, is evenly fired, and has a uniformity that might be lacking if traditional basket-firing is not done perfectly. Tumble-drying is the most common firing process used for the manufacture of moderate to high-quality tea.

One of the oldest of the manufactured green teas, Gunpowder tea is produced using a similar but different style of tumbler. The same logic used to replicate basket-firing with a perforated drum tumbler can be applied to pan-firing. Pan-firing is imitated (and made more efficient) by the use of an apparatus similar to that used to mix concrete or "pan" candies that have a thin candy coating (or shell), such as M&Ms, Jordan Almonds, jelly beans,

Two tea-firers and their charcoal tender accomplish the initial pan-firing of Tai Ping Hou Kui green tea (Anhui Province, China).

and so on. The solid-wall, shallow-finned tumbler used for firing Gunpowder tea is set on an angle, so that the leaf is tossed about in a figure-eight pattern. The potbelly shape of the tumbler combined with the internal tumbling action results in a finished tea that has a pellet-like shape, hence the moniker "gunpowder." Depending on the size of the original leaf put into the tumbler, the resulting Gunpowder tea varies in size from that of a BB to that of a pea. The smaller sizes of balled tea indicate that the youngest and most tender leaf must have been used, and that the firing was carefully accomplished to achieve an "imperial-grade" size and shape.

On a misty morning in the spring of 2000 we visited a modest Gunpowder tea factory in a remote upland of Zhejiang Province in eastern China. We were fascinated by a bank of these tumbler-dryers lined up and ready to be loaded and fired. We could only imagine how much of this famous tea is produced during a tea season, both there and in all the other factories like it throughout Zhejiang. As these belt-driven tumblers are powered by the same motor, many of them can be operated at the same time. Each tumbler has an individual connection to the master belt-drive, so each can be positioned online or offline. This clustering allows the tea factory to easily increase manufacturing capability when demand is heaviest during the peak harvest.

OVEN-DRIED GREEN TEA

This modern variation on basket-firing uses forced hot air to fire the leaf in a contained space. During firing, the leaf is either moved through a chamber on a vibrating conveyor belt (similar to the method employed to bake modern loaves of bread or cookies) or fired in pans that are inserted into an ovenlike cavity and tossed occasionally. This efficient process produces large quantities of uniform product, but leaf

The Lu Shan tea factory's custom-designed oven-drying system (Jiangxi Province, China).

manufactured into tea in this manner lacks the subtlety and individuality of leaf processed by a more traditional method. This manufacture is used primarily in southern China to reduce the heat and energy needed to process tea (and during the warm-weather months, when heat generation is not desired in any tea factory). For much of the run-of-the-harvest leaf, however, this method is satisfactory and yields inexpensive, acceptable-tasting tea.

We recently visited an extraordinary tea factory in the Lu Shan mountains of Jiangxi Province, where they use two huge banks of ovenlike dryers. Similar in appearance to the French-made ovens popular with artisan bread bakers worldwide, these ovens produce a remarkable tea, one of China's most famous and highly regarded: Lu Shan Clouds and Mist. Most assuredly, this factory replicates a type of basket-firing, but the tea produced is exquisite, expensive, and world-renowned.

STEAMED GREEN TEA

This style of tea is used primarily in the production of authentic Japanese or Japanese-style green tea. Steamed green tea is typically leaf that has been mechanically harvested, most often by what is called shearing. Shears can be electric or gas-fired and can be handled by two people walking along garden rows, creating the beautifully manicured gardens one sees in photos of Japan (see "Uniquely Japanese" in chapter 2). There are also single-operator shearing machines that are driven above the row on oversized wheels. For this style of tea the look of the leaf is not a critical element to the enjoyment of the brewed tea the way that the physical appearance of the dried and wet leaf is considered an integral component of Chinese green tea.

To manufacture steamed green tea, the leaf is processed according to the method used for all green tea. To create the signature flavor of steamed green tea, however, an additional step is added during the early stages of processing, during which the primary leaf undergoes a brief period of steaming. This steaming period can vary from a half-minute, while the leaf is transported through a steaming chamber on a conveyor belt, to longer, during which the leaf remains in a chamber (see pages 169 and 175). This deep steaming produces tea such as Fukamushi Sencha and gives the tea more depth of flavor and a focused taste.

Steaming changes the nature of the chlorophyll in the leaf. Steamed-leaf tea presents a more vegetal, sometimes kelpy character, often likened to the flavor of spinach or other leafy greens. This flavor is described as simply being more "green." Steamed green tea is the tea taste of choice in Japan, and everyone has a favorite brand. The art of developing a signature flavor in Japanese tea is based on the blending of primary tea, known in Japan as *aracha.* Be sure to look for this form of green tea in Japan; it is consumed as a relatively inexpensive simple tea. Aracha varies in style, taste, and look, but it is unique in that most finished Japanese green tea is blended.

Because of the dominance of the style (the steaming) in the flavor profile, leaf structure is not as important as it is with handworked green teas. The leaf is reasonably uneven, because dissimilar particle sizes are mixed together in a batch. Steamed green tea liquor brews up cloudy in appearance, the taste is generally heavier on the palate because of the increase in soluble solids in the brew, and the intense flavor lingers longer. The differences in flavor between various batches of steamed green tea are subtle but clear, and the aroma of both dry and wet leaf is quite different than that of Chinese green tea.

Steamed green tea that has been finely powdered is called *matcha.* Ceremonial-grade matcha used for Japanese tea ceremony can be shockingly expensive, while the culinary grade (used to make ice cream and marinades, and for general cooking purposes and everyday drinking) is more reasonable (see "Varieties of Japanese Tea" in chapter 4). Brewing steamed green tea is a bit fussier than brewing other green teas. Extra care must be taken with the water: purity and a cooler infusing temperature are essential. Our Japanese colleagues recommend using soft bottled water such as Volvic. Even though these leaves have been exposed to high heat during the steaming process, they do not tolerate very hot water temperatures when brewed. The inherent sweetness of high-quality Japanese green tea can become bitter if the brewing water temperature is too hot (see chapter 6 for detailed brewing instructions).

Although subtle in difference to one another, steamed green teas are an integral subcategory of the green tea class, and they should be thoroughly explored. A controlled tasting of several sencha teas from Japan is a wonderful way to experience craft rather than terroir—how a tea blender can combine the leaf of several varietals from one or more producers to create a signature taste. This type of comparison is difficult to do with Chinese green teas, however, as the style of leaf preparation nearly always changes with the geography. Sencha is fantastic for cooking and forms the basis for wonderful stock, salad dressings, and marinades, and when powdered, for dusting desserts, confections, chocolates, and baked goods.

TEA WISDOM: A CONVERSATION WITH DEN SHIRAKATA

The following is taken from an interview with Den Shirakata, the president and CEO of Shirakata Denshiro Shoten (Shizuoka, Japan) and Den's Teas (Torrance, California).

Japanese green tea has distinctive characteristics and it is very different from other green teas. Since the freshness is the most important factor for Japanese teas, I believe that the distinctions are pulled out and made clear only when the tea is fresh. It is common for tea companies in Japan to store their teas in chilled warehouses or facilities, but this is a new concept in America. We import our teas directly from our factory by air shipment and store them here in a chilled warehouse. Most of my tea arrives vacuum-sealed, and I have paid a lot of attention to building the best conditions for keeping the quality of Japanese teas as fresh as possible. I want American tea lovers to experience a genuine flavor of Japanese green teas that are kept under the best conditions—as they would experience them in Japan.

In Japan we treasure aroma and flavor. With flavor we examine sweetness, sharpness, and body. Sweetness comes from theanine, a chemical component of the leaf; sharpness comes from bitterness, and body is the mouth feel contributed by the catechins. Aroma has two types—one is the natural, grassy aroma of green tea and the other one is a roasted aroma. The roasted aromas come several different ways—from leaf that has been roasted or from green tea that has the addition of toasted rice (such as *genmaicha*) or from toasted twig (such as *kukicha*). I believe that the most unique process of Japanese tea is in the "roasting." How you handle the final processing of the leaf against the heat with skillful tending determines the unique flavor of each producer.

We purchase most of the tea that we will use in an entire year in May and June during the first flush season. Every time we need to sell our tea, we take some crude tea—*aracha*—inventory from our warehouse and remanufacture it in our factory, which means sifting and cutting, roasting, blending, and packaging. To me tea is so interesting. It seems easy but it is difficult to control. Although the green tea market in the United States is big right now, the market for Japanese tea is still small. I think that the interest in green tea is here to stay, and I am hopeful that our share in the green tea business will grow.

Yellow Tea

Yellow tea is a most unusual and difficult-to-define class of tea. We have offered several selections of it in our store for many years and have an enthusiastic audience for it; nevertheless, it remains cloaked in mystery and misunderstanding. Tea experts outside of Asia have a difficult time explaining exactly what yellow tea is, and in the West the tea is often mistakenly sold as green tea. Yellow tea has its own process, however, and should be correctly understood and offered as such. On a tea-sourcing trip to Sichuan Province, it was our good fortune to find a traditional Chinese tea merchant who was able to accurately describe this limited-production tea (see a related story, "The Imperial Tea Garden and Wu LiZhen's Tea Bushes," in chapter 4).

YELLOW TEA, DEFINED

Yellow tea is wonderfully fresh and does have much in common with early spring green teas, one reason for some of the confusion surrounding yellow teas. It is made from either very early spring buds or a *mao feng* pluck and then processed by the same methods as green tea, up to the point of the initial firing. Following the initial drying, just before the first firing, yellow tea undergoes a significant, additional step called *men huan*, during which yellow tea leaf is lightly and slowly steamed, then covered with a cloth to allow the leaves to breathe (in this case they reabsorb their own aromatics). This step translates into English as "sealing yellow."

This smothering cover can last for several hours or up to several days, during which time fragrance and sweetness increase. This gentle moisture control changes the chemistry of the leaf and makes yellow tea distinctive. Less apt to develop a grassy or assertive flavor, yellow tea is reliably smooth and lush in the cup. Astringency is rare, as the smothering procedure inhibits development of those flavor components in the finished tea. After this extra step the manufacture of yellow tea resumes the identical course as that taken in green tea manufacture. Similar in concept to the processing of Japan's Fukamushi Sencha, yellow tea is also easy to brew, is pleasant to drink, and stores well.

There are very few yellow teas manufactured today because of the extra work involved and the general lack of knowledge of the class. There are several, however, and they are well worth trying. Anhui Province provides our teashop with Huo Mountain Yellow Sprouting, a large-leaf mao feng yellow tea that is reminiscent of the glorious early harvest green teas from the Huang Shan, only softer and more lush. Sichuan Province is famous for Mengding Mountain Snow Buds (Mengding Huang Ya) and Bamboo Tips (Zhu Ye Qing). These two yellow teas are early budset plucks. These buds are short and slender, and brew a pale yellow, sweet, fragrant cup. Sometimes this style of pluck is called sparrow's tongue for its fine, thin, crescent shape. Bamboo Tips is one of our all-time favorite teas and is painstakingly manufactured and hand-sorted (see page 162). In the Chinese view of tea, yellow tea is celebrated as "mature tea," a reference to the mellowing effects of *men huan*, the resting period it is allowed during manufacture.

White Tea

The least complicated class of tea to describe, but not the least difficult to produce, is white tea. The manufacture of white tea is an ancient process that, like the sun-dried green tea of Xishuangbanna in the deep southwest of Yunnan Province, predates all other tea manufacture.

WHITE TEA, DEFINED

White tea in its original, pure form consists of only the tender, unopened budsets of particular varieties of China bush tea plants that are cultivated especially for this class of tea in Fujian Province on the eastern coast of China. Like other famous place-specific teas, such as Hangzhou's Longjing and Tieguanyin from Anxi,

"FRESH" TEA

Yellow tea, a so-called fresh tea, should not be confused with "new" tea. Envision artisanal spring tea production in a remote village, where tradition might dictate that certain local teas be "rested" during their processing. Locally, this tea would be referred to simply as fresh tea. The Chinese apply this term to a range of conventionally made teas that are minimally processed and usually locally consumed. It was not until the 1990s, when Western tea enthusiasts began to discover the amazing world of authentic and traditional Asian teas, that the concept of "fresh" or "spring" tea was introduced and embraced by tea drinkers worldwide.

Asians in general and the Chinese in particular have enjoyed interestingly processed spring teas (that is, fresh teas) for centuries. We believe that much of what the Chinese drink as fresh tea seasonally during March through May, which is processed by traditional local custom, is often yellow tea but is known to them only by Chinese pictorial nomenclature, not the classic color-coded tea term.

The Big Sprout varietal has a bud that is proportionally large to the size of its leaf (Fujian Province, China).

white tea has a specific geographic terroir, style, flavor, and definition. In the best of years the production of authentic Fujian white tea is small.

Fujian white tea is produced in only three restricted locales: Fuding county, Shuijie/Jianyang county, and Zhenghe county—all north of the geographically important Minjiang River. The tea bushes there must be cultivars (developed in the late 1800s) from tea bushes indigenous to these locations, of which 95 percent are members of the Da Hao (Big Sprout) variety of *Camellia sinensis* var. *sinensis*. The vegetation of these specific plants—Fuding Da Bai (Fuding Big White), Zhenghe Da Bai (Zhending Big White), Narcissus, and Xiao Bai (Vegetable or Small White)—is uniquely able to produce buds and leaf that, after processing, reveal a covering of fine, downy white hair. Some white teas are used in the creation of presentation (or so-called blooming-flower) teas and for certain strictly top-shelf jasmine-scented white teas. White tea is picked in the early spring, before the buds have a chance to develop into leaves. For Fujian white tea plucking the weather conditions must be perfect—no rain, dew, or frost can occur during the harvest. The buds must be fully fleshed and plump, not too thin or too long. The tea maker must know how to counter the many slight variations in the condition of the fresh leaf, to coax the best flavor and style from the leaves. The magic of this historic tea lies in its sheer simplicity—light-colored infusions, sweet subtlety (without any of the grassy undertones of green tea), and flavors that suggest honey, chestnut, and peaches.

White tea budsets are shaded for approximately the final three weeks of their time on the bush. Legend tells us that in the days of the early Chinese emperors, only virgins wearing white silk gloves were allowed to pluck the budsets that would become white tea. Today the buds are simply meticulously selected from the few gardens that are esteemed for the production of these superb tea varietals. According to tradition, these budsets are dried only in a shaded area with good air circulation, such as a pavilion. This technique prevents "greening" (chlorophyll development from exposure to the sun) and enables the fresh tea to dry rapidly without the need for externally applied heat. As these variables are difficult to combine, the limited production of genuine Fujian budset white tea commands a high price every year.

Since the days of the Song emperors, the traditional habitat for white tea has been Fujian Province in China. Today, to the dismay of these tea producers, a small amount of traditionally made budset white tea is now produced in Anhui Province and in the tea-growing regions of Assam, Darjeeling, Nilgiri, and Sri Lanka in South Asia. Many tea producers regard white tea as a process of manufacture rather than as a unique product that is the sum total of terroir, history, and experience. We distinguish three types of white tea on offer in today's marketplace.

First is the traditional budset white tea from the recognized original sources in Fujian Province. The premier version of this is Bai Hao Yin Zhen (Flowery White Pekoe or Silver Needle). Second is the "new-style" leaf white tea from many sources, including excellent versions from Fujian Province, such as Bai Mudan and Shou Mei (the latter a more highly oxidized white tea that is popular in dim sum houses in Guangdong Province and Hong Kong). Third is the traditional-style budset white tea from other sources. This might be Anhui Province's glorious Imperial Silver Needles, or a newcomer such as southern India's Craigmore Estate Nilgiri white tea. All three forms of white tea belong to a distinct class and should never be offered as a subvariety of green tea, although white tea does have elements in common with green and other classes of tea. A group of tea masters with whom we explored a white tea withering room in Fujian Province described the key difference between white and green tea as follows: in white tea manufacture there is no de-enzyming, but there is slight oxidation; to manufacture green tea there is de-enzyming, but no oxidation. These opposite early processes in the manufacture of these two classes have a profound effect on the ultimate development of these two teas.

The two versions of the white tea class—traditional-style budset white tea and the modern new-style leaf white tea—should not be offered as being the same (or interchangeable). Their appearances are distinctly different, so they are impossible to confuse. In the marketplace white teas should always be identified by both style and place of origin. If you are purchasing white tea in an opaque container and the label does not reveal what is inside, buyer beware! Furthermore, what the label states should match the tea inside the container. Traditional-style budset white tea (whether from Fujian, Anhui, or elsewhere) should be 100 percent buds (no leaf), and Shou Mei should have no (or very few) buds and be more oxidized.

TRADITIONAL-STYLE BUDSET WHITE TEA

The original, traditional Fujian budset white tea is Bai Hao Yin Zhen (Flowery White Pekoe or Silver Needle) and its first cousins Silver Pekoe, Silver Tip, and so on. Made exclusively from a select picking of plump spring buds, Bai Hao Yin Zhen is the most expensive grade of authentic, traditional-style Fujian white tea. It is estimated that more than ten thousand handpicked buds are needed to produce just 2.2 pounds (1 kilo) of this exquisite tea. As the young buds are plucked only from the Fuding Da Bai or Zhenghe Da Bai tea bush varietals, Bai Hao Yin Zhen is light in color and tinged with a soft greenish-gray cast. The buds are covered with tender, downy hair that gives the tea a velvety appearance. The liquor is pale in color and delicate in flavor, reminiscent of ripe melon, fresh apricots, or peaches.

NEW-STYLE WHITE TEA

Enterprising tea enthusiasts created new-style leaf white tea, a unique subcategory of white tea made from the first leaf bunch of the tea plant, processed as carefully and almost as minimally as is traditional budset white tea. This new-style leaf white tea is essentially just shade-dried tea (as is its traditional budset counterpart). The processing consists of the two steps of traditional white tea manufacture: outdoor withering in the shade and indoor withering with cool air, but a third and final step of bake-drying (not leaf-firing) is added to thoroughly dry the higher moisture content leaf cluster. This processing must happen quickly, before the leaf has a chance to undergo many enzymatic changes.

New-style white tea has a slightly more concentrated flavor profile than true budset white tea (and the healthful benefits) at a significantly reduced cost. Highest-quality new-style white tea contains varying percentages of buds to help maintain a certain consistency of flavor with that of true budset white tea. In our store we offer two versions of new-style white tea: one contains about 40 percent budsets, and the other about 25 percent. Both versions are quite popular.

Because the pluck for new-style white tea can be one of only several choices, new-style white tea is a perfect example of pluck specificity. The choices are: (1) A full-sized, perfectly formed budset and first leaf, still intact. This is the finest quality of the genre, in which all of the elements are first rate. (2) The first leaf alone. The leaves used are the "first leaf," the one just below the budset. This is the same pluck used for the elegant Lu'an Guapian, a famous green tea (*guapian* translates to "melon seed," which is what the leaf looks like when rehydrated), but these Big Sprout first leaf plucks are much larger. The first leaf is the most porous of all the leaves on the bush, a necessary attribute for complete drying when using air only. (3) The budset and first leaf when imperfect. Plucked as a whole, particularly when the bud wasn't perfect enough to be plucked earlier as a true budset white tea, this pluck is often the solution for instances of tip damage. (4) One more leaf may be included: in this instance the budset and first leaf are plucked together with the second true leaf. This "branch" is processed as a whole, remaining intact throughout the first stages of processing.

When manufacturing Shou Mei white tea, the bud is not plucked, only true leaves. This pluck normally shows where the bud only was recently plucked during the budset white tea harvest. This group of leaves is plucked as a branch also and processed as a whole, remaining intact throughout the first stages of processing. Later, during the sorting process, the stems are discarded and the classic "eyebrow" form (*mei*) develops.

New-style white tea significantly increases the available supply of white tea and is a welcome addition to the repertoire of tea available for tea enthusiasts. Several well-known types are Bai Mudan (White Peony), Gong Mei (Tribute Eyebrow), and Shou Mei (Long Life Eyebrow). Bai Mudan, made from a careful plucking of buds and first leaf together, is light to medium gray and tinged with streaks of off-white. This tea is made from the leaves of Fuding Da Bai or Zhenghe Da Bai tea bushes, so it has the signature downy covering on the buds. Gong Mei and Shou Mei are called "eyebrow teas" for their delicately curved shapes and are made from leaves only. They are made after the plucking for Bai Hao Yin Zhen and Bai Mudan from a pluck configuration of large leaves (see "Visiting a White Tea factory" in chapter 4).

Sample trays show true budset white tea (left) and new-style white tea (right) (Fujian Province, China).

WHITE TEA PRODUCTION EXPANDS IN THE GLOBAL MARKET

All forms of white tea are best when made from the budsets or leaf of China bush tea plants. Traditional budset white tea from Anhui Province is called Imperial Silver Needles. Though a budset pluck, the plants used in Anhui are subvarieties of China bush that differ from the tea plants traditionally grown in Fujian Province for manufacture into its authentic budset white tea. Several of the budset white teas coming from Assam, Darjeeling, and Sri Lanka are beginning to rival the original Chinese versions in character and style, but we still prefer the inherent flavor profile of the Chinese production.

Although some tea merchants promote white tea made from Assam bush as being an up-and-comer, we think that Assam bush is the best choice for making many world-famous teas, but not for white tea, either budset or leaf style. What has potential for future high-quality production of both budset and new-style leaf white tea is the use of one or another of the new clonal varieties of *Camellia sinensis* being derived from ancient strains. In the near future exquisite new-style and budset white teas will be available from tea-growing regions other than Fujian Province. Their position will mimic that of sparkling wines that make every effort to taste like authentic Champagne. Food enthusiasts should appreciate these similar comestibles for their individuality.

Budset white teas are expensive by the pound but are quite affordable when one calculates the cost on a per-cup basis. The flavor is superb, so budset white tea is a small treat that should not be missed. For example, extremely rare authentic budset white tea from Fujian that retails for seventy dollars per pound costs less than fifteen cents per cup!

The introduction of new-style leaf white tea is one of the most exciting recent additions to the tea repertoire. It is difficult to increase the quantity of authentic budset Fujian white tea, but with increasing demand, growers have the ability to process larger quantities of the more modern leaf white tea. Increased awareness and production has enabled more tea drinkers to enjoy this tea's fine flavor, and the cost is usually one-third that of true budset white tea.

THE CHEMISTRY OF WHITE TEA

Because of the technique used to dry white tea, particularly the new-style leaf, it does oxidize slightly (from 8 percent to as much as 15 percent), mostly during the initial "no-sun withering" and then a bit more while it air-dries. The increased oxidation of new-style leaf white tea gives it a flavor that is faintly reminiscent of black tea, with a lush, full, oolong-like body—and it has none of the astringency of green tea. The Shou Mei variety is particularly popular with dim sum aficionados in Hong Kong, because of the full flavor and rich color that develops during its intentionally longer oxidation.

All types of white tea are believed to contain slightly less caffeine and fewer polyphenols than other forms of tea, but this analysis is difficult to duplicate consistently because of the many variables involved. Testing shows that the content of both caffeine and polyphenols can also be higher, so white tea proves the rule of exception and complication in the world of tea (see the discussion on caffeine in chapter 8). New-style white tea has the ability to be broken into fragments and packed in teabags, and it blends well with many green teas, full-leaf Formosa oolong, and large-leaf orthodox black teas. One of our most popular house blends is Snow on Jade Mountain, a blend of new-style leaf white tea and several early-harvest green teas.

Oolong Tea (Wulong or Blue Tea)

Oolong teas are the most complicated teas to manufacture. There are a greater number of steps involved in the manufacture of oolong tea than when making any other class of tea. The process inherently affords more opportunity for personal interpretation. Oolongs come in myriad forms, shapes, and colors.

OOLONG TEA, DEFINED

Oolong teas are made from large tea leaves, and the finished tea varies in appearance, ranging in color from rich chestnut brown to greenish-gray. Some oolongs have long, slightly twisted leaves that just barely curl up on the ends, while other oolongs have been loosely folded, and still others have been compressed into small, irregularly shaped balls. Some oolongs have bits of twig attached, while others do not. Many are given a light sideways

There are two types of classic Fujian oolong manufacture, known as Min-Nan and Min-Bei. Although Tieguanyin oolong manufacture requires eighteen steps, most Min-Nan "balled oolong" processing necessitates only ten. These ten basic steps in oolong tea manufacture are the following: After the pluck (step 1) the leaf is spread out and withered in the sun on ventilating screens for several hours (step 2). Next, the leaf is periodically turned to allow for uniform drying (step 3). Withering generates internal heat (step 4), so when the leaf has wilted the desired amount, the leaf is brought inside the tea factory and allowed to cool (step 5).

Then the leaf must be manipulated and rolled for the next seven to nine hours (step 6)—not continuously but only for a few minutes, once every two hours. This rolling action is the most critical in the long process and is called *shajing*, which means "to kill the flowering." Shajing gently disrupts the cell walls and triggers the chemical substances in the leaves (chlorophyll, polyphenols, carbohydrates, and enzymes) to disperse, an essential step toward the final development of the finished leaf. During rolling, the flavor and character of the oolong tea is determined, so it is critical that tea masters constantly evaluate their handwork during this lengthy partial-oxidation process.

Near daybreak, if the overnight work has gone well, heat is applied to the leaf to stop further oxidation (step 7). Laboriously, this step is achieved by partially drying the leaf, by hand, in tea-firing woks about 2 pounds (1 kilo) at a time. After this the leaf is shaped (by hand or machine) by gently twisting and squeezing the leaves (step 8), which draws the juices and oils to the surface of the leaves. Then the leaf is redried or baked in bamboo baskets over charcoal fires (step 9). Over the next eight hours the leaf is baked four separate times, for five to ten minutes each, over decreasingly hot charcoal embers to achieve a medium firing. After baking, the leaf is allowed to cool (step 10). See the further description of "Tieguanyin" in the Southern Fujian Province section of chapter 4.

The Min-Bei oolong style of manufacture (for example, the Phoenix Mountain single-trunk oolong) is no less complicated, but it varies significantly from the "ball-rolled" style described above. The leaves used for this tea are so large that it takes a full thirty hours to process the leaf into finished tea. In addition to patience and fortitude, it takes the combined skills of a series of tea masters to encourage the slow development of flavor required by this varietal.

Picking. Different leaves are plucked depending on the tea that is being made. For the third spring plucking, for instance, the pluck is a segment comprised of three leaves. Tea is sorted at the point of collection and the leaf is evaluated for three qualities—shape, color, and fragrance.

Primary withering. The freshly plucked leaf is spread on tarps or concrete pads (if outdoors) or on the floor (if indoors) in a single layer to begin the withering process. As the leaf withers, heat is generated, which necessitates turning the leaf at least once. After several hours, the leaf is gathered and taken to the factory.

Cooling down/withering. The warmer the days, the more the leaves need to rest and "cool down" before processing begins. The leaves are sprinkled well-spaced in a single layer on large circular bamboo trays in the withering room. When the leaves begin to wilt, flatten, and stick to the tray they are ready to move on to the next step (about thirty minutes).

Rattling. After the leaves have withered, they are "rattled," or shaken, by hand three times. In Chinese this procedure translates as "rocking the green" or "scratching the green." The trays are picked up one by one and the leaves are gently tossed and rattled. This causes the leaf cells to rupture and the cell sap to disperse internally throughout the leaf, which begins oxidation—the series of chemical reactions that occurs within and on the surface of the leaf in the presence of oxygen.

It is this action that is the most critical in the production of this style of oolong. In this step the leaves are primed to successfully complete all of the remaining transformations that the leaf must undergo to yield the tea's essential flavor and aroma. Oolong teas are all semioxidized, so the degree of oxidation must be rigorously controlled, but in single-trunk oolong production the oxidation is extremely finicky due to the open, flat, highly exposed surface area of the leaf being used.

Rattling usually begins in the late afternoon and proceeds until after midnight. Rattling is done seven different times, and the leaf is given a rest between each rattle.

Bruising/tumbling. After rattling, the tea is bruised or tumbled, which is a more vigorous workout for the leaf. Two or three mats' worth of leaf is put inside a horizontal bamboo cylinder-tumbler and the leaf is gently tumbled. The tumbling continues for twenty minutes and then the leaf is rested for two hours. This is repeated three times.

After this, the appearance of the leaf is evaluated. The tea master notes the appearance of the leaf and looks for the characteristic red-tipped edges. The leaf develops these red-tipped edges from the bruising, and the transformation should be presenting 30 percent red and 70 percent green in the leaf at this point. The distinctive oolong fragrance should be beginning to develop. If all is progressing well, the leaf is heaped into one big pile and let to rest an additional four hours.

(continued)

CLASSIC FUJIAN OOLONG MANUFACTURE (CONTINUED)

Firing/tumbling. A small twig fire is built in each of two fireboxes underneath the tea-firing ovens. When the heat has risen to 160°F (71°C) the leaf is put into the first oven and tumbled for fifteen minutes. The leaf is removed and put back into the bamboo cylinder-tumbler for twenty to twenty-five minutes to cool and change. Then the leaf is removed from the tumbler and placed in a second oven on wire mesh screens at a temperature of 100 to 105°F (38 to 41°C) for two to two-and-a-half hours.

At this point the tea is called *gan mao cha*, "half-done" or "primary" tea. The tea is stable at this point and will keep for several weeks in a cool, dry place. But the tea still needs to go through final drying (a six-hour process) to give it its finish-firing.

crimping or folding, and others a hard, ball-rolling. In most cases fine oolongs require several successive infusions for the leaves to unfurl to their full extent.

Oolongs are truly *the* most complicated teas to manufacture. The key to making a successful oolong is in the processing—in the crafting of the leaf. Crafting oolong tea involves a greater number of steps that are conducted over a longer period of time than when making other types of tea. Oolongs are semioxidized, and the range of level of oxidization is generally from 35 to 80 percent, latitude that allows tea makers to tweak the leaf into a tea that reflects their own expression of the style. Many oolongs are plucked as a bud with an accompanying set of leaves—sometimes as many as three leaves down the stem are picked as a unit.

Many of these oolongs are the ball-rolled or the semi-ball-rolled styles, and the connecting bits of stem are quite apparent and necessary. In Fujian Province these are historically known as the Min-Nan oolongs (south of the Min River) and the most famous is Tieguanyin, but this style of oolong is made elsewhere. These teas are in enormous contrast to another traditional style of oolong tea, the single-leaf oolongs, which are made from one large leaf, given a slight twist. These are what is known in Fujian Province as Min-Bei oolongs (north of the Min River) and include the revered Wuyi, or Rock oolongs, and are not seen manufactured in many other tea-producing areas. In between these two extreme leaf styles are the standard and special grades of oolong that most tea enthusiasts outside Asia are familiar with— full-bodied, deliciously soft tea with incredible stone-fruit aromatics. Oolong tea must be made from leaves that have reached a certain size for them to be "chemically balanced to deliver their maximum quality," according to Leo Kwan, the managing director of Ming Cha in Hong Kong. Oolongs are produced after the spring green tea season has finished, and unlike green tea leaf, which is picked in the early morning and rushed to the factory, tea leaf that will be used to produce oolong tea is picked midday. Once the oolong leaf is picked, the process must continue around the clock until each batch of tea is finished.

Many locals drink primary tea, rather than the more expensive finished (or refined) tea. Primary tea is dull in color and lacks the polish that the finish-firing gives the tea. Refined tea has a deeper flavor and more character, and will reinfuse more times. The length of storage time for this style of oolong tea comes from the finishing, as do the characteristic sweetness and aftertaste. Finishing removes the final bit of moisture from the leaf, concentrating the flavors in the leaf and contributing to longevity. Primary tea contains about 8 percent moisture and refined tea about 5 percent. See "Fenghuang Dan Cong" in chapter 4.

As this tasting flight shows, the liquor color of oolong tea varies from pale gold to dark amber (Fujian Province, China).

Oolong teas possess a diverse and appealing range of sophisticated, complex, and richly rewarding flavors and aromas, such as peach, apricot, honey, orchid, melon, leather, amber, and sandalwood. Their finish is long and sweet, with just a suggestion of astringency. Although most green teas yield a second and sometimes third infusion, because oolongs are made from large mature leaves, they do not open to their full, original size until the third or fourth infusion. Oolongs can commonly be infused several more

Top: Each specific pluck yields a different finished leaf.

Above: Wuyi oolong tea (left to right): partially rattled, *gan mao cha*, and finish-fired (Fujian Province, China).

times once fully open, for a total of as many as eight or nine infusions. The degree of partial or semioxidation in oolong tea can range from 10 to 80 percent and is determined during manufacture. Oolongs on the low end of the oxidation scale bear a resemblance to the tightly curled, tippy midseason green teas, and on the high end they look just like a super-large, individual-leaf orthodox black tea.

Fujian oolongs offer all the levels of oxidation possible within the oolong class. We have seen Fujian oolongs at 12 percent oxidation and every stage up to 80 percent oxidation. The difficulty is selecting which to drink first! High-quality Taiwan oolongs are given on average 60 percent oxidization and have an appearance similar to those of similarly oxidized Fujian oolongs—nice, well-rolled buds or leaf that offer a variation of natural color, ranging from greenish-gold to brownish-gold and reddish-brown. The aroma should be strong and intensely floral, and the flavors should be mellow, saturated with stone-fruit flavors.

Oolongs tend to derive from varietal plantings. Fujian is the historical source of oolong tea because the subspecies of the *Camellia sinensis* plants that produce the finest oolong teas grow there. Fujian and Taiwan both have the terroir and shared plantings that best support the growth of first-quality oolong tea plants, both wild and under cultivation. The tea artisans who manufacture this outstanding tea lavish special attention on their tea.

There are many styles of oolong tea and different methods for brewing them. In general, they are very easy drinking and fun to experiment with. They can also be fussed over; the choice is yours. For a genuine oolong-tea-drinking experience, find someone who can perform a *gong fu* tea ceremony for you, together with several friends (see "Gong Fu Tea Service" in chapter 7). This unique oolong brewing ritual has, like all fine rituals, its own set of utensils and teawares and is based on historical tea-brewing methods.

SOUTH ASIAN OOLONG?

During the 1990s the expertise required to manufacture oolong tea was introduced to other tea-growing regions, most ambitiously in Darjeeling and Sri Lanka. What will the future be for these non-Chinese oolongs? The soil is not correct, the climate is different, and the plants are young and not of the subvarieties considered appropriate for the manufacture of fine oolong. The bushes may be in venerable old tea gardens, but there is no local tea tradition for the production or appreciation of oolong tea. It is difficult to imagine that these new-growth teas will be able to compete with the snap and verve of Chinese or Taiwanese oolongs (see "Oolong Teas" in chapter 4).

WORLDWIDE INTEREST IN
SUBVARIETALS

True gong fu service is altogether elegant and somewhat messy (Fujian Province, China).

On our most recent tea-sourcing trip to Fujian and Japan, we discovered that the tea artisans in Fujian are noting renewed interest in the older, more traditional styles of oolong firing: the darker, more exotically pungent styles that they prefer and believe to be more historically "proper." This old-style firing is increasingly popular (again) in Southeast Asia, Hong Kong, Canada, and Japan. The gardens in Fujian are also producing much leaf, and experimentation is ongoing to try to make interesting black tea and green tea from the leaf of specific, older varietals such as Tieguanyin and Rou Gui. In Japan we discovered that oolong is the craze of the moment, and enthusiasm for oolong has spread to the gardens there, where oolong varietals (particularly Tieguanyin) are being planted to see whether or not Fujian's oolong sub-varieties will grow (and produce quality leaf) in Japan. The flavor profiles of these varietals are so unique that if these trials yield quality drinking tea, tea enthusiasts everywhere are in for a treat!

Black Tea (Qi Hong or Red Tea)

The most popular class of tea outside of Asia is the second most popular tea in the world. This incredible leaf is known today as black tea. The Chinese, in their early color-based system of identifying tea by the color of the brewed liquor and not the leaf, identified this class of tea as red tea. This allowed their term *black tea* to be used to designate the deeply dark-brewing liquor of the only truly fermented tea: the highly regarded pu-erh (see the discussion on "Pu-erh Tea" later in this chapter).

BLACK TEA, DEFINED

Black tea is not fermented, it is oxidized; The most common error found in discussing or describing black tea is the improper use of the terms *fermented* and *fermentation* as a phase in the production of this class of tea. One can distinguish between those who are simply repeating information that they have read or heard and those few who have truly taken the time to learn about tea, understand the differences among the great classes of tea, and then be specific about the processes involved in the different manufactures. If you visit a teashop or website and there is any mention of "fermentation" in reference to the production of black tea, run—do not walk—to another tea vendor!

Complete oxidation creates this truly remarkable class of tea. In the production of black tea, the critical component necessary to effect an even and complete oxidation of the "made tea" (finished leaf) is the "juice" trapped naturally inside the leaf structure. How this juice is allowed to release from its native holding cells and the controlled chemical reactions that follow are the processes that make the manufacture of black tea so interesting. An even wither (when required) and the best general results will always be had using either a budset or a fine pluck—the premium pickings from the new growth on the bush. A coarse pluck will contain less moisture but will have a harder epidermis (skin), so more time and careful supervision may be required to wither it successfully. One of the most important factors in a successful wither is the uniformity of the leaf that has been plucked.

A proper wither requires that the leaf within each batch be consistent in size, as withering a quantity of leaf that is heterogeneous is a fool's game. A fine pluck is always the first choice for initiating high-quality tea, because when a pluck is picked uniformly it does not require sorting, which inevitably adds another handling to the leaf, which increases both the cost and the time of the overall process. Thus some argue that the pluck is the single most important element of black tea manufacture.

WITHERING: PREPARATION IS EVERYTHING

The primary drying step in black tea production is called *withering*, the beginning stage of the time-consuming and complicated process of the manufacture of black tea. Withering consists of two distinct phases: *physical withering* and *chemical withering*. These are involved and complex processes that condition the leaf for the processes that follow. Some tea experts argue that withering is the single most important step in black tea manufacture.

The sections of a traditional tea factory where withering takes place are known as the withering loft. They are large, enclosed, but well-ventilated spaces with good natural air circulation that is often supplemented by powerful ceiling fans. If leaves are processed during the rainy season, when the leaf is first introduced to the loft heaters are used for short periods to help drive excess surface moisture from the leaf. If the weather is particularly humid, heaters may be fired up briefly even during withering to aid evaporation. Ideally the ambient air should be sufficient, so tea factories are situated at high elevations or in open locations. The physical wither sets the stage for successful tea processing; it creates the foundation leaf on which all the subsequent processes depend.

Physical withering. The initial drying stage of the withering process is known as physical withering (the reduction of moisture). The sole function of physical withering is to make the fresh leaf pliable and prepared to develop further during the numerous processing steps that follow. There is too much intrinsic moisture in a freshly picked *Camellia sinensis* leaf than will allow that leaf to be twisted without breaking, so the 70 to 77 percent innate moisture content of fresh leaf must be reduced to a more manageable 60 to

65 percent. Only after this portion of its native moisture has been driven out can the leaf be twisted and bruised during the rolling process, the motion that spreads the internal juices over the entirety of the surface of the leaf, thereby facilitating proper oxidation.

Chemical withering. Only through comprehensive withering is the leaf able to yield a quality finished tea. While physical withering is the process that encourages superior oxidization, chemical withering sets in motion the biochemical changes necessary for good cupping quality. As the moisture content of leaf undergoing physical withering reaches that desirable level of 60 to 65 percent, chemical withering begins spontaneously. Then the final 10 to 20 percent of withering is the chemical withering (the conversion of the juices inside a leaf's cells into more complex liquoring compounds).

Natural withering. Traditional natural withering is known as open (*chung*) withering. This simple form of withering is accomplished by spreading a several-inch-thick layer of freshly plucked leaf on what are known as "tats"—trays made of tightly stretched jute hessian (a type of burlap) or occasionally wire or synthetic mesh. The tats are banked vertically in columns, separated by $4^{1}/_{2}$ to 6 inches (12 to 15 centimeters) of airspace. Air circulates through the leaf, driving off both the heat that is generated by the drying process and the evaporating moisture. Natural withering normally takes eighteen to twenty hours and is considered to be the finest form of withering, the method that most likely yields premium tea. Natural withering is most often used when manufacturing premium large-leaf orthodox tea that will command a high price in the marketplace. In Sri Lanka, for instance, many old tea factories have central fans and intake/exhaust systems in the withering lofts that draw fresh dry air from the ground up through the leaf that is withering on vertically stacked tats or in open-top withering troughs.

Trough withering. The most widespread style of withering today is accomplished by the method known as trough withering. These troughs may be open-top or enclosed. An open-top withering trough is a wooden box, commonly 6 feet wide (1.8 meters) and 75 to 100 feet long (23 to 30 meters), rising 2 to $2^{1}/_{2}$ feet (0.6 meters) off the floor. The box has sixteen-gauge wire mesh mounted horizontally throughout, which actually creates the trough. This withering trough is literally a plenum chamber within the box, into which the fresh leaf (8 to 10 inches deep, or 20 to 25 centimeters) is placed. The plenum chamber is a finite space between two controllable openings or vents, the purpose of which is to redirect or manage the volume of the air flowing between. The most modern versions of these plenum chambers are within boxes that are double-wide or wider (12 to 15 feet, or 3.7 to 4.5 meters) and of considerably varying lengths (60 to 120 feet, or 18 to 36 meters).

All sizes of open-top withering troughs typically have fans mounted in the ends of the lower part of the box, below the leaf. These fans are often variable-speed and reversible, and are used prudently to create a current of air that rises through the leaf. This upward current of air can affect uneven withering of the leaf, causing the bottom leaf to wither faster than the upper leaf. Methods of regulating this include reversing the airflow of the fans and turning the leaf during the wither. Turning the leaf is practically difficult when using double-wide troughs and not preferred when processing orthodox leaf, as it may break a significant number of leaves.

For the manufacture of orthodox leaf, tats, traditional single-wide open-top troughs, and small enclosed troughs are most often used. Open-top troughs are generally filled to the top of the box, so that as the leaf becomes flaccid, it shrinks to just below the top edge of the side boards. If fans are used, they are engaged sparingly, and the flow is reversed on a regular basis. Whether on tats or in open-top troughs, the leaf being prepared for orthodox tea is fluffed one or two times, very gently. If heat is incorporated into the air stream, it is applied cautiously, only during the early wither, to prevent the leaf from over-drying prematurely.

Withering troughs at Parkside Estate (Nilgiri, India). Photo courtesy of Eliot Jordan.

If leaf for cut-tear-curl (CTC) production is being withered in open-top troughs, the side boards of the box normally rise above the fresh leaf by several inches, to support the necessary turning of the leaf that occurs once or twice during the withering period for CTC leaf. Fans are commonly used, so the combination of the increase in airflow and the greater exposure of the surface area to evaporation due to the turning make the process go more quickly (only sixteen to eighteen hours).

The newest form of withering trough is the enclosed trough, which is similar in function to an open-top trough, except that the airspace above the plenum chamber is boxed in, mimicking the airspace below. The advantage of this type of trough is that the air current can be maintained at a more even flow and pressure. The trough is situated in the box such that the airspace below the trough is equal to or slightly less than the airspace above the top of the leaf. Fans are mounted on one end and are one-directional, blowing into the box. There is a baffle just inside the fan end that controls whether the airflow goes up through the leaf from under the plenum or goes down through the leaf from the airspace above the plenum. The exit doors for the spent air are placed on the opposite end and are shuttered so that they can be toggled: one open while the other is closed, drawing the blown air through the trough. Because the airflow continues in the same direction for the entirety of the process, pressure builds up in the enclosed trough and the evaporation rate becomes optimal. Turning the leaf is eliminated, as the change in direction of the airflow accomplishes the same result without the damaging physical movement of the leaf.

When withering leaf for CTC manufacture, the enclosed trough becomes an integral part of the more modern, faster manufacture of a greater quantity of leaf tea. Many modifications are currently being researched and implemented to increase the quality and efficiency of the enclosed trough method of withering. Given that energy availability and costs are a constant problem in tea-producing regions, much work is being done to maintain the quality of traditionally withered leaf while simultaneously decreasing energy use. For example, one 5 HP fan running continuously for twelve hours consumes 44,760 watts ($5 \times 746 \times 12 = 44{,}760$). Check your electric bill to see what your per kilowatt charge is, then do the math to determine just one of the many costs that go into the base price of your cup of tea!

An important consideration regarding the modernization of the withering process is that for withering to be complete, both physical withering and chemical withering must happen. Chemical withering will only occur if the withering process continues for a minimum of nine to twelve hours for most CTC tea, and sixteen hours for orthodox tea. Using modern withering equipment, physical withering may reduce the moisture content of the leaf to the desired level well before chemical withering has initiated the internal biochemical changes necessary for a great finished tea. When chemical withering is complete, a distinctive fruity aroma releases from the leaf, the result of the internal breakdown of proteins and carbohydrates into simple sugars and amino acids. While this chemical change is taking place, the concentration of caffeine and polyphenols is increasing. A simple rule of thumb is that the better the wither, the more successful the oxidation will be.

THE PROCESSING OF BLACK TEA

The actual processing of black tea divides into two styles: *orthodox* and *cut-tear-curl* or *crush-tear-curl* (CTC). Orthodox black teas are those that we otherwise call whole-leaf tea. They are graded by size, and the nomenclature varies by country. Orthodox teas are recognized as being of the highest quality, and are the teas of legend, commanding a fair price and representing the skill of the tea artisan. Black teas are graded in a different way than are the other classes of tea, and within the orthodox style, this sieve size is an important factor in the eventual pedigree (see the individual country and region listings in chapter 4 for specific grade designations).

THE ROLLING PROCESS

Withered leaf destined to become orthodox black tea now goes through the rolling process. Following a quick but thorough sifting to sort the leaf into uniform-sized particles, rolling twists, compresses, and turns the leaf over and over. This distorts the leaf and bursts its cellular structure, releasing internally what some call "juice." This rolling action encourages the internal enzymes and polyphenols to mix, setting in motion the enzymic oxidation of the catechins that eventually feed the oxidation process, turning this withered leaf into tasty black tea.

Originally manipulated by hand, by loosely squeezing and wringing bunched piles of tea, or rolling and pressing mounds of tea on a tabletop or woven mat, this process has evolved into one requiring sophisticated machinery that replicates these movements without unnecessarily ripping or tearing the whole leaf.

In the mid-1800s withered leaf was first mechanically rolled in Java, in a machine created by a man named A. Holle. Mechanical rollers were introduced to tea manufacture in Assam in 1872 by William Jackson, at Jorhat, and their use has spread worldwide. Although minor modifications have been made to the equipment and materials have changed, the technique is essentially unchanged since that time. Brass rollers integrated into freestanding platforms that have raised surfaces to generate the necessary folding movement have replaced primitive cast-steel units that were formerly hand-held over a wooden table. This machine is known as a planetary roller.

During rolling for orthodox tea, only internal injury to the cell structure of the leaf is desired; the leaf is not chopped into pieces as is required in rolling CTC teas. A secondary step that may be combined with orthodox rolling is the use of a machine called the Rotorvane. Developed in 1957 by Ian McTear of the Experimental Tea Research Station at Tocklai in Assam, this machine is a motorized tumbler/barrel/drum with a diameter that ranges from 8 to 18 inches. It has a central shaft that acts as an auger, pulling the leaf through the drum. Leaf processed through a Rotorvane is thoroughly distorted, crushed, and mixed, generating heat and furthering the enzymic activity.

This manipulation also spreads the juice to the leaf's surface so that oxidation can begin. Some Rotorvanes are open on the far end, allowing the leaf to exit reasonably whole. This type of Rotorvane is used when making the so-called broken grades of orthodox leaf. A Rotorvane is not used at all in the manufacture of whole- or large-leaf black tea grades, as the process would break the leaves.

ROLL-BREAKING AND SIFTING

For superior oxidation to occur, rolled leaf must be cool, aerated, of a uniform particle size, and evenly coated with the enzymatic juice. Because the release of the enzymatic juice during the rolling process causes the leaf to start to bunch and clump the next step is roll-breaking and sifting. By breaking up the clumping masses of leaf back into individual rolled leaf, this intermediate step aerates the clumps, reduces the temperature of the leaf, and does a preliminary sieving. This process also helps to evenly coat the leaf with the enzymatic juices, ensuring that superior oxidation can take place.

OXIDATION

Finally the leaf is ready for the main event—oxidation, the process so often mislabeled as fermentation. By definition, fermentation can only occur in the absence of oxygen. Oxidation is a chemical process that requires an abundance of moist, oxygen-rich air. Oxidation rooms, or chambers, for tea produc-

A typical oxidation table (Darjeeling, India). Photo courtesy of Eliot Jordan.

tion must have fifteen to twenty exchanges of humidified air per hour to guarantee complete oxidation. The catechins (polyphenols) in the leaf absorb a significant quantity of oxygen, particularly during the early stages of oxidation. Oxidation officially begins during the withering stage and accelerates gradually during the subsequent steps. Within the controlled environment of the official oxidation process, the several chemical reactions that together comprise oxidation now take center stage. In traditional oxidation the sieved leaf is spread out in a thin layer (maximum 2 to 3 inches, or 5 to 8 centimeters) on the floor of the factory, on tables, or on perforated trays that are similar to the withering troughs.

The oxygenation of the catechins stimulates them to start the series of chemical reactions that will yield the flavor components and cup characteristics that we expect in black tea. During the first and most important of the enzymic oxidations the enzymes polyphenol oxidase and peroxidase act on other polyphenols to produce theaflavins. These red-orange compounds then react with more polyphenols to produce thearubigins, the chemicals responsible for changing the leaf's color from green to golden, coppery, or chocolate brown. The thearubigins, meanwhile, are also busy reacting with some of the amino acids and sugars in the leaf to create such distinctive flavor components as the highly polymerized substances. In general, theaflavins contribute to the brisk and bright taste of black tea, while the thearubigins are what provide strength (depth or body) and color. Carbon dioxide is also being driven out of the leaf, and heat is exchanged. If the temperature of the leaf rises too high, oxidation will rage out of control; if it falls too low, oxidation will cease.

At this point the oxidizing leaf takes on a new moniker: *dhool.* Oxidation requires two to four hours and is controlled by experience, not by science. Although there may be technical markers for determining a prospective end to the process, so many variables come into play that the best method for ending oxidation is the nose and eye of the expert monitoring the process. The tea master must control the thickness and raking of the leaf, which determines the exposure of the surface area of the dhool to the air; the ideal ambient temperature (85°F, or 29°C) and relative humidity (98 percent); and the ventilation (fifteen to twenty complete changes of air per hour). Also, the environment must be completely hygienic; bacteria must be prevented from ruining the dhool.

During oxidation the dhool goes through a predictable series of flavor profiles: brisk, high color, and overall strength. The tea master can direct the dhool into a particular style by adjusting the length of time allowed in oxidation in combination with regulating the temperature/humidity of the oxidation chamber. Most tea is manufactured to a balanced cup showing bright liquor, good brightness in the nose, and a solid full body. When the tea master has determined that the dhool is fully oxidized to the desired level, oxidation is halted by the final and also critical process of black tea manufacture: drying.

DRYING AND COOLING

The purpose of drying is to stop all biochemical enzymatic activity (which then halts oxidation) by exposing the dhool to hot air (heated to a minimum 130°F, or 54°C). Drying also reduces the moisture content of the dhool from the mid-60s percent to a mere 3 percent. Residual sugars are also caramelized during drying, changing the color of the dhool from its coppery-red color to a rich brown-black. While all the other processes in the manufacture of black tea have a fairly large window for success, drying happens quickly (fifteen to twenty minutes). Many experts refer to it as the do-or-die moment, because all the work that has gone into bringing the fresh leaf to the dhool stage will be for naught if the drying fails.

The dhool is dried by one of many methods. Originally finished in large pans or baskets over an open fire or charcoal, as artisanal green tea is still final-fired, virtually all black tea today is dried using mechanically forced hot air. Some of the machines that are used to finish dhool into black tea include drum-dryers, tumble-dryers, fluid-bed dryers (similar to an enclosed withering trough), endless-chain-pressure-type dryers (vertically angled conveyors that tumble the dhool down from level to level, increasing the heat as it travels through the machine), and tempest-dryers. Orthodox leaf tea is then cooled quickly and thoroughly to prevent overheating and loss of flavor. When it is cool and shelf-stable, the finished "made tea" is sorted one last time before final grading and being packed for storage and eventual sale.

PROCESSING CTC-MANUFACTURED BLACK TEA

Because CTC manufacture requires chopping the withered leaf, extra care must be taken to eliminate unwanted material before the leaf goes into the cutting machinery. The cutters used are extremely sharp and fast-moving, so sticks, stones, and other miscellaneous objects must not enter this machinery. Leaf destined to be CTC-grade black tea is thus put through what is known as preconditioning. This is a combination sifting-and-shredding procedure. The first step is accomplished by a machine called a green leaf sifter, a perforated vibrating tray that guarantees that a free flow of withered leaf moves on to the next step, free of such extraneous matter as sticks, stones, and sand. Strong magnets remove iron or steel particles that may have found their way into the mix.

Moving quickly, the sifted leaf now goes into the green leaf shredder, which precuts the leaf into small pieces before it goes on to the Rotorvane. The green leaf shredder is a cylinder with a main shaft to which are fastened extremely sharp, lightweight, and well-balanced knives. These knives rotate on their shaft at 2,500 rpm, shredding the leaf as it passes through. The spacing between the knives decreases along the length of the shaft, increasing the machine's cutting ability and ensuring that the leaf particle size is uniformly small when it emerges from the cylinder.

Now that the withered leaf is preconditioned, it is sent to a series of two Rotorvanes for final conditioning. The first Rotorvane has an open exit end but is only 8 inches (20 centimeters) in diameter, so it really crushes and compacts the leaf. Because the size of the leaf entering the second, larger-diameter (15 inches, or 38 centimeters) Rotorvane is so much smaller than that used for orthodox tea, this Rotorvane is set up with a sieve plate or screening at the end, to really scrunch the leaf as it exits the machine. This minced leaf is now called *chutney*, a clear reflection of the English influence on tea production.

ROLLING TO BECOME CTC LEAF

Now that the withered leaf has been meticulously conditioned, it is time for CTC rolling, which means that the chutney is passed through a succession of four or five CTC rollers. A CTC rolling machine consists of two stainless-steel rollers with many sharp cutting teeth. The two rollers are the same size diameter (8 or 13 inches, or 20 or 33 centimeters) and width (variously 24, 30, and 36 inches, or 60, 75, and 90 centimeters). They are mounted parallel to each other and are fixed horizontally. The rollers rotate at different speeds, in opposite directions to one another. The first is the slow roller and the second the fast. The ratio is 1 to 10, with speeds of 70 to 700 rpm to 100 to 1,000 rpm. The chutney, fed from the rear, is let to fall just behind the crown of the slow roller, which rotates forward.

The chutney is drawn between the rollers by the action of the fast roller, which is rotating back, at the faster speed. The slow roller actually performs more as the cutting surface and the fast roller as the cutting knife. Both are kept extremely sharp, however, and together they chop or cut the chutney into the uniformly small particles that will now be oxidized and soon become finished CTC leaf tea. Because the particles are so small, clumping is not a big problem going into the oxidation phase of CTC production, so rolled CTC leaf is not put through the roll-breaking and sifting process that orthodox leaf would be at this stage. Due to the small particle size, good air circulation is the critical element now, so floor oxidation and trough oxidation are not good choices for the oxidation phase of CTC production. To increase the ventilation of the chutney, CTC production uses drum oxidation and continuous oxidation machinery to facilitate the necessary oxidation.

CTC DRUM OXIDATION

In southern India oxidation drums are used most commonly for this next step. A standard drum has a 16-foot-long (5 meters) cylindrical middle section with a 2-foot (60-centimeter) conical end at each extremity. Oxidation drums are mounted horizontally, in groups, and are perforated to aid air circulation. The rolled chutney is placed into these large revolving drums for sixty to ninety minutes. Fresh or conditioned air is pumped through the drum to assure proper aeration of the dhool. Because it is the transfer of oxygen to the leaf particle that causes oxidation, it is critical that fresh air is brought into the oxidation room, which is sometimes saturated with moisture to assure proper oxidation.

The distinctive movement of dhool within the drum guarantees that all the bits of leaf and every drop of the internal juices are spread throughout the dhool repeatedly, completely, and evenly. Drum oxidation also encourages even granulation, increases bulk density, and assures that the finished leaf is consistently blacker in color. CTC leaf processed by drum oxidation often does not require roll-ball breaking as a finishing step, as the tumbling action accomplishes that during the oxidation stage.

CTC CONTINUOUS OXIDATION, ROLL-BALL BREAKING, AND FINISHING

Continuous oxidation machines are the other choice for mechanical oxidation in CTC manufacture. This equipment is fairly straightforward and consists of a conveyor made of interwoven racks on which the rolled chutney is placed. The conveyor racks, or trays, pass under ultraviolet lamps; this activates the polyphenol oxidase and stimulates the oxidation process. The use of ultraviolet light also kills unwanted bacteria and microbial contaminants. This processing is used where humidity is high and conditions necessitate a super-clean environment for a faster, high-volume production of average-grade CTC leaf. CTC dhool processed using continuous oxidation machinery requires roll-ball breaking as a finishing step, as the conveyor system tends to encourage the creation of small clumps during the oxidation stage.

Following the completion of the oxidation stage, CTC leaf manufacture mimics that of orthodox leaf manufacture. The dhool is cooled quickly and thoroughly to prevent overheating and loss of flavor. When cool and shelf-stable, the finished "made tea" is sorted one last time before final grading and being packed for storage and eventual sale.

Pu-erh Tea

Pu-erh, known in old Chinese as "black tea," is tea that is actually fermented. Depending on which type of pu-erh is being manufactured, the leaf may or may not oxidize; however, microbial activity involving several different bacteria takes place both in and on the leaf—this is true fermentation. According to the *Pu-erh Yunnan Local Standard*, there are two main types of pu-erh, with two styles within each type, outlined on the next page.

I received a small brick of tea,

And sipping it, felt cool; I can do with the wind as I will.

Why should I need paradise?

My whole body is floating amid the white clouds.

—GIDŌ SHUSHIN (1325–1388)

1. Sheng pu-erh ("raw" or "green" pu-erh)
    A. *Mao Cha*. "Young green" (good for investment, not immediate consumption!), this tea requires proper storage and aging, and then it becomes 1B).
    B. *Dry storage, naturally aged*. The best of all four choices, both for current consumption and for additional keeping, this is authentic, compressed, caked, or bricked pu-erh.
2. Shou pu-erh ("cooked" or "black" pu-erh)
    A. *Wo Dui ("wet-pile fermented")*. This is almost always loose-leaf, but it is sometimes packed in bamboo or citrus peel or compressed into interesting shapes, generally ready to be consumed.
    B. *Wet storage, quickly aged*. This is usually compressed into a beeng cha. Purists disdain this style of pu-erh, just as traditionalists scorn wine vinified in the modern style for drinking without cellaring, but much pu-erh is manufactured in this style and enjoyed worldwide.

PU-ERH TEA, DEFINED

Pu-erh is a particularly large, richly colored leaf tea that can be made from either oxidized ("cooked") or nonoxidized ("raw") leaf. Pu-erh can be loose-leaf or compressed into the traditional round cakes (known as *beeng cha*) and such other interesting shapes as mushrooms, spheres, cubes, pyramids, coins, and more.

The large leaves used in the manufacture of highest-quality pu-erh are plucked from the long-lived tea bushes that grow abundantly in southern Yunnan Province (see "China" in chapter 4).

The most famous region in Yunnan Province for tea plants of this type is the Six Famous Mountains region in the Xishuangbanna district, bordered by Myanmar to the west and Laos to the south. This lush, subtropical, and mountainous region provides one of the most perfect tea-growing areas in the world; as such, it is one of the locations where "wild" tea may have originated. Many of the tea plants here qualify as being ancient because they are more than a hundred years old (see chapter 1 for a full discussion on tea's origins)

Whereas China primarily grows *Camellia sinensis* var. *sinensis* (the China bush), which is kept pruned and is picked seasonally, the tea plants that grow in subtropical Xishuangbanna are *Camellia sinensis* var. *assamica* (the Assam bush) or minor subvarieties indigenous to the region, known locally as Yunnan Big Leaf, or *dayeh*. These plant varieties grow quite large and are picked continually, allowing rest periods only for the plants to produce and grow new leaf. In a few growing areas, bushes are semicultivated, but because these tea plants are more treelike than bushlike, for the most part they are found growing randomly and sporadically throughout the hillsides and mountain slopes. Gathering their leaf is thus difficult and time-consuming, and transport is complicated.

SHENG PU-ERH MANUFACTURE

Classical, traditionally made Sheng pu-erh is manufactured as follows: Initially, the plucked large leaves are processed by standard tea methodology—following a quick sort and cleaning (primary-leaf pu-erh is easy to sort because of the large leaf size), the leaf is left to air-dry (traditionally in the sun) for a brief period. Then it is fired quickly, to remove the excess surface moisture that large tea leaves often carry. This is a critical step in the processing, because for successful fermentation, the leaf must retain a different moisture content depending on which type of pu-erh it is to become.

Now the decision must be made as to whether the leaf will become a raw or a cooked pu-erh. If it is to become "raw" pu-erh, it is fired almost completely, to stop all enzymatic processes and prevent oxidation, but not so much as to eliminate all internal moisture, which would inhibit internal fermentation. Similar to the phenomenon that occurs when using heirloom apple varieties for cider production (and because the big leaf for making pu-erh tea is

Top: This store in Dali specializes in both traditional and fanciful pu-erh in a multitude of shapes and forms (Yunnan Province, China).

Above: Ancient tea trees in Xishuangbanna (Yunnan Province, China).

harvested from Yunnan's large, older, *dayeh* tea plants), the leaf has plenty of natural bacterium present on its surface to begin the chemical transformation that is necessary for pu-erh to develop.

The leaf is now gathered, usually on the floor (as dhool is for black tea oxidation). Careful supervision is required during the next phase, while the leaf is turned regularly and allowed to ferment. The practical differences between this fermentation stage and the oxidation phase of black tea manufacture are that these piles are much greater in size, the leaf is much drier, and higher heat is generated. So while the exposed portion of the pile permits oxygen absorption as a catalyst for surface oxidation, the core of the pile is robbed of oxygen but becomes very hot for short periods, encouraging the true microbial activity of fermentation.

For the leaf to ferment evenly, the pile must be turned at regular intervals, so that all the leaf has an opportunity to be at the core of the pile— encouraging the crucial microbial activity. In this way the heat generated by the fermentation process can be dispersed and the leaf remains raw. Because the leaf has been dried so much more than dhool, the level of oxidation that occurs is limited. The leaf at this stage is called Mao Cha.

All pu-erh beeng cha are individually wrapped for market (Yunnan Province, China).

FROM MAO CHA TO SHENG PU-ERH

At this point in the manufacture of raw pu-erh, the Mao Cha is packed into either the traditional or the modern compressed shapes. The goal in making raw pu-erh is to cause the leaf to begin to ferment internally, to reduce the moisture content to a very low level, and to limit exposure to fresh oxygen. The Mao Cha is then packed into a compressed form, where it remains, undergoing postfermentation (aging) for the next ten years. It will continue its gradual development as long as conditions are correct for the chemical process to continue.

Years ago, postfermentation was accomplished in caves, each cave having a unique environment that individualized the production of the particular pu-erh artisan. Today, however, the proper conditions are climate-controlled storage facilities where the humidity is maintained at less than 80 percent, and calm but good air circulation must be maintained. The discs are paper-wrapped to allow the tea to breathe, to mark the place and date of manufacture, and to record important storage information (the future provenance). After some time (about six years) the compressed Mao Cha's changed balance of bacteria and moisture slows the postfermentation process. From this point on the beeng cha will simply age and become a *dry storage naturally aged* Sheng pu-erh, ready to be tasted.

Tasting pu-erh through the years to check on its readiness is simple. One carefully removes several whole leaves from the back side of the disc near the dimple (it is easier to remove at this point) and brews some liquid treasure. When it is to the owner's taste, it is ready to be consumed, but the pu-erh will not change further quickly, so there is no hurry to drink it all up. In an effort to satisfy worldwide demand for ready-to-drink pu-erh, tea artisans in the 1970s began to experiment with "accelerated aging," and Shou pu-erh was created.

Shou pu-erh. In the pu-erh Yunnan local standard, there are ten grades of leaf for Shou pu-erh, with grades 1 through 4 reserved for use in the fancier compressed shapes and for the high-quality loose-leaf offerings. Grades 5 through 10 are used for basic beeng cha, rectangles, and market-quality loose-leaf Shou pu-erh. Interestingly, this grading system refers only to the leaf, so it is not a complete indicator of quality, and the consumer may not even have access to the grade designation. In the case of compressed pu-erh, when a beeng cha or other shape has a number stamped on its paper wrapper, the third digit is the grade. However, there is more to it than that: top-grade leaf can be ruined or simply develop incorrectly in the fermenting, or grade 8 leaf may mature into an unbelievable Shou pu-erh with careful fermentation and years of excellent aging. Our best recommendation is to rely on a reliable merchant or, if possible, purchase a sample taste. When purchasing loose-leaf pu-erh, purchase a small quantity at first. When you find a loose leaf that you like, purchase as much of that batch as you can afford, because every lot is different!

Wo Dui Shou pu-erh. To manufacture Wo Dui Shou pu-erh, the same process is followed as for all pu-erh, up to the point of piling the Mao Cha on the factory floor. The moist leaf for Wo Dui Mao Cha is piled more densely than it would be for compressed Shou pu-erh. It is allowed to ferment in that state for the amount of time necessary to produce a finished loose-leaf pu-erh. This process is usually reserved for summer leaf, as the heat and humidity of the muggy summer weather is ideal for generating the heat necessary to regulate fermentation. The leaf is never compressed but is finished as

A collection of pu-erh tongs containing various shapes, including camel's breath mushrooms and tuo cha (Yunnan Province, China).

an oxidized tea would be, with a final firing to expel excess moisture and prevent spoilage.

Wo Dui Shou pu-erh is ready to drink right away and is often sold in wooden mini-chestlets that replicate the historical tea chests once used for oxidized tea. It is also packed in other containers, including bamboo (that is sometimes charred to impart a slight smokiness) and whole dried citrus peel.

In order to manufacture a compressed "wet-storage" Shou pu-erh, the exact same methodology is followed as for Sheng pu-erh, except that the Mao Cha is not fired quite as dry, and after being formed into the beeng cha shape, the discs are kept in storage above 80 percent humidity and are occasionally wetted down. This accelerates the fermentation (aging) process and creates a pu-erh that will not have the complexity of flavor of a Sheng pu-erh, but it will be much less expensive and ready to drink after only two to three years. Usually factory-made, this type of pu-erh is consumed in great quantity worldwide.

Quality beeng cha pu-erhs are traditionally wrapped in paper, which often marks the place and date of manufacture, along with the seal (known as "the chop") of those who have previously owned the disc—a Chinese form of provenance. A stack of seven discs in a bamboo-leaf wrapper is known as a *tong*, which translates as "seven sons." Each tong weighs approximately 5 pounds (2.5 kilograms). Traders wrap four tongs to a bundle (twenty-eight beeng cha total), with a total net weight of 20 to 22 pounds (10 kilograms).

Scented Tea

Flower-scented teas are uniquely Chinese. As China is the historical origin of many varieties of distinctive fruits and aromatic flowers, early Chinese tea masters first experimented with and then excelled at producing scented teas that were esteemed worldwide. Perhaps the most famous example of this is the manufacture of Jasmine tea (for a full discussion, see chapter 4). Tea scented with jasmine flowers was especially prized by the emperors, so during their reign (and continuing today) jasmine tea has been offered as a gift to dignitaries who visit China. The resultant far-flung exposure to this exotic new flavor of the Far East, combined with the movement of similarly mysterious goods along early trade routes, was directly responsible for the popularity of the masterfully blended Chinese scented teas that became the sources of inspiration for the lovely scented teas favored by both Russians and the peoples of the Near East. Outside of China these cultures had an early appreciation of fine tea, and Chinese tea merchants provided the bulk of their supply.

Over time, as the popularity of finished tea spread around the world, flowers, spices, oils, and herbs began to be used to flavor different types of already finished tea locally. As more diverse flavorings became available, the variety of combination used with tea helped to develop what we now consider to be the signature flavors of the cuisines of the modern world. One sees this today with the fresh mint added to green tea in Morocco, the addition of regionally varying blends of "earth spices" to black tea with milk for India's chai, or the addition of the citrus oil bergamot to black tea in England to create the legendary Earl Grey tea. These illustrate the body of tea history that is flavored tea; scented tea, however, refers to the technique practiced at the source of tea manufacture, in which jasmine flowers, wild rosebuds, chrysanthemums, osmanthus (sweet almond flowers), or fragrant varieties of fruit such as lychee or orange are added to partially finished tea. The tea is then finished, imbued with the aromatics given off by these flowers and other ingredients.

Tea drinkers in the Tang dynasty often added onion, jujube fruit, orange peel, dogwood berries, or mint to their tea. Salt was always added.

JASMINE TEA

Manufacturing jasmine tea is a delicate and complicated task. It requires great skill to understand how to obtain the correct level of scenting. Jasmine teas divide into two categories: (1) the premium, traditional jasmine tea whose reputation is renowned, and (2) the standard-grade jasmine tea, both of which are discussed here.

Premium, traditional jasmine tea. The base tea that is scented and subsequently transformed into top-quality traditional jasmine tea requires some of the most precise leaf preparation in the whole of tea production. It falls into none of the standard categories of tea; thus it is not green, black, white, or yellow. The best jasmine teas are made from leaf that has been encouraged to oxidize just a little but remains close in type to green tea. This distinctive initial processing yields a base tea often called *pouchong,* but more correctly *zao bei* (tea readied). This category is used only to designate the base tea that is eventually scented, becoming traditional jasmine tea. This unique process was developed expressly for two reasons: first, it gives this tea the ability to readily absorb the aromatics from the jasmine flowers, and second, its particular flavor counterpoints the sweetness of the jasmine in the cup.

Because first-quality budset zao bei (the base tea) is harvested in the spring, and jasmine vines bloom in the summer, there is an incompatibility in the natural timing. For the top grades of jasmine tea, leaf plucking commences in April and early May (the season known for its "before-the-rain" tea). Because the jasmine vines do not bloom until July and into September, however, this base tea must be kept in storage in anticipation of the arrival of the blossoms. Zao bei, with its remarkable ability to "rest," is set aside after its primary processing until midsummer, when the particular varieties of jasmine used for tea-scenting bloom (see "A Visit to a Jasmine Tea Factory" in chapter 4).

That said, though, an exception to this is Bai Hao or Yin Zhen Jasmine (Silver Needles Jasmine white tea), a glorious marriage of top-grade white tea that is delicately scented with a light touch of jasmine. Because of the slight oxidation inherent in white tea manufacture, this combination works well, but the scenting is the lightest of all the jasmine teas. This ethereal tea exemplifies the exquisite imperial teas once available only to the emperors.

Manufacturing jasmine tea requires at least several days, and the finer quality jasmines necessitate up to a month of scenting. The scenting involves several introductions of fresh jasmine blossoms to acquire the desired level of jasmine aroma. The zao bei leaf readily absorbs the perfume from the blossoms, so it is the fashion of the scent master that determines how long and how many times a new batch of fresh jasmine flowers is added to the base tea. When scenting in the traditional style, fresh jasmine flowers are combined with the zao bei during the hottest period of Fujian Province's sweltering summer.

Starting in the evening, the leaf and jasmine flowers mingle together in a large pile for about six hours. During this time the internal temperature of the pile increases to 113°F (45°C). This buildup of heat encourages the blossoms to open fully, releasing their perfume, and creates the necessary chemistry for a moisture transfer to occur between the flowers and the zao bei.

The size of a scenting pile is adjusted to be in sync with the ambient temperature of the room. The larger the pile, the hotter the internal temperature will become, so the tea makers must keep a watchful eye on the buildup of heat. If the base tea reaches too high a temperature, a bitter, "funny" flavor will develop. After six to seven hours the piles are flattened and the tea is spread out to breathe for a short time. By now it is 2 or 3 a.m., but the scenting process is not over. Each pile of tea must be heaped again and scenting continues for another four to five hours.

After a total of ten to twelve hours, the flowers are sifted out, then after the tea rests for a day, the process is repeated for standard grades of jasmine tea. For the better grades of tea such as First Grade Jasmine, the tea is scented four or five times. The more costly Yin Hao Jasmine is scented as many as eight or nine separate times. The first scenting period is the most important, so large quantities of flowers are used, but the amount is reduced during subsequent scentings. The level of perfume absorbed from the flowers is monitored carefully, and the variables are adjusted as necessary. After each period of scenting, the spent blossoms are removed by sifting and fresh flowers are added. The processing tea needs time to rest between scentings (more scentings require more rest in between), so it can take as long as one month to finish a batch of Yin Hao Jasmine.

When the tea master decides that the zao bei has become jasmine tea all spent blossoms are removed from the tea with high-powered blower fans that send the blossoms scattering. Having blossoms remaining in the leaf is not considered aesthetically pleasing in most of China. Following the scenting phase, the tea is finish-fired and becomes shelf-stable, the perfume having been absorbed into the leaf, waiting to be released when brewed. In Sichuan Province, however, such top grades as Snowflake Jasmine tea have more fresh flowers added at the finish for an extra dose of fragrance and to create a visually interesting contrasting-color look.

Standard-grade jasmine tea. The second type of jasmine tea is the large volume that is manufactured for general consumption by, for instance, the average residents of northern China, where it is extremely popular. Tea enthusiasts worldwide, particularly restaurant patrons in the West, also consume this grade. The procedure for manufacturing this broad category of jasmine tea replicates the process just described but uses summer-harvest leaf pluck of a lesser grade and is given only one or two scentings. This tea may also be created simply by combining fully processed green or oolong tea with jasmine flowers, resulting in a "jasmine tea" that is less deeply scented and has a short shelf life.

A new entry of nonauthentically prepared jasmine tea has entered the marketplace. It is created by spraying jasmine extract on one or another of the types of tea, be it green, oolong, or white tea, from many different source countries. These concoctions may include the use of other flower essences or artificial flavoring and are primarily responsible for the rise of what is popularly known as jasmine green tea or green jasmine tea. Because this modern form of "jasmine tea" exists, the product is arguably green tea. When treated this way, however, it should not technically be called jasmine tea, because if it had been scented by traditional methodology, the base leaf would not have been green tea, but rather zao bei. Strictly speaking, it should therefore be called jasmine-flavored green tea or green tea flavored with jasmine. We recommend that tea enthusiasts make every effort to purchase authentic jasmine tea, of whichever of the two time-honored scenting styles is preferred. In doing so, we all help continue a tea tradition that has a deep-rooted history.

EARL GREY

Earl Grey tea is one of the most classic of the "scented" teas, although it really fits the description of a flavored tea. Whether or not there ever was a real Earl of Grey who drank tea (especially this tea) is a subject of debate, as is which tea company first used bergamot to scent its tea. No matter, the popularity of this flavored tea is so tremendous that none of the details of its history matter much to those who love its wonderful taste.

Earl Grey tea is a blended black tea to which bergamot aroma has been added. The exact blend of tea used will affect the flavor of the finished tea, as will the bergamot. Many tea blenders use natural bergamot, and others use artificial. When natural, the oil will be one of many grades of what is known as "oil of bergamot."

Bergamot is a citrus fruit that looks similar to ugli fruit, and it is the rind, or peel, that is important in commerce. The pulp is edible but sour and extremely small in proportion to the whole of the fruit and has little commercial value. It is the generous rind that contains the essential oil prized by tea aficionados and perfumeries.

We have always blended our own Earl Grey tea and therefore have complete control over the blend of tea and the amount of and style of "scenting." The variables encountered when experimenting with different merchants' Earl Grey are: (1) The overall strength of the tea blend itself and its particular flavor. Teas used range from being a straight Ceylon, Indian, or African black tea to a blend specifically designed to enhance the ultimate combination with the oil of bergamot. (2) The type of oil of bergamot used, natural or synthetic. Natural bergamot has a more subtle but well-defined flavor. It has snap and a genuine citrus intensity. Synthetic bergamot is more one-dimensional; it tastes okay but is timid and short in the cup. (The main reason to use synthetic oil is the small number of customers who have a citrus allergy, so it is mostly multinational companies who use it as a means to avoid potential liability issues. Their lawyers assume that most tea drinkers today do not know that bergamot is a citrus fruit.) Another source of confusion is bee balm bergamot, a biannual plant that is often used in tisanes. This is not the flavoring used in Earl Grey tea. Natural bergamot will vary from being a lightly aromatic and low-concentration inexpensive oil to the intensely flavorful and high-concentration Italian bergamot used also by perfumers. This latter is what we have always chosen to use, and it is very expensive! (3) The amount of bergamot added. This is where house style comes into play. A tea blender may choose to use strong tea and a light hand with the bergamot, a light tea and a heavy hand adding the bergamot, and every possible variation in between. All Earl Greys differ, so buy many and taste for yourself which style you prefer. We use a tremendously full-bodied and brisk blend of black tea, scented highly with natural Italian oil of bergamot. Most (95 percent) of our clientele love it just the way it is, but for those for whom it is too citrusy, we can always blend in more black tea.

Several regional variations are: (1) a bit of Lapsang Souchong added for a smoky-style English Earl Grey; (2) the addition of a handful of lavender, so beloved in France; (3) blue cornflowers added strictly for visual interest; (4) Earl Green, which is blended using green tea rather than the traditional black tea (very difficult to blend properly because green tea is astringent as is the citrus); and (5) Lady Grey—you have to ask the merchant, because we have seen this name on many different concoctions!

LAPSANG SOUCHONG

Lapsang Souchong is reputedly a tea that the Chinese rarely drink; rather, it is manufactured for export only. There is some truth to this; see "Wuyi Shan" in the black tea section in chapter 4 for a detailed relating of the fascinating history of Lapsang Souchong tea.

This interior of a smoking shed in Zen Shan shows all three levels. In the open chamber at lower left, tiled vents in the floor allow smoke to enter the shed from the smoke boxes directly outside and behind the building (Fujian Province, China).

The Lapsang Souchong that the West knows is also known as "Tarry Lapsang," and that moniker really tells it all. When customers of ours request it, they are often immediately balanced by another patron who is cringing at the reminder of a tea with such a distinctive and potent flavor profile. Lapsang Souchong is like licorice and cilantro: one either loves it or detests it. And millions of tea drinkers worldwide love to consume piping hot cups or glasses of this smoky-hot beverage. No milk, no sugar or honey—just the tea, brewed strong.

Lapsang Souchong is produced one of two ways: the rare, artisanal, and authentic Zhen Shan Xiao Zhong described in chapter 4, or the much larger production of tea that has been finish-manufactured and then transported to the smoking sheds of Zen Shan to be heavily smoked before being shipped to demanding tea enthusiasts around the world.

To create this distinctive tea, the black tea manufactured in the large tea-producing area around Wuyi (and from tea growers even further away) is trucked into the smoking sheds deep in the mountains. There it is smoked hard and hot to imbue it with the smokiness desired by the firm to which it will be exported.

A smoking shed is constructed on three levels. Surprisingly, the floors on the top and middle levels are not solid, but are comprised of woven slats of wood that allow one to peek all the way down to the ground level. It also allows the pine smoke to rise up through the floors all the way to the top level.

Fully manufactured tea is laid on mats on the floors and begins to absorb the faint, slightly moist aroma of smoke. From here, the more supple tea is

THE MARK T. WENDELL TEA COMPANY: HU-KWA TEA

During the heyday of the Canton tea trade (1784–1860) foreign traders arriving in Canton were required to stop in the Portuguese colony of Macao. From there the Chinese escorted the foreign ships up the Pearl River to an anchorage in Whampoa. Each ship was then assigned a Hong merchant who was responsible for offloading the Western goods coming into China and for loading the Chinese goods heading to the West. The emperor appointed the Hong merchants; their job was to keep the exchange of tea, silk, and porcelains moving and to make sure that the "foreign devils" did not venture into China proper. The most famous of these Hong merchants was Wu Ping-Chien (1769–1843), whom the Western traders called Houqua.

American merchant Richard Devens, who is said to have personally met with and purchased tea from Houqua during the height of the China tea trade days, established an importing company in Boston in 1852 and began to sell port, sherry, olive oil, and tea using the mark of "XXX," which was then a sign of superior quality. In 1904 the ownership of the tea company passed to Mark T. Wendell, Devens's nephew. Wendell changed the name of this custom-made, tarry, smoky tea from "XXX" to "Hu-kwa" to more clearly underscore the connection between this tea and the venerable Hong merchant. Many Americans were familiar with the name Houqua, as it was associated with fair business practices as well as the finest-quality imported goods from Asia.

Wendell created the iconic black and gold Hu-Kwa packaging, complete with a stylized Russian-inspired crowned eagle. Carrying on a long-standing tradition of tea merchants, Wendell packed the tea into containers by hand and delivered it himself to his loyal customers.

Wendell remained the owner of Hu-kwa tea until he sold the company in the 1960s. Today's owners, Elliot H. Johnson and son Hartley, continue to supply Hu-kwa tea in the familiar black and gold tins and boxes. The firm sells more than sixty teas, but the bestseller is still the smoky Hu-Kwa, "the master's poison," as one Irish maid used to refer to it when placing her employer's orders.

Rumor has it that when Wendell died, his ashes were placed in a black Hu-Kwa tin and buried.

moved downstairs to another area where it is placed in baskets and hung in the smoking chamber for as long as twelve hours.

The tea is exposed only to indirect smoke and never experiences direct heat or flame. The smoke circulates up from specially designed troughs in the floor that direct the moist smoke into the smoking rooms from large fireplaces located outside the building. After smoking, the tea is dried again in tumbler-dryers to fix the finished tea.

It is an acquired taste for sure, but one that appeals to many tea enthusiasts all around the world. Toasty, smoky, tarry, burnt, full-bodied—these descriptors all suggest a certain allure that Lapsang Souchong shares with dark-roast coffee, single-malt scotch, extra-dark hot cocoa, and mescal.

ROSE, OSMANTHUS, AND OTHER FLOWER-SCENTED TEAS

Many exotic and garden flowers may be used to scent tea leaves. Several classics are rose (both mature petals and baby buds), osmanthus (flowering sweet almond), chrysanthemum, orchid, lotus, magnolia, lily, marigold, globe amaranth, and several traditional Chinese choices that you seldom see outside Asia, including bai lan (gardenia) and long zhu (dragon ball).

Three different styles of "presentation" or "blooming" tea, resting on a tray of the white tea budsets from which they were made (Fujian Province, China).

These teas are customarily made by adding fresh or dried flowers to already finished black, oolong, or green tea. The scenting is therefore light but very pleasant.

Recently there has been interest in what are known as "presentation," "display," or "artisan" teas, known in China as "hui fa cha." These are bundles of hand-tied buds from special cultivars of *Camellia sinensis*, which stay supple and can be tied into elegant, striking, and fantastic shapes. Various flower buds are incorporated into the silk-thread-tied tea bundles, which transform into flowers, baskets, and other fun shapes when they "bloom" following exposure to hot water.

Banned during the Cultural Revolution because they were considered wasteful and frivolous, "blooming tea" creations are now part of a renewed appreciation of the artistic enjoyment of tea. "Brewed" in a glass teapot or brandy snifter, these are wonderful to drink and are also a great conversation piece as the centerpiece of a table or on a mantle. Kept under daily refreshed cold water, these maintain their color and interest for almost a week.

LYCHEE AND FRUIT-INFUSED TEAS, FLAVORED TEAS, AND SPICED TEAS

Another time-tested method of incorporating creative flavors into tea is the use of fresh or dried fruit. Almost any fruit can be used, though some appear more often than others: apple, lychee, plum, peach, and apricot; berries (strawberry, raspberry, and blackberry); and of course citrus fruits (lime, lemon, and orange). If the dried fruit or peel is used, then the application falls under the category of fruit-infused tea, whereas if one is simply adding juice, then technically the beverage is a flavored tea. When one starts to combine flavors, the possibilities are almost endless.

It is always interesting to see what other cuisines of the world do to spice things up. In mainland southeast Asia, dragon fruit is often added to tea in dried or pulp form. In France, one will encounter the national favorite cassis (black currant juice). In the Pacific Northwest of the United States, pear (in pulp form or dried) is added to either hot or cold tea, bringing an extra zip of astringency and deliciousness to the cup. And in the Caribbean, it is not unusual to find mango purée being juiced into a tea cooler. Fresh juice can be added, oil can be zested from citrus peel, and pieces of dried fruit can be added all year long; the tea can be drunk hot, cold, or at room temperature.

Spiced tea opens up another range of possibilities, from the classic Indian chai (using at least cardamom, clove, cinnamon, black pepper, nutmeg, and ginger) to the mentholated green tea of Morocco (where dried mint is blended with the tea leaves for brewing and then fresh mint is added at service). While it is unusual to use fresh culinary herbs such as basil and rosemary with real tea, some do work; almost all spices and herbs combine successfully with tea. Some of the most thirst-quenching beverages in the world are combination tea, herb, and spice concoctions.

Now that we have discussed the hows and whys of manufacture, let's take a deeper look at the places and people that tea has enriched, and how it evolved from being consumed in only one particular part of the world to being the popular beverage it is today, enjoyed worldwide.

FROM GARDEN TO CUP: BRINGING TEA TO MARKET

Every facet of the food industry has countless jobs that are vital to keeping the industry running and functioning smoothly, and for bringing products from the growers to consumers around the world. Tea is no exception: it takes the combined efforts of millions of people in fifty-one countries to bring staggering quantities of tea from bush to cup each year.

After the tea growers and tea producers have brought the leaf to market, tea is either sold at auction or sold privately through export brokers and agents to foreign or domestic tea companies or importers. Import brokers or agents are responsible for bringing the tea into the country of final destination. Sometimes this shipment of tea is consigned exclusively to a large, multinational tea company, while other times the shipment will be broken down and sold in large lots to several national or regional tea wholesalers.

Tea wholesalers will in turn sell lesser quantities of tea to smaller wholesalers or to midsized tea companies who market the products themselves. From the small wholesalers tea is distributed to scores of specialty retailers, food co-ops, restaurants, teahouses, and cafés. In tea-exporting countries, the industry relies on the behind-the-scenes work of legions of botanists and soil scientists, plant nutritionists, organic-certification agents, tea researchers, tea estate managers, and tea factory managers to keep things on the right track. Tea tasters, tea blenders, and tea packers are needed in both exporting and importing countries, as well as workers in the chain of distribution, supply, shipping, and freight forwarding. For more, see "Bringing Tea to Market in China" in chapter 4.

CHAPTER 4

JOURNEYING ALONG THE TEA TRAIL

An array of freshly brewed oolong teas invites sampling in a tasting room (Fujian Province, China).

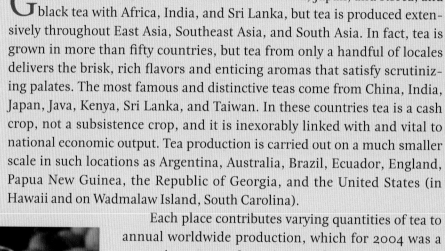

GREEN TEA IS COMMONLY ASSOCIATED WITH China, Japan, and Korea, and black tea with Africa, India, and Sri Lanka, but tea is produced extensively throughout East Asia, Southeast Asia, and South Asia. In fact, tea is grown in more than fifty countries, but tea from only a handful of locales delivers the brisk, rich flavors and enticing aromas that satisfy scrutinizing palates. The most famous and distinctive teas come from China, India, Japan, Java, Kenya, Sri Lanka, and Taiwan. In these countries tea is a cash crop, not a subsistence crop, and it is inexorably linked with and vital to national economic output. Tea production is carried out on a much smaller scale in such locations as Argentina, Australia, Brazil, Ecuador, England, Papua New Guinea, the Republic of Georgia, and the United States (in Hawaii and on Wadmalaw Island, South Carolina).

Each place contributes varying quantities of tea to annual worldwide production, which for 2004 was a staggering 3,233,216 metric tons of tea. The breakdown of tea production by the top ten tea-producing countries was: China, 835 metric tons; India, 820 metric tons; Kenya, 325 metric tons; Sri Lanka, 308 metric tons; Indonesia, 165 metric tons; Turkey, 165 metric tons; Japan, 100 metric tons; Vietnam, 95 metric tons; Argentina, 63 metric tons; and Bangladesh, 56 metric tons.

For the year, 2004 saw a global tea increase of 2.6 percent over 2003, and for the first time in decades China regained her place as the world's largest producer of tea, topping the output of that of historic rival India.

Early morning on the Huang Shan, one of China's premier green tea–growing mountains (Anhui Province, China).

China: The Origins and Unique Traditions of Tea

The West has always been tantalized by the exotic and opulent nature of Oriental material goods—silks, lacquer, porcelains—and the foreign mannerisms of Chinese tea-drinking customs. To us, tea will always be China's drink, forever associated with this enigmatic culture that fascinates us with its ancient legends, whispering walls, and rich oral tradition. Like all good storytelling, China's great oral tradition embellishes and underscores the lessons of life with colorful legends of gods, sages, and the natural world. Chinese people believe in a multitude of auspicious symbols and thoughts that are believed to determine prosperity, health, protection from evil, good luck or bad luck, and of course longevity. In this worldview surely all of the mysteries of life can be explained in one or another legend.

The classic China bush *Camellia sinensis* (Anhui Province, China).

Chinese legend supplies the story of tea's origin long before recorded history provides actual documentation. Shen Nung, the Second Divine Emperor and Celestial God, known as the Divine Husbandman and Father of Agriculture and Medicine, is said to have taught his people to farm and rely on a diet of vegetables rather than animal meats to maintain health. He is also credited with discovering the medicinal values of herbs, which became the basis for China's herbal pharmacopoeia. Shen Nung assigned plants, animals, and minerals and foods with therapeutic values of cooling and warmth, hot and cold, which underscore the dual concepts of yin and yang. He also advocated that people drink boiled hot water (called *bai cha*) for health, something that the poorest Chinese citizen has done during hard times in the poverty-stricken hinterlands of China. Despite knowing of this tradition, we were, however, caught off guard when visiting a modest Buddhist temple in Xishuangbanna, when an elderly monk offered us cups of hot water in simple, well-worn tin cups. His heartfelt welcome charmed us and made the gesture as sincere as if he had offered celestial tea in golden cups. We were pleased to be so well received.

As the Chinese legend goes, one day while Shen Nung was napping, a few leaves from a tea bush blew into his cup of hot water. He found the taste and the invigorating quality of this brew to his liking. He decreed that all Chinese people should from then on drink an infusion of tea leaves for health. Legends aside, however, the first mention of tea was in the *Shuo Wên*, an ancient dictionary of natural plants and objects. In this book, which was presented to the Han emperor Andi (r. 105–126), tea is referred to as *ming* and was described as buds plucked from the *t'u* plant. Other early books refer to *t'u* as the drink of the Chinese people.

Today, China cultivates tea in most every province except for such regions as Mongolia, Qinghai, and Tibet, where dry environments and harsh climate do not support the natural needs of green crops. Nonetheless, this leaves eighteen provinces and the island of Hainan to contribute to the massive collective output of tea. The large tea provinces in the east are stacked geographically one atop the other, defining a substantial portion of the coastline of China, touching first on the Yellow Sea, then the East China Sea, and finally the South China Sea. In the south and west the tea-producing provinces surround China's innermost core, leaving only the agriculturally challenged provinces of the north devoid of tea. China's long history of tea development and centuries of isolation from the rest of the world has resulted in a system of tea cultivation and production that in many ways remains unchanged from the way tea was produced during the Ming dynasty. Unlike all other tea-producing countries, China's tea gardens are found in small patches high in the mountains. The gardens terrace down the mountains in small groupings and are cut off from one another by sheer geography. Numerous tea gardens were planted in small patches here and there during the Tang dynasty, and China's tea gardens have proliferated since then as a loosely connected network of isolated gardens in their natural environment. It is always a joy for us to see patches of tea growing interspersed with plantings of rice, taro, and green vegetables on the village outskirts that we pass as we twist and turn our way along bumpy, broken roads in search of tea.

In China village tea farmers grow a majority of the tea. Their freshly plucked leaves are taken to the village tea factory or local cooperative factory for processing. This is an antiquated system of tea production compared to

Small, wild tea gardens occupy patches of land in the mountains of eastern China (Anhui Province, China).

modern standards employed elsewhere, but it is one that still works for China. Many of China's fine green teas are still handmade, based on this traditional production methodology. So much diversity and regional variation exists in Chinese green teas today because of the continuation of these traditional techniques.

China's immense landmass contributes many unique local teas to the marketplace, each of which is the result of tea-manufacturing and tea-drinking traditions that are strongly rooted in custom and local practices. Regional preferences can be strong in this vast country, and taste preferences differ greatly. Tea production is more complicated than just tossing, bruising, and drying fresh leaf. Factors that contribute to the unique differences in tea are a combination of soil, climate, altitude, air, water, tea bush variety, the care in which the tea was processed, and the taste preferences of the local residents. Each tea-producing region is famous for unique teas whose leaf style, processing, and inherent flavor have been perfected by generations of tea workers.

Each batch of tea from the same tea farm will be slightly different from the previous one as the season progresses. Every day is a new day when it comes to tea production, and part of the joy is that tea will always have a new dimension of style and flavor to reveal in the cup. In China tea is appreciated for the seemingly endless variations of taste and aroma that it offers. The art of tea brewing and tea appreciation is built on these anticipated variations and differences. In Asia, where the choices from one region are plentiful, comparisons can provide seemingly endless fodder for tasting and conversation. And when comparisons need be made between different regions of the same province or different parts of the country, it's no wonder that one sits in a Chinese teahouse for hours on end.

Tea drinking in China still fulfills a need to engage all of the senses in the brewing and the drinking. Tea culture in Asia is not about quaffing a hot cup of caffeine on the run, but about keeping tea culture alive, enjoying the delicious taste of tea, and being in the moment of appreciating the rich, sophisticated tea traditions that were developed centuries ago by scholars and emperors. Tea culture also encourages the participants to visually appreciate the beauty of the tea leaves, the skill of the person preparing the tea, how the tea is brewed and poured, and the attractiveness of the teawares selected for use.

THE MAJOR CLASSES OF TEA PRODUCED IN CHINA

All six major classes of tea are produced throughout China from approximately 340 different plant varieties of *Camellia sinensis*. Each province does not produce all classes of tea but instead excels in certain styles of production. As a result, most residents develop a strong taste preference for the style of tea that is made in their village. In the east, Jiangsu, Anhui, Zhejiang, and Jiangxi Provinces manufacture primarily green tea. The historic specialties of Fujian Province are the exotic and ethereal white teas, the sweet-smelling jasmine teas, the tarry, smoky Lapsang Souchong, and the fine fruity, earthy oolong teas. In the west, Yunnan Province produces both wonderful black and green teas but is most famous for pu-erh tea, a fermented specialty produced in both government-run tea factories and small village tea factories operated by Dai and Bulong villagers. Sichuan, known for tongue-tingling hot and spicy food, contributes elegant black and tender budset green teas to China's market basket.

In a relaxing local teahouse, an experienced tea server shares a brewing of his specially scented jasmine tea (Sichuan Province, China).

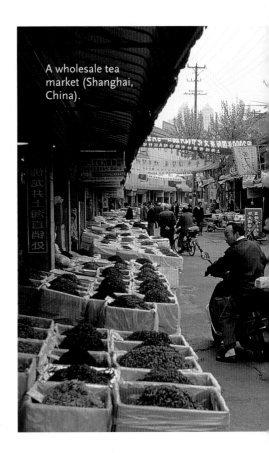

A wholesale tea market (Shanghai, China).

In each of these provinces both regional teas and locally produced and renowned "famous teas" dominate the selections on teahouse menus, in restaurants, and in teashops. In Beijing, Shanghai, and other populous cities, however, recent advances in transit and rising personal incomes have now made it possible for teashops to specialize in hand-crafted teas from all regions of China. This concept did not exist even ten years ago. These shops now provide locals as well as visitors with the opportunity to sample and purchase many styles of tea that were formerly unavailable to them or that were once reserved for export.

TEA EXPERT MADAME WEI

As we progress along the path of our tea education, we treasure the relationships we have with our tea mentors who have been eager to teach us the proper understanding of "tea" in all aspects of its meaning. One of our favorite Chinese colleagues is Madame Wei Cui Lan, one of China's many highly degreed and respected female tea experts. She always meets us at a designated rendezvous point early on in our trip with her boundless enthusiasm, lots of tea samples, and bags of unfamiliar Chinese candies and snacks.

Despite the fact that we do not share a common language, we do share a love and respect for green tea that allows us to comfortably communicate likes and dislikes with exaggerated facial expressions and hand gestures. She has been known to gently slap a person's hand if she sees him or her reaching for a second sip of a cup of tea that she finds inferior. Madame Wei has taught us to always taste the tea before making a judgment about its quality, and not to judge from the appearance of the leaf alone. Many young Chinese tea processors today are very skillful, and they can turn less-than-desirable leaf into nicely finished tea that will fool the eye.

China is a changing country on the move, but as stated earlier many aspects of tea production remain the same. With a great emphasis on handmade tea and traditional styles of leaf manufacture, Mr. Di Yung-zu, a retired tea merchant from Taipei, sums it up as such: "Styles of clothes may change, but the traditional tea doesn't change."

EVALUATING CHINESE GREEN TEAS

Because Chinese green teas come in a visually dizzying array of shapes and styles, our Chinese colleague Madame Wei has taught us to be savvy Chinese tea tasters and to evaluate tea the way she does. We look at the dry tea leaf *before* brewing and also the wet tea leaf *after* brewing. Although all tea should be tasted before judgment is passed, this is especially true with Chinese green teas.

In China tea is purchased based on the region it is from, the method of manufacturer, the flush, the uniformity of leaf, and the taste. After taking into account place and leaf style, we look for the following when tasting green teas: *se* (color), *xiang* (aroma), *wei* (taste), and *xing* (shape). When evaluating samples, we then ask these questions: Does the leaf and the liquor have the color it should? Does it have the aroma it should? Does it taste as it should? Does it look the way it should? These "shoulds" are important with Chinese teas because each tea has a standard that it should aspire to conform to, against which all tea of that type is compared.

The appearance of high-quality, well-made tea is not happenstance but intentional. It accomplishes three things: First, the shape and style of the leaves tell the purchaser what to expect from that tea. For example, tiny Bi Lo Chun tea leaves tell the drinker that these leaves were picked in the early spring, whereas the larger, rolled pellets of Gunpowder tea impart the wisdom that this tea was made from an older, large leaf that the tea maker needed to use in order to have enough length to achieve the roll. Longjing is a flat-leaf tea whose appearance implies that the tea was flattened and pressed by hand against the tea-firing pan. Second, tea leaves flaunt the skill of the tea maker. Although each style of tea needs to fulfill the expectation of how it should look, the skills of an expert tea maker are essential to coax the best appearance from the leaves. Third, a well-made green tea will, after brewing, return to the way it looked as a freshly picked leaf, before firing and shaping process changed it. This full-circle approach reminds the tea drinker of the ephemeral nature and simplicity of green tea, and that the vital seasonal energy or chi of the tea bush has been assimilated through the liquid tea.

This well-worn, tumbler-style, wall-mounted dryer (known as an "oven") removes moisture efficiently and is often used for the finish-firing of green tea (Fujian Province, China).

BRINGING TEA TO MARKET IN CHINA

Tea comes to market in several ways in China, although the traditional means of commerce is changing rapidly. Tea that is picked by individual farmers is usually brought to the village tea factory or collected and brought to a regional tea factory. That fresh leaf is then turned into finished tea, often in true cooperative fashion. State-run tea factories purchase tea from local tea farmers and sometimes oversee production from their own tea gardens as well. Unlike in India, Japan, or Sri Lanka, there is little private ownership of tea in China: farmers do not own their farms and consequently tea has always been sold to the government, which has historically controlled tea production.

In other major tea-producing countries, a majority of tea is sold to buyers through auctions, but there are no buyers' auctions in China. Rather, the provincial tea boards in each tea-producing region are responsible for contributing the annual output of tea from their province to the collective whole. The mood of the Chinese government is changing, however, and today independent tea agents sell Chinese tea abroad directly without government intervention. This change is responsible for bringing some interesting and distinctive regional teas to market. Many tea processors in China feel renewed by the opportunity to have their work recognized and desired by new and larger audiences of appreciative tea drinkers both in China and abroad.

CHINA'S DELICATE AND ELEGANT GREEN TEAS

China's green teas are famous for their finesse, elegance, clean fresh flavors, and artistically shaped leaves, the finest of which are processed by hand with nimble fingers and a series of repeating hand motions. The Ming dynasty (1368–1644) first uncovered the secrets of producing whole-leaf green tea. As the added seasonings that tea lovers once mixed with cake tea began to lose their appeal, tea drinkers began to pay attention to the fine differences in flavor to be savored from the tea leaves themselves. By trial and error, the Ming tea workers established many tea-production methods that became a template for tea workers in the Qing dynasty (1644–1911) to adjust and refine the major classifications of leaf style. In succession, the creation of magnificent flower-scented teas followed the process for green tea manufacture, which in turn led to the discovery of how to fashion the superb aromas of oolong tea. Lastly, and most importantly, Qing dynasty China perfected the process of black tea manufacture, which was instrumental in ensuring that tea traveling across the ocean to the West arrived in sound condition. Both of these dynasties are responsible for creating the fundamental changes in tea production that resulted in today's modern leaf teas.

The main green tea–growing regions of Anhui, Jiangxi, and Zhejiang Provinces are located west of Shanghai, where steep mountains elevate the tea gardens into the zone of cooling clouds and quenching mist. China has a dormant season in the winter when the tea bushes rest. Each year Chinese citizens eagerly await spring green teas as a harbinger of the arrival of the new season and the beginning of the tea harvest. In the first days of spring, just after bud break, tender and delicate newly emerging leaves produce fresh teas known as "before the rain" teas. Picking begins in late March, just before the Qing Ming Festival, which is celebrated around April 5. Tea picked after this date, but before April 20, is called *gu yu*. Tea picked from April 20 through May 6 is called *li xia*. After this time the tea bushes flush rapidly, and the quality of the tea loses nuance every week as the leaf grows larger.

The arrival of the rains in mid-to-late May gives both people and plants a time to recharge. After the rains come to an end in late June, the main tea harvest gets underway, yielding the balance of China's ordinary green teas. Thus, even in the best of seasons, the time for picking tender spring green tea is a race against nature, yielding only small amounts of precious leaf. The seasonal yield for spring green teas is only 10 to 12 percent of the entire harvest for all Chinese green tea. Spring green teas are identified by poetic names that evoke the serenity and classical nature of China's tea culture while also specifying which mountain or region the tea is from. Some of our favorite names are Bubbling Spring, Clouds and Mist, Curled Dragon Silver Tip, Dragon Whiskers, Esteemed Treasure, Gold-Flecked Emerald Tips, Jade in the Clouds, Nine Dragons, Purple Bamboo, Rainflower, Snow Dragon, Snow on Jade Mountain, Snow on Monkey's Tail, Spring Pine Buds, and White Monkey Paw. China's spring green teas are celebrated for their simple deliciousness and unmistakable goodness and flavor. These delicate teas brew pale green colors tinged with gold and have sweet, mild, slightly grassy, herbaceous flavors and striking vegetable aromas.

Today there is a new call from Beijing for the exclusive purchase of many rare, small production teas. The Chinese government is using these teas for diplomatic gifts. When we visited the tea factory in Jingangshan in Jiangzi Province, the manager showed us packages of tea that had been prepared for Beijing. Their preferred tea consists of a select plucking of one leaf and the bud, and it is packed in elegant red and gold tins. The estimated cost of this tea is just under $250 per pound.

A monastery on sacred Jiu Hua Shan offers an excellent mao jian green tea, known locally as Buddha's Tea (Anhui Province, China).

TRIBUTE TEAS AND FAMOUS TEAS

FAMOUS TEAS AND THEIR PROVINCES

At the top of the list of desirability are China's "famous teas," the modern-day name for the former Imperial Tribute Teas. As these teas were of such remarkable and ethereal quality, they were claimed as the exclusive provenance of the emperors of China's last four dynasties: Tang, Song, Ming, and Qing. Each emperor had his favorite, and delivery of the tea was recorded as a tax payment owed to the throne. Tribute tea that did not suit the emperor's taste would be given to court officials, who could drink the tea for their own enjoyment or secretly sell it at a premium price.

When the days of imperial China ended in 1912, the famous tribute teas became available for mere mortals to enjoy. Each of these teas is distinctive and unique, and justifiably the pride and joy of the regions that produce them. Famous teas are instantly recognizable by their characteristic leaf shape, appearance, and flavor. They are named after the mountains from which they come (Huang Shan, Lu Shan, or Tianmu Shan) and are often given poetic descriptive names such as Da Hong Pao, Lu'an Guapian, or Tianmu Clouds and Mist.

Bai Hao Yin Zhen (Fujian)

Da Hong Pao, Wuyi Cliff (Fujian)

Dong Ting Bi Lo Chun (Jiangsu)

Duyun Mao Jian (Guizhou)

Fenghuang Dan Cong (Guangdong)

Huang Shan Mao Feng (Anhui)

Huo Shan Huang Ya, or Yellow Sprouting (Anhui)

Jingangshan (Jiangxi)

Jun Shan Yin Zhen, or Silver Needle (Hunan)

Keemun, or Qimen (Anhui)

Longjing, or Dragon Well (Zhejiang)

Lu Shan Yun Wu (Jiangxi)

Lu'an Guapian, or Lu'an Melon Seeds (Anhui)

Mengding Mountain Snow Buds (Sichuan)

Tai Ping Hou Kui (Anhui)

Tianmu Shan Clouds and Mist (Zhejiang)

Tieguanyin (Fujian)

Xin Yang Mao Jian, or Fur Tip (Henan)

Zhuyeqing, or Bamboo Tips (Sichuan)

CHINA'S GOLDEN TRIANGLE OF TEA: ANHUI, ZHEJIANG, AND JIANGXI PROVINCES AND JIANGSU PROVINCE

The greatest number of famous teas comes from the region in China known as the Golden Triangle. Historically close to the seat of the emperor, this region was a source for many of the imperial tribute teas. On our first tea-buying trip to China in April of 2000 we visited the eastern provinces of Anhui, Jiangsu, Jiangxi, and Zhejiang. The topography of these four provinces is stunning and features steep, rugged mountains claiming much of the land. We were awed by the sight of famous tea mountains—Huang Shan, Mogan Shan, Qi Shan, and Tianmu Shan—which rise to impressive heights of over six thousand feet.

These famous Chinese clouds-and-mist-covered mountains are heavily forested and accentuated with elegant bamboo groves, waterfalls, and stands of pines. Because these mountains still resemble the familiar landscapes depicted in classical Chinese paintings, being in these mountains feels like walking through a page of Song dynasty (960–1279) history. The modern world has not yet invaded these remote places, and the bamboo forests still hide tea-drinking pavilions in their greenery. Rugged foothills lay at the feet of the mountains, forming a densely compacted landscape that reveals only fleeting glimpses of tea bushes. Terraced gardens cover every inch of the land, soothing the eye with rhythmic patterns that drape the landscape in a soft green mantle. Small rivers, which provide essential water, tumble through the fields. We watched in fascination as solitary farmers maneuvered their massive water buffalos through the muddy churnings of rice paddies as they prepared the fields for planting rice or vegetables.

We began this journey in sprawling, congested, and heavily polluted Shanghai but arrived in tea country by the end of a long day. Along the way it seemed as if construction crews were at work around every bend in the road, digging or sorting rocks and gravel. Fortunately, the badly pockmarked roads had little else in the way of vehicular traffic. As we approached the mountains, the roads turned to dirt and became increasingly bumpy and dusty. We passed through strings of lively villages awash with children, chickens, bicycles, pushcarts, ducks, farmers, small restaurants, and quick-moving farmers carrying bamboo slings holding baskets filled with fruits and vegetables.

When we began to encounter groups of farmers trading tea from large sacks lined up on the road sides, we knew we had arrived in the foothills of our first destination: the Huo Mountains of Anhui Province.

Anhui Province. Anhui is the home of the strange and magnificent Huang Shan, one of China's most awe-inspiring and classic topographical regions. These scenic mountains have steep, rocky peaks as well as graceful, ancient pine trees and cold, clear mountain springs. The moist environment produces a natural phenomenon of swirling mist known as "sea of clouds." Huang Shan Mao Feng tea grows in the protection of these revered pinnacles and benefits from its unique microclimate.

Anhui also produces Lu'an Guapian and the rare Tai Ping Hou Kui, two spectacular teas. Unlike most spring-plucked teas, both of these are made from the specific picking of one large single leaf located on a particular spot on the tea branch. Tai Ping tea pickers head out into the tea gardens to pluck from just dawn to mid-morning to capture the leaves before the hot sun changes the balance of moisture within each leaf. The most famous location for prized Tai Ping tea comes from an area outside of Tai Ping called Monkey Ditch. The village is situated at the end of a long and tranquil isolated lake. We journeyed there by boat, catching only a few glimpses of tiny villages beyond the banks of the lake. A few solitary fishermen with long bamboo fishing poles and wide-rimmed bamboo hats dotted the edge of the water. Along the way our skipper carefully skirted around delicate, arching bamboo floats that had been secured in the middle of the lake by local fisherman.

Jiangxi, Zhejiang, and Jiangsu Provinces. Jiangxi contributes Ming Mei, the treasured, slender, "eyebrow" tea gathered from remote villages located on Da Zhang Mountain. Zhejiang Province lays claim to China's most revered famous tea, Longjing, the Dragonwell tea of Hangzhou. Bi Lo Chun or Green Snail Spring is the delicate little curled specialty of Jiangsu Province. These teas differ one from another in specific ways. First, each requires that the fresh leaf be of a certain size and configuration, such as two leaves and the bud, or one leaf and the bud, or a pair of leaves and no bud. Second, the drying and shaping technique used to process the leaf must give each tea its characteristic appearance.

Timing is critical in this early harvest. Every day the leaves on the bush are different than they were the day before, so the picking and processing must constantly be adjusted. Each day will thus produce a slightly different batch of tea. The smaller leaf teas come first in the season. The choicest leaf picking (*mao feng*), consists of two equal-length leaves and a bud; next comes one slightly larger leaf and a bud (*mao jian*). Mao feng teas have a broad, flat shape and a sword-like curve from tip to end, while mao jian teas are thin and delicate, with a wiry twist to the leaf.

CHINA'S VARIATIONS IN LEAF STYLES

China produces the world's largest quantity of green tea and the greatest number of variations in leaf styles. China's ability to turn fresh leaf into an amazing array of fanciful twists, rolls, curls, and slender needles is unmatched by any other country. Because of the staggering number of teas that the country produces, China has the most complicated terminology and categorization of any tea-producing country. It is rumored that there are more than eight thousand distinctions in the Chinese system of labeling and grading teas. Most of these classifications are for green teas, but a smaller number includes black and oolong teas as well.

A confusion of green tea names exists in China due to the breadth of their production and also because sometimes geographical names are included and other times not. Spelling differences abound, and each tea has the potential to include in its name as many as eight different name assignations that refer to the four main plucking times and the four main quality grades of each tea. And confusion is beginning to arise on another front: suddenly, in this new free-market economy, China is beginning to grapple with the notion of "copycat" teas being produced by skillful but, some feel, unethical tea producers in neighboring regions. The need to protect the integrity of China's authentic, famous teas is being brought about by issues from within. China is beginning to deter similar or outright copycat teas from other regions from being falsely marketed as the original by granting unique teas "protected indication" status. This protection policy for unique food products is similar to that used in Europe, where designations such as AOC (Appellation Controlée), DOP (Denomination di Origine Protetta), and PDO (Protected Denomination of Origin) are granted to unique place-specific European food products. In fact, on our most recent trip to eastern China we purchased a very special grade of Lu Shan tea that came with a sticker on the package that read, "Products of Designations of Origin and Geographical Indications of the P.R., China."

KUNG FU STYLE OF POURING TEA

One of the more unusual tea arts in China is the so-called tea-distributing skill or the Kung Fu style of pouring tea. This artful way of pouring hot water for tea was once executed only in the Imperial Palace for the special enjoyment of the emperor's guests, but by the end of China's dynasty era this skill moved into the public teahouses. This method of brewing requires nothing less than perfect concentration and a very good sense of time and space on the part of the server. We have observed this style of extreme water pouring in selected teahouses in Sichuan and Anhui as well as in Hong Kong.

During this tea service the tea master pours hot water from a uniquely designed teakettle that resembles a squat, round metal watering can with an exaggeratedly long, curved spout. The tea master crouches down in a martial arts–style position, one of eighteen various contorted positions, while skillfully directing the stream of hot brewing water into a small *gaiwan*, the classic Chinese teacup. Some of these positions include over his head while looking straight down or over his head while bending backwards and looking up at the ceiling. Very minimal splashing is acceptable. Missing the cup completely is a no-no. Targeting the customer necessitates a career change—fast!

We encountered this tea service for the first time in a hotel atop the Huang Shan mountains when ordering a cup of Babaocha (Eight Treasure Tea). An elegant gaiwan arrived at our table, inside of which were a mélange of colorful dried fruits mixed in with the jasmine tea, including tiny sugar crystals, wolfberry, raisin, bits of walnut, dried longan, dates, and some chrysanthemum blossoms. A young man holding the kettle appeared. We were spellbound by his performance, which included moves with names such as Eagle Spread and Dragon Tail that were replayed every time an empty cup was set down. We drank an unusually large amount of tea that afternoon just to watch him strut his stuff.

In addition, other protections for tea are becoming necessary as China enters the modern world. In the industrialized east, for example, tea acreage is under threat of being lost because of urbanization and development. In Zhejiang Province the Longjing tea-growing areas located outside of the city of Hangzhou have been reduced to sixty-six square miles. In June 2001 the provincial government took action by blocking further construction in the tea areas, thereby protecting the remaining tea gardens from encroachment—a step that unfortunately is still necessary in other parts of China. But these are mere wrinkles in the long and tumultuous history of Chinese tea. Tea drinkers can help by purchasing authentic tea from reputable vendors who know where their tea is from and who can verify the authenticity of these teas. Many wonderful Chinese green teas are available in the United States from tea specialists in stores and online (see "Buyer's Resources" at the end of the book for a list of vendors).

CHINA'S BLACK TEAS (QIHONG OR RED TEAS)

China also produces many spectacular black teas, which are often overlooked by tea drinkers in favor of the green and oolong power players that dominate the spotlight in China's tea arsenal. This is unfortunate, because Chinese black teas are superb and seductively delicious, and they are extremely different than the black teas from India or Sri Lanka. Production quantities of Chinese black teas pale in comparison to the green teas, but they are deliciously stylish and fragrant and the quality is high.

The highest grades of black teas are referred to as *kung fu* teas, a term that is meant to underscore a process or something that is well produced, carefully made, labor intensive, and well executed (see "Kung Fu Style of Pouring Tea," earlier in this chapter). Kung fu teas require extraordinary skills in all steps of their manufacture—from the plucking to the initial sorting to the manufacture and final sorting. Similarly, *gong fu* refers to a style of tea service for oolong teas that originated in Fujian and Guangdong Provinces. This method of preparing and serving tea is labor intensive because of the many carefully orchestrated steps involved in rinsing, brewing, and serving this style of tea (see "Gong Fu Tea Service" in chapter 7 for a full explanation). In the West black tea is named for the color of the fired leaf, but in China these teas are called *hongcha*, or red tea, after the color of the infusion. Historically, Chinese people have preferred to drink green or oolong

JAPANESE-STYLE TEA PRODUCTION IN CHINA

In Zheijang Province we visited a Chinese tea factory that was producing Japanese-style tea from Chinese leaf. The tea factory manager had been trained in Japan, and the Japanese parent company had established this brand-new, state-of-the-art factory to produce tea using Japanese processing techniques. This modern tea factory was spotlessly clean and bright; the high humidity generated by the steaming process gave the workers a healthy, rosy-cheeked glow. These Chinese-produced teas are sold to Japan for use exclusively in such exported items as bottled tea drinks and nonpremium tea blends that ship to Europe and North America. Japanese-produced sencha and matcha (finely powdered steamed green tea) is too expensive to be used for anything other than sipping during moments of appreciative contemplation.

tea, so the bulk of these black teas have always been made for export to "satisfy Western barbarian tea tastes." However, a new generation of young Chinese tea drinkers are incorporating Western ideology, culture, and style into their lives. Hence black tea drinking is on the rise in China, particularly the strong black tea from India that is used to make iced tea beverages.

The Chinese use a lighter touch when withering and oxidizing their black teas, and thus coax elegant, fragrant, soft-style teas from their fresh leaves rather than the strong, fruity, and sometimes more astringent teas of the more major black tea–producing countries. Most Chinese tea drinkers prefer black teas that are unblended and unscented. Such sweet, petal-scented, and fragranced black teas as gardenia, lychee, rose, osmanthus, and plum—once the favorites of tea drinkers during the Ming dynasty—are today made in Guangdong Province in southeastern China, primarily for export to the West.

Anhui Province. This province produces the following black teas: Keemun Hao Ya, Keemun Hao Ya B, Keemun Hairpoint Mao Feng, and Keemun Congou. Keemun (spelled Qimen in the East), sometimes referred to as Keemun Congou or *qihong* tea, is a superb example of an elegant and alluringly fragrant Chinese black tea. The Keemun area is comprised of four growing areas—Dongzhi, Guichi, Shitai, and Yixian—which are located not far from Huang-Shan City and the famous Huang Shan Mountains. Also renowned for celebrated spring green teas, this stunning mountainous vicinity has a temperate climate and abundant rainfall. The microclimate creates moisture-laden blankets of swirling clouds and mist over the tea-producing areas.

Keemun teas are produced from eight different types of tea bushes; locals say that the best Keemun comes from leaves that have a little red vein running down the backside of the leaf. Many small rivers and springs run through this area, creating soil conditions that feed the bushes with a unique combination of nutrients. Small, thin, slightly twisted leaves that are naturally sweet and refreshing characterize the style and flavor of the best Keemun tea. These tiny leaves are painstakingly hand-sorted both before and after processing. Hao Ya A and Hao Ya B are the two highest grades of these tiny leaves. Keemun Mao Feng is larger in size and is a special picking of two leaves and a bud, which yields a rich, full flavor. These elegant teas can range from very dark black to black that is tinged with a soft, matte gray. Keemun teas rarely, if ever, show any light-colored downy tip on the ends of the leaf. The greatest cropping season for high-grade Keemun tea is in spring; little is made from summer or fall pluckings.

Fujian Province. This province produces the following black teas in the Panyang Congou family: Dan Gui, Golden Crab, Golden Monkey, King of Golden Needles, and Panyang Congou. Panyang Congou is little known in America, but it is one of the last of its type of the great historical teas that were produced in China during the days of the tea trade. Produced in the little village of Tan Yang on Taimu Mountain, located outside of Fu'an City, Panyang Congou is primarily sold today to England, the Middle East, and Russia.

ORIGIN-SPECIFIC TEA

In July 2005 the Hangzhou Tea Research Institute informed the World Trade Organization (WTO) that the Chinese tea trade strongly supports a future global scheme for the protection of "high-quality origin teas." Requirements for "origin denomination" teas would thus be: (1) a defined specific botanic species, (2) a delineated geographic area, (3) a traditional process and manufacturing method, and (4) a distinctive flavor. According to the Trademark Office of the State Administration of Industry and Commerce, China has established more than 110 applications for geographic indication status food products, including pears, oranges, fish, tea, vinegar, and wine, and more are in the works.

Table 4.1.
Production Numbers for Chinese Tea

Class of Tea	Percentage of Total Production
Green tea	70 percent
Oolong tea	14 percent
Black tea	13 percent
Pu-erh tea	2 percent
White	less than 1 percent

CHINESE GREEN TEAS AVAILABLE IN THE UNITED STATES

Numerous Chinese teas are now available in this country. Look for these well-known favorites at your local teashop or favorite online specialty vendor.

Anhui Province
Buddha's Peak (Jiu Hua Mao Feng)
Dragon Whiskers (Qi Mountain Mao Feng)
Emerald Green Spouting (Cui Ya)
Huang Shan Mao Feng
Huang Shan Mao Jian
Huo Mountain Yellow Spouting
Jade in the Clouds (Huang Hua Yun Jian)
Jin Shang Tian Hua (display tea with chrysanthemum)
Lu Mudan (display tea)
Lu'an Melon Seeds (Lu'an Guapian)
Tai Ping Hou Kui
Yong Xi Huo Qin

Fujian Province
After the Snow Sprouting
Dragon Pearl Jasmine (Fuding)
Fuding Dabei Cha (display tea)
Fujian Mountain Green (Chao Qing)
Jade Green Butterfly (display tea with rose)
Lotus Heart (Lian Xin Cha)
Phoenix Eyes or Phoenix Eyes Jasmine
Taishun Snow Dragon
Wu Yi Clam Shape (display tea with jasmine and chrysanthemum)

Jiangsu Province
Green Snail Spring (Bi Lo Chun)

Jiangxi Province
Da Zhang Mountain
Lu Shan Yun Wu
Ming Mei

Sichuan Province
Jasmine Snowflakes (Bi Tan Piao Xue)
Mengding Mountain Snow Buds (Mengding Huang Ya)
Prince of the Forest
Snow Orchid (Xue Lan)

Yunnan Province
Bamboo Shoots (display tea)
Bamboo Tips (Zhu Ye Qing)
Jade Rings
Nine Dragons Mao Feng
Sunshine (from ancient dayeh tea trees)

Zhejiang Province
Curled Dragon Silver Tips (Pan Long Yin Hao)
Green Peony Lu Mu Dan (display tea)
Green Spider Leg
Gunpowder (Ping Sui county)
Jiang Shan
Jiang Shan Tian Hua (display tea)
Jingangshan Hao Ya
Jingangshan Mao Jian
Lake of a Thousand Islands
Longjing from the following areas: Lion Peak, Longjing village, Man Jue Long, Shi Feng Longjing, Weng Jai Shan, Xihu Longjing, and Yang Mei Ling
Peach Balls (display tea)
Snow Dragon
Tianmu Shan Green Tips (Tianmu Qing Ding)

According to Mr. Liu Shi Bao, general manager of the Fujian Fu'An Agricultural Tea Company Limited, Panyang is known as Tan Yang Congou in China, and the tea gardens were first established more than three hundred years ago, in the early Qing dynasty (1644–1911). During the heyday of the tea trade with Europe, Panyang Congou, Paklum, and Chingwo were popular teas with the English. Today Paklum is no longer produced, and Chingwo is nearly out of production. Panyang comprises only 5 percent of the four hundred tons of tea produced each year in Tan Yong village; the remaining 95 percent is green tea.

The village makes a handful of other black teas that fall under the Panyang umbrella, and each has a different processing style. Despite its small production, Panyang Congou is given a fine plucking of one bud and one leaf (hence the designation Congou, a spelling variation of Kung Fu meaning "skillfully made") and is sorted into four grades of quality. Of these black teas King of Golden Needle is the finest leaf with the largest amount of tip, Golden Monkey is a slightly larger leaf with less tip, and Golden Crab is larger again. Panyang Congou is the largest leaf with the least amount of tip but the most concentrated flavor.

Wuyi Shan. This region produces the smoky black tea known as Lapsang Souchong. In the nineteenth century this inky black, tarry, smoky tea became popular in England. Still today, Lapsang Souchong is a Continental favorite, and some English companies add a dash of Lapsang Souchong tea to their Earl Grey and Russian Caravan tea blends. Historically, this tea was created by accident, not by careful intention. The Wuyi Mountains have always specialized in exquisite, fragrant, large-leaf oolong teas, but starting in 1646 a change came about that would have a permanent effect on the Wuyi tea industry.

During the reign of the young Qing emperor Shunzhi (r. 1644–1661), the affairs of state were controlled by his uncle, Dorghon. Dorghon wanted to consolidate the provinces of Zheijang, Fujian, and Canton (now Guangdong) under Manchu rule. In 1646 the Qing army invaded the Wuyi Shan in northwest Fujian and the villagers fled. Those with advance warning hid their tea from the soldiers. For safekeeping, they buried it in the mountains. But before doing so, it was necessary for them to first quickly dry the tea to keep it from rotting. Having no choice in this dire situation, they dried the tea over what they had at hand—boughs of freshly cut pinewood culled from the forests surrounding the village.

THE HUANG SHAN

The pointy, barren, and rocky peaks of the Huang Shan have been depicted and romanticized in Chinese brush paintings for centuries. These otherworldly mountains are capped with rocky pinnacles and isolated pines that invoke China's past when aesthetics, scholars, artists, and monks roamed these mountains in search of inspiration, enlightenment, and solitude. Near the Keemun tea-growing region, the well-preserved village of Tunxi contains public buildings and houses built in the southern Anhui Huizhou vernacular style that date from the Ming dynasty (1368–1644). One of these original houses from this area has been dismantled and is now on public display at the Peabody Essex Museum in Salem, Massachusetts.

Porters carry all of the goods that are needed in the hotels and restaurants atop the Huang Shan up the mountain. These athletic men and women drape long bamboo poles across their shoulders and hang their cargo by ropes from the ends of the pole. The goods sway gently as the porters scamper up the stone steps of the steep trails. The porters haul sinks, potted plants, laundry, and sometimes fatigued tourists (not us) all the way to the top.

Later, when they returned and dug up the tea, they considered it ruined. It was dark, it was smoky from the pine-firing, and it was not at all to their liking. All was not lost, however. Dutch traders had been purchasing tea from the Chinese in Canton and bringing it back to Europe for several years. As most of the tea sold in Canton was probably an early version of wulong or oolong tea that came down the river from the Wuyi Shan in Fujian, the Chinese offered this "new" tea to the Dutch. To their surprise, the Dutch traders loved it, purchased it, and returned the following year looking to buy more. In fact, it is said that the Dutch liked it so much, they offered the Chinese twice as much money for it as for the other teas on offer. As the process was easy to replicate, a new tea was born: *bohea*.

The term *bohea* became synonymous for all of the high-quality dark, leafy teas coming from the Wyui Shan at that time. The term *black tea* was not yet in use. This smoky tea eventually became known in local Fuzhou dialect as La ("pine") Sang ("wood") or Lapsang. As the term *bohea* began to be used for more and more types of dark tea, it began to carry a generic meaning. Many of the finer teas from Fujian were renamed. *Souchong* was the term coined for quality large-leaf black teas from this region, and the name Lapsang Souchong became the trade name for this tea. Locals, however, have always called it Ooda or Da. Lapsang Souchong is also manufactured in Taiwan. During various times in the history of China and Taiwan, Mainland Chinese citizens have left China to live across the straits in Taiwan. Many of these people were involved with the tea industry in

Fujian, and they brought tea-making skills with them to Taiwan and seeded a thriving tea industry there.

Lapsang Souchong tea has enjoyed worldwide fame and a renowned reputation for its distinctive character. The styles of the two Lapsang Souchongs are similar but different: the Taiwanese style is stronger and more heavily smoked; in fact, we have tasted some that can just about wrestle your tongue into submission. The Fujian version is milder and softer, however. Lapsang Souchong tea was reported to have been a favorite of cigar-smoking Winston Churchill. Its strong, substantial flavor goes nicely with hot, spicy food or when sitting around a cozy campfire.

On Zhen Shan Mountain, deep in the protected pine and bamboo forest of the Wuyi Mountain Forest Preserve, the small enclave of Xingcun Community still makes the historic, traditional Lapsang Souchong tea: Zhen Shan Xiao Zhong. We held our breath for days hoping that we would be granted permission to visit the Zhen Shan Xiao Zhong and Lapsang Souchong smoking sheds, admission to which is rarely allowed. We got the word that we were "in" late one night and were on our way just after dawn the following day. The journey to the production facility took us through lush forested areas of pristine, serene beauty. We were jolted back to reality when we reached the first of several gated guard posts along the way. There is an air of secrecy to the exact processing of Lapsang Souchong, as the Chinese still want to keep it under wraps. This intrigue harkens back to the days of the China tea trade, China's attempts to keep their tea-processing techniques a secret

A BRIEF HISTORY OF TEA NAMES

During the zenith of the China tea trade, European tea-buying representatives had the daunting task of communicating with the Chinese tea merchants. At that time China produced two types of tea—green tea for domestic consumption and black tea for export. Most of what was purchased by the Westerners was grown just north of the trading port of Canton. Eventually, green tea was exported also, and Westerners distinguished between the many varieties of these teas by naming them with corrupt transliterations of the Chinese names for the tea or for the places where the tea was from.

For example, the term *bohea* was used in reference to the dark, big-leaf teas from the Wuyi Shan. *Singlo* green tea designated that which came from the Songluo Mountains. *Hyson* was used in reference to tea picked in the early spring (*xichun* in Chinese). Gunpowder tea was so named by sea captains for its rolled shape (*zhucha* or "pearl tea" in Chinese). Eventually these terms became more exacting and used to reference particular teas, or they were replaced by names that identified the tea's specific origin or classification.

A traditional Lapsang Souchong smoking shed in the midst of a lush bamboo forest on a watershed-protected mountainside (Fujian Province, China).

from the West, and Robert Fortune's subterfuge in the Wuyi Mountains. The tea is made in thirty-two villages that use special wooden smoking sheds, not the traditional cement and concrete tea-factory buildings, to produce this tea. These lovely old sheds reminded us of the wooden tobacco drying barns that dot the tobacco fields back home in our Connecticut River valley.

Curiously, when we entered our first smoking shed, instead of being greeted with the usual organized chaos of workers busy with tea production, the room was empty. The early production of the finely crafted, traditional tea called Zhen Shan Xiao Zhong was already over for the year. Production of standard Lapsang Souchong would follow several weeks later. Usually thirty people work in each smoking shed, but this one would accommodate seventy workers. The wooden structures retained the distinctive aroma of years of accumulated pine smoke; the wooden boards inside and out have acquired a rich patina and have deepened into a lovely cognac brown.

Mr. Jiang Yuanxun, the owner of the tea company and fifteenth-generation heir to "The Noble Lapsang Souchong Tea-Producing Family," explained that Zhen Shan Xiao Zhong is a special "tips only" pluck of early spring leaf collected from tea gardens located in the surrounding forest. This leaf is plucked by the villagers and carefully processed and smoked before it is fully dried. The tea production that would follow in a few weeks would be comprised of semifinished tea that had been plucked and partially processed elsewhere in the vicinity from larger, older leaf that is then brought to these smoking sheds to be smoked over a fire and given a final drying. In this second processing, there is a trade-off of price versus quality, as the tea produced in this latter manner will absorb more smoke and lose precious delicacy. These two methods of smoked-tea production yield teas that taste vastly different from one another and feature unique styles. The more expensive Zhen Shan Xiao Zhong is essentially cold-smoked, while Lapsang Souchong is hot-smoked; hence the difference in both flavor and price. Zhen Shan Xiao Zhong is rarely seen outside of China, and the Lapsang Souchong teas are more commonly offered for sale in the United States.

Zhen Shan Xiao Zhong is a perfect example of a *zen jhen* tea—tea from a boundary area whose *terroir* (the unique effect that soil and climate in a specific place has on products grown there), history, and unique processing techniques make it genuine, original, and "truthful" to a place and unable to be duplicated elsewhere. To Mr. Jiang, Zhen Shan Xiao Zhong is the "real Lapsang Souchong," the historical tea that made Lapsang Souchong famous so long ago. Because of the short window of opportunity to pluck such small early leaf, not much of this tea is produced in a single season. Most tea lovers never have a chance to taste it or even learn of its existence.

Mr. Jiang served us cups of Zhen Shan Xiao Zhong, which we were anxious to taste. Before sipping the tea, we inhaled the delicious aroma, which tantalized us with delicate wafts of a lightly parched and smoky fragrance. The flavor was familiar yet refined, carrying a sweet undertone reminiscent of caramel and the best sugar-cured smoked Virginia ham. The small leaves and careful smoking yield a beguiling and exotic brew that is light-years away from the sometimes corrosive brew of the coarse-leaf, hot-smoked Chinese and crudely produced Taiwanese Lapsang Souchongs.

Mr. Jiang Yuanxun presents his recently published history of Zhen Shan Xiao Zhong (Fujian Province, China).

Sichuan Province. Sichuan is a mountainous region that features vast, remote areas of unspoiled natural beauty and wilderness as well as such large congested cities as Chengdu (the gateway to Tibet for those flying in from China) and the bustling autonomous municipality of Chongqing, the fourth-largest city in China and the starting point for Yangtze River cruises. About 30 percent of Sichuan's teas are processed into black teas, 60 percent into green teas, and 10 percent into specialty teas like jasmine. Sichuan Province produces the black tea known as Imperial Sichuan (Zao Bei Jian). Another small-leaf, thin, and compact tea, this stunning tea is embellished with a small amount of golden tip. The presence of tip adds fullness and richness to the body of the tea and a slight suggestion of creaminess and maltiness to the flavor.

Tea grows high in the mountains far beyond the confines of the city of Ya'an, where the Sichuan Agricultural University is based. We spent an educational day here as guests of the tea professors. We had the opportunity to taste tea from several clonal varieties of tea bushes that had been developed by the local tea research center, and we listened to a presentation about the recent advances in organic tea production in Sichuan. The professors generously allowed time for us to have a question-and-answer period with them.

Sichuan also produces compressed brick teas, made from mature, coarse tea leaves and used for export to Tibet, Qinghai, and Tibetan-populated areas of Sichuan. These teas, while distinctly different from the aged, postfermented pu-erh teas of neighboring Yunnan, are slightly fermented (but not aged) in order to help Tibetan tea drinkers better digest the proteins in the meat that they consume in their essentially vegetable-less diet. Two other brick-style teas are made for use in temple offerings and for use during festivals.

Yunnan Province. The tip of northwestern Yunnan touches on the Tibetan Himalaya, and in the south it shares a border with Myanmar, Laos, and Vietnam. This is only one example of the contrasts that comprise the province of Yunnan. It is a vast region with spectacular scenery, vivid blue sky, and a multitude of ethnic minorities and ancient cultures far removed from the bureaucracy of Beijing. Yunnan's food is mild, while neighboring Sichuan's is tantalizingly aromatic and fiery. But some of China's most interesting and flavorsome tea comes from Yunnan, many of which have a fascinating history and story to tell.

Yunnan black teas are lush, thirst-quenching treats that are worth the search. Consider yourself blessed by Sheng Nung if you find a supply of Yunnan Buds of Gold or Yunnan Golden Needles—both are made from an indigenous variety of large, broad-leaf tea bushes and trees found in this part of Yunnan. Known to locals as *dayeh* and classified by botanists as a subvariety of *Camellia sinensis* var. *assamica*, dayeh produces lush, full-flavored tea, the leaves of which are a golden-russet color before and after brewing. As in Fujian Province, dozens of varieties of *Camellia sinensis* are found growing in this region. But the dayeh teas are made from old-growth trees (not bushes) that grow naturally in the jungle and forest ecosystems. If you look at the leaves after they have been infused, you will see that the leaves are large and intact. Yunnan Buds of Gold and Yunnan Golden Needles are among the highest grades of Yunnan black tea and are comprised of long tips, which yield an exquisite creamy and malty, sweet-liquoring tea with almost no bite. These teas top our best black tea list.

In the hot and steamy southwestern corner of Yunnan, the tropical region known as Xishuangbanna is home to pu-erh tea. Oddly enough, no pu-erh tea is made in the town of Pu-erh, but the town was important as a distribution and collection point and the beginning of the Tea Horse Route for those about to embark on the long journey north and westward. Pu-erh is one of China's most unusual teas, with a legendary history and venerable reputation.

Once rarely known outside of Yunnan, pu-erh came to be admired and collected by wealthy Hong Kong and Taiwanese businessmen. Today, the tea is having a resurgence of interest with a new audience of tea drinkers in Japan, Southeast Asia, Europe (especially France and countries throughout Eastern Europe), and America. Pu-erh aficionados worldwide are driving up the price for these teas; pu-erh collectors are now able to find interesting examples at high prices for sale in the United States, although most of the very aged and thusly expensive pu-erh is still in Asia.

Xishuangbanna enjoys a mild climate that is conducive to early spring harvest teas that begin production in late February. Yunnan tea does not grow in abundance as do the teas in eastern China, and although much Yunnan tea is cultivated from clonal varieties developed from the indigenous plants, many of the distinctive teas of Xishuangbanna are produced from large, broad-leaf tea bushes. This region is primarily mountainous, interspersed with dense junglelike forests, broad terraced hillsides of vegetables and cultivated tea, and large sweeping valleys that contain twelve natural "basins" where rice is grown.

In this tropical region of Yunnan many of the dayeh tea bushes are actually tea trees that have been producing tea for hundreds of years. These enormous trees—many of which have grown twenty to thirty feet tall—are found in a geographic area that encompasses the towns of Simao, Lancang, Menghai, and Jinghong. This region is home to twelve tea mountains. Six of these are located north of the Lancang (Mekong) River: You Le, Ge Deng, Yi Bang, Mang Zhi, Man Zhuan, and Man Sa. Six others are located south of the river: Nan Nuo, Jing Mai, Meng Hai, Ba Da, Nan Qiao, and Meng Son.

MAKING ARTISAN PU-ERH

In village tea factories we observed stone-pressed pu-erh cakes being shaped with stone weights. Primary tea is put inside of a sock-shaped cloth and pressed flat in the bottom of a large tin can. The tea is lightly steamed, then removed from the form and placed under the first in a series of large stone weights. Each stone weighs slightly more than the previous one. The bottoms of each stone are carved in a slightly concave manner to form the disc shape. Each disc is removed from beneath one stone and placed under the stone beside it in musical-chairs fashion. When the cake is removed from the last weight, the tea is fully shaped and compacted and ready to be wrapped in paper and sent to market.

The village yields as many tea cakes as there are stone weights in the series and in as many days. In contrast, in the government-operated tea factories, metal molds and machine hydraulics are used to shape and compress hundreds of discs a day. Either way, the tea is traditionally marketed as a stack of seven paper-wrapped cakes. Each stack is wrapped in bamboo leaf and packed nine stacks to a basket. We were told that there were seven kingdoms in this region during the Qing dynasty, hence each cake reflects one kingdom.

A tea worker pushes a cart of pu-erh to the aging room (Yunnan Province, China).

Compressed pu-erh tea comes in myriad shapes.

Hidden away in these forests, locals report the existence of tea trees that are five hundred and a thousand years old, including a seventeen-hundred-year-old tree named the King of Tea Trees, which lives on Nan Nuo Mountain.

Eight of China's fifty-six recognized groups of ethnic minorities live in Jinghong county in Xishuangbanna Dai Autonomous prefecture: the Dai, Hani-aini, Ake, Miao, Yao, Bulang, Lahu, and Jinuo peoples. Here the ancient tea trees are a living legacy for the villagers, who climb up into the trees to reach the leaves. These broad tea leaves are used to make genuine pu-erh tea and our organic sun-dried Sunshine green tea.

Pu-erh is sold as loose-leaf tea or in compressed discs or bricks (*zhuang cha*), and understanding the differences in pu-erh seems complicated at first. The distinctions are not easy to grasp without some explanation, and many variables come into play in its manufacture. Both styles of pu-erh come in either raw (*sheng*) or cooked (*shou*) versions. These terms have no equitable definitions; think of them as loosely akin to green versus black tea. Loose-leaf pu-erh is made in eleven grades of quality and can be aged for decades, providing a multitude of taste experiences.

Historically, for convenience, pu-erh was compressed to make it less bulky for the horse caravans to transport as they trekked across the rugged Himalaya. Two distinct trading routes to Tibet developed in China—one in southwestern Yunnan near the town of Pu-erh, and the other from northern Sichuan Province. These routes eventually met in eastern Tibet and merged into one. Pu-erh cakes continued to be made after these trading days, and the emphasis changed to focus on the fact that cakes keep and improve with age under the right storage conditions.

The leaf used to make both cooked and raw pu-erh cakes is sun-dried leaf from the local tea trees that has undergone de-enzyming, rolling, brief steaming, and final-firing. Once the processing reaches this point, the leaf is postfermented in dry storage. To achieve the distinctive flavor and aroma of pu-erh, the tea is heaped into piles and a controlled amount of moisture is introduced to the leaves. As the bacterial process begins to affect the nature of the tea, the piles are carefully turned and monitored as heat begins to generate within the pile. The heat combined with moisture encourages the natural bacterial fermentation integral to the tea's character and flavor.

Raw *ching bings* (green cakes) are made according to a simple but effective process in which dried tea leaves are steamed lightly before being pressed. This little bit of moisture encourages the natural bacteria present in

Above: Beeng cha curing on aging racks (Yunnan Province, China).

the leaves to slowly continue developing within the disc as it ages. Raw, green pu-erh can be made from any of the quality grades of loose-leaf pu-erh, or a combination of leaves.

Newly pressed raw green cakes are not ready for immediate consumption. They must be stored in a warm, moisture-controlled environment to rest and age. During aging, the raw cakes darken in color and slowly evolve into mature cakes that possess the characteristic mellow, beefy, and toasty flavor that pu-erh lovers seek. The quality of the leaf, the precision of the fermentation, the steaming, and the success of the aging results in a good product. At seven to ten years of age the cakes begin to get pricey. If left undisturbed, the cakes will be well on their way to becoming venerable thirty-year-old cakes worth hundreds of dollars apiece. Part of the fun of owning a cache of aging cakes is checking on the progress of the tea from time to time by scraping off just enough tea to make a small pot and observing and appreciating its changing flavor.

The other type of pu-erh cake—the ripe, black "cooked" variety—is a new variation begun in the 1970s as a response to tea drinkers' demand for pu-erh that could be consumed sooner. The dried green tea leaf is lightly steamed just before being pressed. In the government-run tea factories, highly skilled workers grab fistfuls of tea leaves from various baskets surrounding their workstations and layer the tea leaf in a certain order before the tea is quickly steamed and then pressed into the mold. This ensures that the better-looking leaf shows on the outside of the tea cake, while the coarser, less attractive leaf is tucked on the inside. After shaping, one additional step is added. The cakes and classic, bowl-shaped *tuo-cha* pu-erhs are set on racks in heated chambers with moist, circulating steam and allowed to oxidize and darken in color. These quick-ripened pu-erhs supply the marketplace with reasonably priced, affordable pu-erh, which can also be cellared and aged to improve flavor if desired, but most cakes are no doubt consumed right away.

TASTING A FIFTY-YEAR-OLD PU-ERH

THE BENEFITS OF PU-ERH TEA

One afternoon we visited a teashop in Dali, Yunnan, where we were treated to a tasting of tea scraped from a fifty-year-old pu-erh cake. Our tea mistress infused it in a small Yixing clay teapot. Thimble-sized cups of tea were passed around, and we enjoyed thirty reinfusions of this leaf without noticing any loss of flavor. In fact, when we reached the point that we could not drink any more tea, the leaf still had flavor to give.

A tea mistress prepares fifty-year-old pu-erh for serving (Yunnan Province, China).

Today, an occasional cache of old pu-erh cakes is discovered when a venerable Hong Kong teahouse or restaurant closes. These tea cakes, if properly aged, can fetch hundreds of dollars, as would the offerings in a fine wine cellar in the West. Chinese tea drinkers believe that pu-erh lowers blood cholesterol and prevents so-called bad cholesterol (LDL) from forming in the arteries. Researchers at Taiwan National University believe that pu-erh contains the same degree of beneficial, antioxidant catechins as green tea. Chinese people drink pu-erh after a heavy meal to aid with digestion and the metabolism of fats. Chinese women drink pu-erh to stimulate weight loss.

Villagers in Xishuangbanna also make sun-dried green teas from the large, broad dayeh tea leaves. Every Dai and Jinuo village has its own variation of these simple yet delicious teas, which are made by a simple process of de-enzyming the leaves, then rolling and quickly drying them in the sun. These teas are what the locals drink and are similar in appearance to leafy white teas but have a pleasant, mild lingering flavor that is slightly reminiscent of black tea.

But for connoisseurs willing to pay the price, nothing compares to the complexity and nuance of flavor experienced when drinking tea from an aged raw pu-erh cake. Teashops in and around Menghai and the capital city of Kunming feature a seemingly unlimited selection of cooked and raw pu-erh. We spied an eye-popping, desirable selection of cakes in fanciful shapes of discs, squares (*fang cha*), oversized mushrooms (which are sometimes called Camels Breath), rectangles (*zuan cha*), small melons, and tiny, individually wrapped miniature *tuo cha* that resemble hummingbird nests. Our great disappointment was that we could not manage to bring home a stunning, beautifully pressed and molded pu-erh that was shaped like a giant melon. Weighing perhaps more than forty pounds, this pressed tea would have no doubt made a terrific store display and conversation piece.

CHINA'S OOLONG TEAS (BLUE TEAS, CHING CHA, OR WULONG)

Oolong tea is highly revered in China, and to tea aficionados these sophisticated teas represent the pinnacle of much that is exotic, enticing, aromatic, flavorful, visual, captivating, and delicious about Chinese tea. Oolong fanciers can get carried away with the comparisons of various oolongs, finding never-ending joy in discussing the merits of Chinese versus Taiwanese oolongs, Wuyi Shan to Ali Shan, high-grown to low-grown, specificity of oxidation levels, and so on. Distinguished oolongs are less familiar to tea drinkers in the West than are China's green or black teas, but Wulong Cha has been highly revered in China for centuries. Today, the tea is known as oolong, but its original name *wulong* translates into Dark or Black Dragon, a title once bestowed on the large, bulky dark tea leaves from the Wuyi Shan. This is also a possible deferential nod to the fact that the twist given to these magnificently shaped teas resemble the silhouette of the mystical Chinese dragon.

Fujian Province. A treasury of indigenous tea species, Fujian is the home of Chinese oolongs. Each of the famous oolong teas is named for the subspecies of bush from which the leaf is plucked. Production for oolong tea begins later in the spring than it does in green tea–producing regions—May versus March. For details of oolong tea production, please refer to "Oolong Tea" in chapter 3. When the Europeans came knocking on China's door for tea in the early seventeenth century, Chinese historians now believe that these

dark, large-leaf, heavily oxidized, nearly black *wulong* teas from Wuyi Shan were the teas that the Chinese shipped downriver to Canton and set sail for the Continent.

The Wuyi Shan, in northwestern Fujian, is a fairy-tale area of rocky limestone peaks, winding rivers, and lush, thick vegetation with steep roads and sheer cliffs. Atop the peaks the tea bushes are heavily shaded by clouds and mist, and feed on only several hours of sunlight each day. These teas are called "rock teas" or "cliff teas" in reference to the thin layer of soil that supports the growth of the tea bushes. Tea plants grow amid the rocks and crumbling rock shards of the disintegrating cliffs. These harsh and unforgiving conditions provide the plants with vital minerals and nutrients, supplying the backbone of flavor that these teas are famous for. Wuyi Shan is indeed a unique environment that produces tea no other place can duplicate.

Coupled with healthy air and cool, pure mountain water, these conditions have yielded tea that has quenched the thirst of scholars and the philosophical ideals of legions of artists, hermits, and monks. Wuyi Shan is a vibrant part of China's tea culture, and one of the "routes of tea enlightenment" for those experiencing the way of Chinese tea. Wuyi Shan teas have always been associated with health and vigor. If plants have been able to survive and thrive in this threadbare soil for a thousand years, something beneficial must come of drinking this tea.

Above: A charcoal-firing station for basket-fired oolong, in Jian'ou (Fujian Province, China).

Right: A tea worker prepares for a tasting of "rock" oolongs (Fujian Province, China).

Like many other tea-producing places in China, not much has changed regarding how tea is made in the Wuyi Shan region. It is small—only thirty-five to forty square miles in total area—and production cannot increase because the space is so limited. Thus the tea remains as precious and rare as it was during the Ming dynasty. The best teas are still made the traditional way, by hand, by families in the tea business, from bushes cloned and now cultivated from the original species found there. Demand for these specialties far outstrips supply. The mystical and wondrous Wuyi Shan is home to the spectacular "rock" or "cliff" oolong teas, such as Bai Ji Guan (White Cockscomb), Da Hong Pao (Royal Red Robe), Golden Xuan, Huang Jin Gui, Roi Gui (Cinnamon Tea), Shi Ru Xiang (Melted Minerals), Shui Jin Gui (Golden Water Turtle), Shui Xian (Water Sprite), and Tie Luo Han (Iron Arhat). Rock teas grown within the Wuyi Shan origin-specific region are known as Ming Yan teas; those teas grown outside of the designated region are known as Dan Yan teas.

The season for oolong tea in Fujian is the same as for other Chinese teas. The tea bushes go dormant in the winter and return to life in the spring. Oolong teas are large-leaf teas and as a group, very distinctive in style. Some finished tea is long and twisted and features elegant leaves. Others are gnarly and bunched, as if they had been held tightly in someone's fist. Some have a greenish-gray cast, others are flinty black, and several have a brownish hue. A number of oolongs from southern Fujian have zigzag bits of dried stem attached, a thrilling part of the lure of oolongs and a sure sign that the entire top leaf complex was snatched complete from the bush (as opposed to the careful plucking of a specific leaf or leaf and bud).

Oolong teas are often described as a cross between a green and a black tea, which is a poor attempt at describing these exquisite teas. Nor does that description do justice to the superb nature of these distinguished teas and the unique tea bushes from which all of the famous oolong teas are plucked. Oolong teas undergo a partial oxidation, which can vary from 10 to 80 percent, depending on the style of the tea favored in each region and the intentions of the tea maker. This broad oxidation range brings a remarkable number of delicious teas to market, featuring a range of styles and flavors. Lightly oxidized oolongs are fruity or flowery and aromatic. They are light brown and show tinges of green. Traditional, more fully oxidized oolongs have a dark, almost brooding appearance, and they have a deep, rich flavor with aromas that suggest wood and leather rather than flowers and vegetation.

Historically, Fujian oolong teas have been baked or roasted over charcoal fires in bamboo baskets or rotating drums, but China's new environmental concerns are changing that. Except for artisan-produced tea made by individual tea farmers or tea-farming villages, much of today's oolong teas are dried in gas or electric ovens, which do the job but fail to influence the tea's character in the same way that wood charcoal does. Nevertheless, roasting styles vary from light roasting to medium or dark. Lighter roasting is a more contemporary style and highlights the more floral nature of the leaf, while darker roasting, which is the traditional method, brings out a mellower, deeper, toastier flavor.

Many of the modern tea makers give their teas a lighter, greener oxidation, which gives the teas a fresh, exuberant style and an appealing range of fruity and flowery aromas. Perhaps this is just a contemporary change of heart from the once-favored heavily oxidized oolongs. Or it may be a complete reversal and return to what might have been the style of oolong tea first produced in the late days of the Ming dynasty (1368–1644), when Chinese tea makers began experimenting with this new type of tea in the mid-seventeenth century. No matter the style, the best oolongs are painstakingly handmade and replicate the old techniques of handpicking, hand-rolling, and charcoal-firing.

The time is here . . .

Let everything be happiness through the door

Let this fragrance spread happiness all over this place.

—A TRANSLATION OF SCRIPT WRITTEN AROUND THE DOORFRAME OF A TRADITIONAL CHARCOAL–FIRING TEA FACTORY IN JIAN'OU, FUJIAN, A TOWN ONCE FAMOUS FOR IMPERIAL TRIBUTE TEA

DA HONG PAO (ROYAL RED ROBE)

In this region of venerable teas, small clusters of sacred, ancient, wild-growing tea bushes still thrive in near-impossible to reach places atop the cliffs. Local legend believes that tea made from these bushes restored the health of a Ming dynasty official, who in gratitude honored the tea bushes by leaving his magnificent red cape behind to protect them.

Fortunately, cultivated tea bushes have been cloned from these ancient survivors and grow in nearby tea gardens. Da Hong Pao has large and commanding leaves, which curve just slightly with a twist, and are fired to a distinctive flinty black color. It is approximately 80 percent oxidized, making it one of the darkest of the Fujian oolongs. It is then charcoal-fired, which gives the tea a sweet aroma, a slight smoky tinge to the flavor, and a long, mellow finish.

At our hotel we got a tip about where to find some easily accessible wild Da Hong Pao tea bushes. We headed out immediately to the designated spot in a Wuyi Shan nature reserve. A nicely worn trail led us into the forest to an area between two massive rock outcroppings. We continued along the path, following the course of a stream, until we came to a series of stone steps that ascended the hillside along one side of the rocks. At the top of the steps we saw tea bushes, but nothing that resembled what we expected the Da Hong Pao bushes to look like. They were too full, too flush, too groomed, and too pampered looking. We were searching for rugged, untended plants, scrawny and thinly leafed.

We continued on, starting to doubt the advice. We found a little teahouse tucked in the woods around the corner from a small waterfall. Glad for a rest in the shade and a cup of tea, we selected a Wuyi Shan rock tea—an eight-year-old Rou Gui—to drink gong fu style. We chatted with the two women about their tea selections and admired the impressive rock wall facing the terrace of the teahouse. When we told them we were searching for Da Hong Pao tea bushes without any luck, they gave us a curious look and pointed our gaze back to the rock wall facing the teahouse.

There, just a short distance away, growing about thirty feet up the cliff face and clinging to the smallest outcropping of space, were six Da Hong Pao tea bushes. The woman told us that these bushes are about 360 years old, making them the *lao cong* (old tea bushes) that Wuyi Shan is famous for. The bushes were growing in partial shade, without much soil, but safe and happy amid the cracks and crevices of the rocky outcropping.

The color of oolong leaf is as varied as that of green tea, and the shapes are a stylish tribute to China's artistic tea sensibility.

Oolong tea liquor yields a range of color, from russet to russet-orange, golden-green, amber-green, yellow-gold, and pure honey. Oolong tea should be reinfused numerous times; it is common for a fine Fujian oolong to infuse six to eight times in a Yixing teapot or twenty or more times in a gaiwan decanted into tiny gong fu cups. Remember, multiple infusions are essential for these large tea leaves to fully open to their majestic size. Gong fu tea service was created expressly to accommodate the brewing longevity of oolong leaf with its fine aroma and vibrant liquor.

Six three-hundred-year-old Da Hong Pao bushes in the Wuyi mountains (Fujian Province, China).

Northern Fujian (Min-Bei) Province. This region produces the following tea: *Min-Bei* oolongs (which can feature flat leaf, open leaf, twisted leaf, or slightly folded leaf styles) and *Si Da Ming Cong* Wuyi Shan Rock Cliff oolongs (Bai Ji Guan, Da Hong Pao, Shui Jin Gui, and Tie Luo Han). These Si Da Ming Cong oolong teas are made from the four most famous *Camellia sinensis* bush varietals in the Wuyi Shan. These bushes are single-trunk oolongs, which means that the bushes are pruned to have only one central trunk bearing just a few branches. These bushes are thus encouraged to produce only a small quantity of large leaves (the opposite of the usual manner and desired effect of bush growth, with multiple trunks and plentiful small-leaf production).

Southern Fujian (Min-Nan) Province. The Anxi region produces very interesting ball-rolled (not the wide, leafy style of Wuyi Shan) oolong tea. Two very different types of these teas are made in Anxi, each of which expresses a particular style: the Anxi Se Zhong oolongs and the Anxi Tieguanyin oolongs. *Se Zhong* is a term for oolong teas that are blended from the leaves of several different types of local tea bushes. Some of the more famous Se Zhong oolongs are: Golden Osmanthus (Huang Jing Gui), Hairy Crab (Se Zhong Mao Xie), Imperial Gold (Tou Tian Xiang), Orchid Oolong (Qi Lan), and Water Sprite (Se Zhong Shuixian).

• Hairy Crab: This fragrant delicious tea is so named for the abundant fine hairs that appear on the backside of the leaves of this tea bush.

These hairs are reminiscent of the stiff white hairs on the legs of the freshwater crabs known as "hairy crabs" that are beloved in this region of China and that come to market in the fall, coinciding with the last crop of the season of Hairy Crab tea. Slightly more oxidized than Imperial Gold, this ball-shaped rolled tea is extremely aromatic and floral, with overtones of minerals and stone.

- Imperial Gold: The Chinese name for this ball-shaped rolled oolong means "fragrance throughout the sky." It has a fragrance redolent of ripe melons, lilies, and honey.

Anxi Tieguanyin is one of China's most famous teas—in fact, it is the quintessential Chinese oolong tea. Its method of manufacture offers Tieguanyin tea masters an opportunity to create a signature Tieguanyin flavor and aroma yet remain inside the broad dictates of the style. Tieguanyin is made from tieguanyin tea bush cultivars that are local to Anxi. Three main styles of Tieguanyin are produced.

- Clear and fragrant Tieguanyin: This tea fired at a lower temperature for less time results in greenish-gold-colored leaves that possess fresh, herbaceous style with a clear, fragrant aroma and a mild flavor that is reminiscent of orchids (*lan*).

- Traditional Tieguanyin: This dark-colored leaf is rich and toasty and features a persistent flavor and lingering aroma, and what the Chinese call *gan*, sweetness or a lack of astringency. Tieguanyin is an ideal tea for leisurely sipping or accompanying food or something sweet.

- Wild Tieguanyin: Picked from wild-growing plants located on rocky hillsides in the vicinity of Xiping, these teas yield a fruity, leathery flavor with a concentrated, heady aroma.

Anxi: The Home of Tieguanyin. A drive through the main streets of Anxi reveals a city completely dedicated to tea; in fact, the locals proudly say that they are the tea capital of China. Anxi sports an abundance of teashops, ceramics shops, and other necessary auxiliary tea businesses such as bamboo tray and basket makers, tea machinery repair shops, and so on. Almost every open-air storefront featured tea-sorting stations set up with anywhere from one to twelve women gathered around their tables and busy at work. The townships surrounding Anxi City in Anxi county and Yaoyan village,

Songyong village, and Xiping village in Nanyan county are known for consistently flavorful and distinctive Tieguanyin tea. There are many representations of this tea produced by Fujian tea farmers in this area—more than two hundred have been reported. Locals say that the best teas come from mountaintops, where eastward-facing gardens receive more cooling breezes and gentle morning sun.

Tieguanyin or Ti Kuan Yin is legendary among oolong tea lovers. This tea is named for Kuan Yin or Guan Yin, the only female deity in the Chinese pantheon of deities. She is known as the Goddess of Mercy, believed to be the female incarnation of the many-armed compassion Buddha, Avalokitesvara. *Ti*, which means "iron," is a reference to the iron jars that precious tea was once stored in. Legend has it that the Qing emperor Kangxi (r. 1661–1722) prayed to the goddess for the return of his health during a bout with smallpox. She answered his prayers and later appeared to him in a dream. In his dream she brought him to a place where the farmers were very poor but where a few tea bushes were growing on a mountainside. To repay her kindness, she asked him to help the people of this region cultivate these tea bushes and prosper from it in her name. Kuan Yin then showed the emperor that the leaves of these tea bushes bore a marked impression. He plucked one from the bush, after which the leaf bore the impressions of both of their thumbs. These two tiny marks have always distinguished the leaves of true Tieguanyin bush varietals. Emperor Kangxi proclaimed Tieguanyin famous for all eternity in China and from that time on the Tieguanyin tea industry has thrived. The Qing emperor Qianlong (r. 1736–1795) selected Tieguanyin to be one of his tribute teas.

Locally, Tieguanyin is known as Red Heart Goddess tea. In Xiping village Tieguanyin is a family affair; it seems as if everyone is involved in the tea business. From cultivating tea bushes to plucking or sorting freshly plucked leaf in front of their house, tea is the major industry. South Fujian tea producers, which includes Tieguanyin, place a great deal of emphasis on the fragrance of the plucked leaf and the aroma of the finished tea. Their teas are less oxidized than the teas from the north, and less oxidation (or greener oolongs) encourages aroma. In northern Fujian, where the oolongs are more heavily oxidized (or darker), there is more emphasis placed on a rich and deep flavor of the brew. In some cases the teas are leafy in style, in others they are rolled, or semirolled, stems included. Either way, the friendly competition between north versus south Fujian only brings added riches to the

Our first stop in Anxi was to visit the exuberant and charismatic tea man Mr. Wei Yue De. Even though we didn't arrive in Anxi until after 11 p.m. he insisted on dinner together, and then he personally conducted a gong fu tea tasting for us. Before the night ended, after the eleventh or twelfth infusion, he had explained the three distinctive qualities that brewed Tieguanyin tea should express: fragrance, aftertaste (returning flavor), and resonance (lingering, persistent flavor).

The following day, we traveled up into the mountains to see Mr. Wei Yue De's tea garden. It was near the mountaintop, at the end of a series of switchbacks that defined this precipitous drive. We passed through several villages, and nearly all of the ground floor spaces were filled with women sitting around big tables sorting fresh leaf or finished tea. We noticed that many houses were built down into the slope of the mountains, making the rooftops easily accessible from ground level for spreading fresh leaf to wither in the sun.

We picked up a narrow and slippery mud-packed trail downhill through the garden. As we descended further down, the view opened up into an astonishing landscape covered with cascading rows of tea bushes down the hillside in neatly planted tiers. A maze of footpaths and trails headed off in many directions through the garden. We could see tea everywhere—down the hill, beside us, above us, and out across the valley. We came to the place in the garden where a handful of the ancient "mother" tea plants, some of which are 150 years old, were situated. To honor the heritage of these plants, Mr. Wei Yue De had installed a life-sized white marble statue of the goddess Kuan Yin.

The one last remaining hurdle to this "walk in the tea garden" was a strenuous, ver-

Mr. Wei Yue De prepares to brew Tieguanyin tea (Fujian Province, China).

tical climb that brought us out of the garden and up to the tea factory. The physicality of this hike gave us a good sense of what strong physical condition the tea pluckers in Mr. Wei Yue De's beautiful but challenging tea garden must be in.

Right: Kuan Yin protects Mr. Wei Yue De's Anxi tea garden (Fujian Province, China).

Below: The rugged landscape near Anxi yields incredible tea (Fujian Province, China).

table of oolong tea enthusiasts. Within the context of the Tieguanyin style, one can find examples that are earthy, complex, and chewy and others that are floral and sweet and that deliver a long finish.

Tieguanyin processing is the result of two factors that combine to yield the distinctive flavor profile: (1) the variety of tea bush and (2) the method of leaf processing. Tieguanyin is made from leaf plucked from Tieguanyin cultivars grown in twenty-seven villages located in the mountains surrounding Anxi. Red Heart Kuan Yin, White Heart Kuan Yin, and Thin Leaf Kuan Yin are the dominant varieties; the best teas are said to be those made from the Red Heart Kuan Yin cultivars.

Look closely at the spent leaves of Tieguanyin after brewing to notice their lovely russet-brown color and delicate crimson edging. This color is due to the shaking and slight bruising that the leaves undergo during processing and is a signature appearance of well-crafted Tieguanyin. Tieguanyin production incorporates traditional as well as modern processing techniques. This involves eighteen steps and takes a period of thirty-six to forty hours from start to finish, depending on the weather, the humidity levels, and the size of the leaf. We were especially fascinated watching the ball-rolling process, whereby leaf is bundled and secured into large cloth balls and then rolled, turned, and pressed in a rotary rolling machine for several minutes. This action gives the leaf the familiar ball shape. Ball-rolling was once done completely by hand and foot, but few tea producers use that method today.

Although all steps in the manufacture of Tieguanyin are important, the temperature of the firing ovens during the final drying is the most critical. This step needs the hands of a tea master to control the intensity of the heat and to vary the amount of heat as necessary. Firing at a high temperature darkens the leaves and strengthens the flavor, a situation that would lead to ruined tea if not carefully kept in check. The process is as follows:

1. Leaf plucking—only hand-plucked leaf (not sickle-plucked with a knife-like tool) is allowed.
2. Withering, cooling, and resting of the leaf.
3. First sun-drying of the leaf.
4. Bruising and rattling of the leaf.
5. Second sun-drying of the leaf.
6. Second bruising and rattling of the leaf.

7. Light tumbling of the leaf to develop fragrance.
8. Rest, then more tumbling to develop flavor.
9. Rest prior to oxidation.
10. De-enzyming the leaf for moisture removal.
11. Rotary rolling of the leaf to rupture cells internally and release the cell juices and to distribute residual moisture within the leaf evenly.
12. Preliminary leaf drying.
13. Second rotary leaf rolling (for shape).
14. Second leaf drying.
15. Leaf rolling in cloth for shape (ball-rolling).
16. Baking and drying to fix the final shape of the leaf.
17. Sorting leaf from stems.
18. Final drying in baskets over charcoal or in tea-firing ovens.

Tieguanyin leaf is gathered in preparation for the ball-rolling step (Fujian Province, China).

MONKEY-PICKED TEA

One of China's enchanting tea legends, this story suggests that trained monkeys were once employed to pick the most desirous leaves from tea bushes that grew out of humans' reach in isolated locations high in the Wuyi Shan cliffs. Perhaps, behind the bucolic illustrations of monkeys scampering through the tea trees selecting the finest leaf and passing it to the tea workers below, is a veiled commentary on the fact that these tribute teas were "out of the reach" of most people in more ways than one. Or perhaps it was an easy joke on the naive Europeans back in the eighteenth century.

The ball of leaf is horizontally rolled in a machine that replicates the handwork of former tea artisans (Fujian Province, China).

A VISIT TO THE PHOENIX MOUNTAIN

We began in the city of Chaozhou, located in the outskirts of Phoenix Mountain. We came here to see the legendary Fenghuang Dan Cong tea trees, which are reported to be close to two hundred years old. Local history dates production of this tea back to the Tang dynasty (618–907), when indigenous tea bushes in this area were first shaped and pruned to grow as a tree with a single trunk. After a long and winding drive up a notoriously narrow mountain road, we arrived at the elevation where the temperature cools and the clouds and mist begin.

When we reached the tea garden, the old tea trees appeared like ghostly apparitions peering out of the mists. They stood nearly ten feet tall and looked more like fruit trees than tea bushes. A light rustle of wind gently rippled through the trees, created a delicate clacking sound among the leaves. Fenghuang Dan Cong leaf pluckers use ladders to scramble up into these trees to reach the large leaves. Wet stones and muddy paths add to the atmosphere of the place, but make it difficult to walk on the slippery, sloping paths.

These trees are the descendants of the trees that provided tea for export to the West, along with Wuyi Shan's Da Hong Pao oolong tea and the legendary smoky black Lapsang Souchong tea. These trees are part of the nearly three hundred varieties of indigenous tea plants that are unique to northern Guangdong and most of Fujian Province. Thus Fenghuang Dan Cong oolong tea cannot be duplicated elsewhere. Local modifications in leaf-processing techniques, coupled with varying soil and weather conditions, bring distinctive nuances of flavor to these teas. Multiple infusions are the norm with these teas.

Back down the mountain, we visited the tea factory and on the way discovered that in this town the roadside is used as a convenient place by some tea farmers to lay down their tea for withering before shaping and firing. We watched farmers sweep clear a small section of the roadside, quickly remove tea by the handfuls

Stately Fenghuang tea trees show perfect single-trunk oolong form (Fujian Province, China).

from their tea baskets and sprinkle the leaves in a single layer over the asphalt. After a short withering of perhaps one hour, the tea was swept up and put back in the basket as if nothing at all had occurred! We were delighted to observe this ingenious method of withering and marveled at the simplicity and common sense of these farmers. In the tea factory, however, the processing is done in a more controlled environment. We were shown a scaled-down version of the lengthy tumbling, rolling, and drying processes required to make Fenghuang Dan Cong oolong.

Above: During peak tea season, small tea-farming families use any available surface area, even a section of road, to wither fresh leaf (Fujian Province, China).

Right: Traditionally, Fenghuang leaf is withered on bamboo mats on a rack in a local tea factory (Fujian Province, China).

Guangdong Province. The modern name for Canton, the region made famous in the days of the historical tea trade, Guangdong Province is home to Fenghuang Dan Cong (Phoenix Oolong). Bordering on southern Fujian Province, the eastern tea-producing region of Guangdong comes under the influence of moist air from the South China Sea. The teas are grown on and in the vicinity of Fenghuang, Phoenix Mountain, located in Chiuan and Cha-ozhou counties. This is a subtropical region, and the tea grows at altitudes of 4,265 feet in terraced gardens composed of rocky, loose soil.

Fenghuang Dan Cong, or Fonghuang Tan-Chung as it is sometimes called, is made from large, single leaves, and it is classified as a single-trunk oolong. The tea bushes are pruned to grow and develop like a tree, with a single trunk that sports individual branches, much like a stone-fruit tree. The leaves of Fenghuang Dan Cong are long, slender, and slightly twisted, and the tea is sweet and complex; it is very elegant in style with a long, refreshing finish. These teas are difficult to come by in the West and are highly prized in China. Now classified as a famous tea, Fenghuang Dan Cong was once an imperial tribute tea. Although the yield from old trees is not as prolific as it is from younger tea bushes, the tea is long on flavor and very mouth-filling. Occasionally, delicate tiny white Yulan blossoms are used to scent the tea.

Surrounded by luxurious growth of the subvariety of *Camellia sinensis* tea bush that yields the legendary and authentic white tea, this expert budset plucker told us, "Life is good out in the Big Sprout tea garden" (Fujian Province, China).

CHINA'S WHITE TEAS

Under the rule of Tang dynasty Emperor Huizong (r. 626–649) the custom of paying a yearly tribute of rare tea to the emperor was established. During his time these teas came from the mountains of Zhejiang Province, but later, during the reign of Emperor Huizong in the Song dynasty (960–1279), neighboring Fujian Province became the source of the imperial tribute teas. In fact, during the Song era Fujian was quick to develop secret imperial tea gardens, tucked away in the ethereal clouds and mist of the Wuyi Shan.

Emperor Huizong (r. 1101–1125) no doubt sipped white tea that was made from the finest, velvety, gossamer tea powder. The emperor

VISITING A WHITE TEA FACTORY

To make the new-style Shou Mei tea, the factory workers pile fresh leaf in a heap 8 to 12 inches deep (20 to 30 centimeters) outdoors in a covered area and leave it for twenty-four hours to initiate withering. After this step the leaf is gathered up and taken indoors to the withering room. In China, it is common for withering to occur first outside, then inside. We were fortunate to be at the factory at a time when every rack in the withering room was filled with leaf, floor to ceiling. Several large windows along each side of the room were thrown wide open to allow the dry fresh morning air to fill the room and circulate among the withering mats.

Each rack held fifteen open-weave withering trays, and on each tray a single layer of fresh leaf had been loosely spread out to wither. Leaf is always carefully spread in a single layer (*jing zhi*, "gently placed") to avoid bruising the leaf by overcrowding or crushing it under the weight of too many leaves. This efficient configuration of trays was designed to allow the leaf to receive maximum air circulation from both top and bottom. A grand total of approximately twelve hundred withering mats filled the room with tea that would undergo further natural withering from thirty to forty more hours, depending on the weather. The amount of withering combined with rolling and low or high heat during the firing determines the final color of the dried tea. Short withering times yield light-colored buds or leaf, and longer withering gives leaf such as that for Shou Mei a dark, greenish-gray color. When the withering has progressed to the desired result, a quick tug of a rope triggers the trays to release from the front of the rack in a domino-effect fashion, causing the leaf to slide off the trays and onto the floor in neat piles. From there the tea is collected and taken downstairs to be rolled and fired.

Freshly picked leaf for Shou Mei, spread *jing zhi*, airing on custom-designed racks in the withering room of a village tea factory on the outskirts of Fuding, the heart of authentic white tea (Fujian Province, China).

was so devoted to tea that he penned a book about tea, the *Ta Kuan Cha Lun*. Historians theorize that Emperor Huizhong was influenced by Cai Xiang, a Fujian tea master of note who lived during the time of the emperor. Cai Xiang was the first commissioner of tea and kept a ledger book, the *Ch'a Lu*, in which he recorded information for the emperor's knowledge concerning the processing and grading of tribute teas.

Perhaps no other Chinese tea is as misrepresented and misunderstood as Fujian white tea. Poetic gestures to white tea refer to it as being "white like the clouds, green like a dream, pure like snow, and as aromatic as an orchid." Bai Hao Yin Zhen, a descendant of the tribute teas that once supplied the emperor, now appears on the list of China's famous teas and is available to all tea enthusiasts willing to pay the high price for a cup of imperial splendor.

We arrived early one May morning at a village tea factory located on the outskirts of Fuding in Fujian Province. The tea from this village is picked and manufactured completely by about a hundred adult villagers who employ no outside help or seasonal workers to assist them with their tasks. They maintain a high level of quality control this way and are very proud of the careful way that they produce their white tea. Production of the budset white Silver Needle (Bai Hao Yin Zhen) and White Peony (Bai Mudan) had already taken place. This tea factory also makes a white-tip oolong tea from a Shui Xian tea bush varietal called Oriental Beauty Oolong. At this time the villagers were plucking a configuration of four large leaves to make Shou Mei, a coarse-leaf tea made from the Da Bai Mao (Fuding Big Sprout) tea bush varietal.

Elegant in its simplicity, finished authentic Yin Zhen budset tea, ready to be tasted.

As with all Chinese tea methodology and production, the process is exacting. Traditionally, white tea was allowed to wither either outdoors or indoors, away from sunlight or applied heat. After withering, the tea was quickly and simply fired at a low temperature before any bruising or oxidation of the leaf could occur. This is still true of the most expensive budset Bai Hao Yin Zhen. But we learned here that some of the grades of leaf white tea are given a light oxidation and a light bruising (rolling) before bring fired at a higher than normal temperature. This deepens the flavor and darkens the color of the leaf, adding a grayish-green cast to the leaf.

This tweaking of the processing does not classify these teas as black teas, but it introduces a variable that makes them not traditional white tea either. They are referred to as new-style white teas, a variation that was introduced toward the end of the 1960s. This may make perfect sense in the white tea–producing areas of Fujian, but unfortunately only adds confusion and uncertainty to the labeling of product being sold in the West. This style of white tea developed as a way to give teahouses in China a stronger-tasting, lower-cost white tea and to appeal to the tastes of tea drinkers from Guangdong and Hong Kong, who comprise the largest audience in China for white tea.

CHINA'S SCENTED TEAS

Flower-scented teas abound in China. In fact, China has been inexorably linked with lovely scented teas since the Ming dynasty (1368–1644). Fragrant blossoms of many types give delight to tea drinkers—chrysanthemum, gardenia, jasmine, osmanthus, rose, and yulan (magnolia) are the most popular. Later, in the Qing dynasty (1644–1911), teas flavored with the sweet fruity essence of bergamot, litchi, orange, and pomelo introduced the category of flavored teas, which remain popular today.

Jasmine tea. This is the most famous scented tea in China. In all its fragrant, perfumed, and exotic glory, jasmine takes top honors as the jewel in the crown. The jasmine bush that produces these intoxicating flowers is not indigenous to China, however; it is believed to have been brought to China from Persia sometime during the Period of Disunity (220–589).

There are countless varieties of jasmine, but rich Arabian jasmine (Jasmine Sambac) gives Chinese jasmine tea its glorious, intoxicating aroma. In northern China it is customary to serve a cup of fragrant jasmine tea as a welcoming gesture to guests. Many different grades of jasmine tea are available, from everyday grades that are cloyingly sweet and clumsily perfumed to ethereal, fancy grades of such tea as Yin Hao jasmine (there are reputed to be nineteen different grades of Yin Hao jasmine) and the Jasmine Snowflakes from Sichuan Province. The best jasmine teas should caress the senses with delicate allure, not bludgeon them with excess.

Fujian Province is home to white tea with jasmine (Bai Hao Yin Zhen), Dragon Pearls, Jasmine Silver Hair (Yin Hao Jasmine), Jasmine Raindrops, and Jasmine Spring Hao Ya. Sichuan Province produces the Jasmine Snowflakes tea (Bi Tan Piao Xue).

VISITING A JASMINE TEA FACTORY

Jasmine tea has been a historical specialty of northern Fujian Province since the days of the Ming dynasty (1368–1644). The area around the town of Changle is famous for jasmine-flower production, and here jasmine bushes, like tea bushes, are planted in abundance. Visitors to this region in summer can luxuriate in the heady aroma of these blossoms, which drench the surrounding countryside with a languid, sweet perfume. Jasmine tea is made in two steps. In each province that manufactures the tea, the base tea is made appropriate to the taste of its clientele. In Fujian, for example, this base tea (called *zao* or "tea readied") is made from fresh leaf plucked during the spring season. The process of manufacturing *zao bei* into jasmine tea is called *hongqing*.

Zao bei begins by de-enzyming the fresh leaf, which is followed by leaf rolling. Then the leaf is dried, not with direct heat as is used in *chaoqing* or *hon bei* but with indirect heat that is applied by blowing warm air over the leaf's surface as the tea passes through the drying machine. This machine has three levels of adjustment that allow the leaf to pass closer or farther away from the hot air, providing the tea workers with complete control over the process. By using warm air, the leaf curls and rolls less, leaving more surface area exposed, which increases the leaf's ability to absorb the scent of the jasmine blossoms.

After the base tea has been made, it is kept in cool storage until the arrival of the jasmine blossoms in summertime. July through September is the prime season for jasmine blossoms, and those plucked in July are the most fragrant. These flowers are used to scent the most delicate and aromatic jasmine teas. Timing is critical in jasmine tea production: knowing when to pluck the flowers and when the moment is right to introduce the blossoms to the tea are essential to producing top-quality jasmine tea.

Perfect jasmine blossoms are critical to properly scent fragrant jasmine tea (Fujian Province, China).

As with all fine Chinese tea, experienced hand skills come into play to create the fancy rolled and twisted jasmine teas such as Dragon Pearls and Jasmine Raindrops. These popular teas have been enthusiastically embraced by Western tea drinkers. When inhaling the perfume of first-rate jasmine tea, there is a relaxing moment of calm. Close your eyes and imagine what it was like to luxuriate in the splendor of a richly fragranced and lavishly appointed Ming dynasty tea tasting. Additionally, jasmine tea is produced in Hunan, Jiangsu, Jiangxi, Guangdong, Guangxi, and Zhejiang Provinces.

The ideal time to begin gathering the flower buds is noon, which ensures that any lingering remnants of dew from the night before have evaporated. The flower buds are collected during the early afternoon. Experienced pluckers know when to pluck and use two criteria for selecting blossoms: first, the length of the flower shaft (which is plucked when the length increases 50 percent from the day before, or increases from $1/4$ inch to about $1/2$ inch) and second, when the color of the blossom changes from ivory to white. By 4 p.m. it is time to bring the collected flowers into the tea factory. Maintenance of the condition of the flowers is very important. The workers will keep the flowers at a temperature of around 100 to 104°F (38 to 40°C) to encourage development of aroma. The goal is to encourage the flower buds to continue opening enough to see the center of the blossom but not open fully. At 8 p.m. the actual production of jasmine tea begins. The *zao bei* that has been released from storage is now at ambient room temperature, which in Changle in July is 90 to 99°F (32 to 37°C). The fresh jasmine blossoms are introduced to the base tea; the two are mixed together and raked into a pile on the floor.

Because the process of scenting occurs as it does, it is not necessary for the flower blossoms to remain in the finished tea. The spent blossoms are traditionally removed from the finished jasmine tea that is made for the Chinese market. The tea is set in front of large industrial fans that blow the blossoms away, scattering them around the factory floor. In jasmine tea made for export, however, the final scenting blossoms are usually left in the tea. But these are for show only, as the true scenting has already been accomplished. A current crop of jasmine tea does not reach the market until October or November each year. Jasmine tea stays fresh for up to three years because of the minor oxidation that occurs during the heat buildup in the pile during scenting.

Above: A silk bag of freshly picked buds, destined to become Bamboo Tips yellow tea (Sichuan Province, China).

Below: Mengding Mountain, the birthplace of cultivated tea (Sichuan Province, China).

CHINA'S YELLOW TEAS

Yellow teas have a pleasing, slightly golden cast to the leaf. They are reported to have been tribute teas to the emperor as far back as the Song dynasty (960–1279). They are rare and costly but one of the consummate examples of the Chinese art of tea making. Yellow teas are similar to green teas but are given an extra step during the leaf manufacture. Yellow tea is most often made from buds or tips only, which is the most select plucking. A tea plucker might pluck four to five pounds of fresh leaf each day but gather only eight ounces of tiny buds, which makes bud-picked teas the most expensive. Most Westerners have never tasted a yellow tea, and in fact few are even aware of them. This is unfortunate, because yellow teas are delicious and refreshing; they are one of our personal favorite styles of tea. Although they are not commonly found outside of China, yellow teas are worth pursuing. For a description of the manufacture of yellow tea, see "Yellow Tea" in chapter 3.

In central Sichuan Province, Ya'an county is famous for producing flavorful long-leaf *mao feng* teas (the choice picking of two leaves and a bud). Mingshan county, located several hours' drive north of Ya'an, is the historical place where tea was first cultivated in China. According to legend, somewhere around 53 BC (during the

Han dynasty) a young man named Wu LiZhen planted seven tea trees on Mengding Mountain from tea bush cuttings. Wu LiZhen was given the title of Master of Sweet Dew by Emperor Xiaozong of the Song dynasty (960–1279), for whom this was a tribute tea. Wu LiZhen planted the tea bushes near a natural spring that is believed to have a special, sweet scent and the ability to run eternal. After Wu LiZhen passed away, the tea was referred to as *xian cha*, or "tea of the immortals."

In the high elevations sweet, early spring buds are picked when they are covered with soft, fluffy down. They are turned into a refreshing yellow tea known as *gan lu* ("sweet dew," after Wu LiZhen's honorific title) or Mengding Mountain Huang Ya (Mending Mountain Snow Buds). From the environs of Mount Emei, one of China's most sacred Buddhist mountains, comes Bamboo Tips, another of Sichuan's exquisite yellow teas, comprised of many tiny compact and smooth budsets. Snow Shoot Tea from Qing Cheng Mountain is aptly named, as it refers to tea that is plucked from the earliest part of the spring tea harvest.

Yellow tea sold in its own right has only recently begun to appear on the lists of tea merchants in Shanghai, Hong Kong, Chongqing, and Europe, as well as a few specialty tea merchants in the United States. Several yellow teas to look for are Huang Shan Mao Feng and Huo Mountain Yellow Sprouting, Bamboo Tips (Zhu Ye Qing), Mengding Mountain Snow Buds (Mengding Huang Ya), and Snow Shoot Tea.

THE IMPERIAL TEA GARDEN AND WU LIZHEN'S TEA BUSHES

Many temples are tucked throughout the valleys of Mengding Mountain, but only after passing through the Mengding Mountain gate do visitors find the Huangdi Temple, which has stood in this place since the Song dynasty. This is the site of the Imperial Tea Garden and Wu LiZhen's tea bushes. Today a handful of monks still live in this pristine environment and carefully guard these seven sacred tea trees, which are secluded behind a gated stonewall. The garden is also home to a white stone tiger that was placed in the garden to add further protection for the emperor's tea. A few ceremonial tea leaves are picked each spring by dignitaries wearing Song dynasty–style yellow robes to celebrate the seasonal tea harvest and the importance of this former tribute tea. These tea bushes are now only symbolic in meaning, as surely they have been replaced many times over and are connected to Wu LiZhen only in spirit and memory.

Japan: Unique Teas and Introspective Customs

Both China and Japan are famous for their green tea, but the similarities between these two revered teas end there. Each country is famous for a heritage of producing unique and refreshing green teas, but from cultivation to production and leaf style to flavor characteristics, the teas from these two countries are worlds apart. The best Chinese green teas are hand-plucked and hand-processed, and grow in isolated tea gardens tucked away high in the mountains. The leaf is processed in small, rural tea factories that rely on traditional manufacturing styles rather than modern efficiency. In Japan, however, most tea is made from leaf that has been mechanically plucked from tea bushes that grow in meticulously groomed gardens at relatively low elevations. This leaf is usually processed by sophisticated and often computer-driven, high-tech machinery in state-of-the-art modern leaf-processing facilities. Chinese and Japanese teas reflect the different point of view that each country has toward tea. Chinese teas are all about the source of origin and the leaf style, while Japanese teas are all about the manufacture, the modern production process, and the art of blending for specific flavor.

The origins of tea drinking in Japan can perhaps be traced to a time during the eighth-century Nara period (710–794). Under the rule of Emperor Kammu (r. 781–806), Japan dispatched several diplomatic missions to Chang'An, the capital of Tang-era China (618–907). These missions, called *kenyōshi*, also served the purpose of bringing back to Japan knowledge and understanding of China and Chinese culture. Knowledge was garnered by the envoys through experience, observation, learning, and the acquisition of scrolls, paintings, statues, and other material goods brought back to Japan.

On one of these missions two Japanese monks and scholars—Kūkai (774–835) and Saichō (767–822)—reached China sometime around the year 804 and stayed in China for several years studying religion and doctrine. While there, each man perfected the religious school of thought that he introduced to Japan when he returned—Tendai Buddhism (Saichō) and Shingon Buddhism (Kūkai). It is believed that one of these men may have brought the first tea seeds back to Japan, and perhaps also the concept of tea drinking. But envoys had been visiting China since before 618, so familiarity with tea could have been established much earlier. Early writings of this period in Japan make reference to "tea drinking," but light has yet to be shed on exactly who made the introduction, where it occurred, and how the tea was brewed or consumed.

Emperor Shōmu (r. 724–749) is reported to have served tea to a hundred priests in his palace as early as 729. Another reference to tea drinking occurs in 814 in volume four of the *Shooryōshō*, a collection of Kūkai's writings compiled by one of his disciples. This reference notes Kūkai's return from China in 806 and reports that Kūkai presented Emperor Saga (r. 802–823) with books to view. It goes on to say that as he studied, he reportedly drank "hot water with tea" or Chanoyu.

Tea drinking was next recorded in 815, during the Heian era (794–1185), under the reign of the fifty-second imperial ruler, Emperor Saga. A book called the *Kuikū Kokushi* recorded that Abbott Eichu made tea "with his own hands and served it to the emperor." Since then, many writings and poems praising tea and Chinese ways of tea drinking have been penned. But for many years tea drinking in Japan was, as in China, practiced among only a few groups: monks, who considered it a spiritual exercise (they cultivated small patches of tea on temple grounds), the imperial family, and members of the nobility. Japanese monks learned of the virtues of tea from the Chinese sages, who deemed it to be the "elixir of the gods." For the Japanese nobility tea drinking was thought to be a way to transcend the mundane of everyday life.

In Japan's Kamakura period (1192–1333), Myōan Eisai, the founder of the Rinsai sect of Buddhism, encouraged green tea drinking for general health. Eisai (1141–1215), who later became known as Eisai Zenji (Zen Master), made numerous trips to China throughout his lifetime, each time bringing back tea seed for planting. He shared the seed with other monks and priests who planted these tea seeds in various locations throughout Japan, including Kyoto, Kyushu, and Uji. It is believed that Eisai is responsible for starting the old tea gardens at Kyoto's Kozanji Temple.

Eisai wrote the first Japanese book on tea, called the *Kissa Yōjōki* (or "Tea Drinking Good for the Health"). He claimed that tea would "conquer the five

Tea production in Japan is more highly mechanized and modern than it is in China. In this Japanese factory, green tea production still requires the trained eye of a professional to determine how the color and form of early season aracha manufacture is progressing (Shizuoka prefecture, Japan).

A serene temple setting (Kyoto, Japan).

diseases" and "remedy all disorders" and that tea should be consumed by all citizens. With this endorsement interest in tea drinking spread from the aristocracy to the warrior classes. This was the first time that the practice of drinking tea in Japan was for the simple pleasure of drinking tea, and not for some medicinal or healthful benefit. During Japan's Muromachi period (1392–1573) the roots of tea culture took hold and were developed in Uji, a rural area located outside of the imperial city of Kyoto. For a time in Japan tea was synonymous with Uji and was thus called *ujicha*.

Another notable figure in the advancement of tea culture was Shogun Ashikaga Yoshimasa (r. 1449–1474), the battle-worn general, who, after starting the Onin War and nearly destroying Kyoto, handed the country's reins to his son and retired to a life in his Kyoto palace. Thereafter he devoted his life to Zen arts, tea, and poetry. Under his influence and patronage of the tea master Murata Jukō, tea drinking entered the secular realm.

From this point on tea drinking began its elevation into a fine art, which eventually culminated into the tea ceremony known as Chanoyu. Although tea grows throughout Japan, the oldest and most famous tea gardens are still those at Uji, where traditional tea-making skills are devoutly practiced. While images of Samurai warriors, contemplative Zen gardens, the masks of No actors, and the inscrutable perfection of geishas presents an artistic and evocative side of Japanese history and culture, Japan is an industrialized country with large, crowded, fast-paced modern cities. Underneath this bustling outward facade, however, Japan maintains its proud and strong culture based on ancient Shinto beliefs and Zen practices that seek to capture moments of simplicity and to express ideas of beauty and paradox. Japan's enigmatic food culture captures our attention with the ritual of their intricate and precise tea ceremony, while visually stunning food served on dynamic, artistically designed pottery presents these dishes according to established concepts of style, manners, and tradition.

Japan is comprised of four major islands and more than three thousand small islands. More than 80 percent of Japan's landmass is mountainous, which leaves people, cities, and agriculture elbowing for their share of the same usable land. Japan is the second most industrialized country in the world after the United States, but it has managed to rise to the challenge of utilizing every inch of land to its best advantage. Tea, rice, buckwheat, wheat, soy, and other beans are grown intensively on small, scattered tracts of land that sometimes lie just outside of the major cities. Even with their minimal amount of arable land, Japan ranked eighth in world tea production in 2004 and thirteenth for tea exports. Although Japan cannot compete with the volume of tea produced by other major tea producers, it leads the way in efficiency and precision of production methods.

Japan has progressed from crafting handmade tea to the introduction of machine-manufactured tea in the nineteenth century to computer-automated machinery in the twentieth century. Skilled workers perform their duties in state-of-the-art facilities, where they also rely on their eyes, senses, professional palates, and experience to keep things on track. Interestingly, from 1875 until the mid-1950s Japan also produced black tea for export, a practice that was stopped in the face of overwhelming competition in the black tea market from India and Sri Lanka. Happily, Japanese teas are uniquely Japanese. Their flavor profiles suit the palate of Japanese citizens, and they are a perfect match for the wide range and styles of Japanese cooking. Several of Japan's green teas feature the addition of other materials, such as thin-cut stems or roasted rice, or are used in powdered form. Two examples are matcha, the powdered tea used in the Japanese tea ceremony, and genmaicha, which is sencha green tea to which roasted and popped kernels of rice are added.

In most places Japanese tea gardens do not cling to isolated mountainsides in terraced plots as they do in China, nor do they carpet the contour of rugged mountains and valleys as they do in India and Ceylon. Japanese tea gardens are arranged on undulating hills in no-nonsense, straight, well-manicured, and carefully tended rows. Ideally they are situated close to rivers or streams that daily tender a moist blanket of dew over the manicured tea bushes. Wherever rows of tea bushes end and change direction, or when rows are juxtaposed one to the other, astonishingly beautiful and precise tone-on-tone green patterns emerge on the hillsides.

In Japan it is essential that all available space for growing tea be used efficiently and that the greatest yield of tea is realized from each bush. Although some very specialized and expensive tea is plucked by hand, most of Japan's tea is harvested with hand-held mechanical cutting shears or high-volume mechanical shearing machines. Hand-held cutting shears are guided over the tops of bushes by a pair of workers each holding an end of the cutting shears and facing each other across a row of tea bushes. In large gardens, where the rows have been perfectly spaced to accommodate their girth, large shearing machines straddle the rows of bushes, allowing the shears to achieve a uniform, even pluck. Workers rely on these mechanical shearing machines to trim the bushes neatly and keep the pluck uniform while performing the task with great efficiency. The amount of leaf picked using one of these mechanical means is much higher than the amount of shoots plucked by hand—200 to 300 pounds per day per worker, versus 20 to 30 pounds per day per worker. In Japan, even when tea is plucked by hand, efficiency is higher than it is in China because of Japan's less difficult and less vast terrain and the regularity of planting arrangement of the rows of tea bushes. As harvesting efficiency speeds up the plucking time, a fourth harvest can sometimes be gained in the southernmost regions if the weather cooperates.

A herringbone pattern of tea garden perfection (Uji, Japan).

UNIQUELY JAPANESE TEAS

All tea in Japan is manufactured as green tea, but there are ten main types and a handful of regional specialties produced. Several aspects of Japanese tea production lend their teas distinctive flavors and appearances. Nearly all Japanese tea is steamed during its manufacture, although some tea produced on the island of Kyushu is pan-fired in the Chinese style. Tea was introduced to Japan as cake tea made from compressed powdered tea, and it remained this way until leaf tea was introduced in the eighteenth century. Not only was the change to leaf tea significant, but the additional step of steaming the fresh leaf in order to retain flavor and vivid color changed the nature of the tea and made it uniquely Japanese.

It is reported that Soen Nagatani, an Uji tea producer, invented this method of steaming and rolling fresh leaf in the eighteenth century. This became the basic technique that is now used throughout Japan for producing bancha, gyokuro, and sencha. Steaming also preserves the natural enzymes in the leaves and "fixes" the leaf's dark, emerald green color. Sometimes described as tasting like spinach, seaweed, or newly mown grass, the flavors of Japanese tea can often be startling on first sip. But given a second and third taste, the underlying sweetness becomes apparent, along with an abundance of fresh, clean, and complex flavors. The standard steaming process lasts less than one minute and softens the leaf, imparting a characteristic vegetal taste. A lengthier steaming is given to some leaf to give it a darker color and impart a stronger flavor.

All Japanese green tea begins with steaming the leaf (Shizuoka prefecture, Japan).

Most Japanese green teas are recognizable by their distinguishing, thin, needle-shaped leaf as well as by their characteristic color. The steaming process sets the color of the dried leaf, which is why you will notice that there is a similar vivid dark green color to many Japanese teas. The characteristic straight, needle leaf shape is attained by putting the partially dried leaf through a series of rolling/drying machines. These machines use metal "paddles" that move the tea back and forth over a series of fixed metal ridges while gentle heat is applied to slowly form the familiar needle shape.

Some Japanese tea is grown in the shade, such as the famous gyokuro (Jade Dew), kabusecha, and tencha. Gyokuro and kabuse cha are specialty leaf teas manufactured to be sipped and savored. Tencha leaf is grown expressly for deveining and grinding in slow-turning stone mills to turn it into light and delicate tea powder or matcha. Sun shading eliminates astringent qualities in the leaf and imparts a strong vegetal sweetness to the tea.

Some teas are reprocessed, meaning that something has been added to the tea (such as the roasted rice that is added to genmaicha) or that something has been removed (such as the veins from the leaf when making tencha for processing into matcha) or that the leaves or twigs have been roasted (as with hojicha and kukicha).

Tea bushes growing underneath a tana covering (Uji, Japan).

Japan is the only country that produces a significant amount of matcha, the powdered tea that is integral to Chanoyu, the Japanese tea ceremony. Japan has raised the details of matcha production to a fine art and in teashops one can find many choices in flavor and cost in both ceremonial-grade matcha and premium-grade matcha for less formal tea drinking and socializing. Matcha is highly regarded in Japan but not widely used in other tea-drinking countries. China and Vietnam now also produce matcha, but these imitations suffer, as the fresh leaf used for making matcha is dissimilar to that used in Japan. We have yet to see Chinese matcha that compares in flavor, color, astringency, and overall punch to the traditional Japanese product. Some Chinese matcha is made for and sold to the Japanese tea market, but it is used in iced tea beverages, where the flavor of the tea is only part of the taste.

In Japan, all tea is vacuum-packed and kept under refrigeration to maintain maximum freshness. This begins in the tea factories and is maintained up to the time the customer makes a purchase in a teashop. Japanese tea drinkers purchase tea in small, elegantly designed paper pouches or tea tins that contain a sealed envelope of tea inside. Matcha, which is the most perishable form of tea, is sold in small, sealed tin containers of 20 or 40 grams.

SHINCHA: JAPAN'S FIRST TEA OF THE NEW SEASON

In Japan the growing season and the leaf-plucking schedule follow the same agricultural cycle as in other tea-producing countries. Springtime in Japan brings *shincha*, or the first new tea (*shin* = new, *cha* = tea) of the season, to market. Shincha is an early plucking that arrives before the first-flush teas; it is made from tender young leaves plucked just from early April to early May. The shincha season traditionally starts after budbreak, or after the beginning of the lunar new year. In both Japan and China the arrival of new tea is an important rite of spring. Tea drinkers associate the arrival of these teas in their favorite teashop as a sign of a prosperous harvest to come.

Shincha is produced in all tea regions of Japan and reflects the Japanese love of fresh, bright tea flavor that is tinged with grassy sweetness and luminous, light-green color in the cup. Sometimes shincha is sencha, as this is often the earliest tea to come to market, but shincha can refer to the new crop of any style of tea that has been made from leaf plucked during the pre-harvest before the main harvest begins. Shincha has the highest polyphenol content of any Japanese tea; in early spring the tea bushes awaken from winter dormancy and begin to send stored-up nutrients to the tiny buds. When picked at the right moment, the catechin polyphenols in the early buds and leaves is highly concentrated. Because of its seasonal nature, shincha is produced in small quantities, is packaged immediately, and usually sells out by the end of July. As shincha represents only one-fifth of the tea produced during an entire year, it is as expensive as it is exquisite: two ounces can cost twenty to thirty dollars or more.

Despite its popularity with tea lovers, tea producers disagree on the merits of shincha. Some believe that fresh early tea lacks the finesse and richness that tea develops after it has rested for a few months. Most Japanese green tea is processed to a half-finished state called *aracha*, a primary tea that is stable and able to remain like this until it is time to move it on to the final leaf-finishing state. Aracha is kept fresh in vacuum-packed foil bags and refrigerated until it is ready to be finished. Some believe that during this resting period Japanese green teas undergo a necessary mellowing that softens their sometimes sharp edge and helps the tea to gain a deep, rich flavor that is lacking in the first tea of the season.

SHIRAKATA "HASHIRI" SHINCHA

In Shizuoka prefecture the Honeyama Mountains north of Shizuoka City are home to many fine tea gardens. In fact, the prefecture is the largest tea producer in Japan. Here, tea from Honeyama, Kawane, Makinohara, and other tea areas supply much of the tea that passes through the bustling Shizuoka Wholesale Tea Market. The tea gods were smiling upon us when we arrived at the shop of Shirakata-Denshiro Shoten in Shizuoka City late one spring afternoon. The first of the season's crop of shincha tea had just come to market, and we were offered a taste of the Hashiri shincha.

One sip of this pale golden-green tea confirmed all of the characteristics that we had hoped to savor in tea this young. It had a distinctive and expressive vegetal taste that was underscored by a crisp but slightly sweet flavor. The liquor had a smooth, nearly buttery quality, which was unexpected. This tea perfectly captured the essence of tender young tea sprouts. The fresh and lively aroma added yet another element of pleasure to the experience of savoring this tender, young tea.

JAPAN'S SENCHA: A FAVORITE NATIONAL TEA

Sencha is the next tea to come to market after shincha, and heralds the beginning of the main tea harvest. Sencha is produced throughout the tea season, and it is the quintessential tea of Japan. The first sencha of the season, called first-flush sencha, commands a 30 percent higher price for what it offers in the cup—the sweetest taste, the most satisfying rich goodness. Sencha becomes stronger in flavor and darker in color as the leaves are plucked later and later during the season. Each successive flush yields tea of a lesser quality and price. Many of the best teashops in Kyoto and Tokyo feature teas from artisan tea producers, but most sell the teas under the shop name, not the producer. Japanese like their o-cha (tea) to exhibit the three necessary characteristics of a well-made tea: good aroma, good taste, and good appearance.

JAPANESE GREEN TEA PROCESSING

Different teas require different steps in the leaf-manufacturing process, and some tea processors will change various steps to accommodate a particular result that they feel enhances the flavor of their tea. Essentially there are nine basic steps involved in manufacturing Japanese green tea like bancha, gyokuro, and sencha. But as many as twelve to fourteen other intermediary steps can be added. Regional techniques for tweaking flavor also come into play, as does what the age and sophistication of machinery will allow. But no matter what else, the skill of the leaf processor is always paramount for success. The first six preliminary manufacturing steps yield aracha and the remaining three steps are used for final tea refining, or *shiagecha*.

1. Leaf plucking
2. Tea steaming machine
3. Primary roller/dryer
4. Rotary tea roller
5. Secondary roller/dryer
6. Final tea roller/shaper
7. Final dryer
8. Refining machine
9. Tea blending

Soon after the leaf is plucked, it is quickly brought to the tea factory for processing. The leaf is stored in the green leaf pre-server until the production line is ready for it. The tea remains in the pre-server only for several hours and cool air is blown over the top of the leaf to keep it cool while it remains here. The first step in the leaf manufacture is to stop oxidation in the leaf by steaming it, which usually takes 30 to 45 seconds, or longer (up to 120 seconds) when manufacturing a deep-steamed tea such as Fukamushi Sencha. Two types of steamers are used; one is a revolving steaming machine and the other is a conveyor belt steamer. After the leaves undergo the traditional steaming, they are allowed to cool to room temperature. Following this step, the leaf is placed in the primary roller/dryer, which is an enclosed machine that blows gentle, warm air onto the leaf while mechanical hands toss the tea in a continuous motion. Next, the tea is transferred to a rotary rolling machine, which rolls the tea in a slow and steady circular manner over a grooved bottom plate. This machine exerts a slight pressure on the fresh leaf in order to evenly distribute the internal cell juices throughout the leaf.

Next, the leaf is placed in the secondary tea roller/dryer and further dried while it begins to take on its characteristic shape. Following this, the tea is placed in the final roller/dryer, where it encounters a series of mechanical paddles that push the tea back and forth across a grooved plate to shape it into its characteristic long, needle-leaf style.

At this point the moisture in the leaf has been reduced to about 13 percent, and the leaf is now called aracha, or crude tea. All Japanese green tea is processed first into aracha, which must then be skillfully fashioned into a finished product by careful refining. The refining process puts the aracha through a second set of machines for sorting, separating, and final drying (or "roasting") of the leaves. Refining will bring out and balance the flavor, aroma, and color of the leaf, giving the surface of the finished leaf a rich, glossy shine. The moisture content of the leaf will be reduced to 5 percent. Although it is essential that quality leaf be grown and picked in the tea gardens, this critical work of the tea refiner transforms the aracha into a fine, stylish tea that will deliver exquisite flavor and aroma.

Once aracha has been refined, the finished leaf is called *shiagecha*. The largest tea companies down to the smallest artisan tea maker process tea from aracha. The shiagecha method of leaf finishing is unique to Japan, where it is common practice for artisan tea merchants to purchase aracha and then skillfully finish the tea in their own workshops, nurturing the process slowly and carefully.

JAPAN'S CUSTOM BLENDS

Such teas as sencha and gyokuro are blended to suit the taste of their customers, and these teas benefit from the signature touch of these artisans. Because all the leaf tea that Japan grows is used to produce just a handful of tea styles, Japanese tea is almost always blended and sold without specific designation of region, farm, or garden.

This way of selling tea is different from the emphasis on region, elevation, and estate that is attached to premium teas from India or Ceylon, or from the emphasis on leaf appearance and terroir or source that is so important with Chinese teas. Most Japanese tea is sold as a signature brand of a teashop or tea company. Several blends of varying levels of quality are often available, and each blend is priced according to the cost of the teas used in the blend. Tea aficionados have come to rely on their favorite teashops for the tea flavor that they prefer. Japanese tea drinkers know that tasting the tea is essential before purchasing, and teashops routinely brew small samples for consideration. Tea lovers find the taste they like at the price that they wish to pay and they will continue to support that shop or brand for their tea throughout the year.

Of course it was not all that long ago that all Japanese tea was plucked and processed by hand. Some tea in the highest price category is still plucked by hand, but those teas are the exceptions to the rule. Along with price usually goes limited production, so this extra effort is reserved for the more specialized harvests, such as the first-flush gyokuro or sencha from very special gardens. Little tea is hand-rolled anymore; we were told that it takes six hours to properly hand-roll a batch of sencha tea, a task that tea-processing equipment can accomplish in fifty minutes.

Japan's premium teas are limited in quantity, so the small amount that is not consumed domestically is exported and sold abroad, where it commands high prices. To meet the growing demand in Japan for bottled green tea as well as snacks and traditional foods made with green tea, Japan must supplement its tea production with green tea imported from and manufactured in China, in the so-called Japanese style, under the supervision of Japanese firms.

THE 370-YEAR-OLD TEASHOP

As a specialty food retailer who has been in business since 1974 we are used to people responding with surprise when we tell them how long we have operated our shop. Imagine our surprise when we discovered that Mr. Furon-Izumi-en's shop is 370 years old and has always been in the same location! Mr. Furon-Izumi-en is a fifteenth-generation tea blender in Uji.

Mr. Furon-Izumi-en dispenses the third infusion of his family's gyokuro for tasting (Uji, Japan).

Deeply steamed versus traditionally steamed leaf (Shizuoka prefecture, Japan).

JAPAN'S TEA-GROWING REGIONS

Tea gardens are concentrated in three principle areas in Japan: Kyushu island, Uji, and Shizuoka prefecture on Honshu island.

Kyushu. On Japan's southernmost island, Kyushu, tea gardens flourish in its northern and southern regions. Kyushu was once the gateway from China or Korea into Japan, and the cultural influences of pottery making and tea production came early to this part of the country. In the south, Kagoshima prefecture, Japan's second largest tea-producing region, is protected by the Bay of Kagoshima. The bay separates the city and its surrounding region from the brooding and still active volcano Sakurajima, which lies to the west of Kagoshima City. North of the city lies Aso-San, one of the world's largest volcanoes, with a five-peak caldera. Kirishima National Park, also in the north, offers splendid hikes and stunning vistas.

Although tea has been grown in Kyushu for centuries, the tea industry today is modern and efficient. Kagoshima's climate is ideal for encouraging lush growth: warm air mixed with cool bay breezes. There are fifteen tea-growing regions in Kagoshima, and more than eight thousand hectares planted at low elevations in systematic rows that allow for high-volume mechanical harvesting. A broad variety of tea is produced here, including sencha and kamairi-cha from the four harvests that are plucked from April through mid-October. Rich and earthy matcha is also produced from the Sakura-jima variety of tea bushes, which are shaded and covered with traditional kabuse nets. The best matcha from Kagoshima, like that of the Uji district, comes from the earliest tea of the spring, in the pre-season, before the main harvest begins. The green tea known as kamairi-cha forgoes the traditional Japanese leaf-steaming process and instead is processed by pan-firing and hand-rolling in large iron pans over a heat source in the manner of some Chinese green teas. Kagoshima Shincha is the first to arrive in Japanese markets each spring. Most gardens are company-owned and are the most modernized and mechanized in Japan.

Heading north, the prefectures of Kumamoto and Miyazaki also contribute sencha tea, and in the far north Fukuoka and Saga prefectures produce sencha and gyokuro that are rich and sweet. In Saga the Ureshino region specializes in kamairi-cha. The Yame region, located in Fukuoka, enjoys a temperate climate that makes it Japan's largest producer of gyokuro.

Saga and nearby Nagasaki prefectures are historical pottery centers that have contributed to the country's rich history of ceramic teawares. Korean artists who were brought to live in Japan at the end of the sixteenth century were responsible for influencing much of Japan's ceramic sensibilities. Sen Rikyu, the Zen tea master, admired the rough, naive qualities of Korean ceramics more than the smooth style of the Chinese-made porcelain cups. On Kyushu the towns of Arita, Imari, Karatsu, and Okawachi still support a thriving ceramics industry comprised of both large and small pottery workshops. Porcelain tea sets as well as pottery teawares are made here, but pottery collectors know that the handmade pottery is found off in the mountains, where wood can be gathered to fire wood-burning kilns.

Uji (Kyoto). South of the historical city of Kyoto, on the main island of Honshu, are Uji's world-famous tea gardens that produce Japan's most exclusive and expensive teas. Kyoto is Japan's seventh-largest city and also the country's culturally rich serene heart and soul. Despite its modern façade and crowded nature, Kyoto still shelters sublime vestiges of old Japan. From 794 to 1868, Kyoto was Japan's imperial city. During this time the arts flourished and concepts of Japanese understated sensibilities of spare luxury were perfected. The tea arts were perfected in Kyoto, where the major schools of tea study are located today. Under his rule the Shogun Ashikaga Yoshimasa (r. 1449-1474) encouraged the expansion of tea gardens that had been planted several hundred years earlier in Uji, many of which are the oldest tea gardens still in production in Japan. Uji is famous for premium-quality gyokuro, sencha, and matcha. Nara and Mie prefectures, also known for fine tea, lie south and east of Uji.

Shizuoka prefecture. Shizuoka prefecture is the largest tea-growing area in all of Japan. It is situated along the Pacific coast, southwest of Tokyo and due south of Mount Fuji, Japan's tallest peak. The Akaishi Mountains, the southernmost range of the Japanese Alps, end in western Shizuoka prefecture and provide cool, high-elevation locations, rolling foothills, and abundant rivers conducive for vigorous tea growth. In the central part of the prefecture Shizuoka City and its environs are protected by Suruga Bay, which brings a mild microclimate in all four seasons and frequent, nurturing dense coastal fogs. Sencha is the primary tea produced here, and close to 40 percent of all the sencha produced in Japan comes from this region. Shizuoka began to cultivate tea during Japan's Kamakura period (1185–1333). Approximately 39,500 private tea farmers sell their tea directly to tea

SHIZUOKA IS A TEA TOWN

We took the bullet train (the Shinkansen) from Tokyo Station to Shizuoka City, the capital of Shizouka prefecture, a quick ninety-minute ride. Stepping out from the train station in the city center, we detected the aroma of freshly roasting tea leaves. What a pleasant surprise—the slightly parched, toasty fragrance of tumble-dried leaf was a comforting and enticing welcome, and a vestige of a previous time, when a large concentration of tea finishers and tea blenders plied their craft here. Since the 1600s (Japan's Edo period), this city has been a center for tea commerce. Today, tea factory buildings, teashops, tea warehouses, and pottery shops are still located in the vicinity of Chamati and Amzai Streets, tucked away behind the restaurants, shops, residential houses, commercial businesses, and karaoke clubs.

Not far out of town, rows of tea bushes come into view. Some houses feature rows of neatly tended tea bushes where vegetable gardens might have been. Nearly everyone has a classic, elegantly pruned Japanese pine tree planted by his or her doorway, with tidy little Zen gardens with a few stones and a bonsai or two tucked alongside. Further out of town, the spaces open up and the rows of tea bushes begin to sweep away from the road in long, fool-the-eye rows. We stopped to visit with Mr. Ichiro Mochizuki, a retired gentleman who was out tending his tea. Although it was late afternoon and threatening to rain, he wanted to show us his gas-powdered shearing machine in action. We followed him to his barn, which is actually his little tea factory.

With some help from us, he brought one of his shearer machines over to one of the rows. He positioned himself across the row, holding one end of the clippers, and pointed at us to grab the other end. With a loud blast of noise from the gas engine, we moved down the row at a rapid clip, shearing tea from the tops of the bushes. The bag to catch the leaf clippings sailed out from the rear of the machine and trailed behind, partially aloft like a parachute, as it filled with the newly sheared leaf. The machine was surprisingly heavy and difficult to hold steady as it vibrated furiously. The next day, Mr. Mochizuki tracked us down in town and presented us with a bag of the aracha that he had fired from those clippings!

producers and packers in Shizuoka and at the weekly Shizuoka Wholesale Tea Auction.

Central Honshu. Clustered in the center of Honshu, Shiga, Gifu, and Saitama prefectures are known for fresh, earthy, richly textured sencha. Aichi is a production area for premium matcha, supplying many of the finest teashops in Japan.

VARITIES OF JAPANESE TEA

All Japanese green teas are steamed during the processing (except for one not very commonly seen style of tea, which is "parched" or pan-fired in the Chinese style). There are two classifications of green tea according to whether it is shade grown or sun grown. The teas listed below are easily available in the United States; some of Japan's more obscure teas are difficult to find, however, even within Japan and thus have not been included here.

The following is a list of green teas that are steamed and sun grown.

- **Bancha.** This common class of tea is lower in quality than sencha. Leaves for bancha are picked right after the first or second flush of each picking season, when sencha production is over. Bancha has a stronger flavor, which many Japanese people prefer with food.

- **Genmaicha.** This is made from sencha leaf, to which toasted and puffed brown rice is added. The proportion of tea to rice varies, but more rice to tea is generally desired to cut the slight bitterness of the sencha leaf. Sometimes matcha is added to the mix, which covers both leaf and rice with a soft powdery coating, and the tea is then called matcha genmaicha.

- **Guricha.** This steamed green tea is small in size and elegant in presentation. It is not a traditional needle leaf but has acquired the shape of a comma.

- **Konacha.** This powdered tea is made from the small leaves and pieces of leaf that are gathered from sencha processing. It is not as fine as matcha, nor does it command the same price or distinguished place of honor. Known in Japan as *agari*, kona cha is often served in sushi restaurants as a palate-refreshing tea that stands up well to the sweet and oily fish and the savory condiments.

We were thrilled to receive permission to visit this busy place and arrived at the appointed time—5 a.m. Although the official auction hours are from 6:30 a.m. to 10 a.m., it was clear from the size of the crowd and the level of enthusiasm brewing that things were in full swing. From the end of April until the end of June, this is *the place* where buyers and sellers come to trade aracha. From the number of buyers and sellers we saw engaged in business, they move a lot of tea. During the height of the tea season the auction operates every day; if it is raining and no one is picking tea (wet leaves clog the mechanical shearing machines), there is no auction until more tea is picked and more aracha can be made.

This was not the type of hands-waving-in-the-air-bidding-for-antiques-country auction that we were familiar with back home. Instead, those with tea to sell placed the tea out for view in black lacquer trays on long tables. Buyers roamed from table to table, offering comments, fingering the tea, discussing things with one another conspiratorially, and sometimes throwing in a paper bid. Despite the size of the crowd, it was a pretty quiet place. Everyone seemed to be concentrating deeply. In fact, as we wandered and took notes and photographs for the better part of an hour, we were not sure that anyone even noticed we were there. All of the players wore official hats—yellow hats designated auction association members, green hats were reserved for industry and tea association members, and blue hats distinguished the local tea growers and producers. On the side of the room, two tea-cupping sta-

Tea buyers examine the various lots on offer at the Shizuoka tea auction (Shizuoka, Japan).

tions became increasingly busy as the crowd of buyers thickened. Ten industrial-sized water kettles belched out a heady supply of steam, a sign that they were ready to accommodate the volume expected to take place over the next few hours as buyers made their final decisions about prospective purchases.

As the action waned, we left and stopped by the offices of a local *saitori* (tea dealer). We had passed by his shop on our way to the auction and noticed a group of men inside huddled around a tea-tasting table sipping and examining tea. The street was lined with tea dealers, and there was activity everywhere. It was now 7 a.m. and his business was concluded for the day—he had accomplished his goal of selling all of his tea. The *saitori* invited us to sit and taste some tea. We watched with curiosity while he placed a five-yen coin (a *go en*) on the small round platform on one side of his scale and added tiny amounts of tea to the platform on the other side. When the weight of tea reached the correct level and the scale balanced, he had the right amount—five grams—the measure that Japanese tea tasters use when brewing a taste of aracha. He explained to us that a *go en* also has the double meaning of "well connected."

When a buyer determines that a particular lot of aracha is of interest, it goes to the tasting area. Copious kettles of perfectly heated water are supplied by the staff so that buyers can cup, look, taste, and spit over and over for hours, looking for the particular aracha that will complete the desired blend (Shizuoka, Japan).

- **Sencha**. This term has two meanings in Japan. First, it refers to the most popular style of leaf tea produced in Japan. Second, it has a historical reference to a practice of tea drinking that infuses tea leaves rather than the powdered tea of Chanoyu.

Sencha is the most popular tea drunk in Japanese households and restaurants—more than 80 percent of all the tea produced in Japan is sencha. It is plucked three to four times a year, but the first spring picking yields the finest quality. Many quality grades of sencha are produced, including costly handpicked teas made in small quantities. The first plucking is designated as *ichibancha*; the second plucking, which begins about the end of June, is known as *nibancha*; the third plucking, which starts in mid-August, is called *sanbancha*; and the fourth picking, which begins in late September, is known as *yobancha*. Fukamushi Sencha is a deeply steamed variation of sencha that results in a sweeter, richer flavor that is less astringent in style. The following green teas are steamed and shade grown.

Gyokuro. Associated with the ancient tea gardens of Uji in the Kansai region near Kyoto prefecture, gyokuro is Japan's most treasured tea. It is labor intensive to produce and finicky to brew. Although most tea thrives on a balance of weather that brings sunny days interspersed with cloudy days, gyokuro (Jade Dew) grows under a full-shade covering before it is picked. It is only produced in the spring from the first leaf plucking. As soon as the weather stimulates the bushes to flush with new growth, the shade covering is applied. This is done in two ways. In the most elaborate way for the most expensive tea, trellises are erected over the rows of plants to completely cover the rows in large sections. Black netting is spread over the top of the trellis and down the sides, covering the entirety all the way to the ground. This method of covering is called *tana*, and while the bushes are completely covered, the new growth on the bushes is still able to grow freely as the material does not touch the plants. See "Uniquely Japanese" in chapter 2 for more information and photographs of covered tea bushes.

Conversely, many bushes are simply wrapped in the cloth row by row, in a style called *jikagise*. Either way, fine, dappled light is able to filter through the cloth—about 10 percent—but the bushes essentially grow in the shade protected from the sun for twenty-one days. A further refinement is sometimes added, which requires covering the black tana with a thick mat of straw. The mat reduces the light through the netting even more, increasing the darkness within the tent. This step is reserved for the top grades of gyokuro and for tencha, which is processed into the most expensive powdered matcha for thick tea.

The point of shading the bushes is to increase chlorophyll production in the plants by reducing natural photosynthesis in the leaves. This extra boost of green chlorophyll pigment changes the natural balance of caffeine, sugars, and flavanols in the leaf, creating the opportunity for the tea processors to coax added sweetness from the leaf. In addition, the absence of photosynthesis increases the presence of naturally occurring theanine (an amino acid that is believed to induce relaxation), which is the component of tea that is responsible for giving tea its vegetal taste. Usually, photosynthesis reduces theanine and increases tannins.

This reversal of leaf dynamic is one of the factors responsible for gyokuro's distinctive flavor and rich, pine-green color. The best Uji gyokuro is made exclusively from the bud and new leaf, which is hand-plucked. This type of select picking has a limited number of production days possible each year—approximately ten. Gyokuro of this caliber accounts for only 1 percent of Uji's total gyokuro production, which is just under 20 percent of their total tea production. The remaining 80 percent is sencha production, with another small percentage of tencha leaf that will become matcha powder.

When processing gyokuro, the fresh leaf undergoes a different rolling, separating, and drying procedure for the leaves to acquire their characteristic thin, needlelike appearance. Special clonal varieties of tea plants have been developed for gyokuro production that yield small, sweet leaf. When brewed properly at a low water temperature, gyokuro produces a sweet, rich tea with a characteristic, striking vegetal flavor. Because of the specific combination of variables necessary to produce gyokuro, this is the most expensive Japanese leaf green tea and highly regarded among connoisseurs. There is much debate about who makes the best gyokuro; competitions are held yearly to crown the best producer. The most famous gyokuro-growing region is Uji, followed by Okabe in Shizuoka prefecture, and the Yame district in Fukuoka prefecture.

Kabuse cha. This shade-grown tea is grown throughout Japan. Not shaded for as long as gyokuro, kabuse-cha is considered a shade-grown sencha. It combines the green freshness of sencha with the creamy, pungent richness of gyokuro.

CHAMPION GYOKURO PRODUCER MASO KONO

For the past five years running, Maso Kono from Minamiyamashiro village in Uji has been the man to beat in gyokuro competitions. We arrived at his house late one misty spring afternoon just as he was heading out to his new matcha factory to tinker with some equipment. We tagged along, happy for the opportunity to visit his pristine factory and to learn something from this tea master. It was clear that even though he owns nine other sencha and gyokuro tea factories, this new factory was his baby. It had cost him 60,000,000 yen ($550,000) to build this state-of-the-art facility.

He led us back to his house to have a taste of his competition-grade gyokuro. As the water heated, he explained that competition-grade gyokuro is picked and processed differently than gyokuro manufactured for daily tea drinking. Pluckers snatch just the tiny bud or shoot for the competition grade, whereas high-quality gyokuro plucking begins perhaps one week later, and it is the bud and one leaf that will be sought. If you think that this is too subtle a difference to matter, you should know that transient details matter significantly to Japanese tea connoisseurs like Maso Kono. Millimeters and

seconds matter: competition-grade tea is the stuff of minutia and ephemeral detail. Winning a competition significantly raises the amount of money that one can expect to generate from other tea produced throughout the season and bestows great honor on the tea producer.

He grabbed a container of tea on the table and tipped some leaf into a rugged-looking, rust-colored, hand-thrown pottery *kyusu* teapot embellished with a vigorous streak of putty-colored glaze. He poured hot water into a *yuzamashi* to let it cool a few degrees. He explained that when brewing gyokuro, the water temperature is critical. Water that is too hot will brew bitter tea; when water is too cool, the voice of the tea cannot be heard. Just-right temperature brings out the inherent sweetness and vegetal flavors. Then he tipped the water from the yuzamashi into the teapot and gently swirled the pot for one minute. He filled tiny cups only half full with tea from the pot; this was tea meant for sipping and pondering. It was golden yellow, intensely aromatic, and tasted like bamboo, asparagus, and every other deliciously delicate spring taste that the earth musters. What a sublime treat.

Matcha. This bright emerald-green tea powder is whisked to a slightly frothy drink in the Japanese tea ceremony. Matcha is made in many regions of Japan, but it is always made from tencha, shade-grown leaf that is grown under the same conditions as gyokuro. In Japan many people appreciate the unique properties and flavor qualities of matcha and drink it as a simple, refreshing cup of tea. When matcha is consumed this way, the greatest percentage of antioxidants is realized because the entire leaf is consumed, not just an extraction of the leaf.

Freshness is very important to Japanese tea drinkers, and because production of Japanese tea is small, the finest teas are costly. Gyokuro and matcha top the list for cost. Matcha is sold in small containers to maintain the freshness of the powder at its peak, and even in Japan, it is quite expensive. The best matcha is jaw-droppingly expensive. In a teashop in Kyoto we discovered half-ounce (20 gram) containers of matcha selling for $35, $26, $17, and $14. Later, in Uji, we spotted small tins of matcha tins selling for $80, $65, $50, and $40. We were told that the price goes up from this, especially for matcha that has been shaded in the most traditional manner with the grass mats for preparing thick tea. In both cases all of this fresh matcha was custom blended and ground in stone mills by the shops selling it. Depending on the use one has in mind—ceremonial matcha for Chanoyu, for ice cream and baked goods, or for Western-style iced tea or hot tea—the correct matcha is purchased accordingly.

A bank of precisely milled stone matcha grinders. No process powders tencha into matcha as accurately as a stone mill (Uji, Japan).

JAPAN'S ROASTED TEAS

Houjicha. This is made by roasting sencha leaf and kukicha twig tea to create a chestnut-brown-colored tea with a crumpled appearance and a pleasant, toasty flavor. Houjicha can be made at any time throughout the season as long as there is bancha leaf available. Houjicha is often served to Japanese children, as it is low in caffeine.

Ire bancha. This tea offers a delicious smoky flavor. It has an unusual preparation: it is comprised of large, flat tea leaves that are roasted flat and

On a chilly, rainy afternoon we met with Mr. Haruhide Morita, a young and energetic tea grower, producer, and tea merchant in Uji who specializes in the production and blending of gyokuro and matcha teas for his company, Morita-en. We walked (with umbrellas) through his tea garden to view his shaded gyokuro tents. Even in the darkened interior of the tents, we could see the slightly eerie pale-green color of the new growth on the tea plants. Plenty of rain still filtered through the cloths covering the tents; the tea seemed well watered and thriving in the trapped heat of the tent.

Next, Mr. Morita gave us a tour of production at a cooperative tencha factory. He explained that the major difference between leaf plucking for gyokuro and for tencha is as follows: for tencha the pluck is the bud and three leaves, which introduces slightly older, larger leaves, to add "influence" to the final flavor of the matcha, while for gyokuro, the pluck is the bud and two leaves. Technically, tencha production is a variation of gyokuro production, but with an additional difference. The leaf for tencha is steamed and dried but not rolled, as it is for gyokuro. The reason is that the leaf must remain flat so that it can easily be stripped of its stems and the veining. After stripping, the remaining tencha leaf is ground in slow-turning stone mills, which yields silky smooth matcha powder.

In the Japanese tea ceremony matcha is brewed two ways. For more elaborate ceremonies a communal cup of *koicha* (thick tea) is made and passed around for all of the guests to share. In the shorter versions of the ceremony, individual cups of *usucha* (thin tea) are made for each guest. But there is more to it than that. For the fresh leaf that will be plucked to make matcha for koicha, Mr. Morita covers the tents with the extra layer of straw matting, something that he does only for his highest-quality teas. While a cup of usucha is made by whisking matcha and hot water to a frothy consistency with a bamboo whisk, the thin thread of bubbles that form around the edge of the bowl from this action are unwelcome in a bowl of koicha. So, for koicha, the matcha and water are gently mixed together with the bamboo tea scoop until a thickened consistency is achieved and a smooth, level surface forms.

Fresh leaf for tencha is sent into a brand-new factory built to manufacture only this form of tea. After undergoing considerable processing, this leaf will be transformed into highest-quality tencha and ground into matcha (Uji, Japan).

open. The tea is light and bulky and is brewed by adding a fairly large quantity of leaf to a pot of boiled water. Iri bancha is simple and delicious and excellent for sipping before savoring a sampling of sashimi.

Kamairi-cha or Tamaryokucha. This green tea is a specialty of the island of Kyushu, in the vicinity of Ureshino. It is processed "Chinese-style" by pan-firing (roasted or parched) and hand-rolling the leaves in iron pans.

JAPAN'S TWIG TEAS

Karigane cha. This twig tea is made from the stems and twigs of gyokuro. Sometimes sencha leaf is added, in which case the tea is called Karigane Sencha.

Kukicha. This twig-and-leaf blended tea is made from carefully rendered leaf and stalk cuttings of sencha production. The leaf is processed separately from the stalks, and both are cut to create a precise, uniform tea. A specialty made just in the early spring, this tea brews a clear, bright yellow-green color and has a fresh, herbaceous aroma.

Korea: Tea Continues Its Spread

As tea drinking spread in both China and Japan in the sixth, seventh, and eighth centuries, Buddhist monks returning from study in China first introduced the culture of tea to Korea. This was a time of a great exchange of information and ideas among scholars, men of religion, and trade emissaries as travel between these countries blossomed. Although the country is geographically aligned between China and Japan, Korea's history did not allow it to realize as famous or as firmly entrenched a tea culture as was achieved in China and Japan. Korea's tea culture was underway in the early days of the Koryo dynasty (918–1392). It was recorded that King Tae Jo, the first ruler, gave Uh Cha (tea gifts given by the king) to Buddhist priests and monks and to members of his military. As time passed, successive kings gave gifts of tea for loyalty to families who lost a loved one and to those suffering from illness. Tea was referred to as *New Woun Cha,* or "mind origin tea," for clearing the mind and as *Dae Cha,* meaning great tea. Custom was established for placing boxes of tea with the dead when performing funeral rites.

For centuries Buddhist monks had nurtured tea drinking in Korea as an ritual offering to Buddha. Buddhism also extolled the virtues of tea as a contemplative beverage essential for developing mental discipline. During the Koryo dynasty tea began to be used as an offering to the spirits of such natural places as rivers and mountains and to one's ancestral spirits at the New Year and on the full harvest moon ceremonies known as *Ch'a-rye*. Various tea ceremonies developed that were performed as special seasonal rites and events honoring important occasions. Unlike in China and Japan, where tea drinking for many years was reserved as an exclusive practice for aristocrats or warriors, all classes of Koreans practiced tea drinking, including making ritual tea offerings known as *Hon-ta* to statues of Buddha in the temples. A culture of tea drinking followed that developed the tenets and philosophy of this practice in a way that was unique to Korea. During the Koryo dynasty Korean ceramicists had learned the craft of producing fine celadon wares from Chinese potters proficient in the production of Chinese celadon-like wares known as Yue ware. Korean celadon became known as Chongja ware, and these were later followed by white porcelain wares, and then blue-and-white wares with applied decoration.

But this appreciation of tea was destroyed during a time of a shift in power and abrupt religious change.

At the end of the Koryo dynasty (918-1392) in the fourteenth century and the beginning of the Choson dynasty (1392-1910) the Yi family gained power and replaced established Buddhist ideals with Confucian views. This new religion—a radical variant of Chinese Confucianism—pushed the familiar ways of drinking, preparing, and appreciating tea into the background. Despite this, however, Buddhist monks tried to keep interest in the tea ceremonies alive. In retaliation for the influence the Buddhist monks held over society, the ruling government placed a tax on tea as a way to force the monasteries and temples to destroy their tea fields. In fact, so disdainful were the Choson rulers of the Buddhists and their tea that they also destroyed many temples and monasteries and stripped the remaining ones of their wealth and treasures.

By the end of the sixteenth century only a few tea fields remained in southern Korea. Korean literati shunned the new religion and became major proponents of the former tea culture, which they tried to keep alive through poetry and art. Korean potters who continued to make simple tea bowls, along with bowls for rice and food and other utilitarian objects, developed utilitarian *baekja* and *bunch'ong* stonewares.

In the late 1500s the ill-fated Seven Year War with Japan again packed a wallop to what remained of Korea's tea culture. By the war's end Korea was a devastated place that had incurred countless damage to farmlands, villages, and cities.

The human toll was further devastated after the war with the capture of thousands of Korean potters and other craftsmen, who were forcibly removed from their country and sent to live in exile and to ply their skills in Japan. This influx of manpower and skill is largely responsible for the formidable advances that Japan gained in ceramic arts and handmade pottery skills. It was at Korea's expense that the great pottery-making traditions of Japan developed and flourished.

Despite all of this, the late-eighteenth century brought a return to interest in Buddhist ideals and ways, and the first of three men who account for the restoration and slow revival of traditional Korean tea practices. The first was a scholar named Tsan Chong Yak-yong (1762–1836), who learned tea discipline and practice from an enclave of Buddhist monks who grew tea in Jeollanam Province. He in turn introduced a Buddhist monk named Ch'o Ui (1786–1866) to the way of tea. Ch'o Ui cultivated the practice of tea in an isolated tearoom near Haenam county in Jeollanam. He then penned two important books on tea and tea preparation in the nineteenth century.

Fate turned against Korea in 1910, when the country came under Japanese colonial rule and once again the nation was repressed in its ways of tea drinking. But as soon as Korea won independence from the Japanese in 1945, Choi Beom-sul, later known as the Venerable Hyo Dang, a renaissance man active in the independence movement, began his lifelong efforts to rekindle a strong interest in tea. The abrupt arrival of the Korean War (1950–1953) returned Korea to chaos again, but fortunately this strife did not stop the forward advance of tea culture.

A Korean tea bowl and tray, with a hand-carved Korean tea scoop.

Venerable Hyo Dang accomplished three important things in his lifetime: First, he composed the first modern-day study of tea in 1973, which he titled *The Korean Way of Tea.* Second, from the ideals set forth in this work, he codified the "natural" and "open heart" methods of brewing green tea that became known as Panyaro. He also founded the Korean Association for the Way of Tea, the first alliance and resource center for tea historians and devotees interested in reviving the culture of tea in Korea. The Venerable Hyo Dang was an acclaimed teacher of tea to all of the leading figures working today in Korea's revitalized tea industry. After his death in 1979, he was followed by his successor, the great tea master Chae Won-Hwa, a female tea master who continues to promote the Way of Tea to her graduate students in tea culture from her Panyaro Institute for the Way of Tea in Seoul, South Korea.

Today, Panyaro embodies Zen practices of purification and strengthening of body and mind while keeping the practice of the Korean Way of Tea accessible to all. The gestures involved in making tea are simple, and the environment in which tea is served should also be conducive to adopting an appropriate spirit of heart and mind that expresses naturalness, simplicity, moderation, firmness, flexibility, and gratitude. Panyaro is not a ritualized tea ceremony but remains a way of life that embodies simple but essential values of life through the activity of serving tea. The benefits of drinking tea in the Panyaro way include sharper hearing, clearer sight, and enhanced appetite, as well as awakening the mind, ending fatigue, quenching thirst, and inducing warm in winter and cool in summer. In 1979, the Federation of Korean Tea Masters Society was founded to encourage people to rediscover the joys of tea drinking. Today, the society has more than 100,000 members in Korea who are dedicated to helping restore Korea's traditional tea-drinking culture.

METHODS OF KOREAN GREEN TEA PRODUCTION

Korean tea is hand-plucked and the leaf is fired or "parched" or lightly roasted in an iron caldron or a tea-firing pan. The steps are driving off the moisture, rolling and shaping, drying, and parching. These parched teas, known as *puch'o-cha,* are dried over a wood fire or gas flame similar to the way that green teas are pan-fired in China. But there is one difference: for puch'o-cha the fresh leaves are heated in the tea-firing pan to begin to drive the moisture from the leaves. But after a few minutes the leaves are removed from the heat of the pan and placed on a flat work surface where the leaves are exposed to vigorous hand-rolling and shaping. Shaping is usually performed on a bamboo or straw mat, which aids in curling the leaf. Following this, the leaves are hand-separated to declump the moist leaves, which can become sticky from the leaf juices.

After a few minutes the leaves are laid to rest on flat mats to air-dry for a short time before being returned to the heat of the pan. The leaves remain in the pan for another few minutes, and then they are removed once more for shaping, separating, and air-drying. This ritual is repeated as many additional times as is deemed necessary to shape and dry the leaf, after which the leaf is laid out to air-dry for four to five hours. The final charcoal parching follows, which is performed in the same caldron or tea-firing pan but at a much lower temperature. During this stage of processing of "taste giving" (*mat-naegi*) and "fragrance enhancing" (*hyang-olligi*), the tea's character is released.

Chung-ch'a is a variation on the Japanese method of steaming the tea leaves at the initial step. For chung-ch'a the fresh leaves are briefly submerged in a vat of boiling water and then removed and allowed to drain before being put into the tea-firing pans. Once the firing process begins, the tea leaves remain in the tea-firing pan during shaping and rolling. Chung-ch'a is the old, traditional way of tea-firing, and it is more costly to produce. Tea Master Chae Won-Hwa presides over the final finishing of batches of chung-ch'a tea that is prepared for use at the Panyaro Institute for the Way of Tea in Seoul.

KOREA'S TEA GARDENS TODAY

Successful tea gardens have been established in southern Korea in South Jeollanam Province, on the southwestern quadrant of the island in Haenam, Yeongam, and Jangseong counties. Cheju-do Island, the largest of nearly two thousand small islands lying off the eastern and western coastline of South Jeolla, and Mount Wolchul, located in Yeongam county, both offer excellent weather conditions for growing fine tea. Mount Jiri, which spills over into three provinces—North Jeolla, South Jeolla, and South Gyeonsang—provides a sheltering environment for several wild-tea gardens that blanket the slopes in several places. Korean tea is available in limited supplies, and as a result the prices of the most select pluckings are high. The best teas are plucked according to the established dates of the seasonal divisions of the lunar calendar. And, as in China and Japan, the premium teas are plucked the earliest.

The first plucking of the season occurs just before April 20 or *Koku* (the first grain rain), the sixth seasonal division of the year based on the changing location of the sun. This is a bud and single-leaf plucking called Ujon, which is followed a few days later by a second plucking that consists of a bud and two leaves and is known as Sejak. A third plucking, and the first summer plucking, begins around May 5 or *Ipha*. This is followed throughout the summer with pluckings of several lower-quality teas.

India: Diversity of Tea and Place

Images of India conjure up a colorful swirl of people, places, and exotic animals. From Mogul monuments and Buddhist temples to vast deserts and lush tropical jungles, India casts a seductive spell. In the cities daily life is a juxtaposition of tradition and today's fast-paced new economic opportunities. In the country nomadic tribes hold yearly camel fairs, and bustling silk and spice markets entice both locals and tourists with exotic wares. Nature reserves protect large populations of elephants, tigers, and gray rhinos as well as exotic native flora. Every facet of this former jewel in the crown of the British Empire offers another glimpse into the vibrant pulse of this populous continent.

Although India is surrounded by water on three sides—the Bay of Bengal to the east, the Arabian Sea to the west, and the Indian Ocean to the south—the soaring peaks of the magnificent Himalaya define its northern border. Sharing the border with neighbors Bhutan, China, Myanmar, Nepal, and Pakistan, northern India is edged with revered holy mountains, sharply cut vertiginous valleys, a multitude of ethnic populations and religions, and the most famous tea gardens in the world. In the north tea is produced in the geographically diverse states of Assam, Arunachal Pradesh, Bihar, Dooars, Himachal Pradesh, Manipur, Nagaland, Orissa, Sikkim, Tripura, Uttaranchal, and West Bengal (Darjeeling region). In the south tea is produced in Karnataka, Kerala, and Tamil Nadu.

India is the world's largest producer of tea. In 2005 tea production in that country was 927,984 metric tons of tea, a figure that represents the

combined total production from 111,979 tea estates, and the efforts of millions of tea-estate workers. Because much of India's tea is consumed by its own people, the country assumed fourth place in worldwide tea exports in 2005, behind China, Kenya, and Sri Lanka, with 123,620 metric tons of tea exported. Most Indian tea is sold at auction, passing through one of six regional auction centers. In Assam, the capital city of Guwahati provides one location, as does Siliguri in the north. Auction centers are also found in Calcutta, Cochin, Coimbatoor, and Coonoor.

The geography and terrain of India's tea-growing areas feature considerable differences in climate and geography. Northeastern India can be divided into the Brahmaputra and Barak valleys in Assam, the northern Bengal plains of Dooars and Terai, and the Darjeeling Hills. The Nilgiri Mountains provide the only major tea-producing region in southern India, with production in the states of both Kerala and Tamil Nadu.

Left: A clay tea set from India.

Right: Tea pickers queue up to have their shift's pluck weighed and notated. Precise records are kept at every shift to ensure proper compensation for work (Assam, India). Photo courtesy of Saunam Bhattacharjee.

ASSAM: THE BRAHMAPUTRA AND BARAK VALLEYS

Located at the foothills of the eastern Himalaya, in the far northeastern corner of India, Assam's lush, dense jungles are where indigenous, wild-growing India tea plants, called *Camellia sinensis* var. *assamica*, were discovered in 1823. Assam shares a small portion of its northwestern border with the mystical Dragon Kingdom of Bhutan, while the tip of northeastern Assam abuts the jungles of Myanmar. Present-day Assam is encircled by the Indian states of Arunachal Pradesh, Nagaland, Mizoram, and Meghlaya—all of which were carved out of the original Assam state in the British colonial era. The northwestern tip of Bangladesh juts far into Assam, creating a narrow passage of land that isolates and nearly severs Assam from the rest of India. Assam's eastern border is peopled by a diverse mix of nearly four hundred

BASKET-
CARRYING
DAMSELS

Tea pickers are mostly female, and when they fan out into the tea gardens, their garments cut a colorful, multihued swath through the tea fields. Some of these tea pluckers wear woven bamboo hats (in China women in different regions sport different styles of hats), while in India and Ceylon multicolored woven head wraps are favored.

To catch the freshly plucked tea leaves, woven bamboo baskets are slung over the shoulder or carried on the back or steadily held aloft atop one's head in a deft and steady balancing act. Other times cloth sacks are secured and suspended from atop one's head (cloth pads are used to keep the sacks from slipping and from being uncomfortable). The sacks are used in the same manner to catch and contain freshly plucked tea leaves.

The tension applied by slender, nimble fingers to the base of the tea leaf is done with studied skill and care. The pluck of the leaf from the stem must be made with a clean, swift break. The action of separating the leaf from the stalk is done with a twisting motion of the hand that is controlled at the wrist, not by clipping the leaf away with fingernails. Doing so would result in a rust-colored stem end. Efficient tea pickers pluck with both hands at once until they can no longer hold any more leaf. Then they toss their catch into their bag or basket.

Assamese tea pickers tend to use woven head straps to support their tea sacks while they pick. These cloth sacks are lighter in weight than baskets and are made from local fabric (Assam, India). Photo courtesy of Eliot Jordan.

An assortment of tea containers: a ceramic container in the shape of a tea picker from Sri Lanka; an antique tin from Darjeeling, India; and a tin from Nepal.

ethnic groups, including Assamese, Boros, Khasis, Kukis, Nagas, Nishis, Tagins, and Tiwas, to name a few. Today, as in the past, this quadrant of India is a country apart from the mainland, largely undeveloped and left to itself.

Assam is essentially a large, tropical river valley, with few areas of high elevation. In the north and central part of the state the Brahmaputra River courses down through the middle of the region, descending into Assam from the far reaches of Tibet. The Brahmaputra, which is one of the longest rivers in the world, also harbors the largest river island in the world, Majuli. Meeting with the sacred Ganges River in Bangladesh, the Brahmaputra comes to the end of its journey in the Bay of Bengal in Bangladesh. The Brahmaputra watershed provides rich, fertile plains that sustain Assam's plentiful tea gardens. In the southern region of Assam the Barak River forms the Surma valley, where the small Cachar tea district is located. Restricted by the backdrop of the distant Himalaya, the weather of Assam is a microclimate of its own. The sheer height and mass of the Himalaya prevent the hot, humid monsoon air from dispersing north away from Assam, so in turn the rains come and the rivers overflow, washing the fields and plains with a new coat of fertile topsoil each year.

Assam produces the largest quantity of tea in India, which comprises both premium and mass-market quality. Many growers see the high-end, specialty tea market as the means to change their way out of the price slump that Assam's mass-market tea has fallen into. The price for these teas is so low that many growers are giving up and abandoning their gardens. Estimates are that 100 to 150 gardens closed in the thirty-six-month period from 2003 to 2005. There is a lot of tea produced in the world, and much of it competes for the same market. Without a distinctive difference, many of these teas end up playing the pricing game, which always means a lower price for the producer. As the costs of production rise while tea prices fall, many tea gardens go out of business. Assam also has a great deal of political instability, which presents a dangerous situation for visiting foreign tea buyers and discourages both foreign capital investment and investment by local tea garden and factory owners. Tea buyers therefore do not visit Assam, and the Assam market suffers from a lack of hands-on exposure and management. This hinders any improvements that might otherwise be made, out of fear of losing one's investment in these politically charged times.

Fortunately, many Assam tea gardens are striving to upgrade the quality of the leaf produced. As demand for low-grade tea diminishes, interest in the specialty tea market shows no signs of slowing. Worldwide demand for quality leaf has reached its highest pitch ever, and Assam is poised to benefit from this by increasing quality. By law land classified as a tea garden in Assam must be used only to grown tea. So today's tea growers choose between growing tea or not growing anything. Modifications in these land-use laws would allow farmers to expand their cash crops to cover their expenses when tea is losing money. At present, however, upgrading the quality of the tea is the option of choice, but this requires the government's help to upgrade infrastructure and assist with marketing a higher-grade product.

Assam's tea-growing regions. The tea-growing regions in Assam are divided into Upper Assam (at the far end of Assam close to the Chinese–Myanmar border), North Bank (at the northern banks of the Brahmaputra River), Central Assam, and Lower Assam (which lies in the western half of Assam). The tea gardens located in the red loam soil of the Doom Dooma tea belt in Upper Assam generally produce the region's best teas. The tea-growing districts of Upper and Central Assam (such as Dibrugarh, Golagat, Jorhat, Sibsagar, and Tinsukia) produce the largest volume of Assam's tastiest leaf. In British colonial days the Sibsagar region of Upper Assam was known as Burmese Assam, and it was here and in the Lakkimpur region where the British propagated cuttings taken from indigenous tea trees. These cuttings were used to plant the fledgling tea nurseries that eventually resulted in Assam's vast cultivated tea gardens. In this vast region counting the number of tea producers is not an easy task. According to the Indian government, approximately 800 to 850 tea estates (each of which has more than 500 acres of land) are statistically counted and classified in Assam. However, there are another 500 to 800 new tea gardens that are not yet eligible to be clas-

ASSAM'S TWO TYPES OF PRODUCTION

Orthodox tea production in Assam takes place at Balijan Estate, Borbudi Dikom, Doomar, Dulling Estate, Gingia Estate, Greenwood Estate, Hajua Estate, Halmari, Harmutty Estate, Hattiali, Koomsong, Kopili Estate, Mangalam, Marangi, Meleng, Mokalbari, Oaklands Estate, Orangajuli Estate, Rani, Rembeng Estate, Sarupta Estate, Sibsagar Estate, Teen Ali Estate, Tingalimbam Estate, and Toonbarie Estate.

CTC tea production in Assam occurs at Hunwal, Keyhung, Monkooshi, and Tarajulie.

sified; it can take as long as fifteen to twenty years for a garden to be counted as a classified garden. What's more, there are another 200,000 to 300,000 individual tea growers who have landholdings of fewer than ten acres each who turn their freshly plucked leaf over to "bought-leaf" factories. These leaf processors do not own tea gardens but merely process leaf tea for others. These factories easily number between 150 and 200, and neither they nor the individual tea growers are counted in the government's numbers.

According to the government's tea production figures, Assam produces on average 400,000 metric tons of tea each year, a figure that represents 45 to 50 percent of India's total tea output. But remember, these numbers are just production for the classified gardens; if the total production from the small tea growers and nonclassified gardens were included, this estimate could conceivably jump to being closer to accounting for 75 percent of India's total tea output.

Assam's humid, tropical weather. Assam has a humid, lowland climate with ample rain that creates an environment perfectly suited to the India tea bush and for producing characteristically strong, full-bodied, and malty teas. Winter comes to Assam in December and lasts until February, and although temperatures rarely dip below 55°F (13°C) this seasonal change in the weather makes the tea plant go into hibernation until the following spring. March brings the spring harvest of first-flush teas, the most delicate leaves produced in Assam. Late May and early June produce the tippy summer teas, the second-flush teas, which are covered on the

ELEPHANTS IN ASSAM

Our Assamese friend and tea grower Saunam has a pet elephant, Lokhi, who lives and works at one of his tea gardens.

Saunam explained Lokhi's work in the garden: "Lokhi is retired. He came to my family when he was in his mid-thirties. He is a wild-born elephant who was captured when he was a teenager and domesticated. Lokhi spends 50 percent of his time in the jungle just hanging out. The other 30 percent of his time is spent walking up and down, stopping to eat whatever his trunk can reach. The other 20 percent of his time is presently being spent uprooting tea plants in order for us to replace them with new clonal varieties. It is very hard work for humans to dig out the roots of the plants, but it is not much work at all for an elephant—he simply grabs the bush and yanks it out of the ground and then moves on to the next one. Also, if he is around when one of our trucks gets stuck in the mud, he will push it out. He costs me a well-spent ten dollars a day to pay for his maintenance, which includes food, two full-time caretakers, medicines, and supplies."

underside of each leaf with fine, delicate silver hair. Considered by tea connoisseurs to be the most distinctive of Assam teas, these teas have two main flavor profiles: mature, tippy leaves that brew a creamy, full-bodied cup, and crisply defined, brisk flavors with more highly nuanced aromas.

Assam's tea production. Assam produces both orthodox tea and cut-tear-curl (CTC) leaf. Although all Assam tea is picked by hand, the quality of the final product is a result of each particular gardens' focus: producing quality or producing quantity. In the early cropping season, careful, fine plucking and attentive processing ensure a stylish leaf and a smoother cup. CTC teas, which account for most of the annual volume of tea produced in Assam, are given a coarser plucking, and are processed faster during the time of heaviest yield from the gardens. The monsoon season arrives in June, bringing drenching rains and sweltering, hot, humid tropical weather that lingers as late as November. The hearty India tea bush happily thrives in this nurturing heat and moisture, and grows thick and lush with abundant leaves. Last comes the autumn harvest, a late-season October and November picking that is still influenced by the effects of the end of the rainy season. December to March is the off-season, when no plucking occurs. Most tea gardens are plucked on average twenty-five times a season, from March to December, with plucking spaced at least one week apart.

DARJEELING: THE QUEEN OF INDIAN TEAS

In 1835, not many years after the discovery of wild-growing tea trees in Assam, the English established a hill town health resort and sanatorium for military families in the cool, clean air and high elevation of a remote region of western Bengal. The Tibetan Buddhist monks occupying this place had named it "Dorje-ling" (Darjeeling) in honor of the Dorje, the sacred ritual object of holy lamas that symbolizes eternal strength and constancy and a fixed axis point around which all else turns. With its prominent position across the valley from a majestic lineup of soaring Himalayan peaks, this was considered a transcendent place by the Tibetans.

Dr. A. Campbell, the chief government official posted in Darjeeling, tried unsuccessfully to grow an English flower garden, but he did have luck growing some tea bushes nearby his residence that he had started from seeds obtained from the governor general of India in Calcutta. Some of these seeds had been smuggled out of China, although Campbell also used seeds from the newly discovered Assam tea bushes. Other English civil servants in Darjeeling had success cultivating small tea gardens, so much so that by 1856 these experimental government test gardens proved that tea of both types of bush favored the high altitude, cool thin air, ample rains, golden sunshine, and overall lush environment of this remote Shangri-la.

Fewer than a hundred locals lived in this paradise at that time. Workers were brought from Nepal and the northern region of Sikkim to Darjeeling to clear jungles, construct roads, terrace the hillsides, build rudimentary tea-processing factories, and establish towns and villages. The English sent additional men and their families to plant and operate these burgeoning tea gardens. Much like their compatriots in Assam, these early English pioneers had to rely on their own stamina and fortitude to establish the tea industry in Darjeeling, as there was no blueprint of success for them to follow. The rugged terrain and the severe Himalayan weather constantly challenged the mettle of the tea planters.

By 1866 the number of tea gardens in Darjeeling had grown to thirty-nine, and many of today's famous gardens—Ambootia, Badamtam, Makaibari, and Singell, to name a few—were established. By 1881 the population had swelled to 95,000, and the tea gardens numbered just over 100. Eventually, trucks began replacing horses as better roads were being carved out of the mountains. More sophisticated processing factories were built, and living facilities for workers were created on the larger tea estates. In the past few years, however, the number of gardens in the seven valleys of the Darjeeling hills has dwindled from eighty-six to a number that hovers around seventy-five due to garden closings and reopenings and other organizational changes. An estimated 42,000 to 50,000 acres are under cultivation, which makes each garden small in comparison to the large gardens situated in less vertical, high-altitude places. Darjeeling's tea gardens range in elevation from 2,000 to 7,000 feet, and they blanket the hills and valleys in a patchwork of verdant green. Despite the fame and popularity that Darjeeling teas enjoy worldwide, however, the annual output from this region is tiny—about 10 metric tons of tea, only 1 percent of India's total.

Kingdom in the sky. Wedged between Nepal and Bhutan, the Darjeeling region lies just south of Sikkim, the northernmost region of western Bengal, which touches on the Tibetan Himalaya. Visitors wend their way up to Darjeeling town (elevation 7,100 feet), where monasteries and nature reserves provide another facet to the history of this magical place. Signs point to winding roads

THE DARJEELING PLANTERS ASSOCIATION

Formed in 1983 by tea garden owners, this association has created a single platform for the development, promotion, and global protection of the name Darjeeling. The finest plucking of Darjeeling tea is sold as 100 percent Darjeeling estate-specific teas, and these usually indicate which seasonal flush the tea is from. Coarser tea from the summer rainy season is plucked and sold for use in less-expensive Darjeeling blends. Only teas from gardens within the designated parameters of the Darjeeling region are allowed to legally carry the green circular Darjeeling logo that signifies 100 percent pure Darjeeling tea.

For example, Castleton Garden, first-flush Darjeeling, is clearly marked as being a Darjeeling from a specific garden and certain time of year. Tea that is marked 100 percent Darjeeling and bears the Darjeeling logo is more specific about its contents than a package that is just marked as pure Darjeeling. It is important to purchase Darjeeling tea that carries the official government-sanctioned tea logo and from retailers that you can trust. There is more worldwide demand each year for Darjeeling tea than there is enough authentic tea produced to fill the orders. In the best of years Darjeeling tea accounts for less than 1 percent all the tea produced in India.

that twist through valleys toward such tea towns as Ghoom, Kurseong, Mirk, Sonada, Sukhiapokhri, Tiger Hill, Tindharia, and Tung. At Tiger Hill (elevation 8,482 feet) visitors can view a spectacular sunrise over the impressive Kanchenjunga, the third-highest peak in the Himalaya, whose name roughly translates into Five Treasures of the Snow. So named for each of its five massive peaks, Kanchenjunga was once believed to be the highest montain on earth, until that claim was dethroned by Mount Everest in 1849. On a clear day, if the weather cooperates, visitors can catch a glimpse of majestic Mount Everest.

Because of its many high ridges, deep valleys, and changes in elevation throughout the hills, Darjeeling has a great variation of climate. Winters are long and cold, but the summer months of April through June bring cool breezes and lavish, bright sunshine. Late summer brings quenching monsoon rains. Because of the variations in elevation, Darjeeling has several different types of forest: tropical semievergreen in the foothill regions, tropical moist deciduous forests, subtropical forests, eastern Himalayan wet temperate forests, and high alpine forests. Each of these forests contributes to the diversity of flora and fauna. Most of the arable places on the hills are fully planted with tea gardens. Splendid displays of rhododendrons, orchids, and azaleas add splashes of color to the hills and valleys.

Darjeeling's unique terroir. Darjeeling is an exclusive tea—no other tea on earth comes from the combination of geography and climate with which Darjeeling is blessed. A well-drained, slightly acidic, thin, gritty soil anchors tea bushes to the steep pitch of Darjeeling's valley inclines. In gardens that range from 1,800 to 6,300 feet, these high elevations offer thin cool air that slows the maturation of the leaves, yielding harvests of less than half the yield of leaf tea grown in lower elevations in hotter weather. Higher up in Darjeeling the steeply planted slopes are angled sixty to seventy degrees, making the task of planting and picking difficult. Brewed Darjeeling tea is golden amber in color, with a delicate, flowery flavor that has been likened to the sweetness of apricots and peaches. The finished result is a leaf that is stylish, long, and slender, with a significant amount of golden tip.

Many Darjeeling tea gardens cultivate both the China bush and India bush varieties of *Camellia sinensis*, but the proportion of each varies. Many growers argue that the finest tea and the best flavor come from the China bushes, which have acclimated to the high elevation and rugged climate. China bush is smaller than the Assam bush, and it produces a smaller quantity of thinner, more delicate leaves. The size of the tea leaves determines the volume of leaf that it will take to produce a pound of tea. For example, a pound of freshly picked buds is denser and more compact than a pound of the bulkier, freshly picked first leaf. It takes approximately twice as much China bush leaf to equal the same weight of India bush leaf. Not than anyone is counting, but a pound of Darjeeling tea is comprised of more than ten thousand individual tea shoots. It is common in Darjeeling for each tea bush to only yield three to four ounces of finished tea each year.

This comparatively small fraction of the annual yield results in higher labor costs per pound. This is true for China bush tea all over the world, but Darjeeling is one of the more extreme examples because of the restrictions of terrain and altitude. Some Darjeeling tea estates at lower elevations grow Assam bush for its luxurious and abundant habit. Because it is hardy and prolific, many newer gardens are being replanted with Assam bush.

Although Darjeeling is unable to compete with the quantity of tea produced in warmer and more fertile parts of India and other tea-producing regions of the world, Darjeeling gracefully pursues its role as the grower of super-premium desirable tea. Weighing in at only about one-fortieth the volume of tea produced in Assam, Darjeeling tea growers have the time to finesse the flavor and fuss with the withering and oxidation process. Each batch of fresh leaf that comes to the tea factory is processed using intricate variation to the basic technique that takes into account the weather conditions over the season and the condition of the plucked leaf. Because each day's plucking comes from a different section of the garden, each lot is marked and packaged as a separate "invoice." Each invoice represents the individual personality of the particular batch of tea, something unique that cannot be duplicated from one day to the next.

Darjeeling tea is completely handpicked by women, whose brightly colored saris and other clothing bring splashes of color to the tea gardens. Men traditionally work in the tea factories, processing the fresh leaf, and weighing and packing the finished tea. Close to 67,000 workers are employed on a year-round and seasonal basis in Darjeeling. Most of the workers are female, and usually entire families are employed. Each estate has its own tea-processing factory, and many estates produce certified organic tea or practice environmentally friendly growing techniques. Today new tea bushes are no longer planted from seed, although many old tea bushes originally planted from seed still thrive. Nurseries on the estates propagate tea bushes from grafts or clonal varieties, which are more tolerant to variations in weather. It is not unusual in Darjeeling to see tea trees started from seed that are more than seventy years old. Many of the tea estates in Darjeeling have begun utilizing ecological farming methods that are based on Rudolph Steiner's biodynamic principles. This means that they have cast aside the use of artificial pesticides and synthetic fertilizers in favor of using local plants for pest control and readily available, natural fertilizers, such as cow manure, to enrich the soil. The result is less yield per plant but better-tasting tea.

Seasonal flushes. Darjeeling has a clearly delineated seasonal cycle that brings the forces of nature to bear on its tea bushes and gardens. The high altitude of this region brings severe winter weather and many months of dormancy to the bushes. When the last vestige of winter is shrugged off with the arrival of spring rains, the bushes are stimulated to flush with tender, new leaves in February or early March. Connoisseurs worldwide await these fresh, flavorsome Darjeeling teas with anticipation. Picking begins with a fine plucking of two leaves and a bud. The early spring teas are also known as first-flush tea, and they are light, clear, aromatic, and brisk in flavor. First-flush Darjeelings are produced until mid-April, and each bush in the gardens is picked every four to seven days.

In May the second flush is ready for picking and is also given a fine plucking. This leaf is larger in size and more mature, thus less tender. At this stage the tea releases the "muscatel," the dry, currant flavor for which Darjeeling teas are famous. The onset of summer brings the monsoon season to Darjeeling, which lasts from the end of June until October. Tea is still picked during this season, and it is known as the monsoon flush. Hot weather and drenching rains yield large leaves that brew strong flavors, deep red in color but less distinctive overall in flavor nuance. Most monsoon teas are given a coarse plucking, and the tea is sold as nonestate-specific generic Darjeeling.

Lastly, the autumnal flush is ready for picking from October into November. This is the last and final pluck of the season. Autumnal tea is rich and smooth, coppery in color, and round and soft in the mouth. We are often asked which is better, a first- or a second-flush Darjeeling. Truthfully, both are delicious. Each flush represents the unique seasonal effects on leaf style and flavor that occur as the tea season progresses and the leaves mature. Each is unrivaled, and the decision is up to each tea drinker to decide which is preferred—the fresh exuberance of spring tea or the assertive increase of stronger, more forthright flavor.

NILGIRI: THE SOUTHERNMOST TEA GROWN IN INDIA

High in the lush forests and jungles of the Nilgiri (Blue Hill) Mountains in southern India, Nilgiri tea grows on a spectacular series of high altitude ridges that occupy the western portion of the state of Tamil Nadu. Here, inland from the Malabar coast, the Nilgiri range spills over into the Wynaad region of the neighboring state of Kerala, the point at which the Nilgiris meet the magnificent Western Ghat Mountains. The

DARJEELING ESTATES BY VALLEY

Darjeeling East. Arya, Chongtong, Dooteriah, Kalej Valley, Lingia, Marybong, Mim, Orange Valley, Pussimbing, Risheehat, Rungmook & Cedars, and Tumsong.

Darjeeling West. Badamtam, Bannockburn, Barnesbeg, Ging, Happy Valley, North Tukvar, Pandam, Phoobsering, Rangaroon, Rungneet, Singtom, Tukvar, and Vah Tukvar.

Kurseong North. Ambootia, Balasun, Dilaram, Margaret's Hope, Moondakotee, Oaks, Ringtong, Singell, and Springside.

Kurseong South. Castleton, Gidhapahar, Goomtee, Jogmaya, Jungpana, Longview, Mahalderam, Makaibari, Monteviot, Nurbong, Selim Hill, Seepoydhura, Sivitar, and Tindharia.

Mirik. Gayabari, Gopaldhara, Okayti, Phuguri, Seeyok, Singbulli, Soureni, and Thurbo.

Rungbong Valley. Avongrove, Chamong, Dhajea, Nagri, Nagri Farm, Selimbong, and Sungma.

Teesta Valley. Ambiok, Gielle, Glenburn, Kumai (Snowview), Lopchu, Mission Hill, Namring, Runglee Rungliot, Samabeong, Soom, Teesta Valley, and Tukdah.

Nilgiris provide a sweep of elevations that rise from undulating foothills to elevations of 8,202 feet atop the highest peaks. This geographic area is only thirty-five miles long and twenty miles wide, but has 148,263 acres of tea tucked into every hill and valley. This region offers the perfect climate and topography for tea bushes to thrive—lush forests, tropical jungles, misty valleys, sunny high plateaus, gentle grasslands, and numerous streams and rivers.

Two national parks have been created to protect the ecology of the Nilgiris—Mudumalai National Park and Mukurthi National Park. Together, in 1986, these two parks joined with four other natural reserves to form the nucleus of the Nilgiri Biosphere Reserve, the largest of its type in India. Elephants, tigers, wild boar, panthers, and black-faced langur are among the inhabitants that share this oasis with the local residents. The rarest animal, the endangered goatlike Nilgiri tahr, is depicted along with the outline of the Blue Mountains and two leaves and a bud silhouette in the Nilgiri Planters Association logo. An Englishman named Mann is said to have been the first to plant China *jat* (tea planters' term for the China bush subdivision of *Camellia sinensis*) in a Nilgiri experimental tea garden in 1835. The seed had literally been sewn for the English to commercially develop tea in these parts, but the Opium War stayed their interest until 1859, when the conflict was over. Both English and Scottish planters are responsible for developing the tea industry in Nilgiri, and today such estate names as Burnside and Glendale coexist alongside such names as Korakundah and Kairbetta. One of the first and therefore oldest tea estates from 1859 is Thiashola, which is still in production today and acquired organic certification in 2003. More than twenty thousand small landowners and a handful of large estates located in six districts—Coonor, Gudalur, Kothagiri, Kundah, Panthalur, and Udhagamandalam—contribute to the production of Nilgiri tea. Nonviolent resistance to British colonialism led to India's independence from British rule in 1947, and now the majority of tea estates are privately owned.

Nilgiri teas. Two monsoons a year—the southwest and the northeast—give the bushes distinct wet and dry seasons. Each season imparts distinct flavor characteristics to the tea. The tropical climate is similar to that of neighboring Sri Lanka, yielding teas that are more similar in flavor to Ceylon teas than to the Assam or Darjeeling teas from northern India. Plucking occurs all year long, but the prime season is from December through March, when the bushes flush with energy and send out an abundance of new leaves.

Tea from this season is called frost tea, because of the very real threat of frost that hovers over the valleys during this time. While this very chilly weather has a magical effect on the resultant flavor of the tea, if temperatures fall low enough to bring on an actual frost, then the growers suffer damage and crop loss to frostbite. The first flush or spring plucking accounts for approximately 25 percent of the annual crop. The second flush or winter plucking contributes 40 percent of the crop. In total, Nilgiri produces close to 200,000 metric tons of tea, which accounts for 25 percent of India's total tea production.

Nilgiri teas are known as "the fragrant ones" and have fine flavory liquors with pronounced flavor. The teas are bright and dependable and offer something of value in iced-tea blends—the teas do not "cloud" but instead retain a stable, vivid color when iced. Although exceptional orthodox teas are made in this region, most Nilgiri tea is CTC black tea, much of which is consumed locally and purchased by foreign tea companies to add its special, characteristic flavor to spiced chai tea blends. Nearly 50 percent of Nilgiri tea production is exported to the United Kingdom, Europe, and the Commonwealth of Independent States (CIS) from the tea auction center in Coimbatore.

A beautiful landscape of rolling hills (known as the Blue Mountains) are located in the states of Tamil Nadu and Kerala. Here, Nilgiri tea flourishes and is able to be harvested almost year-round due to the mild climate (Nilgiri, India). Photo courtesy of Eliot Jordan.

Nilgiri tea is not as well known as its famous tea cousins from Assam and Darjeeling. The case for quality Nilgiri teas has not been firmly established. Recent shifts in the global economy are changing the sales opportunities for Nilgiri teas. Where Nilgiri once maintained a market lead, CTC black teas from such tea-producing countries as Argentina and Vietnam are now flooding the market and driving down prices, a double strike that is affecting Nilgiri's market share and selling price.

Because an ideal climate allows year-round plucking and processing, Nilgiri allows for a high-yielding crop, producing more tea than the low-yielding areas like Darjeeling. With a worldwide glut of CTC tea, this is not to Nilgiri's advantage. But this situation is starting to turn around as the growers are addressing this question of quality. As was proven when the Sri Lankan tea industry reinvented itself after privatization in 1992 and returned to an emphasis on orthodox tea production, there will always be an ever-growing need in the specialty tea industry for distinguished orthodox leaf. Many Nilgiri producers are committed to producing organic teas and are choosing to single themselves out to the Western market in this way.

NILGIRI TEA AT THE FIRST-EVER AMERICAN TEA AUCTION

In spring 2006 a rare opportunity was presented to the tea buyers attending the World Tea Expo, a trade show devoted to all things tea. The Nilgiri Planters Association in conjunction with twelve member estates conducted the first-ever tea auction on American soil. All the buyers who registered to attend the auction received in advance a sample kit of the teas that would be up for sale. By auction time the event was certainly the buzz of the expo.

The auction was a smashing success. In most cases buyers paid over the value that the growers had hoped to receive for their teas, and all of the tea was purchased. We quickly snapped up six tasty lots for our customers. The auction proved two things: first, that specialty tea buyers will reward the efforts of those who manufacture quality leaf, and second, that these exquisite teas demonstrate that the Nilgiri producers have the ability to match the proficiency and technical skills of top black tea producers anywhere.

The largest tea cooperative in India is named the Indcoserve, located in Coonoor, Nilgiri. Started in 1958, the cooperative supports fifteen member tea factories that process fresh leaf for approximately 20,000 small holder tea growers who farm nearly 32,000 acres of land. It is rare to come across a single-estate Nilgiri tea for sale. But if the opportunity arises, look for fine quality orthodox tea from the following estates: Allada Valley, Beeyu, Burnside, Chamraj, Coonoor, Craigmore, Dunsandle, Glendale, Glenmorgan, Havukal, Kairbetta, Korakundah, Mailoor, Nonsuch, Parkside, Quinshola, Thiashola, Welbeck, and Yellapatty.

The Nilgiri Planters Association. Established in 1891, the NPA works with large tea gardens and tea factories to help the thirty-six member estates maintain their tea at a high level of quality while following ethical, social, and environmental practices. Members of the NPA manufacture their fresh leaf in the twenty-five member-owned tea factories. The NPA tests new clonal varieties of tea bushes and believes that specialty teas, not filler teas, are the way to increase both the market share and the value of tea. Growers and producers are thus being encouraged to bring new types of fancy teas to market, such as white tea, silver tips, and golden tips. These self-drinking teas of single-origin distinction appeal to tea enthusiasts, tea salons, and fine dining restaurants. Many orthodox Nilgiri teas have the body and finesse of mid-level Darjeeling teas, while others are stronger in body. All have fine, delicate aromas and fruity and woodsy flavors that become even more striking because of the lack of tannins or astringency in the cup. Nilgiri winter-picked teas, called frost teas, are particularly unique and flavorsome.

Orthodox tea production and grading. It is twice more costly to produce orthodox leaf than CTC leaf because it is a more time-consuming production process. Many steps are necessary to make a fine orthodox black tea. The subtle nuances of flavor and the distinctive quality of the tea are coaxed out of the leaf during a labor-intensive rolling process. During rolling, the still moist leaves are placed into a rotary rolling machine that, under pressure, rolls but does not rip the leaves in order to bruise and rupture the cells in the leaves. This allows the cells to release cell sap (which contains tannins, caffeine, and proteins, among other substances), a necessary step that begins the oxidation process. The withered leaf is usually rolled three or four separate times, under increased pressure, until the cell rupture is complete.

Seven steps and a great deal of knowledge and experience are required to manufacture a fine orthodox black tea: (1) fine plucking, (2) leaf withering, (3) rotary leaf rolling (cell rupture), (4) oxidation, (5) firing, (6) grading for quality, and (7) final sorting. After firing, the teas are put through revolving or oscillating sorting machines that separate the various grades of tea by using a series of five or more differently sized mesh screens. Each screen is designed to capture one grade size of tea; the rest of the tea passes through to a finer screen. After grading, the tea is sorted one last time to remove any stems or other debris, a task usually done by hand. For more information, see chapter 3.

Have you ever wondered about a seemingly mysterious coding of letters that follow the names of some teas? This code is the technical abbreviation for terminology used to differentiate various grades of leaf. Be sure to look for this the next time you are purchasing tea. If the teashop does not display this information on its jars or bins of loose-leaf tea, ask why not! Without knowing this information, a merchant cannot make a comparative decision about the style or value of the tea when he or she is considering which teas to purchase for resale. Consequently, consumers learn little in their quest to become educated about what they are purchasing. Purchasing tea is similar to purchasing wine; that is, the most expensive products are not always the best or the most suited to one's individual needs. Price is determined by many factors, and goodness is usually one of them, but tea enthusiasts should learn to evaluate tea by its flavor, not its price tag.

Orthodox leaf is classified as whole leaf, broken leaf, fannings, and dust, and is graded by leaf size in each class. For example, whole-leaf teas would be listed from the finest, thinnest leaf to the largest and thickest leaf, from top to bottom. Table 4.2 outlines this system.

CTC (cut-tear-curl) tea production. Instead of undergoing the traditional rolling process, CTC teas are put into cutting machines that chop the tea and distribute the cell sap over the surface of the finely cut bits of tea. Unlike the internal cell sap changes brought on by the rolling of orthodox teas, the cutting machines do not allow for the natural internal changes within the leaf. After cutting, the tea is quickly rolled into granular pieces and then moved to the oxidation room.

The goal of CTC production is the opposite of that behind traditionally made orthodox tea. CTC teas were created to fill the need of teabag packers, who desired tea that would be less bulky and thereby easier to use when filling teabags. Subtlety of style and flavor finesse is not the goal of CTC teas;

Table 4.2. Grades of Orthodox Indian Tea

Whole Leaf	
SFTGFOP	Special fine tippy golden flowery orange pekoe (smallest whole leaf)
FTGFOP	Fine tippy golden flowery orange pekoe (medium whole leaf)
TGFOP	Tippy golden flowery orange pekoe (medium whole leaf)
GFOP	Golden flowery orange pekoe (large whole leaf)
FOP	Flowery orange pekoe (extra-large or large whole leaf)
FP	Flowery pekoe
OP	Orange pekoe
Broken Leaf	
GFBOP	Golden flowery broken orange pekoe
GBOP	Golden broken orange pekoe
FBOP	Flowery broken orange pekoe
BOP 1	Broken orange pekoe one
BOP	Broken orange pekoe
BPS	Broken pekoe souchong

Table 4.3. Grades of CTC Tea

Broken Leaf	
FP	Flowery pekoe
PEK	Pekoe
BOP	Broken orange pekoe
BP 1	Broken pekoe one
BP	Broken pekoe
BPS	Broken pekoe souchong

rather, these teas produce a strong, gutsy, and some would say chewy cup of tea. They are less costly to produce and are now considered by some of the countries who make them to have compromised their tea industries. CTC tea cannot fetch the high price on the world tea market that orthodox tea can, so prices have fallen to a level that makes it difficult for many tea factories to support their manufacture. This overabundance of CTC tea puts many jobs at risk, as the tea factories and tea farmers cannot make the tea pay for the costs involved with bringing the leaf to market. As tea drinkers worldwide become more educated and sophisticated about what tea they choose to drink, CTC tea will be at an even greater disadvantage as demand for specialty orthodox tea increases.

CTC teas are classified as broken leaf, fannings, and dust, and are graded by particle size in each class. For example, broken-leaf CTC teas would be listed from top to bottom in order of largest to smallest particle size. Table 4.3 outlines this system.

The Russian Federation and Georgia: Chinese Tea Crosses the Steppe

In the sixteenth century, Russia explored and conquered the vast territories of Siberia. Cossack soldiers developed towns and settlements, which gave the Russians strategic trading posts for establishing and conducting trade with China and the rest of Asia. Russian soldiers and members of the Russian court would have most likely encountered tea in Siberia or Mongolia some time before official trade with China began, either from firsthand experience from a taste of the intriguing hot beverage or from the tales of those returning from afar who had experienced its potent charms. In 1618 a Russian trade mission left Tobolsk in Siberia for China. The route took them south through Mongolia, where they most likely would have been offered cups of hot tea. This beverage would have been entirely familiar to the Mongols from the former days that Kublai Khan's Yuan dynasty ruled China (1271–1368).

In 1638 a Russian envoy was sent to visit the Mongol Khan Altyn at Lake Ubsa-Nur in Mongolia. The khan is reported to have sent two hundred packages of tea back to Russia to Czar Mikhail Feodorovich Romanov, who, as it was reported, did not care for the superflous articles and would have preferred an "equivalent in sables." Direct contact with the Chinese Manchu emperor Shunzhi (r. 1644–1661) occurred in 1654 and 1658, also resulting in gifts of tea sent by China to Russian, although there are reports of some tea being sold along the way for purchases of jewels. It was not until 1689, however, when the Chinese emperor Kangxi (r. 1661–1722) and the Russia czar Alexei Mikhailovich Romanov signed the Nerchinsky Treaty, that a measurable exchange of goods and materials, including Chinese tea, began to flow between China and Russia through Mongolia and Siberia.

THE CAMEL TEA CARAVANS

The one-way, five-thousand-mile trip from China to Russia was made by the best method of the day—camel caravans consisting of as many as two hundred to three hundred animals each carrying an immense cargo of goods strapped to their backs. These "ships of the desert" would slowly parade single file across the desert thoroughfare, back and forth from Peking to Moscow, laden with all manner of luxury goods. These caravans involved thousands of men and required the support of village outposts along the way to meet their needs and disperse the goods. The route started in the Mongolian city of Kalgan, which lay just beyond China's Great Wall near Peking (today's Bejing), and wended its way to Moscow. In Kalgan, Russian representatives made their purchases of tea from the Chinese, loaded the camels with as many chests of tea and other supplies as each animal could carry, and sent the caravans on their way. These trade routes are now collectively called the Silk Road.

This long and arduous journey took sixteen months on average to complete round-trip. A major trading post for the camel caravans was established at Kiakhta, in Buryatia in southern Siberia. Here chests of tea—heady mixtures of smoky blacks and fragrant oolongs—were received and exchanged for furs, food, and other household goods. Once the tea arrived in Kiakhta, it was unpacked and sorted. Expensive leaf tea bound for the court was wrapped first in paper then in foil and carefully packed into bamboo boxes for safekeeping the remainder of the journey. Lesser-quality tea was packed into animal hides called *tsybics* and brought to the town of Irbit in western Siberia, where it was sold in local markets for disbursement across Russia. Tsybics were eventually replaced by Chinese tea bricks. These ingeniously devised compressed blocks of tea allowed each animal to carry large quantities of tea in a more compact manner and to remain impervious to changes in the weather and traveling conditions.

During the reign of Catherine the Great (r. 1763–1796), Chinese loose-leaf "camel caravan tea" became a necessary luxury at court and for the privileged few. In 1783, the empress gave a gift of tea to Georgia's King Irakli II, although it is most likely that the Georgian court was already familiar with tea, acquired from Turkish traders who bartered Mongolian goods with the Georgians or from Persian traders in Iran. Many of these goods arrived from China, coming by way of camel caravans that roamed across Mongolia, Kazakhstan, Uzbekistan, Turkmenistan, Iran, Azerbaijan, Armenia, and finally reaching Georgia.

TEA CULTIVATED IN GEORGIA

As Russia needed more supplies of tea in the mid-nineteenth century to satisfy the growing appetite for the beverage, agriculturally rich Georgia became the prime site. The western edge of Georgia forms a crescent-shaped shoreline along the Black Sea. Here, as one travels from north to south, the temperate climate becomes almost languid. Against a backdrop of gently rolling hills, this location creates a bountiful agricultural oasis. The first experimental tea gardens were started in Sokhumi in 1847. Success with these gardens led in 1893 to commercial cultivation at Sokhumi and later more gardens along the southern coast of Georgia near Bat'umi, not far from the Turkish border.

The late nineteenth century also brought an increased supply of low-grade tea from China. This change started to occur in 1886, when China began to allow foreign countries to own or lease property and conduct business in certain port or "concession" areas. In the port city of Hankow, located about five hundred miles up the Yangtze River in Hubei Province, the countries of England, France, Germany, Japan, and Russia were granted concession rights. China had previously never allowed foreign operations to establish settlements in ports. Hankow controlled the distribution of tea produced in southern China as well as the production of most of the tea bricks going to Russia. Under the terms of the concession, however, Russian tea companies were able to produce tea bricks in Hankow, significantly reducing the cost of the tea. This extra production at a lower cost allowed many average Russians the opportunity to find warmth and comfort in a daily glass of hot, stimulating tea.

Another change was soon to take place that would alter the Russian supply of tea, as well. Construction for the Trans-Siberian Railway was started in 1891 and completed in 1916, which connected Moscow to Vladivostik via southern Siberia. This brought Russia into the modern age, ending the era of the camel tea caravans. By the time of their disappearance, camels making the trek each year had been estimated to reach ten thousand. Rail shipments of tea could now reach Moscow in a matter of weeks by rail, increasing supply and decreasing prices, which in turn helped incorporate tea drinking into the lives of all Russians.

Obstacles to tea production. Tea continues to be grown in Georgia today. However, war, political instability, and revolution created paralyzing obstacles to tea production in the twentieth century. The Georgian tea industry was decimated by skirmishes during World War I. Ramifications from the February and October Russian revolution (1917), the Russian civil war (1918–1920), and the great famine of 1921 all conspired to reduce tea production to a trickle. The tea industry built itself up again and achieved its greatest point in the mid-1940s, when production reached an output of fifty thousand tons per year from 138 state-owned factories. Internal turmoil developed again when independence was gained from Russia in 1991. The collapse of the Soviet Union left the tea industry without direction, and it is still floundering to regain its place. In 2003 then-president of Georgia Eduard Shevardnadze initiated government-funded programs to rehabilitate the tea plantations and rejuvenate the plantings.

Georgian tea comes from both state-owned and private tea plantations. The private sector is comprised of family-operated village tea producers who are dedicated to returning to producing good-quality tea. Georgia now produces a mere five thousand tons of tea a year, a portion of which is consumed locally and the balance is sold to the Russian Federation, to other countries of the CIS, such as Armenia, Belarus, Kyrgystan, Siberia, and Ukraine, and a small amount to English tea blenders. It is necessary for producers to sell their tea for its cash value even while Georgia must supplement its own tea needs with tea from other places.

For Georgian tea to remain a viable player in the tea market, the growers and producers have realized that they need to upgrade the quality. Their goal is to return Georgian tea to the quality, hand-plucked, orthodox leaf of former days and to be able to stop producing the machine-picked, mass-produced, low-quality CTC tea that they were encouraged to grow during Soviet times. As a consequence of these former practices, the price of Georgian tea is now extremely low. The current ample availability of other low-priced tea in the global marketplace represents a twist from twenty years ago, when Georgia was on top of its game and many new producers had not yet come on line.

Compressed tea bricks. The tea brick (*plitochnyi chai*) business in Georgia is thriving, however. Tonus Limited in the Guria region produces four quality grades of tea bricks, in both black and green tea varieties. The old Chakvi Tea Press Factory, which began pressing tea bricks in 1932 under the direction of the minister of agriculture, is also having a renewal in business. The factory employs 130 people and presses two quality-grade types of green tea bricks. The tea is purchased from five farms, of which 60 percent are privately owned and 40 percent are state owned. The factory hopes to purchase an additional four hundred brick forms to add to their assembly line process.

Recently the Chakvi factory has had to change the design on the back of the tea brick to distinguish the Georgian original from counterfeit tea bricks being peddled by the Chinese in Mongolia. Threats from competition aside, the front of the tea bricks still bears the impression of the hammer and sickle emblem. Just over 50 percent of the Chakvi brick production goes to the Russian Federation and other CIS countries. The remaining tea is earmarked for Mongolia. Sales of this crude, cheap-quality tea move especially briskly in Buriatia, in southern Siberia in the vicinity of Lake Baikal, where Buriat families still prepare tea in traditional ways. Once a nomadic people who migrated to Siberia from Mongolia, they make *Nogoon sai/zelenyi chai* from green brick tea and milk, to which a pinch of salt and some melted butter is added. *Zuttaraan sai* is made from black loose tea or green brick tea, which has been boiled in water and added to a paste of wheat flour that has been fried in mutton and lightly salted. Ironically, despite all of the ups and downs in the tea trade, most Georgians prefer to drink strong Turkish-style coffee.

Taiwan: A Small Country Famous for Tea

Across the Formosa Strait from Fujian Province, China, lies the island of Taiwan, a mere speck of land anchored in the South China Sea. Once named Ilha Formosa by Portuguese traders, the Chinese renamed the island Taiwan in the nineteenth century. Taiwan is 235 miles long and 90 miles wide, about twice the size of New Jersey. Although it is dwarfed in size by Mainland China, it is a power-producer of fine, mountain-grown oolong tea. Taiwan's modern tea industry is relatively new, however. The first exports of tea occurred in 1865, during the Qing dynasty (1644–1911). Taiwan's tea industry was sparked by an exodus of Chinese immigrants to the island from Fujian in the mid-1850s. These migrants brought tea-growing and tea-processing skills with them, as well as tea seeds and tea bush cuttings. It is estimated that by the end of the nineteenth century, close to two million former residents of Fujian had made the trip to Taiwan.

Linguistically speaking, Taiwan's aboriginal inhabitants are not of Chinese descent; rather, they are considered to be of Polynesian background, belonging to the Austronesian language family. Eleven aboriginal tribes still maintain viable populations there, and for members of these tribes tea cultivation and production is a traditional livelihood. Prior to the arrival of the first Fujianese Chinese, these native Taiwanese people cultivated tea from wild-growing tea trees found in the protected high reaches of the mountains. Under Dutch rule, from 1624 to 1662, the Dutch began to relocate Fujian Chinese citizens from China to Taiwan to work as laborers. Many of these Fujianese had experience in the tea trade, and they taught the native aboriginal people Chinese methods of tea cultivation by establishing tea gardens in various locations in the interior mountainous parts of the island with tea bush cuttings that they brought with them from China. After the

Chinese expelled the Dutch from Taiwan in the mid-seventeenth century, Fujianese continued to relocate to Taiwan. Since then, the special nature of Taiwan teas is reflective not just of the geography and climate of the island but also of the unique history of the people involved in developing these fragrant and distinctive teas. The result has been the development of a vibrant tea industry that supports and is maintained by close to six thousand small family-owned tea farms and is world renowned for excellence.

The terrain and climate of Taiwan has proved to be conducive to the growing of high-quality tea. Two-thirds of the island is covered with forested mountains, and a subtropical climate brings summer rains to the southern part of the island and winter rains to the north. The expansion of tea into Taiwan proved to be a profitable venture. In the 1860s Taiwan's tea exports accounted for less than 10 percent of their total export sales, but by the 1890s that amount had increased to almost 65 percent.

During the Japanese occupation of Taiwan some green tea was produced for export to Japan at the end of the first Chinese-Japanese War in 1895. When the Chinese regained control of Taiwan after Japan's defeat at the end of World War II, the green tea industry's export trade remained. Today, Taiwan produces and exports a small quantity of sencha-style green tea to Japan, to cover demand in iced-tea beverages and bottled tea drinks. During the 1970s and 1980s members of the tea farmers associations, tea manufacturers associations, and tea scholars joined forces with the Taiwan Provincial Government's Department of Agriculture and Forestry to develop teahouses throughout the island devoted to the promotion of tea culture.

The Taiwanese take tea so seriously that government business, such as banks and civic offices, serve tea to customers waiting in line. The Taiwanese prefer to drink oolong tea hot, but they also love iced-tea beverages. It is reported that the Taiwanese have concocted more than a hundred different iced-tea flavors. One such modern-day creation is Bubble Tea—a sweet, vividly colored cold beverage concoction of tea, fruit, and tapioca pearls that is slurped through an oversized straw.

Taiwan exports approximately 60 to 70 percent of its annual tea production, and the rest is consumed locally. In recent years demand for high-quality leaf has refocused Taiwan's tea production to emphasize the manufacture of traditional, high-quality, mountain-grown oolong teas that are unique to Taiwan. Although Taiwan produces a small amount of both black tea for local consumption and green tea for export, Taiwan is famous for light, refreshing, and fragrant oolong teas that are distinctively different from those produced in Mainland China.

TAIWAN'S TEA-GROWING REGIONS

Taiwan has three distinct tea-growing regions—north, central, and southern—with the heaviest concentration of tea gardens in the center of the island. Seven prime tea-producing areas dot the landscape, and favorable weather allows for five plucking seasons—spring, summer, second summer, fall, and winter. Winter temperatures hover around 65°F (18°C), providing nearly year-round picking opportunity and year-round sales of these village-made teas.

Each of Taiwan's oolong teas has very different flavor characteristics, color in the cup, and identifiable leaf shape. Some of these teas are rolled into tight balls; others are loosely rolled into a half-ball. Some are lightly withered, brownish, and curled; others are very dark in color, long, and slightly twisted. The main characteristic of Taiwanese oolongs is a tendency to go toward the "greener" side of oolong manufacture; their oxidation levels are lower than that of neighboring Fujian Province, ranging from just 10 percent to 40 percent. This gives the teas a lighter, deliciously drinkable style and slightly woodsy flavor and peachy aroma.

The Taiwan Tea Research and Extension Station has provided farmers with many clonal varieties of tea bushes developed from the Ti Kuan Yin and Shuixian cultivars brought from the mainland by Chinese immigrants. Such new varieties as Qing Xing, Jin Xuan, and Sijichun focus on vigor and hardiness, pest and disease resistance, and weather tolerance.

TAIWAN'S FAMOUS TEAS

Approximately fifty thousand acres of land is planted with tea throughout the island. The mountainous Wenshan area of Taipei county lies east of Taiwan's most populated city, Taipei City. This region is home to Baozhong or WenShen Baochong oolong tea, which is produced in the townships of Pinglin, Shidin, and Hsintien. In Mujha and Shihmen townships Tie Guan Yin tea is a regional production that resembles Taiwan's most famous oolong, Tung Ting. Sansia Longjing tea is a flat-leafed specialty tea from the Sansia district of Taipei county. Many tea farms are located close to Taipei City, and the Taipei City Tie Guan Yin Baozhong Tea Research and Promotion

Center can help visitors tour some of the surrounding tea gardens and local teahouses. In Pinglin, the center of the Baochong production, the Taiwan Pinglin Tea Industry Museum offers visitors a full tea education. Not far from the museum, small tea factories line the road, scenting the air of the surrounding countryside with the aromas of freshly dried tea. For the most intrepid tea enthusiasts, a visit to the Taoyuan Tea Experimental Station in Yangmei district provides opportunity to find out about the latest advances in tea cultivation, processing, and plant breeding.

In the central region of Taiwan, in Nantou county, the area surrounding Luku and Jhushan townships is forested and heartrendingly beautiful. This area of rolling foothills is adjacent to the central mountain range and natural recreation areas, such as the Fenghuang Valley Bird Park and the Hsitou Bamboo Forest, which offer respite to people as well as birds and animals and is a natural ecosystem that benefits the tea. This is serious tea country, and by government accounts Nantou county claims one-third of Taiwan's 44,447 acres of tea gardens and is home to the fragrant Tung Ting oolongs.

Tung Ting oolong. Approximately twelve thousand residents of a total population of twenty thousand are tea farmers. An earthquake in 1999 wreaked serious havoc on this region, but out of the ashes of that disaster the Luku Farmers Association Tea Culture Museum was erected. Now, this town holds an annual tea festival in the spring, celebrating Tung Ting, their most prized product.

This specialty of central Taiwan is oxidized between 15 and 25 percent and has an elegant, earthy flavor, which is the result of a more prolonged roasting than that given to Baozhong oolongs in the north. Central and southern oolong teas are ball-rolled, which results in leaves that are tightly rolled into irregularly shaped balls. This shape, along with a lustrous green-gray color, gives Tung Ting a distinctive appearance. Spring-plucked Tung Ting has a fine, full flavor; winter plucked has a light, fruity flavor. These teas brew clear yellow in color, sometimes tinged with a bit of green.

Once a year the county tea farmers participate in an annual tea-tasting competition. Farmers submit samples of their fresh tea. The grand champion tea usually fetches close to $2,000 for a "chin" (1.25 pounds) of the winning tea. First-place winners can expect to receive $400 to $800 a chin for their winners. A small quantity of black tea called Sun Moon Lake Black Tea is also produced in Nantou county in the Puli and Yuchih townships.

Tung Ting Mountain, which translates as "frozen peak," has an elevation ranging from 1,900 to 2,624 feet. The summit is often enshrouded in clouds and mist, providing the perfect nurturing environment for the cultivation of tea in elevations. Tung Ting was first planted here in the latter part of the Qing dynasty from twelve plants brought from Fujian, China, which were then propagated to establish the first tea gardens. Tung Ting oolong tea producers pride themselves on the quality, not quantity, of their production.

Jin Xuan oolong. In addition to Tung Ting, Luku village also produces oolong tea called Jin Xuan, which is made in either leaf or ball style. Jin Xuan oolongs are mild and naturally sweet tasting, with light, honey-colored infusions. These teas are manufactured from a modern clonal variety of tea bush.

Tianhe oolong. To the west of Nantou county, the East Rift valley in Hualien county is known for Tianhe oolong, a high-end oolong with a distinctive flavor and aroma that is popular with Taiwanese tea connoisseurs.

Fulu oolong. In this remote area tea farming is demanding work. For tea farmers life is hard, but they are dedicated to the tea that has always fulfilled their lives. The southernmost tea grown in Taiwan is Fulu tea from Luye township in Taitung county. Fulu tea is not produced in large quantities, but it is of excellent quality and features some characteristics of both Wenshan Baozhong and Tung Ting oolong teas.

Baozhong or WenShen Paochong oolong. Baozhong is the least oxidized of the Taiwan oolongs; it is given just a 10 to 15 percent oxidation and minimal panning, rolling, and roasting. Its amber-colored leaves are long, twisted, and slightly curled. The tea liquor infuses to a delicate, pale golden color, which locals say is the clear color of a full moon. High-grown Baozhong acquires a creamy, rich flavor, with virtually no astringency and a delicate, flowery aroma.

Bai Hao oolong (Oriental Beauty or White Tip oolong). The best Bai Hao oolong is produced from summer to late-summer leaf that is plucked between July and October. Oriental Beauty has a very distinguishing story and character. The leaves of these tea bushes are home to a little parasitic leaf hopper that feeds on the leaves and discolors the edges. Farmers wait until these little insects are well established on the tea bushes before picking the leaves. The chomping begins an enzymatic process in the leaves that is essential to developing the character of this tea. When these leaves are picked and dried, the chomped edges of the leaves turn white, contrasting like strands of white hair against the darker areas of the leaf. The more tips the tea has, the better the quality. Most Oriental Beauty is oxidized 35 to 40 percent and has a lovely honey, peachy flavor. This tea was developed in Taiwan right after World War II and is sometimes marketed to the West as Champagne oolong, while in Taiwan it is sometimes called Pingfang tea. It is grown in the north, in Bepu and Emei in Hsinchu county and in Toufen in Maioli county.

Alishan oolongs. In Chiayi county the Alishan Mountains are home to the famous peaks in southern Taiwan, where these acclaimed oolong teas are made. Alishan is a place of inspiration and contemplation to the Taiwanese, and it features the nourishing clouds and mist phenomenon so valuable to high-grown tea. Alishan produces oolongs that grow above 7,200 feet, the highest altitudes of any tea in Taiwan. These leaves mature slowly in the thin air and only grow at a rate that allows them to be plucked twice a year. Alishan oolongs are big in size and chewy in style—it is not uncommon for the tea to be made from a series of bud and four or five leaves. Most Alishan oolongs are given a light oxidization to underscore, not overwhelm, the naturally sweet, delicate flavor of the leaves. Local tea producers sing the praises of Gold Lily oolong, which is also known as Jin Xuan, so named for the tea cultivar it is made from.

Ti Kuan Yin. Taiwanese Tie Guan Yin teas are a large, somewhat loose semiball-shaped teas, which are made in the northern part of the island in Mutza and Shimen townships. The oxidation is 35 to 40 percent, which produces a

TEA–TASTING COMPETITIONS

On December 6, 2005, an important national tea tasting and tea auction was conducted in Taipei City. In this competition, for the first time, all of the regional winners of local tea-tasting competitions in Taiwan in 2005 were able to compete against each other in a national contest. Fifty top growers were evaluated in the first tasting round, and from these twenty-five teas were selected to compete in the finals. Seven judges officiated the final tasting, and points were scored on three criteria: appearance of the dry leaf, color of the tea, and aroma and taste of the tea.

The winning tea—an oolong grown by Lin Mei-mei of Taiping village in Meishan township, Chiayi county—fetched a whopping $14,400 for slightly more than one pound of leaf. Although this is an astronomical sum of money, it proves what we tell our customers all the time—that even in China and Taiwan the best teas are costly. The only cheap tea in China is just that, cheap tea.

slightly red color in the cup. The aroma of these teas is distinctive, floral, and sweet, and the flavor is earthy, hearty, and slightly woodsy. Taiwan Tie Guan Yin is produced from clonal varieties of the Tie Guan Yin bushes originally brought from Fujian Province.

Sri Lanka: Small in Size but Mighty in Tea Production

The tropical island paradise of Sri Lanka lies fifty-five miles off the southern tip of neighboring India and has the perfect climate and soil conditions for cultivating tea. Despite its small size—271 miles long and 137 miles wide, roughly the size of West Virginia—Sri Lanka is one of the world's leading tea exporters and the third-largest tea producer. This is an amazing accomplishment, considering how much larger the tea-producing landmass giants India and China are in comparison. The splendid weather and perfect growing conditions in the densely planted tea-growing areas of central Sri Lanka allow for intensive, nearly year-round harvesting.

Thirty-eight subdistricts in six regions of varying sizes located in Sri Lanka's center employ more than a million workers who are responsible for bringing the country's tea to market. The tea industry is the largest employer in Sri Lanka, and most tea workers are Indian Tamils from southern Sri Lanka who are descendants of plantation workers originally brought from southern India by the British in the nineteenth century. Large tea plantations management companies such as Bogawantalawa Plantations and Agalawatte Plantations oversee the management of numerous tea estates. These tea estates are comprised of many smaller tea gardens; the tea is sold under the estate or garden name, and in many cases each garden will produce numerous teas of differing styles each season.

Approximately 650 tea estates covering 481,855 acres of land produce all of Sri Lanka's tea. Large tea estates may have several tea factories to process all of their own tea. There are reported to be just more than two thousand different garden marks for Ceylon teas. Much of Sri Lanka's tea is sold as simple blends and marked 100 percent pure Ceylon tea, which contrasts with the tea that has specific garden marks to signify origin and place. Ceylon tea is found in the marketplace in various ways. The following list, from the most general tea to the most specific, provides some examples:

- Ceylon tea blends: 100 percent pure Ceylon tea.
- Region-specific teas: Dimbula or Nuwara Eliya tea.
- Estate-specific tea: Labookellie Estate Tea.
- Garden-specific estate teas: Bogawantalawa Estate, Loinorn Garden.

Ceylon tea is often hailed as the world's best fruity black tea. It is renowned for its briskness of flavor and clarity in the cup. Sri Lanka excels in the production of fine black tea, and produces only a small amount of green tea. In this tropical, verdant paradise, the mist-shrouded mountains, dense jungles, and deep ravines of Sri Lanka's central highlands provide the perfect combination of high altitude, plentiful rains, and brilliant sunshine, which yields the best leaf. Ceylon teas have distinctive personalities—a rich, brisk taste and a bright golden to rosy red color. Rainfall from the annual monsoons drench the island with forty-five to seventy inches of rainfall a year, providing a sound watering for the island's lush green carpet of tea bushes that blanket both the central highlands and the southern lowlands.

Although tea is grown from the edges of the southern coast near Galle up into the central highlands, the famous Ceylon teas grow in the highlands. Tea is the main agricultural livelihood on the island, and land is planted extensively. Despite Sri Lanka's diminutive size, it has vastly changing growing conditions, varying elevations, and changing weather, all of which affect the tea's taste. Differences in geographic location result in varying soil composition, while the amounts of sun, rain, and wind, and the effects of altitude all conspire to impart singular nuance of flavor and style to the cup. These differences work together to create specific terroir. Crosswinds that blow across the island regulate dryness and humidity, creating a microclimate that is unlike anywhere else on earth. The five highest mountains in Sri Lanka are all located in the high-elevation tea-growing regions, as are more than a hundred waterfalls that sparkle throughout the landscape.

SIX DISTINCT GROWING REGIONS

The six tea-growing regions in Sri Lanka—Dimbula, Kandy, Nuwara Eliya, Ruhuna, Uda Pussellawa, and Uva—are broadly located in six different elevations. The geography of each region is unique, and local microclimates conspire to affect the flavor characteristics and body of the specific teas. Although each tea has the brisk, fruity flavor and clean style that we have come to expect from a Ceylon tea, it also possesses distinctive characters that are a reflection of each one's particular terroir. Whether one is looking for specialty grade tea designated by a single garden or valley, or the popular full-bodied Ceylon blends that deliver satisfying flavor, body, and style, Ceylon teas are known as "the cup that cheers."

As is the case with most tea, the finest tea grows in cool, misty reaches high in the mountains, where thinner air slows the leaf's maturation and growth. Sri Lanka's high-grown tea is perfectly located to maximize the local wind patterns, which bring dry and cool breezes across the island. Ceylon tea is cultivated at three altitudes and is broadly classified as a high-grown tea, a mid-level tea, or a low-grown tea (see below for more on each classification). Whether someone is looking for a stylish self-drinking single-estate beauty, a flavorful mid-level tea for economy, or a low-grown tea for adding strength to a blend, Ceylon tea offers a flavor that is unlike any other and is always in demand.

ORTHODOX TEAS ARE THE FOCUS

Sri Lanka primarily produces orthodox black tea, which is sold as self-drinking tea from single estates, or it is used to contribute style and polish to English-style black tea blends. It is the most expensive tea to produce and is the type of tea that connoisseurs treasure. Ceylon teas are fruity and brisk, thus differing from the flowery teas of Darjeeling or the more astringent and robust teas of Assam. They are thirst-quenching either hot or iced and carry other flavors well. Many fruit-flavored teas (such as lemon, mint, raspberry, and red currant) use flavorful Ceylon tea as a base.

This style of brisk, flavory tea brought Ceylon teas much acclaim during the British colonial days. But the Sri Lanka Tea Board decided to change its production methods in 1994 and to offer incentives to tea factories that were willing to turn production over from orthodox leaf manufacture to CTC manufacture. The idea was to allow Sri Lanka to compete with the tea factories in Indian, Kenya, and Malawi for a market share in CTC tea production. These teas are cheaper to produce and less distinguished in flavor, but there is a huge market for them with commercial tea packers and blenders, who use them to strengthen and fortify tea blends for use in teabags or iced-tea blends.

The scheme was a giant failure. The temporary retreat from traditional orthodox tea production cost Sri Lanka both in tea sales and in world-class status as a producer of luxury tea. This temporary exclusive focus on CTC production removed the romance and glory from Ceylon tea, so the decision was made to convert back to the old ways of orthodox tea production. Today the emphasis is again on quality and leaf style, and although a small amount of CTC is still made there, Sri Lanka has regained its former stature in the world tea market by renewing its commitment to quality flowery, flavorful orthodox tea.

HOT, TROPICAL MICROCLIMATES RESULT IN ABUNDANT LEAF

Sri Lanka is unique among tea-producing countries in that tea is picked and processed year-round. Because of the tropical climate and the monsoon seasons, tea bushes do not have a dormant season; rather, they flush with tender new leaves all year long. This constant plucking means that Ceylon teas do not have a first- or second-flush designation assigned to them. The bushes are forced to rest every four years, by heavy pruning that cuts each plant back to just a few inches above the soil. Within five months of this hard pruning, the bushes will have regrown and begun to leaf out again, and plucking thus resumes. The height of the bush is then kept stable by plucking the bushes to table height.

Sri Lanka's tea bushes are propagated from mother tea bushes that supply close to a thousand cuttings a year. New clonal varieties of tea plants are being introduced by the Sri Lanka Tea Research Institute to increase yield and hardiness. Because of the reliably favorable weather across the island, tea bushes generally flush with their first usable leaves by the third growing season. The average life of tea bushes is longer in the highlands than in the lowlands: approximately fifty years versus thirty-five years.

Ceylon tea grows in a quadrant of the island that is known as the Wet Zone. Although tea is picked year-round (except during the height of the monsoon season), the quality varies from month to month. In some tea areas at certain times of the year, such as Uva and Dimbula, the unique microclimate brings a complex set of factors—mainly temperature, moisture, and winds—to bear on the tea. This results in tea with special style and flavor characters. Known as "seasonal quality" teas, these teas possess clear, light liquor in the cup and brisk, bright flavors. Some areas do not experience the weather changes that bring a seasonal quality period, but they still produce outstanding teas. Sri Lanka's central mountain range divides the country into two distinct climate seasons, resulting in a dry season and a monsoon season on each side of the island. As the monsoons occur during different times of the year, the monsoon season in one area sets up optimal weather conditions on the opposite side of the island.

REGIONS OF HIGH-GROWN TEAS

High-grown tea is found at elevations of 4,000 to 6,500 feet and comprises approximately 25 percent of the harvest. These teas are the finest that Sri Lanka produces—leafy, stylish teas that have distinct personalities, golden color, fragrant aromas, and brisk full-bodied flavor. The perfect conditions found at these elevations provide the right environment for the bushes to grow more slowly, concentrating the flavor in fewer rather than more shoots.

West Highlands. Dimbula is perhaps the most famous of Sri Lanka's tea regions. Here, in the western part of the central highlands, tea grows at 3,500 to 5,000 feet. Influenced by its rich tropical soil, Dimbula tea has a strong, distinctive personality. Lush rainforest, dense jungles, and breathtaking waterfalls surround many of these gardens, adding contrast to the rich green tapestry of tea bushes covering the hillsides and valleys. These gardens are perfectly situated to take advantage of the changing wind patterns that blow over the island, which bring both much needed sun and rain to the bushes.

The best Dimbulas are picked in the dry season of January, February, and March. During these months, while the annual northeast monsoon is drenching the northern and eastern side of the island with rain, Dimbula and the rest of the western side are blessed with cool, clear days and bright sunshine. These aromatic teas have long thin leaves and a fine, clear, and bright character in the cup, with strong, distinctive aromas and rich full-bodied flavors. Dimbula is comprised of eight subdistricts: Agarapatana, Bogawantalawa, Hatton/Dickoya, Nanu Oya/Lindula/Talawakelle, Patana/Kotagala, Punduloya, Ramboda, and Upcot/Maskeliya. Each of these subdistricts features unique microclimates among the blanketing hills and lush valleys that coddle the bushes while adding distinction to the tea leaves. Look for Dimbula tea from the following gardens: Bogahawatte, Bogawantalawa,

Diyagama, Kenilworth, Kew, Kirkoswald, Loinorn, Nadoototen, Norwood, Pettiagalla, Somerset, St. Clair, and Strathspey.

Central Highlands. Nuwara Eliya teas grow at over 6,000 feet, the highest elevation for Ceylon teas. Nuwara Eliya lies at the foot of Pidurutalagala (8,280 feet), the highest mountain in Sri Lanka. The area is a high plateau ringed by hills and mountains. Nuwara Eliya teas yield a light, mellow cup that is exquisitely floral, redolent of apricots and peaches, and golden in color. They vie with Darjeeling tea as being some of the most exquisite in the world. Here, in misty mountain valleys, the best tea is plucked from gardens that are laid out in patchwork patterns of undulating rows, interspersed with shade trees. The scent of wild mint, eucalyptus, and cypress trees waft in the air across the landscape. In many places the incline of the hills pitches on a precipitous gradient, yet the tea pickers rarely seem bothered by these steep inclines.

Like Dimbulas, the best Nuwara Eliya teas are picked in the cooler, dry seasonal quality months of January, February, and March. On the road from Kandy to Nuwara Eliya the Labookellie tea factory offers tourists the opportunity to observe tea processing firsthand. Look for estate tea from these Nuwara Eliya gardens: Court Lodge, Delmar, Inverness, Kenmare, Mackwoods/Labookellie, Mahagastotte/Lover's Leap, Pedro, Tommagong, and Wataalia.

Eastern Highlands. Uva region stretches from 2,800 to 6,000 feet in elevation. Uva teas grow on the easternmost slopes of the central mountains and are known for their pronounced, concentrated flavor, coppery red color, and distinctive mellow aroma. The Uva district seasonal quality period is June through September, yielding a much anticipated summer crop. During this time as the southwest monsoons impact the island's southern and western regions, a hot wind called the Cachan blows down from the northeast into Uva and Uda Pussellawa. The tea bushes respond to this hot, dry air by closing up their leaves, literally turning inward against the merciless wind. This response is as if they were faced with a drought, so the bushes initiate a chemical change within the cells of the leaves to replace lost moisture.

As a result of this harsh weather, which can last for six to eight weeks, Uva teas are especially flavorful during this time and thus command high prices. Uva has eight subdistricts located at various elevations: Bandarawela/Poonagala, Demodera/Hali-Ela/Badulla, Ella/Namunukula, Haputale, Koslanda/Haldummulla, Madulsima, Malwatte/Welimada, and Passara/

Lunugala. Look for teas from these Uva gardens: Ambagasdowa, Dyraaba, Koslanda, Pettiagalla, Rooketanne, and St. James.

Uda Pussellawa. This small region in the eastern part of Sri Lanka lies north of Uva and east of Nuwara Eliya. Uda Pussellawa experiences the dry Cachan winds from July to September, which bring the best-quality tea season and rosy, thirst-quenching tea. In the westernmost parts of Uda Pussellawa the tea gardens are somewhat protected from the worst of the December-to-March monsoons, allowing Uda Pussellawa to produce seasonal quality teas from January to March, which coincides with the seasonal quality periods in Nuwara Eliya and Dimbula. This tea is less flavorful than the summer pluckings but is still bright and brisk in the cup. Uda Pussellawa has two main subdistricts: Maturata and Ragala/Halgranoya.

REGIONS OF MID-LEVEL TEAS

Mid-level teas grow at 2,500 to 4,000 feet and account for 16 percent of the annual harvest. Mid-level teas are rich and mouth-filling, with good flavor and a clear, pleasing reddish-gold color.

Central Highlands. Kandy is located not too far from Polonnaruwa, the ancient capital of Ceylon. Scottish planter James Taylor started some of the first tea gardens in this area in 1867. Here tea shares the land with cinnamon and cacao production. Since the mid-1990s, however, tea production has declined in parts of this region as soil erosion problems have led to reduced productivity. Kandy teas are substantial and strong in flavor and have dark, large, full leaves. Ceylon tea blends often rely on Kandy teas to boost the strength and contribute depth to the flavor. Many Kandy estates produce fine-leaf world-class teas with exceptional fragrance and complex flavors.

In Hantane, a few miles from Kandy, the Ceylon Tea Museum opened in January 2002, not too far from the Peradeniya Botanical Gardens. Visitors to Sri Lanka who are interested in learning more about the tea will find these two places worth a visit. Kandy is the largest of the regions and contains many subdistricts, although the two most notable ones are Matale and Pussellawa/Hewaheta. Look for seasonal quality tea in February and March from the following gardens: Adawatte, Blairmond, Hellbodde, Kenilworth, Loolecondera, Melfort, and St. James.

REGIONS OF LOW-GROWN TEAS

Low-grown teas are found mostly in the southern region, from sea level to 2,500 feet, but these teas comprise the largest share of Sri Lanka's total production, at 55 percent. Low-grown teas are the fastest growing, producing an abundance of large leaves at the expense of concentrated flavor.

The southern coast and Rhunua tea. Ruhuna teas from Sri Lanka's southwestern region thrive in fertile soils and warm, humid temperatures. From Galle to Ratnapura tea grows easily, and growers excel in producing large, leafy, sometimes very tippy teas. Particular soil conditions yield a dark, nearly black leaf, and many of the southern teas have nice, well-proportioned leaves. But without the flavor-enhancing benefit of cooling breezes from high-altitude locales, these teas lack finesse, briskness, and distinct clarity of flavor. The largest market for Ruhuna tea is Russia and the Middle East, where tea drinkers seek the punch of a full-bodied, strong flavored tea to drink alone, and the European market, where small amounts of these are added to Ceylon tea blends for strength.

Ruhuna has four main subdistricts: Deniyaya, Galle, Matara, and Ratnapura/Balangoda. Look for tea from the following gardens: Berubeula, Ceycilian, Dellawa, Galaboda, and Uruwela.

TEA REPLACES COFFEE AS SRI LANKA'S MAIN CROP

Tea became a major crop in Sri Lanka only at the end of the nineteenth century. Tea is not indigenous to Sri Lanka; it was brought to the island by the enterprising English. The tea crop later came to prominence when a series of disastrous coffee blights starting in 1869 infected Ceylon's prosperous coffee crop, subsequently destroying the coffee trees. The disease *Hemileia vastatrix* afflicted the underside of the leaves of the coffee trees with orange blotches. Tea cultivation allowed Ceylon's coffee planters to begin rebuilding their devastated economy. First the Portuguese, then the Dutch, and finally the English held sway over the fortunes of this island formerly known as Ceylon. Primarily trading for cinnamon, cacao, exotic woods, and gemstones, these Western traders left their mark on Sri Lanka.

Beginning with the Portuguese invasion in 1505, Ceylon passed over to Dutch rule in 1658, then to partial British rule in 1796, and ultimately to complete British rule by 1802. At this time local people had been growing coffee on the island for at least a hundred years. Large and small coffee gardens populated the island. Realizing the cash potential this crop could have in this lush paradise, the English cleared land in the virgin jungle in record numbers between 1830 and 1845; they developed new coffee plantations in Dimbula, Kandy, and Nuwara Eliya.

But the English also brought tea and their social customs of drinking tea with them to Ceylon. The Dutch, who had been instrumental in the establishment of tea throughout Indonesia and Taiwan, had tried to cultivate tea in Ceylon, but their experiments had failed. The English introduced the local Singhalese to the daily ritual of tea drinking. The Ceylon ruling class, desirous to retain their former elite status with the new rulers, quickly began to win favor with the English by emulating proper English ways. They adopted the quirks of the English lifestyle, including the social rituals of drinking tea by observing morning and afternoon teatime.

Tea seed was imported from China in 1824 and from Assam in 1839 for experimental purposes and grown in the Botanical Gardens of Peradeniya and Nuwara Eliya on an experimental basis. It was not until the 1860s, however, when Solomon and Gabriel de Worms planted some China tea seed in Labookellie Garden in the Nuwara Eliya district and Scotsman James Taylor experimented with Assam tea seed on Loolecondera Garden in the Hewaheta district in Kandy, that the door opened for serious tea production.

Fear of even worse coffee blights resulted in the creation of many new tea estates, extending the range for tea production to Dimbula and Uda Pussellawa. In 1875 the final blow of *Hemileia vastatrix* was felt throughout the remaining coffee farms, and thousands of acres of coffee trees were ripped out of the ground. Tea gardens were planted in their place. With the entire agricultural industry in ruin, the coffee planters suffered many years of financial hardship before resurrecting their new tea industry. Perhaps the cruelest blow came when dead coffee trees were salvaged for wood and sent back to England to be turned into legs for tea tables. That year the total acreage planted with tea was 10,000 acres. Just ten years later, in 1885, 48,000 acres were under cultivation, and by 1900 the number was up to 300,000 acres. Today the total cultivated tea extent is approximately 481,855 acres.

Table 4.4. Grading System for Ceylon Teas

Orthodox Leaf Grades (90 Percent of Production)	
Silver Tips	
OP	Orange Pekoe
FBOP	Flowery Broken Orange Pekoe
BOP 1	Broken Orange Pekoe One
Pekoe	
Broken Grades (4 Percent of Production)	
BOP	Broken Orange Pekoe
BOPF	Broken Orange Pekoe Fannings (the most commonly used orthodox grade for teabag packing)
Dust 1	
FBOPF Ex. Sp.	Flowery Broken Orange Pekoe Fannings Extra Special
FBOPF1	Flowery Broken Orange Pekoe Fannings One
CTC Grades (6 Percent of Production)	
BP1	Broken Pekoe One
PF1	Pekoe Fannings One (the most commonly used CTC grade for teabag packing)

TEA PRODUCTION IN SRI LANKA

Bringing a delicious and fragrant tea to market requires a joint effort among the tea estate manager, the tea factory manager, the tea pluckers, and the factory workers. Unlike the myriad leaf configurations plucked in China, Ceylon teas are always plucked as a flush (two leaves and a bud). Tea is collected in baskets or cloth sacks that loosely contain the freshly plucked leaf. For the finest teas the baskets or sacks are never filled but emptied several times a day to avoid bruising the tea leaves under excess weight. A skilled plucker can pick nearly sixty pounds of tea a day and is usually paid on the weight of tea delivered at day's end. This quantity of plucked leaf yields approximately sixteen pounds of drinkable tea, a ratio of nearly five to one. Depending on the altitude of the tea garden, plucking is repeated in each garden every seven to fourteen days throughout the year.

As in all tea-producing countries, the plucked leaves are collected and brought to the factory to begin processing. Unlike the early teas in Ceylon, which were rolled by hand on floors and then fired over charcoal fires, today's tea is controlled by a combination of machinery and firsthand experience. Because weather conditions vary so greatly in Sri Lanka, tea managers must know how to interpret and adjust for changes in the weather to bring out the best flavor in their teas. Most tea in Sri Lanka is produced by the orthodox method. After withering the leaves, the shoots are rolled to rupture the cell walls, thus beginning the internal process of cellular change and leaf oxidation. CTC teas are cut and torn in an unorthodox manner, to achieve finely cut leaf particles.

Ceylon teas are graded by size, which makes it easy for tea buyers to ascertain a particular leaf size and style of tea. Grading is not necessarily an indication of quality. Ceylon teas are also marketed by region and district, as blends or estate-specific teas. All genuine Ceylon tea carries the logo of the Sri Lanka Tea Board, which is the stamp mark of a stylized lion holding a sword.

Indonesia: Java, Sumatra, and Sulawesi

Once known as the Dutch East Indies, the Indonesian islands of Java, Sumatra, and Sulawesi are part of the Malay Archipelago. Indonesia is comprised of more than 14,000 islands scattered over a distance of 3,100 miles. Indonesia supports numerous peoples, languages, religions, and cultures, and in the diversity of its island flora and fauna, a small but thriving tea industry. Long before the English East Indies Company arrived in China seeking luxurious silks, porcelains, and tea, Portuguese traders in quest of caches of prized exotic pepper from the Malabar Coast in India arrived in the Molucca Islands—the fabled Spice Islands—in 1513.

Before the Portuguese, the source of cloves, cinnamon, and nutmeg was the exclusive haunt of Arab traders who, with the help of Egyptian facilitators, controlled the European market for spices through Venice. Arab traders in Venice are believed to have introduced pre-Renaissance Venetians to tea in the sixteenth century. Throughout the fifteenth and sixteenth centuries such opulent goods as spices, silks, carpets, majolica, glassware, and lacquer began to flow into Europe across the Silk Road, not just from China but also from eastern markets in Egypt, Turkey, and Persia.

With the arrival of the Portuguese in the Molucca Islands via the route around the Cape of Good Hope, this once secret sea route was revealed. This occurrence changed the history of merchant trading in the East Indies from one of Arab dominance to one of European dominance in a few short years. The stream of Portuguese-controlled spices into Europe undercut the price the Arabs charged by more than half. The opportunity to satisfy demand for costly spices, once a precious luxury afforded only by the richest citizens, became a siren song too intoxicating for Spanish and Dutch traders to ignore. The Spanish reached Molucca in 1522, and by 1602 the Dutch, sailing as the Dutch East Indies Company, had sent four ships to the East Indies, where they formed a collection depot at Batavia on Java for collecting and packing Oriental goods headed back home. The Dutch East Indies Company (known as the VOC, or *Vereenigde Oostindische Compagnie* in Dutch) was an association of merchants that became the most ruthless player in the spice market and the eventual master of the East Indies trade in Indonesia for the next three hundred years.

The great age of trade routes and European supremacy in global trading had begun. Although the Portuguese were the first European traders to bring tea to Europe, the Dutch ultimately dominated tea imports into Europe. From their position in the Indonesian islands the Dutch began to trade with China, Japan, and Macao. They bought tea from both China and Japan and sent it to their collection point in Java. From there, the tea was sent to Amsterdam and distributed. By 1610 the Dutch were sending regular shipments of tea from Amsterdam to France, Holland, and the Baltic coast. The Dutch would keep their fierce lock on tea imports to Europe until the English overcame their position in 1669.

Record of the first tea planted on Java by the Dutch occurred in 1684, with tea seeds procured in Japan from China tea bush. Government-established tea gardens were only barely successful—the plants lived but they did not thrive—and tea cultivation in Java languished until around 1835. Perhaps inspired by the success of the British with tea in Assam, the Dutch began to explore tea cultivation on Java with a renewed degree of seriousness. Dutch tea planters eager to take up the challenge of a lucrative cash crop convinced the Dutch government to give up sole control of the tea industry. The Dutch tea planters realized, as the British did in India, that perhaps the China bush tea plants were not the right cultivar of tea bush for the soil and climate conditions the island offered. The tea planters secured tea seed from Assam bushes in India, and it did not take long for the bushes to flourish in the steamy, tropical climate.

Tea cultivation at last became successful on Java in 1878. Modern tea withering techniques were introduced, and positive reception to the tea's quality and flavor from Europeans established Java tea in a class with Ceylon and British Indian teas. The Dutch expanded tea production onto Sumatra in the early 1900s. Java is Indonesia's most important tea-producing island, followed by Sumatra and Sulawesi. Before the Japanese invasion in 1942, Indonesia had risen to become the world's fourth-largest tea producer. The strategic position of the Indonesian archipelago during World War II had a negative effect on the tea industry, and production was affected for many decades. The condition of the tea factories fell into benign neglect, and the gardens became overgrown and wild.

In the late 1980s, however, the Tea Board of Indonesia began to instigate programs to refurbish the tea gardens and infrastructure of the tea industry. This has encouraged renewed interest in the flagging tea industry, and today Indonesia proudly boasts an export production of 168,000 metric tons of tea from thirteen tea-growing provinces on Java, Sumatra, and Sulawesi.

INDONESIA'S TEA-GROWING REGIONS

Indonesia is biologically one of the richest and most complex regions on earth. On Java much of the land is dominated by mountainous interiors, where high peaks and smoking volcanoes are flanked with forest and fertile terraced fields. The shape of the island is long and slender, featuring a nearly continuous chain of mountains all the way down the middle of the island, from west to east. These mountains feature thirty-eight peaks that were at one time (or are currently) active volcanoes, such as Bromo, Kelut, Merap, and Papandayan.

The principal areas for tea production are found in the island's mountainous western regions, in the highlands outside of the cities of Bogor and Bandung. In these high elevations tea gardens benefit from close proximity to lush rain forest preserves and the region's rich volcanic soil. These forests are thick and verdant, filled with nature preserves, botanical parks, archaeological ruins, and abundant exotic bird life. During the colonial days the Dutch cultivated large tea plantations in the valleys south of Bagor. Coffee plantations were planted further south, near Sikabumi, and rubber plantations were established to the northeast, near Citereup. Southwest of Bandung, in the Pangalengan district, the Chakra Group, one of Indonesia's largest tea producers, operates four estates—Dewata, Gunung Kencana, Megawatie, and Negara Kanaan. The Dewata Tea Estate is located near the Gungung Tilu Rain Forest Preserve and the Perhutani Forest and is typical of the tea plantation communities developed by the Europeans in the nineteenth century.

The dry climate in Indonesia encourages year-round plucking, but the best tea is harvested from July through September at elevations from 2,500 to over 5,000 feet. The finest Indonesian tea is produced by orthodox manufacture, although a large quantity of CTC tea is also produced to meet the needs of teabag packers. Some of the best Indonesian teas are compared in flavor and style to high-grown Ceylon teas for their tasteful finesse and rosy flavors. Lesser amounts of undistinguished green tea are produced. Tea accounts for approximately 17 percent of Indonesia's agricultural production.

Tea auctions are held every week in Jakarta on Java. Although Indonesian teas are not easy to find, tea enthusiasts should seek out orthodox black leaf from these estates in Java (Cibuni, Cisaruni, Kertasarie, Santosa, Taloon, Tjidadap, and Tjubuni) and Sumatra (Bah Butong, Gunong Dempo, and Gunong Rosa).

Nepal: Tea from a Himalayan Kingdom

The eastern border of this Himalayan kingdom lies very close to the Darjeeling region of India. In fact, Nepalese tea growers boast that they can drive to the Darjeeling region in just six hours. With soaring elevations reaching close to seven thousand feet in both places, the rarified, thin air that slows leaf maturation and breeds complexity and finesse in Darjeeling teas also works its magic on the tea grown in this tiny sliver of a country. Nepalese teas are hard to come by and unfortunately have yet to be discovered by the vast majority of tea connoisseurs in the West. This is due to Nepal's relative isolation, a lack of modernization, and the fact that the tea industry did not benefit from development and investment by others. In fact, just the opposite occurred in Nepal, as the tea industry suffered negative consequences from years of ineffectual government control and a long delay in transition from government ownership to private ownership and investment opportunity.

Nepal's major claim to fame and most significant tourist draw is majestic Mount Everest. The capital city of Kathmandu, located between eastern and central Nepal, is a crossroads for visitors to the Himalaya regions as well as for trekkers and climbers. It is also a religious and cultural magnet for Nepalese and Tibetan Buddhists and other pilgrims and zealots. The hodge-podge and chaos of Kathmandu is a cultural stewpot of colorful temples, exotic street bazaars, and Freak Street—the street off of the main square dominated by counterculture American and European hippies in the 1970s seeking momentary "enlightenment" in this high-altitude Zanadu.

NEPAL'S ORTHODOX TEA

Nepal's tea gardens were started in the late nineteenth century in the far corner of the eastern region. Nepal produces both orthodox and CTC teas—the orthodox teas are stylish, tippy, flavorful, and aromatic, often nearly indistinguishable from Darjeeling tea. The fine, hill-grown, orthodox teas are made in the districts of Ilam, Panchthar, Taplejung, and Dhankuta, along the Indian border near Darjeeling. These districts are declared as tea zones; an additional tea zone is located on the fertile, lowland plains of the Terai region, where most of the CTC production is carried out. Nepal does not have any large tea estates; its tea industry is comprised primarily of smallholder tea farmers who sell their fresh leaf to the tea factories or the cooperatives. Although Nepal produces some excellent quality, fragrant orthodox leaf, it has many obstacles to overcome before the tea industry can truly flourish. Isolated locations in rugged pockets of land, poor to nonexistent roads and road conditions, political unrest, severe poverty, and severe mismanagement by the formerly government-controlled tea industry have all conspired in the past to prevent the tea industry from moving forward. Additionally, the Nepalese government does not provide subsidies or incentives to the tea farmers, so the costs of producing tea are high, which is a disadvantage to the tea farmers.

Nepalese tea gardens have become privatized in the past twenty years, and the involvement of private sector interest has made great strides toward increased tea production. From 2002 to 2004, a tenfold increase in tea production was recorded, and export quantity reached just over 1,000 metric tons for the first time. The best orthodox leaf teas comprise just 10 percent of Nepal's entire production and are exported to markets, including Canada, Germany, Japan, and the United States. Much of the CTC production is consumed locally and sold abroad for blends.

Because good prospects for orthodox tea in Nepal have been proven, the Nepalese government has given priority to increased tea production in the eastern districts. In addition, improved cultivation practices, the latest technical know-how, and efficient management systems are bringing the tea industry in

NEPAL–DARJEELING BLENDS

Industry sources suggest that in the past there was such a demand for Darjeeling tea that a large portion of the Nepalese leaves plucked at the gardens in Ilam were (and sometimes still are) blended in with Darjeeling teas to pad out the annual yield or, even worse, sold and marketed completely as Darjeeling. The problem lies in that Nepalese tea is auctioned through India at the Calcutta tea auctions, and from there Nepalese tea can end up in anyone's blend. There is demand for Darjeeling tea far beyond what that region can supply, so the temptation for some to stretch tea exists. Figures suggest that as much as three times the amount of Darjeeling tea is sold than is actually grown. This activity is suspected in warehouses across the world and in Calcutta, where no one is the wiser. To combat this, Darjeeling has instituted a quality protection seal to assure tea buyers and consumers that what they are purchasing is 100 percent pure Darjeeling tea; Nepal is likewise working on such a proof of authenticity label.

CODE OF CONDUCT INITIATIVE

In conjunction with Winrock International, a United States–based organization dedicated to alleviating poverty in Nepal and other parts of South Asia, Nepal has developed a code of conduct policy that they hope will be an inspiration to other tea-producing countries. While the code ensures social responsibility to workers and the environment, it also sets standards for excellence in the workplace and in tea production, and supports integrity in pricing, fulfillment of commitments, and consistency in all transactions. The code maintains to uphold thirty-two points under the four main categories: respect for nature, respect for people, respect for the production system, and transparency of operations.

Nepal, which hopes to garner greater visability in the marketplace for its orthodox teas, is staunchly behind the ethics of the code. The hope is that other tea countries will sign on. The use of an identifying logo is available to members of the code, and those who sign on may find that their profits rise as more tea-drinking consumers want to vote with their dollars in support of this type of environmentally and socially sound policy.

line with other tea-producing countries in the region. Various organizations are working with growers, packers, manufacturers, and exporters to ensure continued success with Nepal's tea industry.

The Nepal Tea Planters Association (NTPA) is comprised of twenty-three CTC factory members, and the Himalayan Orthodox Tea Planters Association (HOTPA) represents 18,000 tea farmer members with eleven orthodox tea factories. HOTPA is a nonpolitical, nonprofit organization established by the joint efforts of small farmers and entrepreneurs with the intention of promoting orthodox tea manufacture in the hilly region of eastern Nepal. HOTPA is hoping to motivate small landholders to cultivate tea and for Nepalese entrepreneurs to invest in tea-processing factories. Nepal is woefully short on leaf-processing ability; unlike the tea estates in India or Ceylon, Nepalese orthodox tea growers must send their leaf out for processing. This results in the inability to offer quantities of estate-grown tea, as the leaf winds up in collective blends that are graded by leaf size.

Members of HOTPA have established five new leaf-processing plants, and another three are being established. HOTPA is calling on the private sector to generate employment in the rural areas and support the Nepalese economy by promoting orthodox tea as a major export commodity. HOTPA believes that Nepal has the potential to devote more than 74,000 acres of land to tea production, which is a five-fold increase, and that the focus must be on manufacturing high-end orthodox leaf for the specialty tea trade. Emphasis needs to be placed on the pure and pollution-free environment in Nepal and the special characteristics of the handmade tea that is produced by the small-holder tea farmers. To achieve this goal, HOTPA has established a marketing arm, the Himalayan Tea Marketing Cooperative (HIMCOOP-NEPAL) to promote Nepalese tea and increase exposure in international markets. HIMCOOP's goal is to position Nepalese tea at the highest level of niche marketing, a fitting goal for tea that is grown on the rooftop of the world.

TEA PRODUCTION IN NEPAL

Most tea gardens in Nepal are privately owned, but a few are still publicly owned. The Nepal Tea Development Corporation, a government agency, now only owns seven tea gardens (two for orthodox tea, five for CTC), compared with the private sector, which touts sixty tea gardens. Smallholders account for approximately 2,468 gardens. One collective venture and a model for other smallholders to follow is the Kanchenjunga Tea Estate, located at Ranitar in the remote hilly region of the Panchthar district. This privately owned 232-acre estate lies at the foothills of Mount Kanchenjunga, the second-highest peak on the Himalayan range. The estate is owned collectively by a hundred tea farmers. The total amount of land under cultivation in Nepal claims close to 25,000 acres. Slightly less than half of that is devoted to orthodox leaf. The greatest concentration of orthodox tea production is made by the efforts of the smallholder tea farmers located in Ilam and in Panchthar.

Nepal enjoys a four-season tea harvest before the bushes go dormant for the winter season. Each season brings tea to market

THE TEA FROM THE HIPPIES ON FREAK STREET

Back in the late 1970s we befriended a sweet young couple in our then café-store. They were low on cash but in need of food and coffee, which we gladly offered them. To repay us for our goodwill, they gave us a colorfully illustrated tin of Nepalese tea that they had purchased on a recent trip. This tea was fragrant and delicious, with a light, pleasing style that was very different from other tea that we sold in our shop. We added the tin to our collection of tea miscellany. The red tin has a picture of Kathmandu on one side and a picture of women picking tea in the gardens on the other. One panel is written in Nepali and the other in English. It says that the tea is from the Ilam Tea Company and is touted as a "golden flowery orange pekoe—a superb hill tea with a delicate flavor."

We were taken by this tea's delicious nature and the notion of traveling to someplace so far away and exotic. We tried to locate the source; it took close to a year! But now we feature this Nepalese tea in our shop. We believe in its greatness. To this day we remain eternally grateful to the nameless hippie couple who shared with us their precious tin of tea from Kathmandu's Freak Street.

that features distinctive character traits and flavor profiles. Spring cropping begins in late February and continues into mid-April, and contributes small-leaf teas that are light in body, fresh in flavor, and delicately aromatic. The second crop of tea is plucked in the summer months of May and June. The leaves have grown somewhat larger; the flavor of the tea is more substantial and full, and the liquor is bright and rose-hued. The monsoon flush starts in eastern Nepal in June and continues until the end of September. During this time the fast-growing leaves reflect the abundant moisture that the plants are being exposed to. The quality is considered standard. Lastly, October brings the autumn flush, the final flush of the year. Autumnal teas are delightful to drink and a real connoisseur's delight. The tea has lingering, rich aromas and deep, smooth flavors. The leaf has lost its rosy color and has taken on a mature, dark amber color.

Africa: The Last Frontier of Tea's Colonial Expansion

Although a relative newcomer to tea, Africa ranks fourth in world production with an impressive 476,641 metric tons produced. Tea is grown primarily in the African nations of Kenya, Malawi, Tanzania, Rwanda, Uganda, and Zimbabwe. Smaller crops are beginning to develop in Burundi, Cameroon, Congo/Zaire, Ethiopia, Mauritius, Mozambique, South Africa, and Zambia. According to the Food and Agriculture Organization of the United Nations, world tea production is expected to grow 1.7 percent annually until 2014. Significant growth in tea output is expected from the African countries of Kenya, Malawi, Uganda, and Tanzania as tea bushes come of age and the skills of the tea workers reach their full potential.

KENYA

Compared to the number of years tea has been under cultivation in such countries as India and Sri Lanka, tea is a relative agricultural newcomer to Kenya. Despite this, Kenya has made excellent progress in developing its tea industry. Tea is a valuable cash crop for Kenyan tea farmers; for many of them it is the sole basis of their yearly income. This direct correlation of crop yield to income is the incentive that has spurred Kenyan tea farmers to achieve astonishing success. In 2004 Kenya ranked as the third-largest producer of black tea in the world and the world leader in tea exports—an astonishing feat to accomplish in less than fifty years. Tea has become the largest subsector of the agricultural community, employing approximately 3 million or 10 percent of all workers in Kenya, and the principal cash crop generated for foreign exchange.

Tea was first cultivated in Limuru in 1903 by a European settler named Caine on a small two-acre piece of land. To regulate and promote this up-and-coming industry, Kenya's tea board was founded in 1959 as an adjunct to the ministry of agriculture. The tea board had responsibilities that focus exclusively on matters of tea growing, research, and manufacture, as well as trade and promotion at home and abroad. Later, in 1964, the Kenya Tea Development Authority was established to promote tea farming by small landholders in the highlands.

The Great Rift Valley. In Kenya tea is grown on both sides of the Great Rift Valley, the vast and wide ecological divide that cuts Kenya in half, right down the middle. This African rift system is the largest in the world and forms a long gash in the earth that begins in Ethiopia and carves its way through Kenya, Tanzania, Malawi, and Mozambique. In Kenya the Rift Valley floor is a hot, dry, and parched place, but the lofty highlands provide the altitude and upland climate necessary for vigorous and exceptional tea growth.

The eastern section of the Rift Valley is home to Mount Kenya, the second highest peak in Africa. Known in the Kikuyu language as Mount Kirinyaga, it is one of the few locations on the equator that maintains glaciers. Mount Kenya, located in Nyandarua or the Aberdare Highlands, is home to the Kikuyu god Ngai. This mountainous area is named after the Englishman Joseph Thompson, the first Westerner to venture into this region of Kenya. In 1950 part of the highlands was designated as the Aberdare National Park, an area that stretches down the mountain slopes to the Nyeri region and the outlying eastern tea-growing district.

From Nyeri the largest concentrations of tea gardens trail one another southward through the regions of Kiambu, Maragua, Muranga, and Thika, and they end just north of the bustling capital city of Nairobi. The tea gardens are positioned at elevations ranging from 4,900 feet to 8,850 feet and grow in rich, volcanic soils in a lush, tropical climate. Bountiful sunshine and copious amounts of rainfall in the vicinity of 47 to 106 inches annually provide a plentiful soaking necessary for lush growth. In the western side of the valley, the majority of tea gardens are found in the highland regions of Bomet, Kericho, Kisii, Nandi, Nyamira, and Sotik. Close to an equal number of tea gardens are located on the east side of the rift in Kiambu, Kirinyaga, Meru, Muranga, and Nyeri, but the gardens on the western side bring the largest quantity of tea to market in most years. The highest-producing regions are Kericho, Nandi, Kianbu, Nyamira, and Nyeri.

Kenya produces black tea almost exclusively; just a very small amount of green tea is made. Because of the warm climate tea bushes flush all year in Kenya; they do not have a dormant period. But the best tea is plucked in the earliest part of the year, from January to early March, and again at the end of June into July. Kenyan tea is cultivated from clonal varieties developed to be pest and disease resistant; consequently pesticides are rarely used.

CTC Tea Dominates Production. Kenya is the recognized leader in CTC technology and uses its expertise to favorably position Kenyan teas in the world market and consequently in the tea blends of many internationally known tea companies. Nearly all production yields CTC black teas; less than 5 percent of production ends up as orthodox leaf. Kenyan teas are tippy in appearance and strong and full-bodied in style. Most Kenyan tea is sold as bulk, used by tea blenders around the world to add flavor, strength, and vigor in the cup. In fact, their pleasing character accounts for much of the backbone in many popular proprietary tea blends from England, Ireland, and Scotland.

Smallholder members of the Kenya Tea Development Agency (KTDA) grow and process more than 60 percent of Kenyan tea. The KTDA markets this tea as one brand, and as a result of the collective efforts of the smallholders, the KTDA functions as the largest producer of tea in the world. The KTDA operates fifty-six tea factories that process the leaf from the farms and gardens of 400,000 smallholders. The tea factories are situated in locations that are central to the surrounding tea gardens. The tea farmers brings their fresh leaf to the weighing center on a daily basis, where the quantity of leaf is credited to their account for future payment. From there the leaf goes to the tea factory, where the lots of tea are graded.

For many of these farmers tea accounts for 90 percent of their yearly income; additional income is generated from other marketable fruits and vegetables. The remaining tea produced in Kenya is brought to market by large estates that are owned by multinational tea or commodities firms. The Kenya Tea Growers Association promotes the tea grown by these estates. An additional thirty-nine privately owned tea factories process leaf from these estates. James Finlay, Unilever, and Williamson Tea (based in the United Kingdom) and the Kenya-based Eastern Producers are four of the largest tea companies in the country.

Production figures from 2004 show that the combined efforts of large and small tea growers in Kenya's thirteen tea-growing districts have paid off: Kenya now ranks third in world tea production (325,000 metric tons) and an impressive first in the world for tea exports (293,000 metric tons). Ironically, tea production is on the rise in Kenya while highland coffee production is on the decline. Value-added incentives, such as Fair Trade certification, organic certification, and the creation of a national brand identity, are being incorporated into promotional efforts to attract consumer attention and command higher prices in the retail marketplace for Kenyan tea.

The second-largest tea auction house in the world is located in Mombasa, Kenya's main port town, situated on the Indian Ocean coast. Here, every Tuesday of the year, brokers sell marked lots of tea to importers from all over the world on behalf of the producers. Close to 85 percent of annual tea production in Kenya is sold this way; the remaining tea is either sold privately to tea importers or consumed locally. Kenyan tea is rarely found unblended in the United States, but look for garden marks from these estates: Gathuthi, Githambo, Imenti, Kangaita, Keigoi, Kinoro, Marinyn, Mugania, Mununga, Rukuriri, Theta, and Thumaita.

TANZANIA

Tea is among Tanzania's dominant agricultural products, which also include cloves, cashews, coffee, and maize. Located along the Indian Ocean south of Kenya in East Africa, Tanzania is another relative newcomer to the tea trade. More than fifty thousand families make their living in the tea industry. Tanzania's tea history began with German settlers, but commercial cultivation did not begin until British interests took over the tea plantations after World War II. From 1934 until 1960 the production of Tanzanian tea tripled. Independence for Tanzania in 1961 brought about a change to the old Tea Board of Tanganyika, now named the Tea Board of Tanzania. Before independence the British estate system of private tea garden ownership was in effect in Tanzania. Large tea estates primarily dominated production, but after 1961 programs were established to encourage the involvement of smallholder tea growers, whose contribution to the total tea production in Tanzania was now strongly encouraged.

Unfortunately, the situation in Tanzania has not mirrored the success story of Kenya, which is buzzing with worker effort and opportunity. Initially, smallholder involvement contributed as much as 29 percent of tea production up to the 1985–1986 season, but by 1988 it had severely fallen back to just below 5 percent. Reasons for this decline range from farmers not being paid by the government for tea that was previously delivered to crumbling or nonexistent infrastructure. A lack of working roads prevents fresh leaf from reaching the factories in time, and rundown transport equipment and facilities are also in generally poor condition. In the former Tanzanian socialist government incentives for worker productivity did not exist; consequently efficiency was not encouraged or rewarded. This laid-back attitude plagues the tea industry today.

Matters only became worse from the early 1960s to the early 1970s, when the Tanzanian government began to nationalize most of the tea factories in the private sector. Some tea estates were exempt from this, but two of the largest tea estates were nationalized. The lack of overall infrastructure in Tanzania affected these tea factories and tea estates, as it did the smallholders. Government tea research programs were woefully underfunded and ignored, stalling progress in clonal plant development, effective plant maintenance and pest control, and proper cultivation and soil maintenance techniques.

Relief came in the way of government reform right before the complete collapse of the tea industry. First, the two nationalized tea estates and four nationalized tea factories were privatized. Now these factories are being renovated and brought back on line from investments that have been made to ensure their future success. The two remaining government-owned tea factories are in the process of being privatized. The government-funded Tea Research Institute of Tanzania, which works in conjunction with tea research institutes of Ngwanzi in the south and Marikitanda in the east, was formed to advance tea production for both the smallholders and the large estates. Since 1995, government funding stopped, however, and today large tea estates are privately funding the work of the Tea Research Institute. Efforts are being made to replant with clonal hybrids developed for each growing region and to educate tea farmers in water and soil conservation as well as the use of fertilizers.

The Tanzania Smallholder Tea Development Agency was formed in 1997 to promote and develop tea production in the smallholder section of the industry. To date, smallholders contribute about 10 percent to the total tea output per year, significantly less than the output of smallholders in Kenya. Reports from the World Bank are optimistic for this overhaul of the tea industry: production figures of marketable tea rose in Tanzania from 20,000 metric tons in the 1990–91 season to close to 29,482 metric tons in the 2001–02 season. But perhaps more telling than figures of quantity are figures that underscore a directional return to quality for Tanzanian tea. Tea traders working the Mombasa tea auction in 1996 reported that sales of Tanzanian tea sold for the lowest price of any African tea at auction that year. Today the prices have climbed above that of Uganda and Malawi but still below that of Burundi, Rwanda, and top-rated Kenyan highland tea.

Tea production in the north of Tanzania is centered in the high-plateau regions of the Masai Steppe near Mount Kilimanjaro and the highlands of the Usambara Mountains. In the south tea grows around the Njombe and Mufindi districts of the Iringa region, not too far from the Livingston Mountains that rise up to the Great Rift Valley and Lake Malawi to the south. Most Tanzanian tea is processed by the CTC method and is used to add strength and vigor to tea blends. Look for Tanzanian tea from Ambangulu Estate in Usambara.

Vietnam:
A Modern Tea Industry Begins

Like Laos, Myanmar, and Thailand, Vietnam has a long history of tea consumption. For centuries village residents have consumed tea brewed from the leaves of indigenous tea trees found growing wild in the jungles of northern Vietnam. This tea is called *shan* tea and is now recognized as a subclass of tea known as *Camellia sinensis* var. *shan*. In the mid-1800s the French were responsible for establishing the first cultivated tea gardens in the north midlands region of Vietnam in Phu Tho, in what was then called French Indochina. From then until 1945 the French established tea research stations in three locations in northern Vietnam; they had 33,000 acres of land under tea cultivation.

During World War II the tea gardens were abandoned and left to fall into a state of decline. Production reached a near standstill. After the war Vietnam began to rebuild its tea industry from a hodgepodge of assistance and influence from other tea-producing countries. Russian tea-processing technology and Russian tea machinery were used in the mid-1950s for exports of Vietnamese tea to Russia. In the 1980s assistance from Japanese firms helped establish the production of sencha-style green tea, to augment Japan's growing tea needs. Later, Vietnam turned to India for technical help with black tea production, a style of tea that the green tea–drinking Vietnamese people were not familiar with. Taiwan provided expertise in pouchong-style oolong tea production, much of which is manufactured today in Lam Dong Province in the central highlands.

In 1986 the Communist Party of Vietnam instituted sweeping economic reforms. Known as "the Renovation," this was necessary for the tea industry; one outcome was that the government began to transfer landownership to individual farmers. In addition, the Vietnam National Tea Corporation (Vinatea), the government arm in charge of the tea industry, emerged to improve productivity and marketing. Vinatea is the largest tea producer and exporter in Vietnam, and manages more than thirty-four tea factories and six thousand acres of tea gardens, sixty tea producers, and six joint ventures with Belgium, Iraq, Japan, and Taiwan.

In all, 108,000 acres of tea gardens are under cultivation in Vietnam and 2.5 million people are involved in the tea industry. In the 1990s the government began to privatize a portion of its ownership in the tea factories. This new open-door policy was designed to provide growth opportunities and expansion by attracting joint ventures with foreign partners. But despite twenty years of active restructuring since 1986, this country is still grappling with a struggling socioeconomic situation. The growing pains of modernization are difficult, and results take a long time to be realized, but the benefits are widespread and important. Agriculture adds positively to the national economy and the health and independence of farming communities; tea holds the promise of great potential for Vietnam.

The Viet Nam Tea Association (VITAS) advises the government and outside investors of necessary tea projects on how to further develop the industry's infrastructure and productivity of the tea gardens. VITAS also works with issues of quality and high standards and workers' rights. Through the efforts of VITAS injections of capital and foreign investment from private companies and limited partnerships have allowed tea growers and tea exporters to update to new and efficient processing equipment. This will allow them to keep up with projected increased output from the tea gardens. Dozens of vigorous new tea bush cultivars have been selected from China, India, and Sri Lanka and planted in Vietnam's existing tea gardens to bolster cropping yields and cupping quality.

A Vietnamese teapot in the shape of a water buffalo.

In addition, problems of inconsistent leaf quality are being addressed. Guidelines have been established to help farmers maintain strict quality control and product consistency from year to year. For instance, from north to south, cultivation and harvesting skills are weak; many farmers do not follow standard methods for growing and harvesting tea, and the hand skills that China excels at from centuries of practice are not deeply rooted in Vietnam. Low levels of productivity can often be blamed on former plantings with the wrong choices of tea cultivars for the soil and climate of a specific region, or from tea gardens that have become too old or overexploited and are thus unable to deliver leaf with yield and flavor. Additionlly, Vietnam

LOTUS TEA

Lotus tea is said to combine the essences of the flower, the earth, and the sky. It is extremely delicate and does not lend to export. In fact, lotus tea can be difficult to acquire in Vietnam because of its fragile and ethereal nature. Lotus tea is made from lotus blossoms that are hand-harvested by boat from Hanoi's West Lake. Only thirty families still make this labor-intensive tea from May to July, prime time for picking lotus blossoms before they open.

Lotus tea scenting is an art in Vietnam. In the past the flower buds were gently opened and the tea was placed inside the buds at night, when the nectar was fullest. Today, however, expert tea scenters select their favorite varieties of lotus flowers and disassemble the flowers to remove the stamens and the aromatic pollen. Expert scenters use between 1,300 and 1,500 flower blossoms to fragrance just over a kilo (2.2 pounds) of tea. The pollen is applied to the dried tea in several small applications over the course of two weeks. Such exquisite lotus tea, made from Thai Nguyen or shan tea, sells for more than $125 per kilo in Vietnam.

is subject to problems of prolonged droughts, which lead to decreased production, poor harvests, and inferior quality.

Until recently, Vietnam did not have a recognizable trademark to identify its tea. The Vietnam Tea Association has created a national brand—Cheviet—that establishes national identity and a guarantee of origin. Now Vietnam's tea producers and tea exporters will have the value-added strength of national identity to help them compete in the global marketplace. Additional trademark protection is being applied to prevent fraudulent use of the names of Vietnam's most unique teas—Shan Tuyet, Thai Nguyen, and Lotus tea.

VIETNAM'S TEA-PRODUCING AREAS

In 2005 the French Development Agency and Vietnam's finance ministry signed a deal for an 8.5-million-euro credit agreement to fund a project for tea development in the Phu Tho Province. This money will allow new farmers to begin cultivating tea and for the Phu Tho authorities to expand existing tea gardens. Some of the funds will be used to improve the road system in this area, which will facilitate transportation of the tea from garden to market. It is estimated that three thousand families will directly benefit from this loan and program.

Vietnam's harvest season runs from April into October. Tea grows in thirty-four provinces spread throughout the north, central, and southern coastal regions. In the mountainous north subtropical weather brings all of the benefits of warm days and cool nights. In the central regions tropical, humid weather brings much needed moisture during the hot summer months. Table 4.5 shows how the regions compare for average annual output of tea, based on production figures.

Vietnam produces CTC black tea and some orthodox leaf (60 percent of production), green tea (35 percent of production), jasmine tea, lotus tea, oolong tea, and a specialty highland green tea called Shan Tuyet or Snow Green tea (5 percent of production combined). Shan Tuyet is made from the leaves of indigenous tea trees found in the mountainous provinces in the northern uplands. In these forests the shan tea trees are found in groups of thirty to forty trees that are interspersed in between other types of trees on steep mountain slopes. This region—comprised of Ha Gaing, Lao Cai, Son La, Lai Chau, Tuyen Quang, and Yen Bai Provinces—is large and shares a border with China's Yunnan and Guizhou Provinces, locations of other indigenous tea trees. Local varieties of shan trees include green leaf shan (*shan la xanh*), small leaf shan (*shan la nho*), yellow leaf shan (*shan la vang*), and snow shan (*tuyet*). The Yen Bai Province is home to a region with five-hundred-year-old tea trees that workers must climb up into to gather the leaves.

The populations of Kinh, Nunh, Giao, and Hmong peoples in these provinces also produce several other unique Vietnamese teas—Bat Tien, Keop Am Tich, and Kim Tuyen tea. Given the geographic location of this region to Myanmar, Laos, and Yunnan, one would expect this region to have a history of making compressed cake teas and other preserved styles of tea. Ha Giang brown tea is a traditional tea made from shan leaf that is quickly dried in a cast-iron pan, hand rubbed to shape the leaves, and then laid in the sun to dry. The finished tea is stuffed into a hollow bamboo tube and set aside to age and mellow.

Table 4.5. Vietnam's Annual Tea Production Figures, by Region

Region	Percentage of Annual Tea Production
Northern Uplands and Northern Midlands, including the provinces of Lai Chau, Lao Cai, Yen Bai, Quang Ninh, Son La, Thai Nguyen, and Phu Tho	65 percent
Red River Delta	4 percent
North Center, including Nghe An Province	2 percent
Central Highlands, including Lam Dong Province	6 percent
South-Central Coast	23 percent

VIETNAM'S INCREASED TEA CULTIVATION

Most Vietnam tea today is mass-produced and not made by village artisans, however. CTC tea production dominates in the world of foreign needs and foreign investments, and that is where Vietnam's production efforts are being directed. Although the country is embracing modern, high-tech tea production, it also plans to put more emphasis on these high-grown Shan teas from the border region with China for the specialty trade. Today the total amount of land in Vietnam under tea cultivation is 185,000 acres, and projections for 2010 are that this will increase to 222,300 acres. Annual output of tea has risen dramatically, from 40,000 tons in 1985 to 95,000 tons in 2004. The Vietnamese tea industry is poised to become a vital force in world tea commerce. Vietnam is ranked eighth in the world for tea production, with an annual yield of 83,000 metric tons.

Thailand: Home to Wild-Growing Tea Trees

In the remote jungle regions of northern Thailand both cultural diversity and tea thrive where the borders with Myanmar and Laos surround Thailand. Mountain populations of such ethnic minority tribes as the Akha, Hmong, Kosen, Labu, Lisu, and Lua originated in Mainland China and Myanmar; these groups have been settled in this region for centuries. Their well-established foot trails through the jungles allow them easy access across the borders, where they sell their goods and trade at village markets for cloth, tea, food, and herbal remedies. Tea flourishes in the tropical environment of the thickly forested mountainous Chiang Rai Province in Thailand.

Anthropologists and tea historians believe that the birthplace of tea is a wide swath of adjoining areas in the remote jungle wilderness extending from Assam, India, to southern Yunnan Province, China, across the top of Myanmar and Laos, down into northern Thailand, and across the northern regions of Vietnam. In these jungles centuries-old wild tea plants have grown into stately trees. Local populations have always concocted tea from these leaves, as well as from roots and herbs found in the forests. For generations people across these regions have made slightly differing versions of pickled tea known as *letpet* or *miang*. Letpet is still a diet staple of many of these people, and it is used as an offering on religious occasions, served as a sign of respect to elders, and brought out for special social occasions. Letpet is made by steaming fresh tea leaf and then packing the leaf into large stalks of bamboo that are buried for several months. The letpet will slowly ferment and take on a characteristically pungent flavor and aroma. Pickled tea is not served as tea but instead is usually mixed with oil and garlic and served accompanied by fried peanuts, sesame seeds, fried shrimp, fresh tomatoes, and fresh green chilies. It is only since the 1960s that *Camellia sinensis* has been cultivated in the mountain villages of Chiang Rai and Chiang Mai Provinces.

THAILAND'S TEA-GROWING REGIONS

In Chiang Rai the village of Mae Salong has become famous for its unusual tea—Thai-style Taiwan oolong tea. How Chinese tea came to be produced in Thailand is an interesting chapter in the history of this region. In the 1950s members of Chiang Kai-shek's Chinese Nationalist Kuomintang Army fled Mainland China after being defeated by Mao Tse-tung's People's Liberation Army during the Chinese Civil War. While Chiang Kai-shek and more than 700,000 of his soldiers and political refugees escaped across the Taiwan Strait to the island of Taiwan, other Kuomintang soldiers posted in the border region of Yunnan fled south into Myanmar.

Myanmar had gained independence from the British in 1948. For many years refugee Nationalist Chinese troops assisted Myanmar in rebuilding the country after years of war and strife. But in 1960 guerrilla war with the communists broke out, and the Nationalist Chinese soldiers and their families fled Myanmar for northern Thailand. They were allowed by the Thai government to settle in Chiang Rai Province, and today the area surrounding Mae Salong has a decidedly Chinese feeling to it. One of the first tasks in their new home was to plant tea bushes. But due to their status as Chinese refugees, these former soldiers could not return to China for tea bush cuttings, so they had to rely on their connections residing in Taiwan.

From the Taiwanese they received clonal varieties of tea bushes that had been developed for the manufacture of Taiwan's famous semioxidized oolong teas. In this way oolong tea production came to be a way of life and eventually a thriving livelihood in northern Thailand's remote mountain regions. In this lush, tropical environment the tea bushes flourished, and cultivated tea gardens multiplied rapidly. After not too many years, unforeseen government assistance helped to bolster this fledgling industry.

THAILAND'S TEA PRODUCTION AND MANUFACTURING

In the early 1970s a project initiative started by the Thai king Bhumibol Adulyadej focused on eliminating the lucrative but destructive opium poppy cultivation that had become deeply rooted in Thailand's northern highlands. The project encompassed numerous programs that also focused on eliminating slash-and-burn land use, conserving highland soils by reforestation, and creating profitable cash crops such as stone-fruit trees, vegetables, flowers, and shiitake mushrooms, as well as Chinese tea that would improve the lives of the mountain inhabitants.

Today almost fifteen thousand families grow more than eighty market crops, thanks to the creation of thirty-four extension programs in northern Thailand. From those early beginnings, scientific research and advanced techniques in tea cultivation have helped the tea industry grow. Throughout the 1970s and 1980s tea experts from the Taiwan Tea Agricultural Research Center visited Thailand and supplied the tea producers with tea-processing equipment and provided extensive training to farmers in the highland areas in such subjects as soil management, effective farming techniques, and improvements in manufacturing. Of equal importance were new clonal varieties of oolong tea hybrids supplied by the Taiwanese to increase production in the tea gardens. Today Thai tea farmers speak proudly about their Number 17 (soft stem) and Number 12 plant varietals and the tea-making skills they have learned.

In this region days are warm while night temperatures are cool, creating perfect conditions for the bushes to have daily contact with a cooling cover of mist. Sharply delineated mountains ascend in elevation from 3,900 to 4,420 feet, and from a distance the hillsides are blanketed with neatly placed rows of carefully maintained tea bushes in well-tended tea gardens.

The yearly output of Thailand's oolong tea is small, and much of it is consumed internally. Thai oolong tea is also dispersed throughout Southeast Asia via the booming crossroads hub of Bangkok and to tourists visiting the resorts in Chiang Mai. In Chiang Rai the Chinese village of Mae Salong is being marketed as a colorful tourist destination with a special emphasis on Hmong and Aka fabric and jewelry arts, fantastic Chinese and Thai food, and the production of fragrant and flowery local tea. It's an easy day trip from

Chiang Mai to Chiang Rai—take the bus from Chiang Mai as far as you can, then take a cab the rest of the way—and be sure to visit the 101 Tea Factory.

New Tea Beginnings

Generations of tea drinkers have looked to China, Japan, India, and Sri Lanka for their favorite teas and familiar, trusted tea blends. Now the old dominions of tea production are being joined by new tea gardens elsewhere in the world, including Argentina, Australia, Bangladesh, Iran, Malawi, New Zealand, Turkey, and the United States (in both Hawaii and South Carolina). New ideas for tea, such as bottled tea beverages, tea extracts, instant tea, and tea blends formulated exclusively for making iced tea beverages, are driving much of this tea production in other directions.

Argentina. From wine to olive oil and now tea, the rapid development of fully mechanized tea production in 1960 has resulted today in an industry with an average annual production of 60,000 metric tons.

Australia. Another country that excels in wine, olive oil, and now tea, Australia has the soil and climate for it all. Most of the tea is grown in North Queensland, followed by a small amount grown in New South Wales. Annual production averages 1,500 metric tons.

Bangladesh. Commercial tea cultivation started in Sylhet in 1854. The main growing areas are the Surma valley and the Halda valley. Approximately 90 percent of production in Bangladesh is CTC black tea. Extremely large internal consumption of tea taps into close to half of the country's annual production of 56,853 metric tons of tea.

England. Yes, England. After all the years of angst over tea during the China tea trade, a family-owned estate known as Tregothnan, which has been owned by the Boscawen family since 1335, is taking up the challenge of growing *Camellia sinensis.* Tregothnan is a horticultural specialist in rare plants and ornamental camellias in particular. So it is no surprise that today a new path is being forged. Thirty varieties of *Camellia sinensis* are being cultivated on just over twenty acres of land, and Tregothnan manufactures this leaf into a line of three estate-produced black teas.

Hawaii. Hawaii's rugged Kona Coast is known for its fine specialty coffees. Today adventurous locals are experimenting with whether tea cultivation can repeat that success. The weather is blessed, the location is killer, and the players are optimistic. The Hawaiian Tea Society boasts that its Big Island Association of home tea growers has close to forty members, each of whom cultivates tea in half-acre or less backyard gardens. So far the tea is thriving and appears to be doing well, but no one is sure about how the flavor will intimately fare. Will the proper techniques of firing and shaping be mastered? Is it possible to coax the best from the leaves when "tea knowledge" has not been passed from one set of hands to another over generations? Research is being conducted to develop quality-control standards in Hawaii and to learn the age-old art of processing tea by hand. The U.S. Department of Agriculture in conjunction with the University of Hawaii has been cultivating small plots of tea at different altitudes, ranging from 600 to 4,000 feet above sea level. At best, meaningful production is several years away.

Iran. Tea cultivation in Iran began in 1900, and today tea is grown mostly by smallholders in Rasht, Lahizan, Lanagroud, Rudasar, and Tunekabun, located in the northern part of the country near the Caspian Sea. Originally seedlings were brought from the Himachal Pradesh region of India. Iran is tenth in the world for tea production, with 58,051 metric tons, but the country exports very little tea. Internal demand requires that Iran buy tea to augment its own production.

Malawi. The second-largest producer of African tea following Kenya, Malawi was actually the location where tea was first cultivated in Africa. Smallholders in the areas of Mulanje and Thyolo produce most of the tea, which has an annual production of 41,963 metric tons. The United Kingdom is the largest importer of Malawian tea.

South Carolina. Tea cultivation in South Carolina has an interesting history. Three attempts at serious tea cultivation have been tried since 1790, when the French botanist Andre Michaux first experimented with planting tea shrubs on land outside of Charleston. The nineteenth century saw two commercial tea enterprises fail. Another attempt by philanthropist Charles Shepard resulted in the creation of the Pinehurst Tea Plantation in Summerville, near Charleston, in 1888. By the time that Shepard passed away in 1915, he had reached a degree of success with tea production that no one else before him had achieved in South Carolina. But after his death, however, the tea plantation was abandoned. In 1960 the Thomas J. Lipton Company purchased Shepard's plantation and removed the bushes to replant them on Wadmalaw Island, a well-watered ten-mile-long and six-mile-wide oasis south of Charleston.

Numerous varieties of tea bush cultivars were added to the mix, and the plantation served as a tea research station. The plantation was sold again in 1987 to William B. Hall, who renamed it the Charleston Tea Plantation and began to market American Classic tea from production on the thirty-acre plantation. Today Hall and the Bigelow Tea Company jointly own the tea plantation, and plans for further expansion and increased production are in the works. Their product is the only tea commercially produced in the United States.

Turkey. Turkish tea grows close to the border with Georgia along the Black Sea. Smallholders, who comprise the bulk of the landowners, grow most of the tea. The first tea plantation was started in 1924 in Rize with tea seeds brought from Georgia. Turkey ranks fifth in world tea production, with an average annual yield of 155,000 metric tons of black tea.

New Zealand. No tea is commercially cultivated in New Zealand, but an archival collection of tea varieties is being established on the Purangi Estate, located on the North Island. The collection maintains sixty-six specimen varieties of *Camellia sinensis* and is being propagated and maintained with the idea of selecting the best clonal varieties to use to generate eventual tea gardens planned for future development.

Tea has always been one of the world's most powerful commodities. During the heyday of the China trade in the eighteenth and nineteenth centuries, the mesmerizing effects of Chinese tea on the West and the subsequent interactions between China and England had profound effects on the development of these two countries. Tea also played a role in the independence of a fledgling American nation and the transformation of England from an agrarian society into an industrialized nation. Today, tea is enjoyed and appreciated in countries around the world, and in many cultures the tenets of social order have been established over the practices and habits around a tea table.

CHAPTER 5

AN ENCYCLOPEDIA OF TEA

O<small>N THIS GLOBAL SHOPPING TRIP WE EXPLORE THE WORLD OF TEA</small>, one leaf at a time. Because so many countless teas are available today, we have chosen to illustrate and describe them organized by leaf style. This method yields good results both with face-to-face customers in our store and with our off-premise shoppers. Most tea drinkers establish their custom for enjoying tea using a particular method that remains quite consistent in their daily life. Our categorization is compatible with probable cultural predilections, familial tendencies, brewing techniques, and individual taste preferences. But it also encourages the exploration of new tea.

Some tea drinkers are enthusiasts, but many are not. If you are perfectly happy driving down the same road every day, perhaps we can convince you to stop on the other side of the road to try a new tea. And if you are ready to take that fork in the road that you have always wondered about, this guide ensures that you won't get lost along the new route. If you are an enthusiast, this section melds perfectly with your discovery process as well, because we intend to further stimulate your zeal. There are so many teas in the world that there should be at least a few new ones discussed in this chapter that spark your interest!

For each class of tea (see chapter 3 for detailed descriptions of each class) we profile one or more tea growths in that class. There are far too many teas in the world to attempt a complete encyclopedia of tea growths, however. Furthermore, teas change regularly (similar to wine vintages) and go in and out of season, production, and availability, especially from country to country and importer to importer. So rather than get you excited about a specific single-growth tea, only to discover that you will never be able to find that particular one wherever you happen to be, this guide helps you to

recognize styles and then bracket tea growths into groups. This knowledge is helpful when you are trying to decide between a superb golden-tipped Yunnan black tea and a competition-grade Tung Ting oolong from the tea-producing heart of Taiwan.

In this chapter we move through the six great classes of tea in an expansive order based on the overall strength of flavor of each tea's brewed cup characteristics—from the most exquisite budset white tea to the darkest pu-erh. We start with the largest leaf style in each class and move through that class with examples representing the variety within each class. At the chapter's end, we take a side excursion to encounter a few extraordinary teas, such as jasmine and Lapsang Souchong.

It is imperative that you refer to other chapters throughout this book to fill in the details of production technique, trace a bit of history, find explanations of leaf processing, and explore the comprehensive brewing procedures. The mission of this chapter's journey is simply to portray various styles of leaf and their attributes, to give you a feeling for what these particular teas represent. There are often several equally correct spellings for the same Chinese tea. This is the result of the changes in translation from Chinese to English over the years (tea vendors primarily use pinyin and occasionally the Wade-Giles spellings). It is rarely difficult to ascertain which tea is which, as the spellings are most often quite similar.

Much like wine, olive oil, and other artisanal products, tea has developed a rich and nuanced vocabulary to describe its origins and flavors. See the glossary at the end of this book for a full list of terms, including words used for classic leaf styles, dry leaf, and brewed tea, as well as descriptions of each specific class of tea.

The journey begins with one of the most pure and time-honored of Chinese tribute teas: traditional budset white tea.

White Tea

BAI HAO YIN ZHEN (SILVER NEEDLE)

Region: Fujian Province, China
Manufacture: Air-dried white tea (about 5 percent oxidation)
Style: Full budset with downy hairs
Flavor: Smooth, sweet, soft
Aroma: Clean, floral
Liquor: Pale silver
Brewing: Brew numerous short infusions at 160 to 170°F. Drink plain.

The real McCoy, Silver Needle is true white tea from the proper varietal, grown in the correct place. As Champagne has specificity, so does this tea. It must be tasted at least once in a tea drinker's lifetime. Beware of very expensive budset white tea, however, as it is now being produced essentially everywhere that tea grows. For details, see "White Tea" in chapter 3.

BAI MUDAN

Region: Fujian Province, China (and many other locations worldwide)
Manufacture: Air-dried white tea (about 8 percent oxidation)
Style: Open leaf, usually blended with budsets
Flavor: Smooth, sweet, soft
Aroma: Clean, floral
Liquor: Rich straw
Brewing: Brew numerous short infusions at 160 to 170°F. Drink plain.

This new-style white tea is from China bush if sourced from Chinese gardens, and from China or Assam bush if sourced from most anywhere else. Perfectly good and tasty tea, Bai Mudan is an inexpensive source of a delicious light tea.

Yellow Tea

MENGDING MOUNTAIN SNOW BUDS

Region: Sichuan Province, China
Manufacture: Pan-fired, rare yellow tea
Style: Sword-leaf/budset tea (often called sparrow-tongue)
Flavor: Toasty, brisk, but smooth
Aroma: Clean, fresh
Liquor: Clear tinged with pale green
Brewing: Brew two or three two-minute infusions at 170 to 180°F.
  Drink plain.

Mengding Mountain on the Tibetan Plateau in northwestern Sichuan Province is likely the birthplace of cultivated tea. The garden that grows Mengding Mountain Snow Buds is located just northwest of Mount Emei, one of the four sacred mountains in Chinese Buddhism. The tea is picked as a budset in the garden and gathered in small fabric bags rather than in baskets.

Green Tea

SUN-DRIED TEA FROM XISHUANGBANNA

Region: Yunnan Province, China
Manufacture: Sun-dried green tea
Style: Open budset and leaf
Flavor: Deep, rich
Aroma: Clean, earthy
Liquor: Straw to golden
Brewing: Brew two or three two-minute infusions at 170 to 180°F.
  Drink plain.

One of the most original and authentic teas manufactured anywhere, this sun-dried tea is from one of the birthplaces of tea, protected and harvested by the ethnic minorities who live in one of China's last wild places, the Mekong River valley region of southwestern China that shares a border with Laos and Myanmar.

TAI PING HOU KUI

Region: Anhui Province, China
Manufacture: Both pan-fired and basket-fired green tea
Style: Flat, needle leaf
Flavor: Earthy, rich, vegetal
Aroma: Toasty
Liquor: Deep straw
Brewing: Brew two or three two-minute infusions at 170 to 180°F.
    Drink plain.

Tai Ping Hou Kui is one of the Ten Famous Teas of Chinese lore. Grown in a protected area bordering a pristine lake just north of the Huang Shan, this is one of very few teas that is both pan-fired and basket-fired, blotted in between firings with the rice paper made locally for scroll painting. The impression of this paper displays on authentic Tai Ping Hou Kui.

MING MEI

Region: Jiangxi Province, China
Manufacture: Basket-fired green tea
Style: Twisted-leaf
Flavor: Mineral, slightly grassy
Aroma: Pure, clean, grassy
Liquor: Bright straw tending toward silver
Brewing: Brew two or three two-minute infusions at 170 to 180°F.
    Drink plain.

Ming Mei, an "eyebrow" tea (so named for its distinctive shape), comes from Jiangxi Province, where all tea is possible! Although the tea artisans in this province produce many styles of tea, Ming Mei is their trademark tea and the one for which they have no equal.

DRAGON WELL (LONGJING)

Region: Zhejiang Province, China
Manufacture: Pan-fired green tea
Style: Flat-leaf or bird's beak budsets
Flavor: Soft, rich, toasty
Aroma: Nutty, full
Liquor: Straw tending toward amber, with a tea-oil sheen
Brewing: Brew two or three two-minute infusions at 170 to 180°F.
   Drink plain.

One of the Ten Famous Teas, Dragon Well is one of the most beloved teas in China. Longjing has a toasty, yeasty flavor with chestnut overtones. It is pan-fired in wood charcoal–stoked woks, and the artisans who create this tea are masters of their craft. "Competition-grade" Longjing is traditionally manufactured from tiny dark budsets that form to the shape of bird beaks. High-quality, First Grade Longjing is comprised of flattened budsets that have a distinct straw-yellow tinge to the budset. Both are distinctive and often come in sealed boxes with provenance.

CURLED DRAGON SILVER TIPS (PAN LONG YIN HAO)

Region: Zhejiang Province, China
Manufacture: Pan-fired green tea
Style: Spiral-leaf showing significant tip
Flavor: Vegetal, assertive
Aroma: Clean, earthy
Liquor: Pale straw
Brewing: Brew two or three two-minute infusions at 170 to 180°F.
   Drink plain.

Curled Dragon Silver Tips is a magnificent green tea. Fairly tightly crimped spirals show tip that unfurls to sizable leaf. One of the smoothest but most highly flavored pan-fired teas that you will encounter, this is only produced in limited quantities each year. Be sure to seek out the *authentic* version.

GREEN SNAIL SPRING (BI LO CHUN)

Region: Jiangsu Province, China
Manufacture: Hot-air-fired (sometimes wok-fired) green tea
Style: Bi Lo Chun–spiral-leaf
Flavor: Assertive, thirst-quenching, and astringent
Aroma: Deceptively soft and mild, fresh
Liquor: Clear golden
Brewing: Brew two or three minutes at 175 to 185°F (a second infusion is usually possible). Drink plain.

This is a brisk green tea made famous by the tea artisans of Jiangsu Province, north of Shanghai. Prepared from a beautiful pluck of tiny budsets, this tea demands careful brewing and will reward with a marvelous cup. Properly fired Bi Lo Chun will have a tiny "tail" at the end of its spiral that is unique to the subvariety used for this tea.

In some ways Bi Lo Chun–style teas are the "Darjeelings" of green tea: finicky, quirky, demanding, and ever-changing. The resulting brew is worth the little bit of extra attention needed.

GUNPOWDER (IMPERIAL PINHEAD)

Region: Zhejiang Province, China
Manufacture: Tumble-fired green tea
Style: Rolled-leaf, ball, or pellet
Flavor: Robust, sweet
Aroma: Fresh, slightly nutty
Liquor: Clear green tinged with olive
Brewing: Brew three or four minutes at 175 to 185°F (a second infusion is usually possible). Drink plain.

Gunpowder tea is one of the best known and most liked of all the standard green teas. It is among the easiest and most forgiving of green teas to brew. Simple to measure, Gunpower tea tolerates a range of water temperatures and is fun to watch brew. It is also the base tea used most commonly for the minted tea of Morocco. It was originally shaped into its pellet form for quality and keeping purposes, as it shipped more compactly and retained its fresh flavor better with so little surface area exposed.

SENCHA

Region: Japan
Manufacture: Steamed and oven-fired green tea
Style: Flat-leaf
Flavor: Robust, vegetal
Aroma: Fresh, slightly vegetal, "green"
Liquor: Deep artichoke tinged with olive
Brewing: Brew a short infusion at 160 to 170°F (can be brewed again with cooler water). Drink plain.

Sencha needs to be brewed carefully, with water that is not too hot; it can be a fussy tea. It has the wonderful "green" flavor so highly regarded in Japan. Usually consumed in small cups, sencha should be sipped and is a fantastic accompaniment to snacks or savory bites.

GYOKURO (JADE DEW)

Region: Japan
Manufacture: Steamed and oven-fired green tea
Style: Twisted-needle shape
Flavor: Robust, vegetal
Aroma: Fresh, kelpy, "green"
Liquor: Pale emerald
Brewing: Brew at a maximum 165°F (a second infusion is possible using even cooler water). Drink plain.

Gyokuro is the connoisseur's Japanese green tea. Its rich and full flavor really stimulates the palate. Gyokuro is the green tea that is the most highly revered in Japan, for purity of flavor, depth of the "green" taste, and the robust breadth of flavor that is so uniquely Japanese. It is one of the few Japanese teas that is still plucked by hand.

Oolong Tea

ROYAL RED ROBE WU YI MOUNTAIN (DA HONG PAO)

Region: Min-Bei region (north of Min River), Fujian Province, China
Manufacture: Oolong tea (80 percent oxidation)
Style: Open-crepey leaf
Flavor: Deep, rich
Aroma: Fresh, clean "tea"
Liquor: Golden amber
Brewing: Brew three or perhaps four times at 180 to 190°F (slightly higher than normal oolong-brewing temperature). Drink plain.

Royal Red Robe is as oxidized as oolong ever is. It looks like a black tea, only the leaves are huge, much larger than 98 percent of the black tea on the market. Oolong teas are generally plucked from particular cultivars that are favorable to the oolong being processed. Royal Red Robe oolong is a perfect example of this phenomenon.

FORMOSA FANCY SILVERTIPS

Region: Taiwan, China
Manufacture: Oolong tea (50–60 percent oxidation)
Style: Open folded-leaf
Flavor: Sweet, fresh, "stone fruit"
Aroma: Pure, clean, "stone fruit"
Liquor: Clear golden
Brewing: Brew numerous short infusions at 160 to 180°F. Drink plain.

Traditional-style Formosa oolongs have the stone-fruit flavor and aroma that make for an excellent cup of sipping tea, and uncomplicated ones can be enjoyed with food, especially sweet or slightly savory snacks. Formosa Fancy oolong tea can be infused several times but not the numerous times that the Fujian ball-rolled style oolongs should be steeped. Serve in small cups with a light-colored, clear interior. Formosa Fancy oolong tea brews with an unbelievable aroma and clean taste.

WILD-GROWN TIEGUANYIN

Region: Min-Nan region (south of the Min River), Fujian Province, China
Manufacture: Oolong tea (60–70 percent oxidation)
Style: Folded-leaf or ball-rolled (with many stems)
Flavor: Deep, richly sweet
Aroma: Very fresh, "stone fruit"
Liquor: Golden amber
Brewing: Brew with water slightly hotter than for other Tieguanyins, from 175 to 185°F, thus the temperature may only be increased slightly for subsequent infusions. Drink plain.

This type of oolong is often referred to as "monkey-picked oolong." Wild-grown, traditional-style Tieguanyin is grown on rugged slopes near Anxi. Tieguanyin should be brewed many times, each for a short time. The infusions will vary, initially being light and clear, then very rich and mouth-filling, finally returning to an aromatic, clear brew. The leaves will swell and open gradually until the full leaf is exposed, showing off the lovely crimson-tinged edges of the leaf. This demonstrates the expertise of the tea artisan. Top-grade Tieguanyins may infuse twelve to fifteen times.

TUNG TING

Region: Taiwan, China
Manufacture: Oolong tea (40–50 percent oxidation)
Style: Folded-leaf or ball-rolled (with few stems)
Flavor: Smooth, sweet, soft
Aroma: Clean, floral
Liquor: Golden-green
Brewing: Brew numerous short infusions at 170 to 180°F. Drink plain.

Tung Ting oolong is often referred to as one of the "Orchid Oolongs" or "Jade Oolongs" from Nantou county, Taiwan's premiere oolong-growing region. Tung Ting oolong offers complex aromatics, lush mouth-feel, and varying flavors throughout the multiple infusions that it yields. Authentic Tung Ting oolong is made only in the high mountains, where it is known as "frozen peak" tea. It is one of the most highly regarded oolongs, demanding a premium price because of high demand worldwide.

Black Tea

ASSAM KAMA BLACK

Region: Assam Valley, India
Manufacture: Fully oxidized black tea
Style: Huge, crepey single-leaf pluck
Flavor: Smooth, biscuity, robustly malty
Aroma: Nutty, herbaceous
Liquor: Burnt sienna tinged with copper
Brewing: Brew two to four minutes at 180 to 190°F (super-large-leaf black tea can often be short-brewed twice). Drink plain or with milk and/or sweetener.

This is the style of tea that true Assamese tea lovers drink. Huge intact leaves expertly picked and processed show off the difficult art of oxidizing this size leaf. Search out ultra-large-leaf teas such as this for their complex flavor. This leaf really shows how the term "the agony of the leaves" developed!

YUNNAN GOLDEN BUDS

Region: Yunnan Province, China
Manufacture: Fully oxidized black tea
Style: Full budset in an open spiral
Flavor: Smooth, rich, mouth-filling
Aroma: Clean, nutty
Liquor: Clear, deep golden
Brewing: Brew two or three minutes at 180 to 190°F (budset black tea can often be short-brewed twice). Drink plain.

This tea is manufactured from older tea bushes of varietals indigenous to the subtropical area where southwestern China meets Myanmar. These full, long, and elegant budsets could be made into green tea, but instead they yield this fantastic black tea with incredible depth of flavor and style with subtle nuance. Yunnan Golden Buds must be tasted at least once in a tea lover's lifetime.

CEYLON NUWARA ELIYA

Region: Central Highlands of Sri Lanka
Manufacture: Fully oxidized black tea
Style: Orange Pekoe or Flowery Broken Orange Pekoe, generally in twist or crimped form
Flavor: Brisk, colory, with point
Aroma: Clean, bright
Liquor: Bright copper
Brewing: Brew three to five minutes at 185 to 200°F. Drink plain or with milk, sweetener, or lemon.

Nuwara Eliya gardens at a little altitude yield a large share of the finest Ceylon teas. Potentially lighter and brisker than their better-known cousins the Dimbulas, Nuwara Eliya teas are renown for their polish and finesse, accompanied by a brisk astringency. The best are made with a fairly large leaf, evenly graded into an open crimp or twist.

CEYLON DIMBULA (FANCY SILVERTIPS FOP)

Region: Central Highlands of Sri Lanka
Manufacture: Fully oxidized black tea
Style: Flowery Orange Pekoe and Orange Pekoe, generally wiry or needle, very neat
Flavor: Brisk, coppery, with point
Aroma: Clean, pungent
Liquor: Bright copper
Brewing: Brew three to five minutes at 185 to 200°F. Drink plain or with milk, sweetener, or lemon.

First-rate Dimbulas are known for their polish, finesse, and purity of character, assuring a brisk astringency. The best are evenly graded into a perfect, wiry, classic Flowery Orange Pekoe or Orange Pekoe manufactured tea style. Dimbulas drink well, showing classic black tea disposition. Our customers often remark that this tea tastes as they expect a proper tea should taste.

DARJEELING CASTLETON GARDEN (FTGFOP)

Region: Darjeeling, India
Manufacture: Fully oxidized black tea
Style: Fine Tippy Golden Flowery Orange Pekoe to Flowery Broken Orange
   Pekoe, more often referenced by flush (first/second/autumnal)
Flavor: Brisk, astringent, "muscatel"
Aroma: Pungent, crisp
Liquor: Pale to medium golden
Brewing: Brew three to five minutes at 180 to 195°F (or cooler); check first-
   flush teas at two minutes. Drink plain.

Darjeeling, the "Champagne of teas," is unusual in its briskness and has a peculiar flavor described as "muscatel." We recommend tasting a Darjeeling every twenty to thirty seconds following the first two minutes of infusion, as a Darjeeling may "bolt" all of a sudden, which contributes a distinct sharpness of flavor that isn't always pleasant. The modern European preference for finishing a Darjeeling is more "green" than the traditional firing. The gardens vary tremendously in style, finishing technique, and base tea subvariety, even those adjacent on a hillside.

DARJEELING AUTUMNAL (TGFOP)

Region: Darjeeling, India
Manufacture: Fully oxidized black tea
Style: Autumnal flush is often Tippy Golden Flowery Orange Pekoe
Flavor: Soft "muscatel" with some colory depth
Aroma: Clean, herbaceous
Liquor: Medium golden
Brewing: Brew three to five minutes at 180 to 195°F (or cooler); check at two
   minutes. Drink plain.

Autumnals are definitely worth looking for, as they generally offer a smoother cup behind the big Darjeeling flavor profile. Maturing through the frequently unforgiving first and second flushes, the autumnals have a lot more body and heft than the early year plucks. We find that autumnals often unite the best features of the complex Darjeeling palate with body similar to that of a Nepalese or Yunnan black tea. There is rarely any "green" in the firing of an autumnal.

KEEMUN (HAO YA A)

Region: Keemun (Qimen), Anhui Province, China
Manufacture: Fully oxidized black tea
Style: Wiry, very small, neat
Flavor: Brisk, full-bodied, "winey"
Aroma: Penetrating floral, but clean
Liquor: Golden-red tinged with copper
Brewing: Brew three to five minutes at 185 to 200°F. Drink plain or with
   milk and/or sweetener.

The original English Breakfast Tea, Keemun is no longer plentiful enough (or inexpensive enough) for any but the finest teashops to base their blends on it (as we do). Keemun, in central China, is now a protected area and thus foreigners are not allowed. It continues to be famous as a source for world-class tea. The focused flavor of this tea is superb, and the lingering aftertaste is a real treat.

TANZANIA CTC

Region: Tanzania, Africa
Manufacture: Fully oxidized black tea
Style: Granular, neat
Flavor: Full, rich, malty
Aroma: Nutty, biscuity
Liquor: Burnt umber tinged with orange
Brewing: Brew three to five minutes at 185 to 200°F. Drink plain or with
   milk, sweetener, or lemon.

Most of the Tanzanian tea manufactured today was developed from Assam bush plants grafted onto "native" Kenyan rootstock. This gives the finished tea a good dose of the maltiness of an Assam; however, the clarity of the Kenyan style lightens and softens the whole. Being a moderate-sized CTC, Tanzanian tea brews at about the same rate (or even more slowly) as an orthodox tea.

Pu-erh

PU-ERH, "RAW" (OR "GREEN")

Region: Yunnan Province, China
Manufacture: Not oxidized, then fermented pu-erh
Style: Open leaf and buds
Flavor: Smoothly sweet and lingering, deep (can be woody)
Aroma: Herbaceous, penetratingly floral
Liquor: Dark, burnt umber tinged with red-orange
Brewing: Brew numerous short infusions at 205 to 210°F. Drink plain.

Pu-erh is an acquired taste! "Raw" pu-erh has incredible depth with a lingering sweet, floral, nutty, herbaceous, and vegetal flavor. It is said that pu-erh tastes "of the earth." Developed with years of experimentation going back to the Tea Horse Route days, pu-erh is one of those unique examples of terroir that happily exist to help us celebrate centuries-old tradition. Pu-erh comes in many interesting shapes and sizes. The shapes are usually wrapped and include the provenance, most often the origin and date of manufacture, and are sometimes marked with the seal (or "the chop") of the artisan or previous owner.

PU-ERH, "COOKED" (OR "BLACK")

Region: Yunnan Province, China
Manufacture: Oxidized, then fermented pu-erh
Style: Open leaf and buds
Flavor: Smoothly sweet and lingering, deep
Aroma: Herbaceous, floral, earthy
Liquor: Burnt umber tinged with red-orange
Brewing: Brew numerous short infusions at 205 to 210°F. Drink plain.

"Cooked" pu-erh is not as challenging an acquired taste as so-called "raw" pu-erh and is much less complex and potentially "odd." A modern adaptation of pu-erh abbreviated from the "raw" technique, the base leaf in cooked pu-erh is oxidized before being molded and encouraged to ferment, thus accelerating the progress toward a finished product. Cooked pu-erh is commonly found in loose-leaf form as well as compressed shapes.

Scented Tea

JASMINE DRAGON PEARLS

Region: Fujian Province, China (and other provinces)
Manufacture: True jasmine tea (about 10 percent oxidation)
Style: Budsets scented before, during, and after being rolled into "pearls"
Flavor: Smooth, sweet, soft; traditionally scented
Aroma: Clean, floral
Liquor: Clear silver
Brewing: Brew numerous short infusions at 165 to 180°F (the scenting will dissipate slightly after the first infusion). Drink plain.

Jasmine Dragon Pearls have been popular for several centuries. With the essence of the jasmine flowers captured within the tightly rolled buds, the minimal surface area of Dragon Pearls guarantees that they hold their scent well. Fun to watch unfurl and delicious to drink, Dragon Pearls captivate the tea enthusiast.

TRADITIONAL-STYLE JASMINE (WITHOUT VISIBLE FLOWERS)

Region: Fujian Province, China (and other provinces)
Manufacture: Jasmine tea (about 10 percent oxidation)
Style: Budset and leaf, scented during manufacture only (flower petals are removed from the finished tea)
Flavor: Smooth, sweet, soft; traditionally scented
Aroma: Clean, floral
Liquor: Clear silver
Brewing: Brew numerous short infusions at 160 to 170°F (the scenting will dissipate after the first infusion). Drink plain.

The Chinese mastered the art of scenting the leaf of *Camellia sinensis*, using various flowers and fruits. In traditional-style jasmine tea the essence of jasmine is perceptible in the brewed tea, but no flower petals are visually evident in most Chinese-style jasmine teas.

MODERN-STYLE JASMINE
(WITH VISIBLE FLOWERS)

Region: Sichuan Province, China (and a few other provinces)
Manufacture: Jasmine tea (about 10 percent oxidation)
Style: Budset and leaf, scented during manufacture, then fresh flowers are added to the finished tea
Flavor: Smooth, sweet, focused; highly scented, lingering finish
Aroma: Bright, floral
Liquor: Clear silver
Brewing: Brew numerous short infusions at 160 to 170°F (the scenting dissipates after the first infusion). Drink plain; in Sichuan Province this is sometimes consumed with spicy-hot cuisine.

Modern-style jasmine tea differs significantly from traditional-style jasmine tea. The scenting of the leaf is much higher, requiring that more flowers be added to the base leaf. Flowers are also added to the finished tea, a visual appearance appreciated in Sichuan Province and parts of northern China.

LAPSANG SOUCHONG

Region: Fujian Province, China, and Taiwan
Manufacture: Smoked, fully oxidized black tea
Style: Crepey, open twist
Flavor: Biscuity, robustly smoked
Aroma: Smoky
Liquor: Burnt sienna tinged with copper
Brewing: Brew two to four minutes at 190 to 210°F. Drink plain.

Lapsang Souchong is often referred to as Tarry Lapsang. When a large-leaf black tea is smoked over green pine or other resinous wood, the result is this love-it or hate-it tea. Variation occurs in the strength and inherent flavor profile of the base tea and the amount of and intensity of the smokiness. We often blend a small amount of Lapsang Souchong into other leaf teas to contribute a bit of smoke for those who like "just a whiff." (See "Fujian Province" under "China's Black Teas" in chapter 4 for the fascinating history of Zhen Shan Xiao Zhong, the original Lapsang Souchong.)

EARL GREY

Region: The tea blender's choice of black tea
Manufacture: Fully oxidized black tea
Style: Orange Pekoe, generally in twist or crimp, must be neat
Flavor: Brisk, colory, clean
Aroma: Bright citrus
Liquor: Bright copper tinged with green (from the natural citrus oil)
Brewing: Brew three to five minutes at 185 to 200°F. Drink plain or with
    sweetener or lemon.

Earl Grey is one of the classics. The best are made with a medium-large leaf, evenly graded into a crimp or twist. The addition of natural oil of bergamot provides the citrusy snap and aroma. The character of the base tea combined with the amount of and quality of the citrus oil determine the overall strength, intensity, and aromatic quality of each individual blender's Earl Grey. Sometimes a bit of Lapsang Souchong or lavender is added. Earl Grey tea varies considerably from shop to shop, so be sure to inquire about the house style before stocking up.

Artisan, Presentation, or Display Tea

Presentation teas are a historically rich form of tea elaboration that has recently been revitalized and now captures the fancy of tea enthusiasts worldwide. From simple peony-shaped clusters of green or black tea buds, to intricate bundles of exquisite elongated white tea buds that gracefully unfurl to release silk-thread–strung flower blossoms of jasmine or rose, artisan teas are fun, entertaining, and generally made from high-quality tea. Because so much work goes into these miniature works of art, there is no sense manufacturing them with poor-quality buds.

JADE INGOT, CHINESE LANTERN, JASMINE PEARL-IN-A-SHELL, BLOOMING HEART, DOUBLE-DRAGON WITH PEARL, SHOOTING STAR, ETC.

Region: Historically China but tied today in most tea-growing regions

Style: Elongated-budset base tea; tea buds bundle-wrapped in a fanciful shape and designed to brew open into the likeness of a flower

Flavor: Smooth, sweet, soft; sometimes jasmine-scented

Aroma: Clean, floral

Liquor: Clear silver or pale green-gold

Brewing: Brew numerous short infusions at 165 to 180°F (most scenting dissipates significantly after the first infusion). Drink plain.

Fun to watch and delicious to drink, presentation teas captivate the observer and are best enjoyed brewed in an oversized wine glass, brandy snifter, or glass teapot. Once brewed and enjoyed as a beverage, the opened "flower" can be set in cold water (change daily) and enjoyed for many days as a table centerpiece, a mini bouquet of a sort.

CHAPTER **6**

BREWING THE PERFECT CUP

T^AI CHI, TANGO, AND TEA BREWING are studied but never mastered. Most tea drinkers brew tea the way that their grandmother or familial community does, or by the method used for the first cup of tea that interested them. Today, with the increasing availability of leaf tea from all over the world, of every type of tea manufacture known, and with varying sizes of leaf in each style, a specific explanation of brewing methodology is required for those who want to brew tea with precision. This chapter describes the key components for an incredible tea-drinking experience: purchasing tea, tea storage, the yield, measuring the tea, the water, the water temperature, brewing hot tea, the steeping time, miscellaneous tips for brewing, and finally tasting the tea.

Purchasing Tea

Tea is the second-most consumed beverage in the world, after water; it is also the second-least expensive. It is essential to use fresh, high-quality leaf tea. Many rare and highly regarded teas cost only pennies per cup more than the standard grades, so it is unnecessary to ever brew poor-quality tea. We always tell our customers to "purchase the best tea that you can afford, as often as is necessary to provide convenience for you and to freshen your larder" (see "Tea Storage" later in this chapter).

As with wine, cheese, and coffee, a bit of knowledge regarding production cycles and harvest times will increase your satisfaction with the teas that you select. A new crop of tea comes to market seasonally, so you need to adjust your larder by tea variety, keeping only a sensible quantity on hand,

274

Traditional Korean tea service.

taking particular care with the more delicate fresh teas. A pound of leaf tea, regardless of the variety, always yields two hundred "measures" of tea. This means two hundred cups of tea if brewing a single infusion (most black teas). Teas brewed with multiple infusions (most greens, oolongs, whites, and pu-erhs) may yield as many as six hundred to a thousand cups of tea from those two hundred measures. So there is no reason to have more tea in your pantry than your household can realistically consume. Neither is there any reason to purchase an undersized quantity in the potentially mistaken belief that the tea might remain fresher under the merchant's care. Use these common-sense tips when purchasing tea:

- Support reliable merchants who offer a reasonable selection of tea.

- Keep in mind that your tea merchant should follow the same storage guidelines as you, so more choices do not necessarily mean better tea.

- Shop where there is a steadily moving inventory of a carefully selected assortment of high-quality tea, rather than where there is an enormous variety of poorly chosen tea that has seen better days.

So what is a reasonable selection? The customer base of the merchant dictates that. When a busy tea merchant has a large and diverse clientele, more variety can be offered while maintaining freshness. Selection is nice, but the larger the assortment, the more likely it is that many of the teas are not fresh. If you have a local British provisions shop, we would expect to find tea there from Kenya and India. While shopping a small tea store in China-town, finding any black tea at all may prove impossible, as its clientele most likely drinks only green and oolong tea; this is where you should hope to discover an interesting new flavor, such as a quirky, musty oolong. To recognize merchants who are busy and have an active turnover, regardless of their breadth of selection, ask yourself the following questions:

- Are the dispensing containers clean? Dirty containers show a lack of respect for the tradition established by the tea growers and processors, who have created a fresh, clean product. Avoid merchants who do not understand this relationship.

- Are the signs and related information clear and educational, and is the staff knowledgeable? Well-informed tea purveyors want to share information with you so that a better dialogue can develop, and finer tea can be procured for all to enjoy. Avoid tea stores that are uninteresting or routine.

- Is there obvious enthusiasm for the tea being offered? There should be, fulfilling the connection between the tea grower and the consumer. If this link is dull, chances are the tea will be lifeless as well. Selecting tea is similar to choosing cheese or fish: you need to have a bit of knowledge and find an enthusiastic and reliable source; beyond that, variety is a bonus.

It is critical to learn to distinguish between marketing puff and sincere reverence. If your tea merchant does not provide these positive elements, find another who can offer you a quality product. Bad tea will always be obvious, and questionable tea should be avoided, but great tea is difficult to hide. Most tea merchants are generalists, although a few may elect to specialize in a particular type of tea. Tea on offer must be clearly identified, including the specific garden or estate of origin, when applicable. For example, Castleton Garden is a highly regarded, individual garden in the Darjeeling district of northern India, whereas the highest quality Keemun Hao Ya A will not have further place specificity other than that it is from the Keemun region of Anhui Province, in eastern China.

It is possible to be an expert in the flavor and brewing of tea without having ever set foot in a tea garden, just as one need not be a fisherman to recognize a great fillet of Dover sole or necessarily be able to distinguish goat from ewe to enjoy superlative cheese. When you are interested in learning more about "the way of tea," many knowledgeable tea enthusiasts are ready to share information with you. Professional tea tasters, ourselves included, taste far more tea around our tasting table than on location; the experience of tasting and learning far outweighs being temporarily at the tea's point of origin. All of us drink most of our tea right at home, with local water, so that is how tea should be tasted. That being said, however, if your local tea merchant has observed tea processing at its source and has personal knowledge of tea production, that experience should add to your appreciation of tea as well.

BUYING FRESH TEA

So how fresh is this tea that you are buying, anyway? Basically, there are three ways to purchase leaf tea: (1) bulk, weighed-to-order by your merchant or perhaps self-service; (2) packaged, as a "proprietary" tea, by your tea merchant, in a tin, foil sack, or tin-tie bag; and (3) packaged, so-called branded tea put up by one of the major tea blenders and packers. Each method has its pros and cons, with the most important factors being sourcing the highest-quality tea available in any given year, knowledge of what a singular tea's flavor profile is so that an authentic version of it can be offered, and selling the tea while it is at its peak.

Leaf tea sold in bulk and weighed to order as well as proprietary tea packed by your merchant, near or far, is typically fresher than the packaged branded teas. Just take a look at the tea. Smelling dry tea leaves indicates freshness only for those teas that are scented or flavored, or that should have a toasty or smoky character. It is essential to introduce water to tea leaves to really determine quality. You can tell a lot from the look once you become familiar with quality tea and its visual attributes. Visual clues are particularly important when selecting Chinese green tea.

Many tea lovers can only source high-quality leaf tea by mail order, however, so it is necessary to know how to select tea without the assistance of a merchant. Many of the same tips for buying tea in a store apply to purchasing by mail. What you cannot establish before purchase by mail, of course, are the cleanliness of the facility and the true attitude of the merchant and staff. But you can glean clues by examining the tone of the catalog or website. Is the information clear, accurate, plentiful, and current? Is the presentation cluttered and boring, or fresh and precise? Is everything too slick and marketing-driven, or are you genuinely intrigued with the offerings and stimulated to purchase? Are the prices fair and typical, or mysteriously odd?

HIGHS AND LOWS OF THE TEA-PRICING SPECTRUM

We recently came across an online purveyor selling a particular tea from the exact same source from whom we purchase this tea, but for five times what we charge at retail. This was a fantastic tea, and not inexpensive, but its fair price in the market was $15 per quarter pound, not $70. Even at this hefty price of $280 per pound, the $1.40 per cup cost is still less than a Tetley teabag would be, served to you in any diner. All of this purveyor's prices were extravagant, so this context created a standard. The particular tea we noted was so good that we are sure that many online shoppers were completely happy with their purchase. At this extreme price the purveyor was selling "special" by inflating the price for only those who could afford it. When tea enthusiasts encounter tea that is either very expensive or has a too-good-to-be-true low price, we recommend caution. It is always more important to be wary of cheap tea than expensive tea. Cheap tea is always cheap tea, whereas costly tea (especially when it is priced fairly) is a fantastic value and can provide unforgettable moments of pleasure.

Upon receipt of mail-order tea, you should always confirm that you received what you ordered, check the package for hints as to the care that the tea received during storage and processing, and report immediately any discrepancies or problems. If something is amiss, discuss it thoroughly with the purveyor. Mistakes happen, but they should be resolved to the satisfaction of both parties involved.

SHOPPING FOR BRANDED TEA

Well-known tea companies exist today that have built their reputation on purveying acceptable-leaf tea for generations. These brands are generally available through mass merchandisers and grocers worldwide. You know their names; they are the "old reliables" and quite possibly were your first cup of tea or even the tea that you had this morning. The whole point of creating a "branded" tea is to market a consistent product at a competitive price. A branded tea normally makes use of as many as ten to fifteen teas in its blend to maintain its flavor profile, so you will not find any specific source information on the package.

This is not only okay, it is imperative, as the flavor profile for these teas is the reason to purchase one or another. When clients ask us for PG Tips, they do not want Bewley's flavor profile. We find no fault with blends; they are the equalizers of the tea world. Although we prefer an individual garden's uniqueness and appreciate the inevitable variation from batch to batch, if you prefer to have your morning "cuppa" be reliable and consistent, these teas will provide that for you. Packaged, branded tea generally requires a minimum of four to six months (and often a year or more) to move from harvest to your shopping bag; this processing time should be factored into your purchasing pattern.

WORTH THE PRICE

Diners readily pay $7 to $10 per glass of wine or Champagne with a restaurant meal. Consumed at home, a bottle of wine that retails for $20 costs about $4 per serving. It is not unusual to be charged $3.50 for a cup of coffee or tea after a meal or in a café. It is easy to enjoy a splendid cup of tea from one's own teapot for a fraction of that. At $30 per pound for high-quality black tea, you are paying 15¢ per cup, and at $30 to $40 for fancy oolongs and spring-crop green teas, the price per cup stays about the same or may actually decrease to 5¢ to 7¢ a cup. The most luxurious and unusual teas rarely cost 40¢ per cup, which extrapolates out to $80 per pound for black teas or $160 to $240 for oolong, green, and white teas. Considering that a pound of such highest-quality budset green or traditional white tea may require 40,000 buds (picked one at a time by hand), 40¢ a cup is a steal.

Tea Storage

Tea storage is uncomplicated. Leaf tea should be stored in a cool airtight location, away from strong odors and direct sunlight. The different types of tea have varying internal moisture requirements. An airtight container maintains the proper atmosphere that was established during the manufacture of each specific tea. Recent research indicates that it is possible that some fresh green teas will maintain their flavor best in a very cool environment, such as wine cellar conditions or in the refrigerator. Studies on this are inconclusive, however, so a well-sealed container at ambient room (cool) temperature should be sufficient for the quantity of tea normally kept at home.

Here is a quick reference on guidelines for home storage and consumption:

- Black teas, highly oxidized oolong teas, and budset white teas should be consumed within one year of purchase.

- Less-oxidized oolong teas, modern-leaf white teas, and standard green teas should be consumed within six months to a year.

- Fresh, spring-picked green teas should be consumed within several months to a half-year.

- Pu-erh tea will keep for years if loose leaf, and may improve with age if it is a Sheng Pu-erh (see "Pu-erh" section in chapter 3).

These guidelines assume that you are purchasing leaf tea from the current harvest and that storage conditions from harvest to retail purchase have been excellent. Remember, tea is harvested on a yearly cycle, so you want to capitalize on the seasonal changes that occur throughout the year. Scented and flavored teas show dissipation of the scenting over time, depending on the type of scenting or flavoring and how closely the container is sealed. No accurate prediction can be made for these teas, however, so assume a shelf life of approximately six months.

Yield

As previously stated, regardless of variations in the volume, leaf tea yields two hundred measures per pound for all tea. Using that measure of at least 2 grams of leaf tea for each 6 fluid ounces of water will yield the 50 cups of brewed tea per quarter pound of leaf tea that taste experts recommend. This yield applies to most traditional black teas as well as some standard-grade green and oolong teas. Varieties of tea that allow for multiple infusions (most oolongs, jasmines, whites, and greens), depending on the individual tea and brewing method used, should be able to brew 100 to 150 servings per quarter pound, two to three times the normal yield. The measure of leaf tea remains constant by weight; the factor that increases the number of servings is the capacity of the leaves to be reinfused in fresh water.

Calculated using 2006 prices for high-quality leaf tea in the United States, this is a price per serving of 4¢ to 30¢ per cup, depending on the tea and the number of infusions. As most leaf tea is handpicked from the bush, sorted, manufactured, and handled many times after, then shipped intact around the world, tea continues to be an incredible value.

Measuring the Tea

Professional tea tasters and experienced tea drinkers alike carefully measure the appropriate amount of leaf tea to water. Quality, name-brand tea packers also use a specific proper quantity of tea per teabag (this ranges from 1.8 to 2.2 grams per teabag). In the 1920s, when modern food pioneers perfected the ratios for brewing tea and coffee, their objective was the scientific exploration of pure taste. The measures of "2 level tablespoons" of coffee and

"1 teaspoon" of tea "per cup" are derived from the gram weight of substance held by these common volume-measuring implements.

Tea tasters determined that 2 grams of leaf tea per 6 ounces (180 grams) water (by weight measure) yielded excellent flavor that contained the proper level of soluble solids considered to be the perfect cup of brewed tea. A standard-sized black tea leaf of the day was used for this 2-gram measure and, translated into volume, was that "teaspoon per cup." Six ounces of water by weight (180 grams) is 6 fluid ounces by volume. Both ground coffee and leaf teas generally absorb .5 ounce of every 6 ounces of the brewing water; this suited perfectly the standard cup and saucer developed in 1700s England that holds 5.5 ounces of liquid.

Measuring tea with a simple, inexpensive digital scale is infallible. Whether you are experienced with or are new to tea, and choose to weigh your tea or not, if you enthusiastically aspire to decipher the complexities of the various styles of tea available today, there are two main considerations when measuring tea: the proper measure to use for the type of tea being brewed, and any adjustment for the individual bulkiness of the particular tea being used. Here are the basics and a few variables:

Proper measure by weight. In general, black, oolong, and standard green teas are measured at the customary 2 grams per 6 fluid ounces of water. There are tippy black, spring green, and oolong teas for which one should use 2.5 or 3 grams per 6 fluid ounces. This increased amount is used when a tea will be brewed numerous times, for only 90 seconds to 2 minutes per steeping. Using 2 grams of tea for each 6 fluid ounces of water will yield the fifty cups of brewed tea per quarter pound that taste experts expect. Whether you are weighing your leaf tea or measuring it by volume, it is essential to have a good sense of volume to weight.

Adjustment for differences in volume. First, it must be determined whether the leaf you are using is of the particle size on which the historical base measure of 2 grams (1 teaspoon) per cup was set. The "teaspoon per cup" is based on a standard, medium-long, moderately twisted-leaf black tea. Several well-known examples of this particle size in the black tea class are Keemun Congou, Ceylon BOP, Assam OP, and nearly all Darjeelings. Gunpowder green and Tieguanyin oolong are also of this particle size. Tippy Yunnan, Ceylon FOP, large-leaf Assam, and Lapsang Souchong black teas are all made from a larger leaf (as are most traditional Formosa oolongs and basket-fired spring green teas). These are therefore bulkier, by volume, than the historical base measure, so a larger amount by volume must be used.

Conversely, a cut-tear-curl (CTC) Assam, small-leaf Ceylon, or Keemun Hao Ya A black tea weighs heavy for its bulk and so must be measured "short." A phenomenon that we noticed years ago is that, when using traditional (orthodox) leaf tea, the volume of the spent tea leaves is very similar, whatever the variety of tea being brewed. This is helpful when learning about tea measure and the varieties of leaf style (especially if you choose not to weigh your tea leaves), as observing the structure of the leaf wet versus dry will assist you in determining the correct amount to use.

If the leaf is large, open, and flat, or slightly twisted, as with such bulky oolongs as Formosa Fancy Silvertips or Fujian Da Hong Pao and such big leafy greens as Tai Ping Hou Kui, or when brewing full budset white tea, the tea will not increase much in volume during steeping. Therefore you need to use two or three times the amount of dry leaf by volume than when you are brewing a "standard" particle-sized tea, such as Keemun Congou or a jasmine that will swell significantly when rehydrated. If you do not weigh your dry tea, you can knowledgeably select differently sized scoops that are appropriate to the volume that they need to have for proper brewing of your various teas. See individual tea variety descriptions in chapter 5 for particularly unusual weight and volume correlations.

The Water

Tea should be brewed using fresh, pure cold water. This may be your tap water but will more likely be filtered water or bottled spring water. If you are purchasing bottled water, you should be certain that it is truly spring water, not just someone else's tap water. All spring water sold in the United States and the European Union must have the source of the water identified on the label.

Brewed tea is 99 percent water, so it is essential that it is odor-free and as untreated as is possible. Lu Yu, the Chinese tea scholar (see "Lu Yu: The Father of Tea" in chapter 1), recommended that his Chinese counterparts use water from a spring in the same region from which the tea they were brewing was grown. Of course this is not a practical solution for most of us, although it is a delightful objective when traveling in a tea-producing region. So this is

WATER BOILING VISUAL CLUES

Chinese tea scholars delightfully visualize the four primary temperatures of water used for brewing tea as follows:

- **"Column of steam steadily rising."** This is the period during which a visible pillar of steam materializes, approximately 170 to 180°F (72 to 82°C).

- **"Fish eyes."** This is when large lazy bubbles start to break the surface, approximately 180 to 200°F (82 to 93°C).

- **"String of pearls."** This is the moment almost at the boil, when tiny bubbles appear to loop near the perimeter, approximately 190 to 200°F (88 to 93°C).

- **"Turbulent waters."** This is a full rolling boil, when the water becomes highly oxygenated, approximately 200 to 212°F (93 to 100°C).

our rule of thumb: if we won't drink a particular water, we won't brew tea in it. Conversely, not all great drinking waters are good tea-brewing waters. We love Evian for drinking, but we wouldn't brew tea with it, as it is too soft.

Most tea brews best in moderate to soft water. A few teas (such as tippy Yunnan blacks or full-bodied oolongs) brew well in moderate to slightly hard water with a bit of mineral content. For dependable results when we taste tea professionally, we use water from one of the natural springs in Maine; it consistently has the qualities that we prefer in our tea-brewing water. These springs are relatively nearby our teashop, so the water is fresh. This water is similar to the tap water that our local clientele accesses, but we also regularly taste tea with local tap water, to stay in touch with its flavor.

Experimentation will determine which teas brew well in the water that you drink, or the source for water that complements the tea that you prefer. To evaluate brewing waters, bring a portion of several types of water to a boil, let them cool, then smell and taste each one. Note any positive and negative factors and then test-brew some of your favorite teas with the waters that scored positively. With any luck this will be the water that you drink regularly!

Water Temperature

There are three ideal methods used to heat water for brewing tea. Apply heat to a vessel containing freshly drawn, cold water until: (1) the water reaches the temperature appropriate to the type of tea being brewed; (2) the water comes to a full, rolling boil, then "shock" the temperature down by the addition of a small amount of cold water; (3) the water comes to a full, rolling boil, then allow it to rest until it has cooled to the proper temperature. When the quality of the water is in question, this method must be used.

There are some excellent and easy rules of thumb to follow: For brewing black or oolong teas, the fewer the number of tips and the more highly oxidized the tea leaves, the higher the water temperature should be. For brewing white and most green teas, the lighter the color of the tea leaves, the cooler the water must be. There are important exceptions to this, however: Japanese green teas (which are generally very dark in color but are brewed with cool water) and yellow teas (which are traditionally light in color but are less sensitive to brewing temperature than are many other more darkly colored, early harvest teas). See Table 6.1 for some guidelines on water temperature for brewing the various types of tea.

Table. 6.1. Water Temperature for Brewing Tea, by Type

Tea Type	Temperature
White tea, Japanese green tea, and many new or spring green teas	160–170°F (71–77°C)
Green tea (standard)	"Column of steam steadily rising," 170–180°F (77–82°C)
Oolong tea	"Fish eyes," 180–200°F (82–93°C)
Black tea	"String of pearls," 190–200°F (88–93°C)
Pu-erh tea	"Turbulent waters," 200–212°F (93–100°C)

Sitting at night in a mountain pavilion, drawing spring water to boil tea

As the water and fire battle it out, the scent of the pine billows through the trees

as I pour a cup, bathed in light from the clouds.

The profound pleasure of this moment is hard to convey in words to those of common tastes.

—MING DYNASTY LITERATI

Brewing Hot Tea

Brewing leaf tea requires minimal equipment and a modicum of attention. Preparing tea is not difficult; it should be a pleasurable moment of your day. Millions of people the world over make tea under the most primitive of conditions, so there is no need to complicate it. Allow the leaves to circulate freely in the cup or teapot. We advise our customers to never "contain" bulky spring green tea, oolongs, white tea, or tippy black teas in a tea ball. Tea balls are fine for CTC or very finely cut orthodox tea leaves, but using them for larger leaf will do one of two things. First, using a tea ball might force you to break the leaves into pieces, negating the care with which they have been handled all the way from the tea garden to your kitchen counter. Second, your tea ball might not hold the proper amount of tea because it is too small; or, if the tea ball is large enough, it will displace so much water that the brewing proportions will be wrong. So, while there are many clever filtering and straining devices on the market that will assist you in removing the leaves from your brewed tea, tea balls are not among our recommended choices for this task.

Various cultures have developed creative and legitimate techniques for removing the spent leaves from brewed tea. Five time-tested options are outlined below:

1. **The two-pot method.** Steep the tea in one teapot and pour the brewed tea off into a second pot for serving, straining as necessary. This is by far the easiest, most flexible method for brewing any quantity of any style of tea. An added bonus is that you get to use two teapots from your collection every time rather than just one!

2. **A traditional, single teapot.** Select an appropriately sized teapot, brew the precise quantity of tea that you need, and then steep more if you need it. The English style of this teapot most often has a ceramic "web" or "cage" built into the base of the spout so that the leaves cannot enter the spout. If there is no such cage, there are simple and fancy strainers alike that one can hold between the spout tip and cup to filter errant leaves. Chinese Yixing teapots also have this cage built into the spout base, but this teapot is traditionally used for brewing oolongs. The Japanese tea-brewing rule of thumb is: *The better the tea, the smaller the teapot.* If you are brewing Indian chai, chaiwalla-style, then the water,

milk, tea, and spices will all be brought to a simmer in the same pot. The single-teapot method, whichever type of tea you brew, in whatever style of teapot you use, produces a fixed quantity of fresh tea every time, as you only brew what you will drink at that moment.

3. **Leaf-containing device.** Use a device for containing the leaves, such as a bamboo, twenty-three-carat gold, or stainless-steel basket, a paper tea filter, or a cloth "sock," or use a teapot with a built-in infuser of glass, nylon, ceramic, or stainless steel. Using this method, you can remove the leaves from the brewing water at precisely the steeping time that you prefer and then discard or reinfuse them, depending on the tea leaf being used. Unless all you drink is a small-leaf black tea the utensil that you never want to be tempted with is a tea-ball. This old-fashioned, egg-shaped perforated metal or stainless mesh tea leaf container usually hangs from a chain into the teapot or cup to theoretically infuse the tea. These and most of their variations, while aesthetically pleasing and "cute" are far too small to contain enough tea to properly infuse any tea other than a finely cut black tea and other small leaf teas. Remember, you want the brewing water to circulate around and infuse the leaf, replicating the open pot method but with the convenience of easy elimination of the spent leaf.

4. **A tea glass.** Brew the tea in the vessel from which you will drink. A modern rendition of the classic *gaiwan*, the Chinese have many such tea glasses, ranging from a simple mason-type jar to an elegant stainless-steel cylinder to hold the green tea. These have a filter screen at the top to keep the leaves from coming out of the jar, keeping them in the container for further steeping. Chinese tea drinkers will steep the same leaves many times during the course of the day and refresh them as needed. This is an excellent way to drink green tea.

5. **Make a concentrate.** From Turkish tea to the Russian samovar to the 1970s "sun tea" to institutional iced-tea preparations to present-day chai concentrates, making an essence and then diluting it to taste is a practical method of brewing tea. This concentrate can be prepared using either hot or cold water.

Steeping Time

Now that you have the brewing equipment assembled, fresh water at the proper temperature, and the measure of your favorite tea (or perhaps a new selection) prepared, what is the correct steeping time? We encourage the reinfusion of some types of tea. This is standard with green, oolong, and white tea and pu-erh, plus a few others, such as many of the presentation teas and jasmines. We have been experimenting with the extremely tippy black tea subvarietals from Yunnan and super-large-leaf clonals from northern India that brew wonderfully for a second infusion, but you must infuse them properly and not brew a long first infusion.

This ability to reinfuse is because of a combination of the short brewing time and the tippy nature of the leaf being used. The ability to infuse oolongs multiple times results from the fact that oolongs are traditionally brewed that way, and the process of partial oxidation in the manufacture of oolongs requires the use of a larger, more mature leaf that yields a more flavor-packed leaf that demands reinfusion (see "Oolong Tea, Defined" in chapter 3 for more information). When you know that you will be infusing multiple times, the brew time is kept short, from sixty seconds to slightly more than two minutes per infusion. Some teas that can be brewed multiple times can also be brewed once (or twice) for a longer, more traditional period of time. See Table 6.2 for guidelines on correct steeping times for teas by type.

If you have one pot
And can make your tea in it
That will do quite well.
How much does he lack himself
Who must have a lot of things.

—SEN RIKYU

Table 6.2. Steeping Time for Brewing Tea, by Type

Tea Type	Time
Black tea	3–5 minutes (one steeping only)
Oolong tea	90 seconds to 2 minutes (several steepings)
Green tea	2–3 minutes (several steepings)
Spring (or new) green tea	90 seconds to 2 minutes (several steepings)
White tea	90 seconds to 2 minutes (several steepings)
Pu-erh tea	2–5 minutes (many steepings)

Miscellaneous Brewing Tips

Throughout our collective sixty-plus years of tea-drinking experience, we have observed, learned, and refined several other tea-brewing tips.

1. When brewing green, yellow, white, and oolong teas, do not scorch the tea. Tea leaves of these classes of tea do not benefit from being blasted with boiling hot water, or water at the top of the range at which it could be brewed. Rather, pour some of the water down the side of the brewing vessel to temper the leaves, then pour all over to wet the leaves. Never scorch them, as they will bite back with nasty astringency, especially green tea.

2. For the spring green teas that carry a lot of "down" in their folds, a quick, fresh water rinse is often recommended before steeping. This removes the pollen that would float on the surface of the brewed tea. Many tea experts (such as Eliot Jordan, tea taster for Peets) prefer that their early spring teas have this character, so you decide: to rinse or not to rinse?

3. Cover the tea while it is brewing. Tea always brews better and tastes superior when the brewing vessel is covered during steeping. Tea leaves will unfurl properly only if covered. Try it with two identical portions of tea and you will be amazed; the uncovered portion will not have the character or interest of the covered.

4. Regular harvest China greens and oolongs are generally rebrewed with water that is *hotter* than the temperature of the water first used. Without exceeding the temperature range given in Table 6.1, using water that is at the upper end of the range is often better for rebrewing these teas. Also, we frequently increase the amount of steeping time (perhaps a minute longer), especially when attempting a third or fourth infusion.

5. Early harvest China greens, white teas, and Japanese green teas are generally rebrewed with water that is *cooler* than the temperature of the water first used. Without going below the temperature range given in Table 6.1, using water that is at the lower end of the range is often better for rebrewing these teas. Because the white teas and early greens are delicate tips, and because the Japanese greens have been steamed

already during their processing, the use of cooler water when infusing multiple times will greatly increase the quality of the brewed tea.

6. While millions of avid tea drinkers around the world "take the teapot to the kettle" to use water that is as hot as possible to brew "proper English tea," we find that even the stoutest black teas prefer to be brewed in water that is slightly off the boil. Any perceived reduction in strength can be made up by steeping the tea a little longer.

7. "Creaming" is the term used to describe the phenomenon of a brewed tea becoming cloudy as it cools. The degree of cloudiness is determined by the specific amino acid content of the soluble solids in the brewed tea in combination with the exact composition of the polyphenols. While historically creaming was considered to be an indicator of highest-quality tea in countries that grow and produce Assam bush tea, now, with the rising popularity of iced tea beverages, the presence of cloudiness is no longer the positive factor it once was. Many iced tea blenders today use a significant percentage of Nilgiri black tea and other high-altitude-grown tea from China bush plantings to moderate this effect, as they tend to "cream" less and sparkle more.

   About all we can do to mitigate this chemistry is to (1) use untreated but soft water when possible (a high mineral content water will exacerbate the situation); (2) use tea leaf from China bush growths and accept a typically lighter-color brewed tea; (3) add citrus juice (lemon, lime, or even orange), as the increased acidity will hold the liquor brighter (hence, there is often citric acid in bottled iced tea); and (4) cool the brewed tea slowly and do not refrigerate it. Brewed tea can be kept at room temperature for several days in most climates. Our opinion is that, as with the "down" mentioned above, this aspect of tea brewing is completely natural and should not be cause for concern.

8. You brew a second or third steeping of green or white tea (or the sixth or seventh of oolong) and don't want to drink it at that time. So you put it in a glass pitcher on the counter to hold until later. When you come back to it several hours later, it has changed from its sparklingly clear pale green liquor to a gorgeous but dark golden-amber color. This effect is oxidation, not creaming. The soluble solids in tea liquor brewed from nonoxidized tea leaf will ultimately oxidize even in sus-

pension. As in tip #7 above, if you add acid in the form of citrus juice to the brewed tea before it cools, the darkening will be significantly reduced. Just remember, however you choose to prepare cooled tea, the colors are beautiful, varying, and natural, so enjoy the diversity.

Tea Tasters

Tea tasters are an experienced lot—it can take up to four years of serious, practiced tasting to develop the necessary skills. Tea tasters serve several functions and work in different capacities throughout the tea industry. Some tea tasters must be able to cup two hundred to four hundred samples of tea each day. Depending on the position of the tea taster, he or she must be able to easily distinguish between the flavor characteristics of nearly two thousand types of tea. Their palate and sense of smell must be finely tuned, and they must have the ability to retain a taste memory that allows them to evaluate multiple offerings of the same style of tea from different estates over the course of an entire crop year.

Tea tasters who work for large tea estates in tea-producing countries cup hundreds of samples of tea each day during the heavy cropping season. Their sharp palates detect positive elements as well as any flaws in the daily tea production, and they report this to the tea production manager so that adjustments can be made to the production routine. Tea tasters also work for auction houses, evaluating the continual flow of tea samples. Outside the tea-producing countries, many tea tasters work for specialty tea purveyors. Their experience allows them to zero in on the best teas quickly and accurately and recommend the correct purchases. Still other tea tasters are employed by national tea companies and are responsible for purchasing vast quantities of particularly flavored leaf in order to maintain the recognized flavor of a regional or national tea brand. Additionally, they execute the purchase of large quantities of those teas to keep the brand in production.

Professional tea tasters taste tea several ways. Old-school tasters use the trade custom established by the Tea Act of 1833, in which the weight of tea for tasting was set at thirty-five grains, the weight of the silver half-dime of the era. This quantity of leaf, about 2.25 grams, is put into a 5-ounce cup, properly heated water is added to fill, and tasting ensues.

THE BREATHING AND STRETCHING OF THE TEA LEAVES

In simple terms this is the unfurling of the tea leaves. The British refer to it as the "agony of the leaves," the process of rehydration that dried tea leaves undergo when returning to their original, softened, and pliable state after the introduction of hot water. Hot water is the sap that reinvigorates tea with the blush of new life in the teacup or teapot. The leaves become deliciously drinkable thanks to the flavor and aroma that was coddled and tamed into being by skillful tea-processing hands. The Chinese can be counted on to create the most poetic allusions in this regard. For instance, how much more lovely it is to think about this process as they do—the breathing and stretching of the leaves—rather than as "an agony." Think of it as a rebirth from a hibernation of a sort.

Coincidentally, professional Japanese tea tasters use their five-cent coin as the official tea-weight measure, as well. Weighing 5 grams, the five-yen coin translates to *go en*. For tasting, 200 cc (6.68 ounces) of 165°F (75°F) freshly heated water is added to this *go en* measure.

In most modern tea tasting rooms, 6 grams of tea is the required amount used for tasting. A specially designed three-piece tea-tasting cup set is used. Hot water is poured over the leaves in the tea-steeping cup, and the lid is quickly placed over the cup. The tea is steeped for a specified number of minutes (depends on the tea, but it is usually five) and then, holding the lid in place, the steeping cup is turned over and set to rest in a wide but shallow bowl-like tasting cup. The tea liquor drains from the steeping cup into the tasting bowl through dentals cut into the lip of the steeping cup opposite the handle. Once the liquor has been decanted, some of the wet, infused leaf is tapped onto the underside of the lid. The lid is inverted and set to rest atop the steeping cup for examination. The taster raises a teaspoon of tea to his or her lips and slurps the tea with a loud sucking noise. The tea is then swirled in the mouth and over the tongue, and the taster draws the aroma back into the olfactory area. The tongue judges taste, but other parts of the mouth evaluate hot, sour, bitter, and sweet. The astringency of the tea is felt in the cheeks and on the gums. The lingering aftertaste of the tea is appreciated and noted.

No one expects the casual tea enthusiast at home to supervise and labor over tea brewing in the manner that professionals do at the tasting table; however, we know that many of the particulars of tea brewing are identical, and the processes are similar. While home tea making is more casual, a bit of attention paid to the brewing will reward you with a cup that is well made and shows off the attributes of the tea you sought out in the marketplace.

Now stir the fire, and close the shutters fast,

Let fall the curtains, wheel the sofa round;

And while the bubbling and loud-hissing urn

Throws up a steamy column, and the cups

That cheer wait on each,

So let us welcome peaceful evening in.

—WILLIAM COWPER (1731–1800)

CHAPTER 7

TEA CUSTOMS AND CULTURE

I MAGINE THE FOLLOWING: a Japanese tea master wishing to teach his student the importance of perception dashes a cup of tea to the ground, breaking the cup and spilling the tea. The tea master wished to illustrate the point that the broken cup was no longer a cup but just a pile of shards, while the tea was still tea, immutable and unchanged. But as the tea could no longer be consumed without the cup to hold it, the true importance of the cup becomes clear. It is the empty space of a teacup that performs the most essential duty, one with greater importance than merely the fleeting beauty of a pleasing shape, fetching design, or lustrous glaze.

While this essential point defines the relationship between the drinking vessel and the intended beverage, man's desire to surround himself with objects of beauty has nevertheless placed great emphasis on the pleasing, visual nature of teawares. Over the centuries each tea culture has expressed its passion for tea drinking by creating a rich repository of teacups and teapots that pays homage to form and fancy and to the civilizing power of tea rituals. From highly refined, painted, and gilt-decorated porcelain teacups to rough-textured, slightly asymmetrical, simple cups, teawares are the visual expression of a society's attitudes regarding the importance of tea drinking and the delineation of class in each society. But difference of style and material aside, once tea enters a culture's daily life, it is no longer just a beverage: it becomes a way of life.

No matter where you are or what tea is being enjoyed, the requisite elements of tea drinking are the same: water, tea-brewing vessels, drinking cups, the tea itself, and the expected pleasure of the brew. We have observed in other tea cultures around the world a complex set of practices that is based on history, tradition, and philosophy, as well as daily and ritual necessity.

Gong fu tea service tea sets are made of natural-colored Yixing clay and can be purchased in reddish-brown or dark brown. Each gong fu setting includes a short drinking cup and a tall aroma cup, to capture the delicate floral aroma of a fine oolong tea.

The various traditions uphold a strong, historical tea-drinking practice, as each society has adapted tea drinking in its own exacting ways. From China to India, Japan to Thailand, Tibet to Georgia and the Russian Federation, England to Morocco, tea drinking is expressed differently and passionately. As the second-most widely consumed beverage on the planet, tea brings a vibrant and colorful array of utensils and teawares to the global marketplace, creating a seemingly endless collection of necessities for tea enthusiasts everywhere.

Tea Culture in China

Chinese tea history follows a long and detailed pathway to the creation of the first teacups, water ewers, and teapots, each of which directly influenced the pottery traditions of first Korea and later Japan. Approximately five thousand years ago, the earliest Chinese people made crude, simple tablewares of rudimentary, unglazed clay. Later, by the time of the Shang (1766–1050 BC) and Zhou dynasties (1122–256 BC), cookwares and tablewares were fashioned of heavy, durable, and decorative bronze. By the end of the Zhou dynasty these somber pieces were replaced with lightweight and colorful lacquer tablewares.

Under the Han dynasty (206 BC–220 AD) the variety of materials used for food increased to include wood and bamboo. From a document written from 59 BC titled *Tongyue*, we know that tea was being consumed as a beverage at that time. This text reveals that the duties of a servant boy were to include "tea making and utensil cleaning and buying of tea," although there is no reference to the utensils used for the tea. During the Eastern Jin dynasty (317–419) the first handle-less tea bowl emerged. In the prose poem on tea titled *Chuanfu*, author Du Yu muses regarding the appearance of a freshly prepared cup of tea. Referring to tea brewed from powdered tea and the requisite water temperature necessary to create the desirable surface foam, he writes: "bubbles subside and froth floats/resplendent as snow."

THE WORLDLY ERA OF THE TANG DYNASTY

By the time of the Tang dynasty (618–907), China had developed a diverse food culture comprised of numerous regional cuisines that incorporated various culinary implements. An increased variety of foodstuffs coupled with a growing culinary sophistication brought a sense of refinement to cookware and tableware. As tea transformed in use from medicine to a stimulating, healthful brew, and then to a refined, pleasure beverage, the functionality of teawares changed and the aesthetics increased.

Tea drinking became increasingly fashionable, and social tea drinking became an intellectual pursuit shared and enjoyed by the upper class. For the first time a highly elaborate system of teawares was developed to meet the need for sophisticated tea bowls, water pitchers, and containers for salt and spices, as well as tea grinding, boiling, and measuring devices.

In the early part of the Tang period tea making consisted of grinding a piece of cake tea (made from compressed tea leaves) into a powder and then putting the powdered tea into a caldron of boiling water with spices and or bits of fruit. The mixture would be stirred until frothy, and then the clear tea was ladled into the tea bowls for drinking. In the later days of the Tang, tea drinkers began placing the powdered tea directly into the tea bowls in a method called *diancha fa*. Hot water was poured over the tea from tall, handled water ewers, and the tea was stirred in the bowl until it became frothy.

In the progression from the stirred powdered tea of the Tang dynasty to the whipped powdered tea of the following Song dynasty (960–1279) and finally the steeped tea leaves of the Ming dynasty (1368–1644), each successive emperor commissioned new styles of imperial teawares for use in the court. Imperial porcelains were sometimes called "celestial" porcelain, a reference to their exquisite colors and subtle hues that emulate the shades of precious jade. Only such a delicate material could be considered for a cup that would hold the heavenly liquid that would moisten the lips and quench the thirst of the emperor. During the reign of Emperor Taizong (r. 626–649) fine, light greenish-blue celadon porcelains were being made in the Yue kiln in Zhejiang Province. A little later, white-glazed porcelain wares from the Xing kiln in Hubei Province were lauded by Emperor Xuanzong (r. 712–756). Embossed metal teacups were also used by the upper class. Commoners used earthenware tea ceramics, yet in both cases teawares had suddenly become a category apart from other everyday food utensils. Tea cakes were stored in porcelain, wood, or bamboo jars, although precious silver and jade tea jars were preferred by wealthy citizens.

In the early days of the Tang tea drinkers continued using the diancha fa method but favored low-sided, shallow tea bowls known as *qians*, which accentuated the appearance of the powdered tea in the bowl. Tea bowls still required bowl stands for elevating the cup and to give the bowl a stable base on which to rest. Early tea bowls were often made with a narrow foot and were sometimes unable to stand on their own without tipping over.

THE SONG DYNASTY: ROMANTIC PERIOD OF CHINESE TEA DRINKING

The arrival of the Song dynasty (960–1279), often referred to as the romantic period of Chinese tea drinking, brought a change to the manufacture of cake tea and a new level of sophistication to tea making. Cake tea was now compressed from steamed leaf that had been dried and powdered (rather than being compressed from steamed and dried whole-leaf tea). The molds were smaller, and the designs impressed on the cakes were more elaborate. For high officials tea was compressed in silver tea molds. These elegant teas were called white tea, but they bear no relation to today's white teas. Modern methods of leaf manufacture—green, black, and oolong—had not yet been discovered. These white teas were the result of a very select plucking of tender tea buds that were steamed and then quickly dried and powdered.

This new cake tea provided Song tea drinkers with a cake that was easier to scrape, and which, after grinding and sieving the tea, would produce much finer powder than previous cakes. Now tea powder could be placed directly into the cup, and after the addition of hot water, a bamboo whisk was used to create a "heavenly jade froth." Tea that was properly powdered would float, while coarse, improperly prepared tea would sink to the bottom of the cup, a concern of much embarrassment for the person preparing the tea.

This change of tea preparation necessitated ceramic teacups with a more accommodating shape for this new procedure. The result was a swing away from the wide tea bowl and the introduction of a narrower and taller tea bowl that allowed for the easy movement of the bamboo whisk inside of the cup. These bowls were called *jianzhan* and stunning, very black-brown sensuous glazes were introduced to complement the color of the tea liquor. Kilns in Fujian Province supplied the bowls, and several glaze styles were favored during this time: a streaky brown glaze called "hare's fur" was popular, as was an underglaze of paper-cut stencils in designs of phoenix birds, fruit, flowers, and dragons. Intricate oil-spot, tortoiseshell, and partridge feather glazes also appeared in the Song dynasty. Collecting tea accoutrements was a testament to social status to the Song, and tea bowls became an object of admiration and envy.

These bowls were also favored by the monks in Buddhist temples at Mount Tianmu on the border of Anhui and Zhejiang Province. During this time, many Japanese priests and monks came to visit these famous temples for study and exchange of ideas. Visiting monks returned home to Japan, bringing with them caches of tea bowls for fellow priests and monks to use in their budding tea practice. In Japan, these Chinese bowls were called *tenmoku* tea bowls, in reference to the mountain where they were made. Today, this style of tea bowl is still referred to as tenmoku in both China and Japan and fine examples are still being made in the kilns in Fujian, China.

Some of these tea bowls were intended to rest in elevated tea stands called *tenmoku-dai.* Stands or daises were built as one piece and consisted of a saucerlike base with a raised ring in the center into which the tea bowl was set and securely held in place. This clever design elevated the bowl from the table and allowed the tea drinker to lift the stand and the bowl to his mouth to easily sip the tea without having to touch the hot bowl. For elite members of society, this was another way to enjoy the ritual and protocol of drinking the "celestial beverage of the gods."

Reproduction *tenmoku*-style tea bowls made in Fujian, China, illustrate two popular ceramic styles from the southern Song period: paper-cut designs featuring flying phoenix birds (*feifenhwen*) and black-brown hare's fur glazes.

Water with bubbles like crabs' eyes

Retains the youthful zest.

Bowls with fur's hair glaze

Show the color at its best.

—SHU ZHE (1039–1112)

A stylish pair of Japanese lacquered tenmoku-dai, circa 1955, and two contemporary Japanese tenmoku (Chinese-style) tea bowls.

Sophistication, refined elegance and a degree of opulent showmanship defined Song tea drinking.

Tea-brewing competitions became fashionable during this time, and one type of competition focused on the skills of whipping the powdered tea. For this practice dark glazes were favored for tea bowls, as their color would best show the tea marks on the sides of the cup. If the tea froth was skillfully prepared, the powdered tea would leave a marking on the side of the bowl that would confirm this. Or, on the occasion of a tea that failed to obtain the proper froth, the bowl would simply show a waterline, signifying that the froth failed.

THE ADVENT OF TEAPOTS

It is recorded that close to 130 kilns were operating throughout eastern China during the Song dynasty. Kilns were responsible for producing different types of shapes, glazes, and decorating techniques, and six major schools of ceramics style evolved. Kilns produced both imperial wares (*gong yu*) and everyday wares (*min yao*), although there were restrictions on colors and designs that were reserved for imperial use only. Two of the most colorful Song glazes were Jun ware (which featured an abstract design pattern using light blue and purple glazes) and Ge ware (which featured some of the first dark-lined crackle glazes).

The first teapots began to appear toward the end of the Song dynasty, at a time when tea drinkers began to experiment with tea brewed from tea leaf. These early teapots were made from unglazed *zisha*, or purple sand clay, and evolved from the shape of tall, handled wine pots and water ewers. Tea was consumed in small quantities during the Song dynasty, resulting in teapots that were small and wider at the base than at the top. Unlike water pitchers or ewers for pouring wine, teapots were given a lid, as the Chinese realized that the tea flavor of steeped leaf tea was better when the steam was prevented from escaping from the pot. For balance in pouring and in consideration of the lids that needed to be put on and taken off, handles were often attached to the side of the vessel rather than placed across the top.

Song literati scholars and artists praised the simplicity of these unglazed purple Yixing clay teapots for their spare form, simple design, and hand-carved shapes. The smooth finish of these teapots likened them to a "priceless pearl" and "purple jade." These teapots fulfilled the mindful and natural tea-drinking experience that the literati sought, which allowed them to retreat from the overwrought tea practices of their day. Their careful approach to tea appreciation not only advanced tea culture in China but also later influenced tea culture and customs in Japan.

JINGDEZHEN: CHINA'S PORCELAIN CAPITAL

By the end of the Song dynasty and the beginning of Kublai Khan's Yuan dynasty (1271–1368), ceramics production in China began its ascent to glory. Imperial teawares were no longer made in the kilns in the outlying provinces but were now commissioned in porcelain factories located in the city of Jingdezhen, in Jiangxi Province. Up to this point Jingdezhen had been known for its monochromatic bluish-white Qingbai porcelain wares. The creation of an imperial factory created within China a center for porcelain production that would become world famous for innovations in design and glazes that would forever place China in the vanguard of porcelain production.

For the pleasure of the Yuan rulers, Jing-dezhen produced off-white teawares with carefully incised designs. Later, once the secret for obtaining pure white hard-paste clay-bodied porcelain was discovered, white porcelain objects decorated with elaborate cobalt blue underglaze decorations became a favorite of the Yuan emperors and the Ming emperors (1368–1644) who followed. Ming emperors also

Limited-edition reproduction Ming dynasty teapots made in the famous Jingdenzhen kilns. The original of the tall over-handle teapot was made during the reign of the eighth Ming emperor Wanli (r. 1573–1620).

favored solid color glazes, including yellow, which was prohibited from use by anyone other than the imperial family.

For everyday citizens simple utilitarian *zisha* teapots remained the fashion until the beginning of the second half of the Ming dynasty. Although all classes of citizens used zisha teapots, the imperial palace and upper-class citizens coveted zisha teapots fashioned by famous potters. One such notable zisha potter, Gongchun, was the first to gain notoriety for designing bold new teapot shapes. He inspired a handful of zisha potters who followed after him, namely Dong Han, Shi Dabin, and Hui Mengchen. These potters began to fashion innovative teapots that featured organic shapes borrowed from nature or incorporated a poem or inscription into a pleasing shape.

Ming-era tea drinkers also had the option of using porcelain teapots and drinking from teacups, rather than tea bowls, as was the fashion in the past. As loose-leaf tea steeping became the customary way to brew tea during the naturalistic Ming era, teapots became essential and increasingly popular. Following the lead of the individually sized zisha teapots, porcelain teapots were made similarly small in capacity. It became the Ming custom to add leaf tea to the pot, steep the leaves, pour the tea into a teacup, and quickly return the brewed tea to the pot for additional steeping. It was considered good form to do this twice before drinking the tea, bad form to do it three times.

THE QING DYNASTY: SECRETS OF VIVID GLAZES

With the overthrow of the Ming dynasty, porcelain production continued at Jingdezhen during the arrival of the Manchu rulers and their Qing dynasty. This transition of power was plagued by many rebellions, some of which disrupted porcelain production in Jingdezhen and damaged many of the kilns. Later, the Manchu restored the kilns at Jingdezhen and for the first time created separate kilns for porcelains that would be used to produce wares for the palace from those producing wares for ordinary citizens. This separate imperial porcelain factory created some of the most brilliant pieces of porcelain ever designed in China during the Qing dynasty.

Experiments in bold, opaque monochrome colors ushered in the use of orange, yellow, lime-green, and red glaze colors, many of which are still in production today. Early Qing emperors had a voracious appetite for collecting teawares and embraced solid colors for use in the court. Social ranking dictated which color porcelain wares one could use at the table, and the emperor strictly controlled the use of these colors. For the Qing upper class added amusement came in the form of pewter teapots that imitated zisha teapots or were shaped in the likeness of squatting ducks. During these last two dynasties the porcelain works at Jingdezhen produced exquisitely detailed and innovative designs laden with auspicious symbols on porcelains of such fine delicacy that they immediately became objects of desire to the Western traders arriving in the seventeenth century.

One of the last great contributions of the Qing dynasty to porcelain making was the invention of *fencai*, an elaborate style of raised overglaze enamel decorating that replicated the look of cloisonné design and allowed the use of bright colors and elaborately painted designs on porcelain objects, including teapots and cups. Several techniques were used: *famille verte*, which employed bright green translucent enamels, and *famille rose*, which featured a pallet of pink opaque enamels.

CHINA'S TEAWARES OF TODAY

Today every major museum in China has on display wonderful examples of valuable and historical porcelain teawares from these early periods. Amazingly, many of these items are very contemporary in feeling and would fit right in to the offerings of a fine ceramics shop; the pieces are fresh and lively and still imbued with a spirit that beckons the tea drinker to pick up the piece and take a sip of tea. In fact, we have seen throughout our travels in China that most of these types of teawares are still being used. China's tea history is in some ways a living history: much from the past is still relevant. In today's fast-changing world, everything old is still new in the world of tea leaves and teahouses.

Contemporary Chinese potters and ceramic artists continue to follow tradition while forging new artistic designs in familiar teawares. In Hong Kong the Flagstaff House Museum of Tea Ware pays tribute once a year to the new generation of ceramic artists by hosting a teawares exhibition. This vital showcase presents the work of young Chinese artists who capture the attention of ceramics collectors around the world. Today, one is apt to see many aspects of China's tea history being kept alive in teashops and teahouses. New interpretations of classic teawares, such as handle-less cups, zisha teapots, fencai teacups and teapots, gong fu tea sets, and *gaiwans* (thin-walled, lidded porcelain cups), are still popular. This is a tribute to the genius and functionality of these teawares; after all these years it is inconceivable that any better teacup or teapot design is still waiting to be discovered in China.

CHINA'S FAVORITE TEACUP: THE GAIWAN

China's most popular tea tool is a thin-walled, lidded porcelain cup called the gaiwan. This simple but brilliantly conceived piece of engineering was developed in the Ming dynasty, and nothing better has yet come along to replace it. This palm-sized cup performs as a teapot and provides the tea drinker with all of the apparatus that he or she needs in one easy design— saucer, cup, and lid. Gaiwans are still used in every teahouse in China today as well as in all of the tea research centers and tea factories that we have visited.

Hand-painted Chinese gaiwans.

The gaiwan is comprised of three pieces—a saucer that holds the cup (a much smaller version of the tea bowl and bowl holder of the Song dynasty), a small cup with a flared lip, and a lid. When using a gaiwan, the leaves of black, oolong, or pu-erh teas (but not green or white teas) are washed with a quick rinse of water, a procedure started by tea drinkers in the Ming dynasty. This rinse water is quickly drained away, and the tea drinker takes a moment to appreciate the aroma of the moistened leaf by sniffing the underside of the lid.

More water is slowly poured down the side of the gaiwan, which allows the tea leaves to float and then sink. The lid is replaced while the tea is steeping. The saucer allows the drinker to pick up the hot cup without burning one's fingers. Although gaiwans are simple in design, they require a bit of manual dexterity to properly maneuver them. Two hands are never used for the same task; rather, one hand is used to elevate the gaiwan to the lips, and the other works the lid to brush back the tea leaves that are floating in the cup before taking a sip. Because the infused leaf remains in the cup, tea drinkers are able to visually assess the quality of the leaf. The aroma of the tea collects in the slightly concave underside of the lid, and smelling the aroma is encouraged. Additional infusions are easily obtained by simply adding more water to the leaf in the gaiwan.

Perhaps spurred on by the advantageous ability to see the tea leaves in the bottom of the gaiwan, the superstitious art of tea-leaf reading flourished as a popular teahouse art in Ming-era China. Gaiwans are for sale everywhere in China, from a few dollars each to several thousand. Imagine our surprise when we asked about a lovely gaiwan decorated with delicate butterflies in a Hong Kong teahouse and were told that it was Ming dynasty and for sale for a mere two thousand dollars!

Above: A gaiwan and a zisha teapot are both called into service for an oolong tasting (Fujian Province, China).

Left: In Anxi, tea expert Peter Wu appreciates the subtle aroma of a new spring Tieguanyin oolong tea that has gathered on the underside of a gaiwan lid (Fujian Province, China).

Two contemporary Yixing teapots (the green melon teapot and the Chinese bamboo steamer teapot) are featured with reproductions modeled after two famous Yixing teapots. The magnolia blossom teapot (the original is in the Falstaff House Museum of Tea Ware in Hong Kong) was made by the artist Shi Dabin who lived during the reign of the eighth Ming emperor Wanli (r. 1573–1620). The original version of the large bridge-handle Yixing teapot was excavated in a burial site in the twentieth century and thought to date from 1533, the time of the sixth Ming emperor Jiajing (r. 1522–1567).

ARTISTIC YIXING TEAPOTS

Since the Song dynasty, artists have fashioned these simple teapots by hand from clay deposits found in the vicinity of the town of Yixing near Lake Tai in Jiangsu Province. These skillfully made unglazed small teapots represent one of China's most practical art forms. Early clay teapots were slightly larger than later teapots, and at first their shapes were made into simple rounds or pots that featured geometric, faceted sides. Later, in the Ming and Qing dynasties, teapot artists began to make smaller teapots specifically for brewing oolong teas. The scholar class of tea literati delighted in these teapots, and artists fueled their interest by fashioning teapots that incorporated such nature themes as flowers, fruits, bamboo, and animals into their teapot designs. Over time different schools of teapot artists developed, just as landscape painters represented different schools of thought and technique.

In the twenty-first century contemporary Chinese artists have turned back to spare, simple shapes that feature contour, texture, and a soft sheen finish. These artists are respecting tradition while elevating the teapots to a new level of sophistication. It is as Confucius said: "To search the old is to find the new." Zisha clay is found in a range of natural earth tones—red, yellow, rose-brown, light brown, purple-red, and black—according to the earth pigments in the clay. Most teapots are rubbed with a piece of water buffalo horn to smooth and burnish the surface of the teapot both inside and out, and the pots are signed with the chop mark of the potter on the bottom of the teapot as well as on the lid.

Despite their fragile appearance, Yixing teapots offer the user a practical tool for brewing tea. Zisha clay can tolerate near boiling water without cracking, the color of the teapot does not fade or change, and the clay does not impart or retain any odor. The lids fit tightly to expose the leaf to the beneficial heat and steam of the water. The surface of the teapots gain a fine patina with repeated use, and with careful handling, they will last a lifetime. Bear in mind that there are four levels of price for Yixing teapots, which are determined by the fame of the potter who made it, the intricacy of the design or style, the fineness of the clay, and the amount of surface smoothing and polishing the pot received.

The first category is comprised of the largest production of clay teapots—the basic, simple wares that fetch about $10 to $15 in China. Next come the standard pots, also in the large production category but offering more style and flair, which range from $35 to $60. These are followed by the collectors' pots, pieces crafted by well-known artists from traditional designs or modern interpretations, which can sell from $150 to $800 apiece. Finally, it is not uncommon in China to see antique teapots for sale, which can fetch prices of $3,000 and higher.

But no matter the price, the purpose of a Yixing teapot is for steeping tea. When purchasing one of these teapots, look for a lid that fits snugly and for teapots that have a smooth finish inside and out. The intrigue with these clay teapots lies in the fact that over time the inside of the teapot begins to absorb the flavor of the tea brewed in it. Do as the Chinese do and reserve a different teapot for green tea and for oolong tea, and *never* use these teapots to brew scented or flavored tea such as Earl Grey or jasmine. It is not uncommon to see antique teapots that are fifty, eighty, even a hundred years old in Chinese shops that show no discernable ware or age marks.

But please beware of new "yellow" clay teapots coming from China. These teapots are oversized and clunky, and the spiritual opposite of a graceful, timeless Yixing teapot. These faux teapots are popping up in shops in Chinatown in New York and San Francisco, and they usually appear in the shape of bamboo shoots or stalks of bamboo, dragons, or Chinese coins. Although they are interesting, they are clumsy and made from rough, crude clay that gives off a strong, unpleasant odor, which will taint the flavor of your tea. A true zisha teapot never adulterates the flavor or aroma of the tea, and the smooth, hard clay does not have a discernable aroma.

Zisha teapots find their way into teapot collections around the world, and whether one purchases them here or in China, the choice of designs seems delightfully endless. If you find yourself in Hong Kong, be sure to visit the Flagstaff House Museum of Tea Wares. In addition to housing the K. S. Lo Collection of Yixing teapots that features historical antique teapots made by master potters, the museum has a terrific selection of tea books (most are in English and Chinese), gaiwans, teapots, wooden tea scoops, and many other intriguing tea accessories. Plan your visit as we did and after visiting the museum stop in next door at the teahouse for some tasty dim sum and a soothing pot of tea before heading back out onto the bustling streets of Hong Kong.

GONG FU TEA SERVICE

In China gong fu tea preparation fits the concept behind the name. It is a skillful, labor-intensive practice designed to allow tea drinkers to appreciate the prolonged flavor and distinctive aroma of fine oolong teas. The skill of the tea master preparing and dispensing the tea is also observed and appreciated. The roots of gong fu tea service began in Guangdong Province, close to the border with Fujian Province. Specifically designed for use with big leafy oolong teas, such as Fenghuang Don Cong, gong fu tea service is also performed in Yunnan for tasting costly, aged pu-erh tea, the perfect vehicle to showcase the broad dayeh leaf that these teas are made from.

Gong fu uses small Yixing clay teapots to brew the tea, which is then dispensed into tiny clay cups. Small teapots and cups fulfill the Asian experience that allows tea drinkers to enjoy the changing flavor of the tea over the course of multiple infusions of the same leaf. Tall "aroma" cups are also used to capture the fragrance of these oolongs, which adds to the sensory appreciation of the tea by creating anticipation for the flavor that will follow. Depending on the type of leaf used, the number of infusions can be quite numerous. In Dali, Yunnan, we were treated to a gong fu tasting of an old pu-erh tea that yielded thirty flavorful infusions. By that time we had reached our limit of how much tea we could consume, but the leaf still had flavor to give.

When performing gong fu, it is necessary to wash the cups and teapots for the guests while seated at the table with them. Gong fu tea trays or water

catch basins are specifically designed to catch this overflow water and keep the water from spilling all over the table. Traditional gong fu tea sets come with a clay or ceramic washing bowl (*cha chuan*) as well as a round clay or ceramic platform that is fit with a removable water-draining plate, which rests on top. Modern gong fu sets utilize attractive and decorative wooden or bamboo draining trays that feature a built-in plastic slide-out tray for catching the wash water. Either way, one needs to have a way to pour hot water over the teapot and rinse the cups while seated.

In addition, for gong fu tea service one also needs: one set of wooden tools for handling the wet and dry tea leaves, a tea measuring scoop, a tea presentation bowl for displaying the selected tea leaf and for guiding the tea into the teapot, a small Yixing teapot, a small strainer, a tea-dispensing pitcher for pouring the brewed tea, one tall narrow "aroma" cup (*wen xiang bei*) and a short wide "drinking" cup (*cha bei*) for each participant, and one little clay tray to hold the two cups for each guest.

Conducting gong fu. All of the senses are engaged in gong fu, so it is essential to allow your guests to see and smell the dried tea leaf, to see and smell the wet tea leaf, and to smell and taste the brewed tea. And of course, for your guests to appreciate the skills of the tea master or host, gong fu is performed in front of your guests for their pleasure. Dexterity in executing the steps of gong fu is important to its concept and principle.

An elegantly carved wooden tea washing table arranged for a gaiwan-style tea tasting. The underside of the gaiwan lid captures the aroma of the tea and it is passed around from guest to guest in place of individual aroma cups.

Have your tea table set with all of the tools and equipment that you will need. As host, you will be sitting and the etiquette does not make allowances for getting up to fetch forgotten items. Once your guests are seated, the initial procedure requires that you prepare the cups, teapot, and tea-dispensing pitcher by washing them with hot water (to respectfully cleanse and purify them in anticipation of the tea) before your begin. Follow these steps when performing a gong fu tea service:

1. Put the teapot into the clay tea boat and place all of the cups that you will need on the teapot platform (ideally four teacups and four aroma cups or fewer).

2. Fill the teapot with hot water. Pour additional hot water over the outside of the covered teapot. Let the teapot sit in the water while you move on to washing the cups. Pour equal amounts of hot water into each of the aroma cups and drinking cups, allowing excess water to overflow and drain away.

3. Using the tongs from the tool set, pick up the first cup by the lip and drain the water into the tea platform. Turn the cup sideways and roll the sides of the cup in the water in the second cup to wash the cup. Drain the water from the second cup and repeat the washing in the third cup. Repeat by washing the third cup in the fourth cup. After draining the water from the fourth cup, remove the teapot from the tea boat and set the teapot on a discretely folded tea towel to dry the bottom. Rinse the last cup with water from the teapot.

4. In a similar manner rinse each of the aroma cups and the tea-dispensing pitcher.

5. Scoop the necessary amount of oolong tea into the tea presentation bowl and show the tea to each of your guests, beginning with the most senior member. Initiate a short discussion about the tea and its origin and its expected virtues of flavor and style.

6. Carefully slide the tea into the teapot with one of the tea tools (fill the teapot to approximately three-quarters capacity) and set the teapot back into the clay tea boat. Fill the pot to overflowing with hot water. Set the lid in place and pour the additional hot water over the teapot. Let the pot sit for about one minute.

7. Lift the teapot from the bowl and set the teapot on a discretely folded tea towel to dry off the bottom. Lift the teapot and pour an equal amount of tea into each teacup. *It is important to do this correctly*: do not simply fill each cup one at a time. Rather, use a swift motion to quickly dispense the tea in a continuous stream by moving the teapot back and forth over all of the cups until the cups are filled equally and all of the tea has been dispensed from the pot. By doing so, the tea in each cup will taste the same; that is, no single cup will contain the weakest portion or strongest portion of tea, and the tea will all be the same temperature.

8. Pick up each cup with the tongs and discard this first infusion of tea. This first infusion, known as "foot tea" in China, is only for rinsing and preparing the tea leaf. Fill the teapot again with hot water, pour the additional hot water over the covered teapot, and allow the tea to brew for one minute.

9. Decant this second infusion of tea into the tea-dispensing pitcher or pour from the teapot into the tall aroma cups using the same decanting technique just described. After the aroma cups are filled, place the drinking cup over the top of the aroma cup and, while holding them tightly together, flip each set over so that the contents from the aroma cup drains into the drinking cup. Leave the cups in this position and place the cups on the individual trays and hand one to each of your guests.

10. Invite your guests to carefully lift out the aroma cup and enjoy the delightful fragrance of the tea that lingers in the cup. After appreciating the tea's perfume, the guests are invited to sip the tea from the drinking cups.

11. Use this opportunity to discard the rinse water in your clay bowl; do this as discretely as possible and without a lot of fuss. (In China a bucket is kept under the table for this use.) After your guests have drunk the first cup of tea, reinfuse the leaf as many times as the tea continues to deliver delicious flavor. Depending on the type of oolong tea used, this may be as many as fifteen to thirty times. You may choose to continue filling the aroma cup each time or not.

Using a modern gong fu tea set. The steps are essentially the same; the only difference is that a wooden or bamboo tea tray with a built-in catch basin takes the place of both the clay or ceramic tea bowl and the tea platform. Place your cups, teapot, and dispensing pitcher on the tray and follow the rinsing instructions as just described. The excess water will drain into the catch basin attached underneath the tray; just be aware of the size of the catch basin. Proceed with the remaining steps of the tea service.

Tea Culture in Japan

When thinking of Japanese ceramics, two images come to mind: the first is of richly decorated hard-paste porcelains, vibrant in color and sumptuous in design, executed with precise and exacting workmanship. Collectors of Japanese porcelain seek fine examples from the famous porcelain centers— Arita, Hirado, Imari, Kakiemon, Kutani, and Satsuma. Japan's history of porcelain making can be dated to the beginning of the seventeenth century in Arita, on the island of Kyushu in southern Japan. Today lovely porcelain teapots and teacups continue to be made in Japan and are available in a range of prices and styles. Porcelain is sleek and cool, and remains immutable and constant. Conversely, the second image is of traditionally made pottery tea bowls and teacups made from hand-thrown stoneware and fired in wood-burning kilns. Their simple style is fetching and seductive, and the sometimes rough texture and forceful feeling of these humble teacups resonates with Japanese tea drinkers.

Avid collectors of Japanese teawares are drawn to pieces that have appealing simplicity, a rustic, uneven form and style, and earthy, muted colors and glazes. These pieces exude a naturalistic feeling and show the hand of the maker in their shape and design. In their humble simplicity of form and craftsmanship their beauty and cultural connection lie. Pottery, not porcelain, changes and "wears" over time, developing a patina and character that adds to the beauty and personality of the piece. Japan reveres the ancient traditions of handmade pottery and celebrates living ceramic artists perhaps more than any other country. These teacups and tea bowls, no matter how humble in appearance, can cost many hundreds of dollars and will be passed down to successive generations. For more everyday needs, Japan also has many ceramics factories that manufacture mass-produced teawares suitable

for everyday use in homes, restaurants, and teashops. These colorful and good-looking items are available at a fraction of the cost of fine porcelain or handcrafted pottery, and are widely available in the United States.

THE LINK WITH CHINESE TEA CULTURE

Traditional Japanese tea bowls underscore the link that Japanese tea culture has with Chinese tea culture. Japan's culture of tea drinking began during the Heian (794–1185) and Kamakura periods (1192–1333), the time of China's Song dynasty (960–1279). While tea drinking was initially enjoyed by priests and the aristocracy, its popularity eventually spread to the warrior classes. As Japanese tea drinkers adopted the culture of tea drinking, they also sought to use tea utensils and simple yet elegant tea bowls that were made in China.

The Sanage pottery kilns in Aichi prefecture were known for making utilitarian pottery for nearly eight hundred years, from the fifth century to the fourteenth century. In the early thirteenth century much of this pottery production relocated to Seto, where production began to imitate China's white and green celadon pottery. By the end of that century, Seto had become famous for the technique of ash-fired glazed pottery; it was here

A wood-fired pottery tea set crafted by contemporary Kyoto ceramic artist Ken Nagai. The rustic, hand-formed teapot is modeled after a nineteenth-century skirted-style *tetsubin*, a Japanese cast-iron water kettle. The design is full of clever details; for example, the tiny ceramic knob on the lid spins and makes a little noise—a nod to the tinkling sound that the knob on a tetsubin lid makes when water is boiling.

that the craftsman tradition of handcrafted pottery began in Japan. It is said that a potter named Kato Shirozaemon Kagemasa (1169–1249) returned from visiting the Buddhist temples of Mount Tianmu in Zhejiang, China. He established a pottery kiln in Seto and began to make uncomplicated tea bowls that featured shiny, dark brown glazes with distinctive foot rings in the shape and style of tenmoku tea bowls that he had seen in China. Over time hundreds of potters settled in Seto. Collectively this region became famous for some of Japan's most distinctive handmade pottery, and by the end of the fourteenth century, the ceramic teawares from Seto were second only to China's in quality.

During Japan's late Muromachi period (1336–1573) tea culture began to spread throughout Japan through the port of Sakai (modern-day Osaka), but it was not until the Momoyama period (1568–1600) that Japan's unique tea culture found its own voice. Influences from China, Korea, and Vietnam introduced beautiful and interesting teawares and utensils to Japan, which were quickly snapped up by wealthy businessmen who paid handsomely for these objects. Many of these items, such as tea jars and tea bowls, eventually became part of Japanese tea practice or influenced shapes and styles of tea caddies, teacups, and teapots to come. But the Japanese borrowed and adapted from Chinese and Korean tea cultures and refined tea drinking to a sublime art. They embellished it with customs and practices uniquely their own and named their highest form of tea drinking practice Chanoyu. Tea bowls influenced by the style of Korean Ido ware began to take on a distinctly Japanese look in the Momoyama period. Unglazed stoneware in earth tones began the tradition of drinking bowls that featured rough textures and asymmetrical shapes with uneven rims. Tea bowls were given a wide bottom bt a narrow foot and walls with bulging hips that tipped inward near the top.

THE ART OF CHANOYU

In a line of succession from tea master to student, four Japanese tea masters—Murata Jukō, Takeno Jōō, Sen Rikyu, and Furuta Oribe—adapted, defined, and clarified the philosophical tenets of Chanoyu. In fifteenth century Kyoto the shogun Ashikaga Yoshimasa built a retirement villa called Ginkakuji (Temple of the Silver Pavilion) for his pleasure. Today Ginkakuji belongs to the Shōkōkuji school of the Rinsai school of Buddhism and is listed as a World Heritage Site of the United Nations Educational, Scientific, and Cultural Organization. Here, tea master Murata Jukō is said to have conducted private tea ceremonies for Ashikaga Yoshimasa in what is reported to be the oldest tearoom in Japan.

Murata Jukō created this tearoom as an austere, humble place that replicated the idea of a simple hut in the woods, a place where one could blend the culture of tea with introspection and the spiritual ideals of Zen Buddhism. By creating this unity of tea and religion, which became known as the Way of Tea, Jukō was speaking out against the custom of the Japanese aristocracy to hold elaborate tea-drinking parties and tea-drinking contests as sheer decadent entertainment in elegant, well-appointed pavilions. As the first to link tea drinking with the philosophical ideals of Zen, Jukō advocated placing the tearoom in the separate environment of a quiet teahouse surrounded by nature, rather than locating it inside a villa, pavilion, or temple.

This simple, rustic hut in the woods embodies the ideal space to appreciate the contemplative nature of tea drinking (Kyoto, Japan).

Each of these men—Murata Jukō, Takeno Jōō, Sen Rikyu, and Furuta Oribe—contributed to the order and philosophy of Chanoyu. Murata Jukō developed the spiritual aspect of the tea ceremony and linked the Way of Tea to Zen ideals, and Takeno Jōō ushered in new thoughts about the spirit of tea drinking that involved the interplay of hosts and guests. He espoused ideas that tea should neither be drunk in isolation nor in tea-drinking contests. He believed that appreciation of tea's spirit was established when host and guests quietly enjoy the moment with the right attitude of heart and spirit and preparation of mind. Takeno Jōō developed twelve precepts of conduct that one should follow to develop the right attitude ("straightforward, considerate, and not arrogant") to enjoy the Way of Tea.

The Japanese express ideals of religion, harmony, simplicity, attention to beauty, and appreciation of ephemeral moments in life through their deeply evolved culture of the Way of Tea, Chanoyu. Sen Rikyu, perhaps the most familiar name to those who study Chado, or the

Way of Tea, shaped the principles of *temae* (etiquette) for Chanoyu: *wa* (harmony), *kei* (respect), *sei* (purity), and *jaku* (tranquility). When asked what one needed to do to follow the Way of Tea, Sen Rikyu replied that it was nothing more than boiling water and drinking it, for which he espoused observing seven rules:

1. Make a satisfying bowl of tea.

2. Lay the charcoal so that the water boils efficiently.

3. Provide a sense of warmth in the winter and coolness in the summer.

4. Arrange the flowers as though they were in the field.

5. Be ready ahead of time.

6. Be prepared in case it should rain.

7. Act with utmost consideration toward your guests.

On the surface these steps seem simple and such that anyone could carry them out well. When presented with this type of comment, Sen Rikyu would respond that he would become a disciple of the person who could observe all seven rules without fail. The point is that although the Way of Tea is fundamentally concerned with actions that are a part of everyday life, it takes great effort and practice to master their simplicity. Sen Rikyu believed that the still concentration exercised when whisking a bowl of tea was indeed a meditation and that through practicing the Way of Tea it was possible to reach enlightenment. To this end, he espoused *wabi* concepts of rustic simplicity and deliberate austerity; he disdained artificiality in the practice of tea. For Sen Rikyu, the culture of tea stressed the values of simplicity, self-control, and restraint, and embodied a moral, an ethic, and eventually an aesthetic meaning.

After the death of Sen Rikyu, one of his students, tea master Furuta Oribe, became the second tea master to military leader Toyotomi Hideyoshi. Furuta Oribe introduced a feeling of modernism in ceramics and encouraged the use of cream, green, and black glazes, unique shapes, and spontaneous, contrasting designs. This pottery is thus known as Oribe, and beautiful examples of these wares are still being made today in Aichi prefecture. His influence and the exuberant spirit of his pottery ushered in a collaboration of expression among Japanese painters and other artists in the decorative arts in the sixteenth century that was never before witnessed in the history of Japanese art. He also further refined the design and make-up of tea gardens by contributing ideas for additions and changes to layout and composition as well as the placement of materials. (See the image on page 334 for an example of a contemporary Oribe teapot.)

In late-sixteenth-century Japan tastes in ceramics began to change. Japanese tastes for Chinese-style wares was diminishing, and both Korean ceramics influences and Japanese styles were becoming the new favorites. Sen Rikyu was disdainful of excess in form or design and believed in Zen concepts of unadorned elegance. He taught Chanoyu participants that humble, less than perfectly shaped bowls would serve to focus attention on the tea first and the bowl second. Until this time most tea bowls or *chawan* (not to be confused with *meshi chawan*, which are used for rice) made in Japan came from Seto kilns and were based on smooth, even-shaped, dark brown, and black-brown glazed Chinese tenmoku tea bowls.

FROM TENMOKU TO RAKU:
THE EVOLUTION OF JAPANESE TEA BOWLS

Sen Rikyu found the regularity and smoothness of tenmoku bowls to be unfavorable to the touch. Instead, he preferred the simplicity and honest style of rough-textured, slightly thick, and uneven stoneware rice bowls that were made by Korean potters living in Japan. Looking to incorporate the shape of Chinese tea bowls with the sensibility of the Korean style and feel, Sen Rikyu found his ideal cup in the unglazed, low-fired, and hand-built Raku pottery of a Korean potter named Chōjirō.

These ceramics suited Sen Rikyu's belief in the greatness of small things and in the equal importance of the mundane as well as the sublime. Chōjirō had been given the family name Raku by the warrior statesman and military leader Toyotomi Hideyoshi, who also honored Chōjirō by appointing him as one of the elite craftsmen chosen to make pottery for use in Chanoyu. Today Raku ware is still made by Raku Kichizaemon, the fifteenth generation and current head of the Raku family. His tea bowls can be purchased in Kyoto (although they are quite expensive and the wait is long). Visitors to the Raku Museum can appreciate a display of historic tea bowls made by successive members of the Raku family. Many of the famous, historic tea bowls in Japan—such as Chôjirô's Omokage, Miwa, and Tarobo—are named, and

This sophisticated Tokoname *kyusu*-style teapot, accentuated with a faceted honeycomb design, fits the expectation of Japanese elegance in spare design.

some have significant cultural greatness that they are considered Important Cultural Property.

As a result of Japanese-Korean conflicts, scores of Korean potters were relocated to Karatsu on the island of Kyushu in the late sixteenth century. A major pottery center was ultimately established on the island. Today the tradition of crafting hand-thrown pottery fired in traditional wood-burning kilns continues in the studios of pottery artists living throughout Kyushu.

As interest in Chanoyu spread into Japan in the seventeenth century, the need for rustic, simply glazed teawares in natural styles as well as a battery of tea utensils to use with Chanoyu arose. Many potters switched from making utilitarian wares to developing teawares that fulfilled this new Japanese aesthetic. Kilns in Seto (in Aichi prefecture) and old Mino Province (in Gifu prefecture) were kept busy from the demands of tea drinkers for appropriate tea bowls. Seto is home to scores of kilns that developed many of the famous Mino styles of Japanese pottery—white-glazed Shino, red-glazed Shino, black Setoguro, yellow Kiseto, and the spontaneous brushwork designs of Furuta Oribe.

Today these pottery-producing areas are collectively known as the Six Old Kilns of Japan. They are Bizen, Echizen, Seto, Shigaraki/Iga, Tamba, and Tokoname. Many of these kilns are still in operation today and are thriving; in the old atmospheric ceramics town Tokoname, for example, walking tours have been designed to let visitors enjoy both the centuries-old kilns and the more modern ceramics factories.

THE SENCHA TEA CEREMONY

During Japan's Edo period (1600–1867) a simpler style of tea drinking came into popularity. Many Japanese intellectuals were looking to break away from the formal nature of the Chanoyu powdered tea ceremony. They wanted to drink tea in an unaffected, less restrictive, and conventional way. During this time, it became fashionable among Japanese philosophers and artists to

emulate the refined method of classical tea drinking developed by Chinese scholars and the elite literati of the Ming dynasty (1368–1644). They were drawn to the simplicity of the Chinese method of steeping loose-leaf tea, and sought to emulate Ming scholar-recluses who led spiritually enlightened lives. By aligning themselves with the Ming literati through tea drinking, these Japanese intellectuals created a new way to drink tea in Japan, which first became known as the sencha tea ceremony and later as the sencha tea service or simply as sencha.

For the sencha tea ceremony, small teapots with loop handles attached to the sides were used. These teapots were styled after the Yixing teapots favored by the Chinese Ming literati. Japan took a step away from Chinese customs, however, and drank the tea not in tea bowls but from small, short cylinder-shaped or round *yunomi chawan* teacups. With these simple changes the sencha tea ceremony ushered in a new style of tea brewing that was the precursor of modern tea drinking. The word *sencha* thus came to mean the practice of preparing and drinking Japanese leaf tea that was imbued with an appreciation of Chinese art, culture, and philosophy. Today the term *sencha* refers both to a specific manufacture of Japanese green tea and to the style of brewing green teas such as sencha and gyokuro. In Japan, it is not uncommon to be asked to join someone in "drinking sencha," a phrase that means, "Let's have some tea together."

A small black plate adds color contrast to the pleasing harmony created by the white glaze of this kyusu teapot and teacup. Japanese notions of desirable contrasts are often achieved by pairing teawares of opposing colors, glazes, and textures.

Teapots for sencha were designed with the size of small Chinese teapots in mind, but they were made of porcelain and often painted with fanciful Japanese-inspired motifs. In nineteenth-century Japan potters began making small clay teapots with an easy-to-grasp single handle that projected straight out from the side of the teapot. Known as a *kyusu* teapot, this style of teapot is still popular today, and can be found in both handmade and production versions. Most production-made kyusu are fit with a stainless-steel mesh strainer that lines the inside of the teapot and is designed to keep fine, thin bits of tea leaf out of the cup. The best kyusu teapots are handmade and have a fine clay strainer fashioned into the teapot spout. Very small and delicate kyusu teapots or handle-less teapots called *houbin* are especially made and perfectly suited for brewing tiny amounts of sweet and expensive gyokuro tea.

This small, palm-sized, unglazed teapot is called a houbin. It is perfectly suited to brewing and dosing out small sips of sweet sencha or gyokuro green tea.

JAPANESE CERAMICS FOR THE EXPORT MARKET: THEN AND NOW

After World War II Japanese export wares were mass-produced and quickly painted with simple one-dimensional designs. These images were supposed to convey an idealized sense of Japan to foreigners in the overseas markets. Fortunately, those times are over, and today's ceramics respect the traditional ways and speak the universal language of quality and good design. Today, a seemingly unending array of colors, design, shapes, and patterns in pottery has emerged, underscoring the Japanese preference toward striking and bold or restful and contemplative tablewares featuring contrasting shapes, differing glaze colors, and opposing but harmonious materials.

Japanese cooks observe strict ideas of seasonality regarding food. Pottery also enters the discourse of the meal; the pottery is not complete without the meal and vice versa. Japanese cooks thus use dishes and bowls in a stunning juxtaposition of shapes and sizes to create a mood or express a sensibility or to let the color, weight, feel, and designs of the dishes and serving pieces simply entertain the senses. Repetition in design breeds boredom, hence the desire to hold attention with teasingly diverse tablewares. Seasonality is also taken into account with tablewares, and these notions will be reflected in the choices made by the host or cook concerning color, heft and type of clay, and glaze. Pottery is a part of everyday Japanese life, a national obsession that leads to ambitious collections and an unending quest for the perfect piece.

Over the course of a Japanese meal, for example, table settings might feature a selection of condiments, pickles, and delicately sized portions of fish or vegetables in small bowls and plates featuring appealing colors, thick molten glazes, and unique shapes. A beautiful wooden tray might hold a red and black lacquer lidded bowl, a square ceramic dish with a pebbled surface, and a boldly asymmetrical plate, each chosen to compliment another course of food. An anonymous Japanese satirical poet once commented on the boring sameness of Western taste in table settings: "Western food—every damn plate is round."

Chawan. No tea table is complete without a collection of Japanese dishes and teacups that reflect this mix-and-match heritage. Feel free to serve Japanese tea in handle-less cups but remember to reserve *chawan* tea bowls only for use in Chanoyu. Chawans must be generously wide to accommodate the rapid back-and-forth mixing action of the bamboo whisk and stand about three inches tall. The overall girth of a chawan made by a ceramic artist is hefty and a bit stocky; its size and weight commands respect and it is intended to be held in two hands, as if tenderly holding the soul of the artist. Chawans are squat and chunky, and can feature an uneven rim along the top and either a glazed or an unglazed foot on the bottom of the bowl, which keeps the bowl raised off the table. There are specific styles of chawans used for thin (usucha) tea and thick (koicha) tea and for seasonal tea ceremonies honoring the four seasons. There are also chawans used when recognizing more specific timeframes, such as moon viewing or cherry blossom viewing, or for celebrating the first tea ceremony of the year, Hatsu Gama. Chawans are made by many potters in the famous ceramics areas of Japan and teaware collectors seek out examples made in all of the various types of glazes and clays. Expensive chawans come packed in their own custom-made wooden box with the signature of the artist displayed on the box or under the lid.

Chawans made by famous potters are sometimes passed down from teacher to student or purchased from a tea utensil store. In fine ceramics

A visually interesting and tactile collection of contemporary Japanese yunomi chawan ceramic teacups in assorted styles, materials, colors, shapes, and designs.

shops in Kyoto, we saw handmade pottery tea bowls that started at $250 and quickly escalated toward $1,000 per bowl, depending on the potter's fame and skill. Antique bowls command even higher prices. Because of the value of the chawans in use at a tea ceremony, a Japanese tea master explained to us: "When we admire the bottom of the tea bowl after drinking the tea during Chanoyu we lean forward from a kneeling position and keep our elbows on our thighs or knees while we admire the tea bowl. This way, if the bowl falls, it only falls a few inches onto the cushioning tatami mat and will not suffer a break."

Yunomi chawan. Less expensive, commercially made Japanese teacups are used for all of the everyday types of Japanese tea. Our customers love these cups in all of their infinite variations and styles. Some teacups have glazes that are lighthearted and fun, while others are serious, flashy, austere, and at times wildly colorful. Some are short and wide and bowl-shaped, while others are tall and narrow. Despite having a short stature, these simple cups exude customer appeal. They beguile shoppers from the shelf and, without a lot of show or hype, simply beg to be picked up and held. Show your Japanese spirit and aesthetic sense and collect an unmatched set of teacups. When you serve tea to your friends, be sure to watch how much interest they show in the cups; it will be up to you to extol the virtue and personality of each cup.

CHANOYU: THE JAPANESE TEA CEREMONY

Chanoyu began in Japan the fourteenth century, stemming from a style of powdered tea drinking that had been popularized by the Chinese during the Song dynasty. Initially, tea drinking was practiced by Zen priests, but the rise of a succession of tea masters beginning with Jukō (1422–1502) created the concept of an orderly and formalized tea ceremony. Today this tea practice and these principles are upheld by three main tea schools in Japan—Urasenke, Omotesenke, and Mushanokōjisenke. These schools were founded by descendants and disciples of early tea masters and have active branch schools in locations worldwide.

Under tea master Jukō the harmonious practice of tea drinking brought together various members of society—powerful samurai warlords, artists, scholars, and religious philosophers alike. By the late sixteenth century, it began to influence Japanese life and culture, providing participants in Chanoyu with a sense of peace, well-being and harmony, oneness and unity, and attention to the moment. Chanoyu is always mindful of Japanese aesthetic traditions and principles of Zen simplicity and restraint. Despite the rules of Chanoyu, the practice does not remain stagnant. By its nature every Chanoyu performed has a beginning and an ending and is a moment in time spent in reflection and concentration that cannot be exactly duplicated. Each principle of Chanoyu is expressed through the gestures and movements of the tea master, the objects chosen for the tea, and the environment created in the tearoom.

As no two Chanoyu experiences can ever be the same, this spirit of continued new beginnings imbues Chanoyu with the ability to remain fresh and timely yet authentic and deeply rooted in tradition. Since the time of Sen Rikyu, a phrase for the ephemeral notion of transient time came into use. *Ichi-go ichi-e* literally means "one time, one meeting" or "one time chance in a lifetime" and is a fitting description of the evanescent nature of each Chanoyu experience. Close to fifty different tools and tea-brewing implements are used during Chanoyu, compared with fewer than a dozen for the Chinese gong fu–style tea service. Many items owned by the tea master, such as the bamboo tea-measuring spoon and the lacquered tea caddy that contains the powdered tea, may very likely be priceless antiques, to be used and handled only by the tea master. Other pieces may be valued items that were given to a tea master by his or her teacher or family members.

Top: Some of the necessary accoutrements used for Chanoyu: *chawan, chasen, chashaku, hishaku,* and *usuchaki.*

Above: A richly gilded and decorated antique lacquer matcha caddy contains matcha for usucha, or thin tea.

In Chanoyu the host begins by preparing the tearoom or "empty house," an unadorned, plain space that is reserved for this purpose only. Wood, bamboo, rice paper shoji screens, and tatami mats are the simple architectural elements found inside of the tearoom. In fact, the interior of traditional Japanese teahouses is only as big as the dimensions of four a half tatami mats—nine by nine feet—and is meant to accommodate only five guests. The first teahouse in Japan to use this configuration of tatami mats was in the shogun Ashikaga Yoshimasa's Ginkakuji (Temple of the Silver Pavilion) in Kyoto. This size restriction kept the experience intimate and closely connected for both the host and the guests.

The host takes into account all aspects of sensation and perception that the guests might experience in the teahouse environment, such as wall decor, flower arrangement, lighting, seating, and aromas—all of which must underscore the season of the year and the time of day or night. In a special alcove devoted to art, called the *tokonoma*, the host hangs a scroll (*kakemono*) emblazoned with a phrase in calligraphy (or featuring a painting with calligraphy) that has been written by a Zen priest or tea master. This scroll reflects the mood of the season and theme of the evening.

The Tokonoma and Chabana. A simple and natural arrangement of seasonal flowers and grasses is also placed in the tokonoma. Vases (*hanaire*) are chosen by season and by materials; for example, bamboo containers and baskets arc used in summer, while bronze, porcelain, or unglazed pottery is selected in winter. Flower arrangements created for the tea ceremony are called *chabana*. Just a few flowers are chosen to best communicate thoughts of the momentary and fleeting nature of blossoms in nature, as well as the emotions in the host's heart that best express his or her theme for the evening. Centuries ago in Japan, the art of formalized flower arranging began. Collectively called Ikebana, today there are many different Ikebana schools, such as Ikenobo, Sogetso, and Ohara, with branch schools located worldwide. Whereas Ikebana teaches disciplined art forms, chabana flower arranging strives to be simple, casual, and natural. Flowers are placed in the vase in an informal manner to emphasis the natural, unfussy expressiveness of flowers. Chabana arrangements are restrained and rely on the simple beauty of a few well-chosen stems, pieces of bamboo, and grasses.

CHANOYU TERMS DEFINED

Chagama: Cast-iron kettle for hot water.

Chaire: Ceramic tea caddy for *koicha* (thick tea).

Chasen: Bamboo whisk.

Chashaku: Bamboo tea-measuring scoop.

Chawan: Tea bowl.

Hishaku: Bamboo ladle for drawing water.

Mizusash: Cold water container.

Shifuku: Silk pouch for *chaire*.

Usuchaki: Lacquered tea caddy for *usucha* (thin tea).

It is important that the mood for Chanoyu is set as soon as guests arrive outside of the environs of the tearoom. To evoke a sense of progressively entering deeper into a new world, guests will pass through a series of thresholds that take them from the everyday world into the inner world of the tea garden and the teahouse beyond. If it is evening or early in the morning, guests will follow the glow from the warm, soft light cast from a stone lantern to find their way down a stepping-stone path, which leads them into the tea garden. At the garden entrance guests will begin to undergo the mental transformation from outside to inside, allowing the natural environment of the garden to cleanse them of the cares of the outside world. In cities, where the teahouse is located inside of a large building, the interior design of the

*If asked
the nature of Chanoyu
Say it's the sound
of windblown pines
in a painting.*

—SEN SOTAN

ATTENDING CHANOYU IN JAPAN

At the Eishunnji Temple we had the opportunity to attend a midmorning tea ceremony. The head priest explained the theme that he had selected for the tea ceremony that morning. As it was May, he had chosen the theme of "running water" and followed through with this idea in the sentiment expressed in the broad brushstrokes of the calligraphy he had hung in the tokonoma. He also placed a tall, white Shino vase in the tokonoma, which was decorated in a swirling red design and which held a single branch of cascading white flowers. The tea master began by serving us a typical Japanese sweet called a *wagashi*. This soft sweet was intricately made; it was shaped and decorated to look like a stream of water coursing its way down a riverbed.

The priest explained the steps that the tea master executed as she prepared the tea. We noticed that the thin tea bowls she was using were embellished with a design that pertained to his theme—a little painted cricket on one bowl, bold slashes of color on another that resembled waves, a third had been given a solid blue glaze of the deepest color, and the last tea bowl was glazed in earth tones and decorated with light gray swirls.

surrounding space will be designed to allow for a representation of all of the above welcoming elements.

Roji: A path of dewy ground. Teahouses are traditionally found deep within a meticulously tended and artistically designed garden. One of the main elements of the tea garden is the sixteenth-century concept of *roji*—a path of dewy ground where moss gathers on stones and leaves are scattered as in the forest and where thoughtfully placed pines, nonflowering shrubs, pines, trees, and clumps of bamboo enfold and surround the guests with a feeling of calm. A stone water basin is filled with fresh water and is a place where guests may wash their hands in a gesture of ritual purification that eliminates "the dust of the world," helping them to transcend from the mundane world to the pure serenity of the teahouse.

Nijiriguchi: The crawling-in entrance. Guests may enter the teahouse through a standard door or through the *nijiriguchi*, the crawling-in entrance. This low-placed door is built into the side of the teahouse; it is raised up from the ground two to three feet. The idea behind the nijiriguchi is credited to tea master Sen Rikyu. In the past it was required that all guests crawl head first into the teahouse through this low door, a gesture of casting off their egos and becoming equal to each other in stature inside of the teahouse. In Samurai times sword racks were placed by the nijiriguchi to collect weapons while the owners entered the teahouse to participate in Chanoyu.

Once inside the teahouse, both guests and the host kneel on ivory-colored rice straw tatami mats in the tearoom. Sometimes an ele-

gantly presented *kaiseki* meal is served at the beginning of the tea. This meal consists of small portions of seasonal foods that are light, fresh, and visually enticing. The host selects and prepares the dishes for the kaiseki meal with an eye to presenting a pleasing selection of contrasting textures, tastes, and colors. Dishes, trays, and serving utensils are carefully chosen for visual interest and to offer variation in texture and materials. After the meal guests adjourn to the garden for ten to fifteen minutes, and when they return, the host will have replaced the scroll with flowers and the tea utensils will have been laid out, ready for use. When the host reenters the room, he or she will be dressed in a silk kimono and carrying the tea bowl.

A natural stone water basin (*tsukubai*) is essential in all Japanese tea gardens, and it also makes a charming design element in public and private garden spaces (Kyoto, Japan).

Now the guests leave all worldly thoughts behind as they watch the practiced and seamless movements of the tea master. They listen to the sounds of the heated water in the kettle, which is called *matsukaze*, or the "sound of wind in the pines," as the tea master carefully cleanses the tea bowls. The only sounds heard during the tea preparation are these: the low tone of the lid being replaced on the cast-iron water kettle, the quiet sound of the water as it is gently poured from the bamboo ladle into the tea bowl, and the single, deliberate clink of the tea scoop on the ceramic tea bowl.

Each guest observes and appreciates in silence the wordless concentration and precision with which the tea master proceeds. He

Even though the dewy path is nothing more than a path away from the world's bustle, it frees the heart from its impurity.

—SEN RIKYU

or she carefully measures the matcha into the tea bowl, then lifts a ladleful of water from the kettle with the bamboo hishaku. The water is carefully poured into the tea bowl and after soundlessly resting the hishaku against the water kettle, the tea master uses a bamboo whisk to froth the tea, using a gentle back-and-forth motion that is interspersed with vigorous whisking. Matcha that has been stone ground mixes differently with the water than matcha that has been ground by machine; the stone-ground powder seems to float in the water and maintains a presence in the bowl rather than completely dissolving into the water. Each tea school has its own preferred style of matcha powder, which is based on the school's method for whisking the tea.

A tea master dips a hishaku into hot water in preparation for making a bowl of matcha during a Japanese tea ceremony at the Eishunnji Temple (Kyoto, Japan).

Koicha and usacha. In some tea ceremonies both thick and thin tea is made. In others just one or the other is offered. When both styles of tea are served, the first bowl is the thick tea (*koicha*). This bowl is placed on the mat, and the guest slides up to take the bowl. The guest holds the bowl in his left hand and takes a sip of the koicha. The guest then wipes the bowl from whence he sipped and passes the tea bowl to the next guest, who repeats the action and so on, until all of the guests have sipped the koicha. The tea bowl (along with the tea caddy, water container, and iron tea kettle) may be quite old and of great value, and time is taken for the guests to discuss the utensils and show their appreciation for them. The host may then prepare individual bowls of tea for each guest (*usacha*), which is thinner in consistency than the first bowl of koicha. Koicha is served in undecorated matcha bowls, and usacha is served in matcha bowls that have been selected for their seasonal designs and patterns that fit the theme of the tea. Usacha signals that the tea ceremony is ending and that the guests must prepare themselves to reenter the world outside of the tearoom.

WAGASHI: ARTISTIC SWEETS

When visiting Japan, spend time wandering through the food halls of the Takashimaya department store or any one of the Toraya confectionary shops to see a fascinating array of these small, artistic Japanese sweets known as wagashi. We become spellbound when we see a selection of wagashi, which to us is a distillation of everything that we find compelling about Japanese food and the art of presentation: perfection in shape; pleasing and amusing designs; exquisite use of color in soft tones, texture, and composition; attention to seasonal representation; and of course intriguing flavors, textures, and tastes.

Wagashi began during Japan's Nara period (710–784) and grew into a refined art in Kyoto during the Edo period (1600–1867). Today hundreds of variations of wagashi exist in a few main categories of style. The most common type is *namagashi*, a panoply of bean-filled confections that celebrate the seasons or holidays. Namagashi are made from glutinous rice flour, water, and sugar and are gloriously colored and shaped to represent seasonal flowers or fruits. *Manju* are steamed buns, and *higashi* are dry sweets

that are molded into shapes of flowers and clouds that are a delicate counterpoint to the bitterness of Japanese tea. *Monaka* are crisp rice wafers that contain a sweet bean filling, and *yokan* are jellied confections. Wagashi are made primarily from glutinous rice flour, sweetened adzuki bean paste, kanten (vegetable-based gelatin made from seaweed), and superfine *wasambonto* cane sugar. Their beauty and ability to delight and surprise children and adults alike relies on the dexterity and imagination of trained Japanese confectionary chefs.

A tray of wagashi in an array of colors, shapes, and seasonal designs, in a Takashimaya department store (Tokyo, Japan).

*Above the fir trees
clouds expand,
and above the flowers
the mist hovers.
They stand one before
the other
and compete in abundant
magnificence.
I say, both are foremost
enjoyments of the world:
wine as wine and tea
as tea.*

—RANSHUKU RONSHU (1576)

A Japanese clay kyusu teapot.

Wabi tea bowls. Many Chanoyu tea bowls are handmade and slightly oversized, and made from rough-textured stoneware that accentuates the bowl's humble nature and its sensation in the hand. Or they can be very refined and thin-walled. Rough-textured stoneware tea bowls demonstrate the Japanese concept of beauty found in imperfect, simple, earthy things that have a weathered or worn appearance and an "accidental" beauty. This concept of Zen philosophy known as *wabi* became an essential part of Japanese tea culture under the tea master Takeno Jōō (1504–1555) and his student, tea master Sen Rikyu (1522–1591).

SENCHA TEA CEREMONY

At first the sencha ceremony followed a loose structure, but devotees of the ceremony later codified the tea service into several presentations that use a prescribed nomenclature of accoutrements. Although this seems to contradict the original basis for the sencha ceremony, which was the lack of restriction and formal order, the ideals of veneration of the Chinese literati and their culture of tea drinking still remains. Several large schools of tea etiquette for sencha continue to this day in Japan, including the Issa-an School and the Kagetsuan School in Osaka, and the Ogawa School in Kyoto. Each school follows the general style with slightly differing rules surrounding *temae* (etiquette). The National Japanese Sencha Association, founded in 1956, attempts to serve the needs of the nearly one hundred sencha schools reported to exist. In 1970, the Japanese government raised sencha tea ceremony to an officially sanctioned elite art.

The sencha ceremony evolved into several styles of tea brewing. A monk named Baisao, who spent the latter part of his life as a tea merchant, began the sencha tradition in the early 1720s. He extolled the flavor of tea made with tea leaves rather than powdered tea. His praises of leaf tea drinking caught on with Japanese intellectuals and artists of that time who deeply admired the Chinese literati and the scholar-elites of the Ming dynasty (1368–1644).

Accordingly, some of the tools of the tea equipage remained the same, while some utensils changed depending on the type of service. Baisao's traditional method of sencha preparation added the tea leaf to a teapot filled with simmering water, whereas the later practice of *encha* placed the tea leaves in the teapot first and then followed with hot water from the kettle. Leaving behind the whipped, powdered tea of the Song dynasty (960–1279), the Ming began to brew tea from loose leaves. The sencha tea tradition followed this thinking. While Baisao and the later practitioners of sencha sought to reject formality and embrace a more natural, social approach to tea drinking, Chanoyu remained firmly entrenched with the upper class and the warrior class, and was aligned with the Zen temples. Both tea practices flourished and found their own niche and followers. Today each of these approaches to "teaism" adds to the rich well of Japanese tea history. Each underlying philosophy espouses and follows a disciplined mind-set that continues to inspire and quench the collective thirst of Japan.

CHASENS: THE TEA WHISK

At the Takayama Tea Whisk Productive Cooperative, in Nara prefecture, tea whisks are serious business. In fact, tea whisks have been made by hand here for five hundred years, since the middle of the Muromachi period (1333–1568). The cooperative makes 90 percent of all whisks in Japan, a must-have item for preparing powdered tea. Depending on the type of tea whisk, which differs according to the discipline taught at each tea school, the whisks can have from 60 to 180 light and feathery tines. Every whisk is cut manually from one joint of bamboo with a small knife. Skills are passed from one generation to the other; men perform the tasks of bamboo cutting while women cut the thin and delicate tines. The craft of whisk making has been designated as one of Japan's traditional crafts.

CHA KAISEKI OR TEA KAISEKI

This piece is written by Victoria Abbott Riccardi, author of Untangling My Chopsticks: A Culinary Sojourn in Kyoto *(Broadway, 2003).*

It is important to understand that there are two types of *kaiseki*—restaurant kaiseki and tea kaiseki. Restaurant kaiseki is available to the public and considered "party food." It is multi-course tasting and concludes with dessert. Tea kaiseki is part of an extremely formal Japanese tea ceremony and consists of a ritualized series of small seasonal dishes served before the ceremonial tea.

Kaiseki evolved in the Zen temples of Kyoto. *Kai* means "bosom pocket" and *seki* means "stone." The monks used to place hot stones in the front pocket fold of their kimono to ward off hunger. Over time simple vegetarian dishes replaced the stones. As the monks began making tea for the imperial court, the dishes became more elaborate because the Emperor wanted more than miso soup and tofu before his whipped green tea. The meal that evolved is tea kaiseki, a light seasonal meal based on rice.

An ideal tea kaiseki takes place in a small teahouse with four guests, plus the tea master. The meal can have up to nine or more courses, depending upon the nature of the guests attending. For example, if a famous potter is coming to the tea, the kaiseki meal might include an extra course to show off the potter's wares. The format is somewhat flexible to accommodate these gestures. Unlike restaurant kaiseki, tea kaiseki dishes arrive in a set order. Also, there are certain restrictions with the foods. For example, at a restaurant kaiseki you will encounter fried foods, which you would never encounter at a tea kaiseki because the oils would coat the tongue and ruin the taste of the tea to come.

Here is the standard format for a tea kaiseki:

1. **First Tray.** Every guest receives a square black lacquer tray containing what is considered the first "course," which consists of the following three dishes: Rice (a bowl holding a small amount of steamed white rice), Miso soup (a bowl of miso soup), and Mukozuke (a small dish of marinated fish or vegetables). Some sake is served at this point.

2. **Wanmori.** This is the climax of the kaiseki because it is considered the chef's greatest effort. It is a soup-like dish consisting of a beautiful clear broth filled with seasonal ingredients and garnishes.

3. **Yakimono.** This is a grilled dish and could feature a few bites of grilled fish or several grilled mushroom caps, depending upon the tea master's whim and the season.

4. **Shiizakana.** This is an optional dish composed of fish that is served at this point in the kaiseki if the guests want more sake.

5. **Azukebachi.** This is another optional dish made from any leftover ingredients used to prepare the other dishes in the kaiseki. It would be served, for example, as a way to showcase a famous potter's bowl.

6. **Hashiarai.** This dish is called a "chopstick wash" and is usually some hot water flavored with something in season, such as a spring cherry blossom. This course enables diners to rinse the smoky grilled flavors from the grilled dish off their chopsticks, particularly if no optional dishes are served.

7. **Hassun.** This course consists of a beautiful pink cedar tray holding a seasonal item from the mountains (maybe a wild green) and something from the ocean (perhaps a few shrimp).

8. **Konomono.** This is the pickle course consisting of a few pickled vegetables, such as turnip.

9. **Yuto.** This dish is made from the crispy bits of rice that have stuck to the bottom of the cooking pot mixed with warm salted water. The monks used to make this in the temples.

This ends the tea kaiseki, although the tea master/chef can offer an extra course anywhere along the way. Guests then leave the teahouse, return and enjoy a sweet before the ceremonial whipped green tea.

For restaurant kaiseki and tea kaiseki, cooks aim to offer diners different textures, colors, and flavors throughout the meal for variety and pleasure. Grilling, steaming, and simmering, for example, are used to prepare various courses and ingredients are chosen to offer a variety of colors (white, red, yellow, purple-black, and blue-green) and flavors (salty, sweet, sour, spicy, and bitter) to each dish.

The goal of a tea kaiseki is to transport the diner to another world—away from the cares of everyday life—so that he/she might reach enlightenment. The diner enters the tearoom and focuses on nothing more than the sensual pleasures of all that exists: the poetic nature of the flowers and scroll in the alcove, the beauty of the serving pieces, the seasonal symbolism of the ingredients, the artful presentation of the courses, and the chef's heartfelt desire to please his guests.

When a tea master holds a tea ceremony, the event is considered incredibly precious because he and the guests know that they will never gather together again at that moment, on that day, in that year, in their lifetime. There is a famous saying in tea: "*ichi go ichi e*," meaning, "one chance in one's lifetime." Like the eagerly anticipated cherry blossoms, which burst into bloom in the spring and then quickly die, so is the kaiseki meal—an ephemeral experience that, for a brief moment in time, offers guests a rare taste of the divine.

JAPANESE TETSUBIN

Exemplary craftsmanship is the hallmark of every Japanese iron teakettle and teapot. Supported by a tradition that goes back more than four hundred years, *tetsubin* have been faithful servants to emperors, scholars, artists, and tea connoisseurs. Tetsubin originated as Japanese household pot-bellied cast-iron teakettles and were a class apart from *chagama*, the handle-less and spoutless iron water kettles used in Chanoyu. Because these kettles were given both handles and spouts, tetsubin were expressly meant for heating water for brewing everyday tea.

Although class and status were displayed by the intricacy of the tetsubin's design and surface embellishment, these teakettles were not meant to be status objects but rather something functional to place over the hearth and provide hot water. The classic tetsubin has a dark brown or black pebbled surface that is embossed with simple designs that underscore the simple yet austere nature of these kettles. During the mid-nineteenth century tetsubins were taken out of the kitchen and elevated to the position of status symbol among the elites using them to serve tea. Consequently, the size of tetsubins became sleeker and smaller, and the designs more pleasing and artistic.

Today beautiful tetsubin are made by companies such as Kunsan, Nambu, and Iwachu in Iwate prefecture or by artisan ironworkers in Yamagata prefecture, and the direction is toward teapots rather than teakettles. Interior enamel coating and stainless-steel tea infusers have been added to today's vessels, creating the perfect combination of form and function in a teapot. This new direction is bringing contemporary colors to traditional tetsubin shapes, as well as heat-proof trivets and iron teacups, which complete the tea presentation.

A large Japanese cast-iron water kettle (tetsubin) is a household item used to heat water for filling sencha teapots, such as the brown-and-white Tokonoma teapot and a green Oribe teapot shown here.

Tea Culture in Europe

In seventeenth-century Europe there was a lust for all things Chinese. Chinese tea traders fanned the flames of the Western tea craze by including first porcelain teacups, then porcelain teapots, with each shipment of tea to Europe. In fact, the Chinese were savvy businessmen who satisfied many different markets with their porcelain goods. In addition to their trade with the Near East and India, the Chinese eventually shipped great quantities of export porcelains to America, Europe, Japan, and Southeast Asia.

While Portuguese traders first brought tea to Portugal in the late 1500s, it was Dutch traders who created a frenzy for drinking tea in Amsterdam in 1610. By the time that the first public tea auction was held in London in 1669, a strong secondary market for ceramic paraphernalia from which to serve and drink this new hot beverage had developed. Up to the mid-1600s, Europeans reveled in a few luxury Chinese export items—silks, spices, and lacquer wares. With the arrival of tea and its dissemination among the social classes throughout the seventeenth century, it became necessary to acquire the appropriate drink wares and tablewares for the proper enjoyment of these beverages.

Cottage rose patterns and chintz-inspired designs are perennial favorites with contemporary English teaware manufacturers.

Although it is hard to imagine today, prior to the mid-seventeenth century, most citizens of Europe did not have a history of consuming hot beverages other than medicated potions for the sick or ailing or herbal brews known as possets. Alcohol was the drink of the day, but as world trade commenced and Europe was introduced to the three stimulating social beverages—coffee, tea, and chocolate—that literally changed their world, beverage consumption changed.

CHINESE PORCELAIN FINDS A RIVAL

In the beginning of the tea-drinking boom, Europeans embraced the handle-less porcelain teacups that Dutch traders purchased from China. While the Chinese could brew tea and sip

it all from the same cup, these cups presented a problem for the Europeans, who puzzled over how to prepare and drink this wondrous and strange costly hot beverage. From 1669 to 1690 Dutch and English East India trading ships heading back home from China began to bring in their cargo small Yixing teapots, and later, small blanc-de-chine white porcelain pots decorated in green, red, and orange colors. At the end of the seventeenth century, blue and white overglazed porcelain pots were exported. Except for the Yixing teapots, these teapots were made expressly for export and varied in the placement of spouts and handles, in the overall shape of the teapot, and in how the lids fit. They were also small in size. The influence of these early Chinese export porcelains was absorbed, then later reinvented by European ceramics factories eager to supply their own market with these desirable objects and to keep the profits that were now going to China. For some time the Europeans were successful at producing "soft-paste" porcelain, but the secrets of Chinese "hard-paste" porcelain eluded them. And it was necessary for them to be able to produce a hard-paste porcelain as it was this material that was able to absorb the shock of the hot water used in tea brewing.

A Chinese polychrome China Trade teapot.

It was not until 1707 that a German alchemist named Johann Friedrich Böttger added some kaolin clay to his porcelain recipe and discovered that this ingredient added the missing hardness to the pottery. This unlocked the secret that the Europeans had been searching for. In 1710 a porcelain factory was established in Meissen, Germany, which began producing hard-paste porcelains. This opened the door for eventual porcelain production in Sèvres and Limoges in France beginning in 1767 and shortly after in several English factories, such as Coalport, Spode, and Worcester.

TEA EQUIPAGE IS GIVEN A WESTERN FLAVOR

Across Europe in the early part of the eighteenth century tea drinking was a socially prominent activity reserved for the upper class, and it required teawares that reflected this fashion and the position one held in society. Once the Europeans could manufacture their own porcelain teawares, there was no stopping the highly elaborate nature of the teawares produced, nor the volume of helpful accoutrements deemed necessary to decorate and augment service at the tea table. The need for paraphernalia such as tea caddies for keeping tea fresh and to protect it from contamination were ideas borrowed from the pottery and metal jars in which the Chinese stored tea. Sterling silver scoops to measure the dry leaf were fashioned by silversmiths and made to replicate the real seashell scoops that Chinese tea men would enclose with containers of tea heading to England. Inevitably, other accessory objects were required to support European tea service, such as tea tables, elaborate silver tea caddies, ornate silver vessels for heating water, and serving trays. The Europeans began to produce teacups that were larger than those the Chinese used and handles were added, which made the cups easier to hold when filled with hot liquid. Generously sized saucers served to catch overflows and spills and larger capacity teapots allowed for tea to be made for the entire family at once. For the wealthy, porcelain teawares were fashioned into grandly shaped elaborations and decorated with real and imagined scenes that appealed to worldly and adventurous Western tastes. Traveling tea sets were custom fit into protective leather carrying cases for outfitting day trips and journeys near or far.

Even before the successful discovery of porcelain in Europe, potters tried to copy the style and design of Chinese teapots. From 1670 to 1708 a Dutch potter named Ary de Milde fashioned teapots that imitated Yixing ware in smoothness of finish, shape, and fineness of detail. With the advent of European-produced porcelain wares, it became fashionable for designers to painstakingly hand-paint Western-style, idealized versions of Chinese-inspired designs and motifs. This style of decorating was called *chinoiserie* but was later abandoned in favor of elaborate and realistic paintings of fruits and flowers or pastoral scenes of ladies and gentlemen at leisure.

The addition of milk and sugar to tea is a Western convention credited to the Dutch, who were the first Europeans to bring Chinese tea back home to the Continent on a steady basis. Although the Han Chinese have no history of diluting their tea with anything other than with the juice extracts of fresh fruits or delicately scented flower petals or savory spices such as ginger, the Dutch most likely observed or learned of this milk tea custom from the Manchu emperors of the Qing dynasty (1644–1911).

THE ADVENT OF THE TEACUP HANDLE

With a tea-drinking population desirous of adding milk and sugar to their tea, it was necessary for European porcelain producers to accommodate these whims with the appropriate tewares. As there were no Chinese prototypes to copy, European manufacturers had to devise such accessories that English tea service required, such as creamers and sugar bowls, fanciful silver sugar tongs, and dainty spoons to stir in cream and sugar, along with locked boxes, sugar caddies, and grand water dispensers for hot water.

Let's have a nice cup of tea and a sit down.

—ENGLISH SAYING

At first, Europeans copied the Chinese style of handle-less teacups, but handles and saucers were soon deemed necessary to a citizenry not used to drinking hot beverages and thus they became standard additions. Teapots grew in size as the middle class joined the ranks of tea drinkers, and social opportunities for taking tea increased as the cost of purchasing tea declined. As tea drinking reached all of the classes of society, and tea drinking became a social habit conducted in public as well as in private, teapots and teacups and saucers began to appear in more affordable stoneware and earthenware materials. Tea began to come in packages that sufficed for storage; the average family no longer needed to pay for an expensive tea caddy.

Tea Culture in the United States

By the late 1700s China's porcelain trade with Europe was on the decline, but by 1784, shortly after independence from Britain, America began to purchase both tea and porcelain directly and, most importantly, tax-free from China. The young nation's exuberance over its newly found freedom created a market within America for tea sets festooned with patriotic symbols, freedom motifs, family crests, and fraternal insignias. Before tea became the symbol of and the catalyst behind the American Revolution, expanding world trade and the strengthening of industry in America allowed every tea-drinking citizen to put an English teapot on his or her table. New England silversmiths such as Paul Revere brought a new clean line and a fresh design sense to English-inspired silver teapots and tea sets.

In New England, Ohio, and Virginia early American potters initially created utilitarian kitchenwares from heavy clays, and painted dark brown or red-brown glazed backgrounds with simply drawn mustard yellow designs. Yellow pottery and blue-gray pottery followed, as did soft-paste white creamware, but it was not until the mid to late nineteenth century that the influence of European porcelain factories began to affect the style of American wares. Immigrant pottery workers from England and Germany came to America and established new pottery firms or put their experienced skills to use in fledgling American pottery factories.

These workers introduced changes in the raw materials used, which were followed by changes in the look and style of American ceramic and porcelain wares. Wares became less dark and heavy, and soft-paste china began to sport floral designs and pleasing modern lines and shapes. Pottery factories were located throughout New York, New Jersey, Pennsylvania, and West Virginia, but the largest concentration settled in East Liverpool, Ohio. By the late nineteenth century porcelain factories, such as Lenox, began production, but formal, highly decorated porcelain tea sets never reached the zenith of production in America that they did in Europe. Companies such as Knowles, Taylor & Knowles; Harker Pottery Company; Metlox; Homer Laughlin; Steubenville Pottery Company; Taylor, Smith & Taylor Co.; and countless hundreds of others all produced casual, everyday teapots and tea sets. Although most of these early factories have closed or gone out of business, charming examples of these teapots and oftentimes complete tea sets can still be found in antique shops and at antique shows across the country for reasonable prices.

Tea Culture in the Russian Federation

Before the introduction of tea into Russia in the mid-1600s, Russians drank a mixture of hot water, honey, and herbs known as *sbiten*. The water for this brew was heated in an open, hot-pot type, broad-based vessel known as a *sbitennik*, a devise introduced to them by the Tartars in the fourteenth century. Eventually samovars replaced the sbitennek, but the origin of the samovar is a discussion about which no conclusive agreement has yet been reached. One possibility is that samovars were influenced by the sbitennik or other similar open, spigot-less cooking vessels used in China and Central Asia at that time.

Other possibilities exist. In the late 1600s and early 1700s tall, vase-style, charcoal-burning urns that stood on a base were in use in England and Holland for heating water. Like the later samovars, these urns had a central heating tube, but unlike the sbitennik they had a lid and a spigot from which to dispense the hot water. From the early 1770s, when samovars were first made in Russia, until they became somewhat commonplace in the 1890s, outside cultural ideas from the Middle East and Europe as well as from China and Central Asia influenced Russian culture. But luckily for tea fanciers, the samovar did become the four-legged, fanciful, ornate urn that will forever be the icon of Russian tea culture. Samovars are closely associated with all social levels of Russian life and are in the palace of the tsars as well as in modest homes, teahouses, and train stations. Samovars are mentioned in the works of such Russian literary giants as Chekov, Gogol, and Pushkin.

Samovars are elaborately designed vessels that boil water and keep it heated to the proper tea-brewing temperature. Water is filled from the top and heated and stored in the middle section. Today most samovars are electric, but in the past a center tube running up the middle of the samovar held charcoal or hot coals necessary for heating the water. The town of Tula, which is located south of Moscow, is the center of samovar production in Russia, and production here dates from the late 1700s.

SAMOVAR STYLES

No matter which style of samovar one has, hot water, not tea, is dispensed from an ornate spigot located at the bottom of the urn. The samovar's size gives it an impressive stature; most are tall and come in several different shapes—spherical, cylindrical, barrel-shaped, or urn-shaped. Samovars are made of brass, silver, or stainless steel, and range from plain and utilitarian to excessively ornate and garish versions painted with pink flowers on a black background. Many beautiful old samovars once brought to America by Russian immigrants can be found for sale in specialty antique shops in the Lower East Side of New York and in Brooklyn, but be ready to pay steep prices for spectacular examples or samovars that have been restored to near perfect condition.

At the top of the samovar a crownlike top (*komforka*) is made to hold a small metal or porcelain teapot (*chainik*) and keep the contents warm. In folk tradition the chainik is sometimes covered with a tea cozy doll made in the folk-art likeness of an old woman; her abundant skirt billows out and covers the teapot, keeping the heat in. The chainik contains strong concentrated tea known as *zavarka*. When it is time for a cup of tea, the user pours a small amount of zavarka into a teacup or a straight-sided tea glass that sits in a fanciful filigree silver or enamel holder with an attached handle (*podstakannik*). Hot boiled water (*kipyatok*) is released from the spigot, and the tea is diluted to taste. The usual ratio is ten parts kipyatok to one part zavarka, but adjustments are always made for individual taste.

THE RUSSIAN PORCELAIN TRADITION
OF EMPRESS ELIZABETH

Russia is known for exquisite decorative porcelain tewares, with designs that are uniquely Russian in style. As tea drinking filtered its way through all levels of society, Russia developed unique customs. Under the rule of Tsar Peter the Great (r. 1687–1725), Russia was brought out from under the dark mantle of medieval times and fashioned into a Western-style European power. Backed with a strong heritage and a unique, vibrant culture, Tsar Peter hired artisans and craftsmen from the European continent to create a luxurious Russian lifestyle for his imperial court that would reflect the worldliness and good taste of Russia. In keeping with his desire to establish credibility with the rest of Europe, he moved the capital from Moscow to the new city of St. Petersburg, a city that he created to reflect his sophisticated ideals for Russia.

Peter's daughter Empress Elizabeth continued to blend refinement and art with Russian culture when she ascended the throne in 1741. Instead of commissioning objects from Europe for the court, however, she established the Imperial Porcelain Factory in St. Petersburg in 1744, something that Peter desired but never accomplished. Although the overall direction of production in the Imperial Porcelain Factory remained truly Russian, the influences of German and French artisans combined to produce stunning porcelain tablewares and decorative accessories that featured opulent uses of gold and highly decorative, elaborate hand-painted scenes. In Elizabeth's day Russian state banquets were complicated and structured affairs, lasting many hours

A Soviet-era
tea brick, with
a hammer-and-
sickle design
embossed in
the center of the
brick.

and requiring abundant and sophisticated sets of dishes, serving pieces, and grand decorative objects to grace the banquet tables. The Imperial Porcelain Factory served all of Elizabeth's needs, an accomplishment equaled only by the courts of Germany and France and an achievement that was a matter of great pride to Elizabeth.

Under the rule of Catherine the Great (r. 1793–1796) European customs became even more firmly entrenched at court, and tea drinking, which had become fashionable among the nobility and the upper classes in Europe, became a daily habit of the Russian court. Catherine reorganized the Imperial Porcelain Factory and called for the creation of specialized tea sets and dishes that mirrored the elegance of Continental wares but reflected a bolder, more expressive Russian style. Among the elite porcelain factories were Gardner and Kuznetsov, A. Popov, and the Kornilov Brothers.

By the nineteenth century tea drinking had spread throughout all of the Russian provinces and all classes of society. But expensive leaf tea could only be afforded by the elite, while coarse, brick tea was consumed by the general population. As in China and Europe, tea drinking found its greatest audience when it became available to working-class people. For the average Russian citizen a cup of tea would bolster sagging spirits and supply a quick jolt of energy to housewives and workers. Today Russians drink tea throughout the day: as a pick-me-up during the day, with dessert, at an afternoon zakuska buffet, and in the evening, but never with a meal.

In 1925, a few years into the post-revolutionary Soviet era, the Imperial Porcelain Factory underwent a name change to the Lomonosov Porcelain Factory, in tribute to the celebrated eighteenth-century Russian chemist Mikhail V. Lomonosov. Today, fine, artistically designed porcelain tewares

are still being produced in this factory and many pieces are available in the United States. The distinctive combination of bold cobalt blue and gold set against a white background maintains a strong visual presence that reflects the daring artistic influence heralded by Catherine the Great.

No matter the style of teacup or samovar in use, Russian hospitality and goodwill is legendary. Russian tea is consumed strong and black. It is sometimes accompanied by lemon or orange slices and pots of honey or jam to spread on rolls and bread. Russians never use milk with their tea, but their sweet tooth welcomes sugary accompaniments. In the past Russians often held a sugar cube in their mouth while sucking in the tea, a practice that is not commonly carried out today.

Contemporary blue-and-white Lomonosov porcelain teawares are joined by decorative Russian silver tea glass holders (*podstakanniks*) outfitted with handle-less tea glasses.

Tea Culture in Tibet

Tea was first introduced to Tibet in the early days of the Tang dynasty (618–907), when a marriage occurred between the Chinese princess Wen Cheng and the king of Tibet, Songtsan Gambo. Introduction of this invigorating and hot beverage to Tibetans provided them with warmth and supplemented their meager diet. Rather than follow the lead of the Chinese tea-drinking habit, however, Tibetans concocted their own ways of enriching and preparing the brew. By adding yak butter, yak milk, and salt to the brewed tea, Tibetans bolstered an energizing cup of tea into an enriching "soup."

A young woman operates an old wooden butter churn *(dogmo)* in a family-run teahouse in eastern Tibet. Photo courtesy of Sonam Zoskang.

The Tibetans desire for tea began an interesting episode in China's tea history. Tibet and Mongolia each has a long history of horsemanship and husbandry skills in breeding strong, healthy horses. During the Tang dynasty the Chinese emperor needed horses to supply his army with quick, reliable transportation, so the Chinese began to barter tea supplies with these border populations in exchange for a supply of powerful horses. Tea came to be valued as a food supplement and as a form of currency by the Tibetans and other border groups. This trading practice established the historic Tea for Horse Caravan Route, which extended from Sichuan to Lhasa, Tibet. This dangerous route followed treacherously narrow paths that skirted the sides of mountains and scaled stretches of barren, windswept plains. Turbulent river crossings were particularly dangerous, and trips took months to complete at the cost of many human and animal lives. Tea caravan routes continued to be the sole means of tea transport from China to Tibet until the advent of paved roads in the twentieth century replaced these routes with safer and quicker transport.

YAK TEA CARAVANS

During the height of trading, two hundred to three hundred yak caravans left Sichuan for Tibet and Mongolia each day in addition to horse caravans. Also, there was a need to hire local tea porters to strap bundles of yak hide and bamboo-wrapped tea bricks to their backs and carry them across areas that were too narrow for the animals to traverse. The tea sent to Tibet and Mongolia was not of the same quality as that consumed in China. Border tea, as it was called, was for the most part a mixture of the coarsest leaf and twigs, compressed into bricks for easy transport on the arduous and treacherous journey across rugged terrain and inhospitable weather. Several grades of tea did exist– pure-leaf tea for wealthy merchants in Lhasa and members of the royal family—but it was brick twig tea for the poorest nomads.

Tibetan tea drinking is associated with butter tea, although simple everyday "quick tea" to which salt and milk is added is also consumed. Making authentic butter tea is a lengthy process, and it begins by pounding bits of tea brick into a powder and adding the tea to a pan of cold water. The tea is boiled in the water until the water turns dark in color and the brew becomes strong. The tea is strained into a tall and narrow wooden tea churn, which is followed by the addition of yak milk, salt, and yak butter. The mixture must be churned vigorously with the long plunger until it is well blended and emulsified. We were told that today many shortcuts are taken when making Tibetan tea, and that most families do not use the butter churn except on special occasions.

TIBETAN TEA BOWLS

When the tea is ready to drink, it is poured into traditional, plain Tibetan earthenware teapots. Many families own fanciful brass and silver gilt metal teapots, but these are rarely used except for special occasions such as weddings. Most Tibetans use tea bowls that are crafted from various Asian burlwoods. Elaborate and expensive tea bowls are fit with a silver lining that covers the inside of the bowl as well as the lip. A small band of wood is allowed to show around the middle of the bowl; otherwise, the bottom of the bowl is also encased in silver to create a protective base for the bottom of the bowl. Very fancy bowls feature *repoussé* silver embossed with the Eight Auspicious Symbols of Tibetan Buddhism. Small pieces of coral and turquoise are often used to stud the bands of the silver in simple patterns. Tibetan tea bowls are also used as food bowls for *tsampa*, a mixture of ground, roasted barley flour that is mixed with tea or water to form a soft paste. Tibetan nomads carry

On the last day of the Tibetan New Year, a family makes its way up to Yumbu Lagang, a Buddhist chapel and the former palace of the first king of Tibet. Decked out in finery for the occasion, the yak carries temple offerings (Yarlung valley, Tibet).

For us, no trip to Tibet would have been complete without a taste of Tibetan tea. Our friend Tashi knew where to take us to find a *real* cup of yak butter tea, something that he said is becoming a rarity these days in Tibet. Outside the city we climbed up a hill to a cave hidden away in the mountains in the vicinity of the Drephung Monastery. Once inside the cave, we were in the home of two Buddhist nuns who have lived there for sixteen and twenty-five years, respectively. Tashi made the introductions and the nuns showed us their butter urn and other tea utensils. They were beaming when they handed us little tin cups of yak butter tea that they poured steaming hot from a ubiquitous Chinese red thermos.

At first we were hesitant to take a sip, but politeness always overrules qualms when hospitality is involved. To be honest, the tea was not to our liking, but it was not as off-putting as we expected. The yak milk gave it an oily and very fatty texture, which coated our mouths and in comparison made our familiar cow's milk seem quite bland and unassuming. It was easy to understand why this rich beverage is consumed in such quantities all day long by Tibetans trying to stave off their harsh weather conditions.

A cave dwelling provides cozy shelter from the elements for two Buddhist nuns living a simple life in solitude and prayer (Llasa, Tibet).

their tea bowls with them wherever they go; this is how great their reliance is on a hot cup of tea. Most wooden tea bowls build up a patina of fat from the yak butter in the tea; bowls are rinsed and dried but never thoroughly washed.

It is a custom in Tibet when drinking butter tea to dip the third finger from your thumb into the cup and flick drops of tea three times to pay respect to the gods. Guests are always served tea, and it is not unusual for Tibetans to drink close to forty cups of tea a day. Yak butter tea is believed to aid in the digestion of the vegetable-less Tibetan diet of barley flour and meat, and it is also necessary to boost stamina against the harsh weather environment.

Today Chinese glass and metal tea thermoses are widely used throughout Tibet, and teacups are as apt to be porcelain or enameled tin as wood and silver. In the monasteries tea is still consumed in vast quantities. When we visited the Jokhang Temple in Lhasa, we arrived early in the morning, just in time to observe young monks preparing the morning tea by heating water on a solar heater in one of the side courtyards of the temple. A fleet of insulated thermos jugs were lined up waiting to be filled with the hot tea. Sheets of metal had been cut and fashioned onto metal legs to create solar-powered heat reflectors, an effective way to heat oversized kettles of water in the thin air of this extremely high altitude. Inside of the temple we spied a stack of crude, unwrapped tea on a table near a doorway. The monk in charge of that room was kind enough to let us take a picture of the tea bricks in exchange for a few coins.

Top: Stacks of Tibetan tea bowls. Old, well-worn, and well-used traditional wooden bowls and more recent porcelain bowls decorated with Tibetan Buddhist symbols.

Above: A cache of crude tea bricks in the Jokhang Temple, the holiest temple in Tibet (Llasa, Tibet).

Tea Culture in Morocco

In Morocco exotic silver teapots fashioned with long spouts dispense streams of hot mint tea into short, colorful, gilded tea glasses at all times of day and night. These teapots are fashioned by artisans who hand-hammer festive geometric or arabesque designs into tin, brass, aluminum, or silver alloys. For wealthy clients teapots may bear motifs in gold plate, but all Moroccans use essentially the same tea equipment at home and in restaurants.

Morocco's hot, dry climate is conducive to cooling off in a restful, shady place with a hot cup of sweet mint tea. To make this national beverage, a fistful of fresh mint is stuffed into the teapot along with a few tablespoons of sugar. Chinese Gunpowder green tea is the favorite tea, and the ratio of mint to tea used allows the tea to dominate the flavor. It is important to the Moroccan sense of hospitality that a welcome cup of tea be extended to all guests and visitors. Experienced tea servers like to engage in a bit of flair and

Fancy silver teapots and colorful glasses add panache to tea drinking in Morocco.

gracefully dispense the tea into the cups from a foot or so in the air—hence the necessity for the long and arched pouring spout. Optional sprigs of fresh mint can be added to the glass.

Moroccan tea glasses come in a rainbow of colors—blues, purples, greens, reds, gold, rose, and amber—and are usually purchased in sets of six glasses in the same color. Some patterns use an abundance of gold trim; others are more modest in their decoration. Handle-less silver holders with plain tea glasses are fashionable now, as well as frosted glasses decorated with modern designs. Some glasses have a little handle and a curvaceous shape and are accompanied by a flat little saucer. Moroccan tea trays are round or oval and are made in silver or brass. They are hand-hammered with similar designs to those used on the teapots. Silver receptacles for sugar and tea are used, and portable wooden tea stands hold the tray and accoutrements wherever needed. Platters of fragrant, honeyed, and spiced pastries featuring nut and fruit fillings and fresh fruit usually accompany Moroccan tea.

Tea has gone from the drink of the emperor to the beverage of everyman, consumed daily by people of all ages in all walks of life. Despite the colorful differences in tea culture around the world, tea's role and purpose is viewed in much the same way: with the power to rejuvenate and energize or provide a moment of calm and tranquility, tea reaches out to all of us and lifts the spirit

CHAPTER 8

THE HEALTH BENEFITS OF TEA

WESTERN RESEARCHERS ARE BEGINNING TO DISCOVER what tea drinkers in the East have believed for centuries—that tea is beneficial for maintaining health and vigor. Chinese anecdotal attitudes about the healthful benefits of tea have been shaped and groomed since tea's first mention in early Chinese scripts from the Shang (1766–1050 BC) and Zhou (1122–256 BC) dynasties. Early chronicles associated tea with monks and learned holy men, important for establishing the loftier philosophical and religious merits of tea drinking and for keeping awake during long meditations.

Asian cultures believe strongly in the beneficial cause and effect of food on human health; in effect, what we eat is reflected in how we feel. In her book *Watching the Tree* author Adeline Yen Mah recalls her Aunt Baba telling her as a child that "tea sharpens the mind, soothes the stomach, and nourishes your qi." Chinese health focuses on qi (or chi) as the vital energy within one's body, an internal life force. A qi out of balance therefore results in sickness or disease. A familiar Chinese proverb is "Let food be medicine" (*Yi shi wei liao*).

Because of their long history of practice and discourse with tea, Asians are said to be born with "tea in their veins"; their psyches are thus hardwired to the subtle nuances that permeate their tea cultures in ways that Westerners, despite our nearly three hundred years of tea drinking, are not connected to. But as Westerners begin to tune in to more healthy eating habits and look to beneficial foods for proper nutrition, tea has risen to the top of the charts, joining the list of such power foods as soy, fish, green leafy vegetables, and most fruits. Researchers are studying both green and black tea to understand the potential healthful benefits of their naturally occurring antioxidants.

THE CHARACTER OF TEA 茶

The Chinese character for tea is comprised of three parts: the upper part symbolizes "plant" or "grass"; the middle section refers to "man," especially man's locale on earth; the bottom portion represents "tree" or "being rooted." The sum of this character's elements creates the Chinese pictorial for tea as, "The revered plant that sustains man in his situation on earth."

Although each class of tea offers different antioxidants, the reports coming in for both types of tea are positive.

Tea buds and leaves have a complex chemical structure and contain all of the carbohydrates, proteins, lipids, enzymes, and genetic material pertaining to leaf growth and photosynthesis. The tea beverage is an expression of methylxanthine alkaloids (caffeine, which gives tea its bitter taste; theobromine; and theophylline); polyphenols, the catchin and catchin-derived antioxidants; and theanine, an amino acid that is believed to act as the neurotransmitter responsible for tea's ability to induce relaxation despite the caffeine present. In Japan gyokuro tea is made from leaf that is plucked from shaded tea bushes. Shading interrupts the normal leaf activity and stimulates an abundance of theanine production; the Japanese believe that shaded teas contain the highest amount of theanine possible. In addition, tea contains proteins, polysaccharides; minerals; vitamins B1, B2, and C; and fluoride. It is often erroneously stated that tea contains tannic acid—this is not true. Tea does contain tannins, however; these are complex members of the flavonoid group that give tea its characteristic astringency.

Although fresh tea buds and leaves are comprised of 75 to 80 percent water, the polyphenol components of tea reside in the remaining 20 to 25 percent of solid matter, and the percent will differ between classes of tea. Polyphenols are antioxidants, a broad class of phytochemical compounds found in most plant matter, vegetables, and fruits, as well as in such beverages as beer, coffee, cocoa, wine, and tea. Food chemists have counted more than eight thousand known polyphenols in the plant world (more than 50 percent of these are flavonoids). Researchers are putting these naturally occurring compounds under the microscope to study the potential role they play in boosting our immune systems, maintaining healthy bacteria in the gastrointestinal tract, and preventing or delaying the onset of disease.

Tea polyphenols are important because they halt the damaging effects of oxidation, a process of molecular DNA damage that occurs when the formation of unstable toxic molecules known as free radicals develop within the human body. If left unchecked, deficiencies in our antioxidant quotient will allow these rogue molecules to change the ability of our normal, healthy cells to function properly, a process known as oxidative damage. Free radicals scavenge healthy cells and rob them of their vital cell material, creating a chain reaction of cellular damage that can lead to immune system malfunctions, chronic illness, premature physical deterioration, and organ disease. Oxidation deficiencies can also occur within the human body as a result of repeated exposure to unhealthful conditions that we encounter every day. Some of these risks are eating processed foods that lack vitamins and minerals and that contain an abundance of fats and sugars, secondhand cigarette smoke, exposure to cleaning solvents and chemicals, and of course cigarette smoking, and drug and alcohol abuse.

Tea's Beneficial Antioxidants

Our bodies respond to the negative effects of free radicals by utilizing defensive antioxidant molecules present in our systems to detoxify or counterattack these harmful effects. Scientists and nutritionists encourage us to make deposits into the bank account of good health and long life by increasing the level of antioxidants in our bodies. This is easily and sensibly achieved by adding to our diets delicious foods that are rich in naturally occurring antioxidants, such as fruits and vegetables. Another way is by following the Asian lead of drinking several cups of tea each day.

Tea buds and leaves plucked from *Camellia sinensis* (not "tisanes" or "herbal" infusions made from herbs, twigs, or flowers or fruit infusions made from citrus, berries, and spices) contain a specific group of antioxidant compounds known as flavonoids. The flavonoids in tea are composed of two groups of substances—*flavonols* and *flavanols*. Tea is richest in flavanols, and tea researchers are zeroing in on this group. The tea flavanol group contains substances known as catechins—tea's most important antioxidant arsenal of defense against free radicals.

The fact that green tea undergoes less internal change from fresh leaf means that it contains the largest quantity of intact catechins. Green tea catechins consist of four antioxidant compounds—EC (epicatechin), ECG (epicatechin gallate), EGC (epigallocatechin), and EGCG (epigallocatechin gallate). This last compound is the most abundant catechin in green tea and the most bioactive of the group. These compounds also contribute the light-yellow to golden-green color of brewed green tea and the fresh, clean, vegetal "green jade" flavors that connoisseurs seek in early spring-plucked green tea.

Despite the recent attention paid to the healthful nature of green and white tea, all classes of tea contain polyphenols. The differing methods of leaf manufacture for black, green, oolong, scented, and white teas (see chapter 3) also results in the formation of different polyphenols within the leaves in each class of tea. For black tea, after leaf withering and during the leaf-rolling stages of manufacture, polyphenol oxidaze enzymes that are present in the fresh leaf interact to cause the catechins to oxidize. These oxidized catechins link together to form derived tannins known as theaflavins (catechin dimers), antioxidant substances that contribute to the characteristic orange/red color, brightness, briskness, and flavor of black tea. These substances combine with caffeine to influence astringency.

Theaflavins consist of several fractions—theaflavin, theaflavin 3-gallate, and theaflavin 3,3'-digallate. During this process other catechin compounds oxidize into thearubigins, additional derived tannins formed in tea during oxidation. The method and conditions of oxidized tea manufacture affects the proportions of antioxidant theaflavins to thearubigins present in the tea and thus the corresponding flavor, character, and astringency found in the cup. The longer tea is oxidized and the darker in color it is, the more thearubigins it contains. Both theaflavins and thearubigins contribute the orange-red and red-brown color spectrum that defines the appearance of oxidized tea.

White tea is more aligned with green tea (although some leaf styles of white tea undergo a slight withering) and pu-erh tea more closely follows suit with black tea. Oolong tea, a semioxidized tea, contains the reverse antioxidant proportions of black tea; it has a higher concentration of theaflavins and a lower concentration of thearubigins. But, in fact, some researchers believe that the activation of tea enzymes during the manufacture of black tea may result in the formation of antioxidant compounds that are more powerful in preventing some disease than those contained in green tea.

Research on Tea

Much tea research is ongoing in private laboratories and university research centers across the United States, including the Beltsville Human Nutrition Research Center, the University of Kansas at Lawrence, the National Cancer Institute, the USDA Human Nutrition Research Center on Aging at Tufts University, and the Linus Pauling Institute at Oregon State University. Many questions remain unanswered about the potential that tea has for fighting and preventing disease.

Although it is too soon to know tea's role in disease prevention and cure, tea drinking does provide many healthful benefits. Tea contains no additives or artificial sweeteners, and when consumed without the addition of sugar or dairy, it contains no calories. Tea drinking increases daily fluid intake, helps to maintain a healthy, active metabolism and circulatory system, acts as an antiviral, contributes to oral health by inhibiting bacterial plaque, acts as an anti-inflammatory, and is a rich source of vitamins. The antioxidant levels in green tea have been reported to be a hundred times more effective than vitamin C and twenty-five times better than vitamin E in protecting our immune systems.

The list of medical conditions and diseases that researchers hope to find tea useful for combating or forestalling focuses on certain cancers, heart disease, diabetes, stroke, the onset of Alzheimer's, and liver diseases. To date, clinical studies regarding tea consumption and health remain inconclusive when it comes to understanding just how far tea can go to prevent or delay the onset of disease. Early reporting about the potential healthful benefits of tea took great liberties assigning tea with much hoped for but unproven disease prevention and fighting abilities. Although much tea research and hundreds of clinical trials are actively being conducted in the areas of health and disease, it is vital, however, for consumers to be able to discern between fact and overstatement. A study published by the U.S. Department of Agriculture has reported that "the number of well-designed, carefully controlled dietary intervention studies, which show cause and effect, is limited, and this represents a critical gap in our understanding of these compounds as they relate to health promotion and disease prevention." Until concrete facts have been proven, the buzzwords surrounding tea as a potential disease fighter should be discussed as just that. We would be wise to use such qualifiers for tea as "it has the potential to" or "is thought to aid in" or "may assist with."

Laboratory testing is sometimes at odds in determining the actual measurable antioxidant content of tea within each class. In fact, a study conducted by the UCLA Center for Human Nutrition tested more than eight national brands of green and black tea and came up with staggeringly different antioxidant levels, not only for each class of tea but for each tea tested within its own class. This is disheartening for those looking for pat answers but should come as no surprise. Many variables pertaining to tea and the production of tea arise that make standardization difficult to control and predict. Once one adds any number of variables particular to human biology and disease into the picture, many additional conditions occur to further cloud the results.

Consider the following reports on antioxidant content. In the September 2001 issue of the *Journal of Nutrition*, a research study by Lai Kwok Leung and others addressed the question of the antioxidant content in black and green teas. To quote their findings: "All data presented here suggest that drinking black tea has benefits equal to those of drinking green tea in terms of the antioxidant capacity."

But in a separate study reported in a letter to the editor of the *Journal of Nutrition* in 2002 by Ki Won Lee and others, these researchers reached a different conclusion. This group reported in their findings "the antioxidant capacity per serving of green tea (463 milligrams) was much higher than that of black tea (239 milligrams)." And another report conducted by the Antioxidants Research Laboratory within the Human Nutrition Research Center on Aging concluded findings of 235 milligrams of antioxidants in one six-ounce cup of green tea. The UCLA Center for Nutrition Study found the antioxidant content of several brands of green tea to range from 217 to 53 milligrams and from 164 to 38 milligrams in black tea in a three-minute infusion of each type of tea. Research conducted by Jeffrey Blumberg, associate director of the Jean Mayer USDA Human Nurtrition Research Center on Aging at Tufts University, concludes that the same percentage of flavonoids is present in a brewed cup of green (16 percent) or black (15.6 percent) tea.

Conflicting conclusions underscore the fact that different batches of green tea will contain unequal quantities of catechin, just as the theaflavin/thearubigin content of black tea will also vary. This is to be expected. The polyphenol content of fresh tea leaf varies from country of origin and from region to region within each country (because of the clonal varieties of tea bushes in question). There are also variances based on the time of the season that the leaf was plucked and the position of the leaf on the bush (the younger the leaf, the more antioxidants it contains). Fresh leaf that has been subjected to the least amount of oxidation during manufacture (green tea incurs no oxidation, and budset white tea incurs little oxidation) contains the most catechins. In the case of black and oolong teas the oxidation levels reached when producing these teas vary by percentage-point differences (15 to 80 percent oxidation) that make it impossible to measure percentages of theaflavin/theagrubigin content with any consistency.

Even when comparing green teas to other green teas, or black teas to other black teas, these geographic and seasonal differences present different circumstances that yield differing amounts of polyphenols. Tea researchers at the Sichuan Agricultural University in Ya'an explained to us that they believe that the optimum polyphenol content in green tea is realized in tea that is made using one leaf and a bud. But the argument can also be made that the polyphenol content of budset green or budset white tea is even higher. Whole-leaf tea will no doubt yield different results than tea found in a teabag, and each will differ when tea is consumed hot or with ice, or with milk or sugar. One must also take into account the size of the measure of tea used, the length of time that the tea steeps, and the temperature of the water.

Many studies have also shown positive indicators for tea polyphenols when performed in tests in vitro, but the same tests often fail to confirm results or do not show consistent results when conducted in clinical trials on human study participants. Individual variations in the ability of people or groups of people with different ethnicities to absorb the available bionutrients in tea and to metabolize them efficiently yield differing results. Body type, age, gender, diet, and nutritional habits add further to the variables.

In June 2005 the Food and Drug Administration (FDA) addressed green tea's role as a cancer preventive or cancer fighter. Their ruling declared that there was "no credible evidence" that green tea cuts breast cancer or prostate cancer risk, or is a fighter of other cancers, including lung, gastric, colon, rectal, pancreatic, esophageal, skin, ovarian, or liver cancers. And again in

2006 the FDA denied a Japanese tea company use of the advertising claims that green tea may reduce the risk of cardiovascular disease by stating that there was "no credible evidence" to support this claim.

Despite this broad-based rejection, tea may yet prove itself as a chemopreventive mechanism that can fight disease and maintain wellness in certain situations. From all of these questions one thing is clear, however: research and human clinical studies must continue. The reasons to drink tea are the same now as they have been for centuries: Tea is a pleasure beverage with a sensory appeal and an enormous feel-good attitude that delivers great, satisfying flavor. Tea has virtually no negative side effects, and helps students and workers maintain alertness and mental clarity.

Surely there are many possible benefits from drinking tea that have not yet been discovered. For instance, at Pace University in New York City, Milton Schiffenbauer, PhD, professor of microbiology, has conducted research that concludes that white tea is more effective than green tea as an antiviral and antibacterial when added to toothpaste or used as an oral agent.

So, when it comes to tea, think tonic not curative, healthful collaborator not redeemer. Mix it up and drink tea from all of the fascinating classes of tea. Drink tea to relax and connect with the spiritual nature of life's simple pleasures. Enjoy the flavors and the subtle and not so subtle differences waiting to be discovered in the world of tea offerings, and should the rich doses of flavanoids in each cup of tea be determined to cure what ails you, you will be ahead of the curve.

Caffeine in Tea

Reminiscent of the legends regarding early coffee consumption, the record of humankind's use of the tea plant suggests that if it did not contain caffeine, the beverage that we know today would not have evolved. Were it not for caffeine, the people of mainland Southeast Asia might not have tolerated the bitter, nasty taste of early tea preparations long enough to allow it to evolve into the pleasure beverage that we know today. Throughout tea's journey from fresh leaves chewed for their mild stimulation, then to their use as a component of primitive concoctions of fresh or dried leaf combined with other edibles (trail mix of a sort), to a boiled tincture central to Eastern medicine, caffeine was the constant that inspired experimentation.

In its native wild state *Camellia sinensis* is a rugged plant indeed, both in habit and in taste. As with most indigenous medicinals, the passage of time and changes in use have led to the extraction of caffeine in a pure, more refined form. Botanical improvements and experimentation with brewing techniques persuaded the world to embrace an incredibly pleasant beverage that hid for centuries beneath the veil of folk medicine. The quixotic narratives of the "origin" of both coffee and tea, while romantic and lovely, overlook the practical and valuable roles that these two plants have played in the evolution of stimulants and thirst-quenching beverages. The 1820s were quite an invigorating decade for stimulants: caffeine was first discovered in coffee in 1820, and the stimulant theine was discovered in tea in 1827. Theine was later identified as the primary stimulant in several other ingestible plants, most notably maté, the South American shrub or tree. It didn't take long for chemists to recognize that caffeine and theine were one and the same, so the term *theine* is rarely used today.

Caffeine is a bitter alkaloid, the methylxanthine known as 1,3,7-trimethylxanthine, and is found naturally in at least sixty-three types of plants, most notably coffee, tea, and cacao. It acts as a stimulant to the central nervous system. It is extremely close in chemical structure to theobromine, the main alkaloid in cacao. Caffeine is considered to be safe for most people when consumed at a dose of 0.3 grams or less per day. This equates to approximately five cups of tea, each brewed full-strength. Having followed many of the studies on caffeine as well as volumes of speculative writing about the caffeine content of tea, we can say only this truth with certainty: there is caffeine in tea.

Depending on which study you read and whose analysis you accept as true, the amount of caffeine in your teacup can vary greatly or not at all. Nevertheless, several constants do exist that affect the stimulant intensity of our cups of tea.

> *Drinking tea bespeaks a quest that one offers to his friends for the beauty of gestures, of objects and of the heart.*
>
> —SOGAKU OF THE HAYAMI SCHOOL

CAFFEINE CONSTANTS SPECIFIC TO THE FRESH LEAF

The caffeine content of fresh leaf manufactured into the different classes of tea from the same base leaf is theoretically the same, all other conditions being equal. The leaves of all varieties of the *Camellia sinensis* plant are infused to brew tea. This infusion can be from any of the traditional classes of tea—black, oolong, green, and white, or such minor manufactures as jasmine. An example of this would be a tippy black tea and a budset spring green tea, both made from the same *Camellia sinensis* plantings in Yunnan Province, picked during the same season, and then manufactured into their respective tea styles.

The choice of leaf that is plucked partially determines the caffeine content of that leaf. As with herbs and most flowering plants, the emerging bud (the budset) contains a larger proportion of the lifeblood of a plant than do the other leaves. Therefore the budset of the tea plant has more caffeine. As one moves down the pluck, the amount of caffeine decreases incrementally. Spring green budset teas that have a large amount of "down" (the tea bush's natural pollen) still clinging to them may have an additional source of caffeine in this down. The down is trapped within the budset and remains dusted on it in the spring, when the bud emerges (similar to the green dusty haze released by some conifers). Although it is not scientifically demonstrated in contemporary studies, this influence has been noted in earlier empirical evidence. Any potential variation because of the presence of down varies tremendously from tea to tea, whereas the difference between the budset and the lower leaf is constant.

The age of the plucked leaf has an influence on the amount of caffeine in the leaf. The age of the fresh leaf (the amount of time the leaf has been on the plant) has an effect on the amount of caffeine present. The younger the budset or leaf being plucked, the higher the amount of caffeine, because the "juice" of the plant disperses downward as the plant matures, carrying with it some of the caffeine. The fourth leaf (also known as a coarse plucking) may have 30 percent less caffeine than the same branch's budset.

The period during the plant's growth cycle when the leaf is plucked also affects the caffeine content. The amount of caffeine present in the pluck can be influenced by the specific time during the season at which the harvest occurs. Following a hard pruning (for rejuvenation or shaping), severe winterkill, maintenance pruning, or wind damage, for instance, the tea bush is known to increase the amount of nutrient sent to the emerging growth. This also increases the amount of caffeine. This factor is somewhat untraceable but is another variable that may explain why a certain tea may, for no other reason, have a noticeable kick to it. Even prior plucks can increase the caffeine content of leaf picked from the same plant later that season.

REDUCTION OF CAFFEINE BY THE QUICK RINSE METHOD

After thirty seconds of extraction it is reasonable to expect a reduction in the caffeine content of black leaf tea by 50 to 70 percent. This is not decaffeination, as that term implies (and legally requires) the removal of 97 percent or more of the caffeine that was originally present in the leaf. But it is a significant reduction in caffeine and may be enough for those wishing to moderate their caffeine consumption.

Although the speed of extraction from different leaf styles may make a minor difference in this phenomenon, the premise is sound. A good rule of thumb is the same as that used for the steeping times for teas that permit multiple infusions: the greater the surface area exposed, the faster the soluble solids release from the leaf. This caffeine reduction method only works with fully oxidized black tea.

BREWING TECHNIQUES AND THE RELEASE OF CAFFEINE

Different types of tea require different brewing techniques, each of which affects the release of caffeine into the liquid tea. Below are the variables specific to the brewing techniques.

The temperature of the brewing water used affects the amount of caffeine extracted from the tea leaf. One can inadvertently alter the caffeine extraction from the different styles of tea by using water that is either too hot or too cool for the type of tea being brewed. Any such change alters the normal extraction of caffeine usual for that style of tea. Using water that is hotter than is required extracts more caffeine than desired from the tea leaves, and using water that is too cool extracts less caffeine. This variation is most noticeable when brewing green tea.

The amount of time the tea leaf is allowed to brew affects the amount of caffeine in the liquid tea. This is one of the most critical elements of tea brewing. In addition to the goal of correctly brewing one's cup of tea to develop optimal flavor, the length of steeping time affects the amount of caffeine extracted. It cannot be said whether this is more or less significant when using one style of tea or another. Every style of tea has a specific brewing tradition that should be observed; however, the rate of caffeine extraction relative to the length of time that any particular tea leaf is steeped remains constant, so tea from the same source, steeped according to two different cultural traditions, may vary in caffeine content.

When tea leaves are steeped longer than five minutes, there may be a reduction in stimulant from the brewed tea. This phenomenon is due to one of two reasons: First, the leaf is being brewed multiple times (as with white, green, oolong, and pu-erh teas). As this leaf will have already been infused for a short initial brew or two and the liquor subsequently poured off once or twice (along with the majority of the caffeine), this five-minute marker would only occur during a second, third, or even fourth infusion (for which there is less caffeine remaining to be extracted from the leaf).

Second, if the leaf is being brewed once (most black teas), a long steeping releases many more soluble solids into the brewed tea than does a short steeping. Although the increase in total soluble solids after five minutes likely reduces the percentage of caffeine, the actual amount of caffeine remains constant. There may, however, be other extractives that act as calmatives (for example, the amino acid theanine as well as an abundance of polyphenols, which are proven to bind to caffeine and can prevent absorption) that might negate some of the influence or absorption of the caffeine when consumed. Teabag users who only quickly dunk often extract more caffeine than they realize, because the caffeine extraction rate is very high initially when brewing tea leaves of the size used for most teabags.

Teas that are infused multiple times release varying amounts of caffeine into the different infusions. Green, white, and oolong tea leaves are normally infused multiple times, for a short period (often a maximum of two minutes each) using water that is cooler than that used for brewing black tea. These individual infusions contain varying amounts of caffeine. Different traditions of tea brewing alter the temperature of the water and the brewing time for these individual infusions, but a rough guide to the caffeine content of three infusions of tea brewed from the same green, white, or oolong tea leaves is thus: first brew 60 percent, second brew 30 percent, and third brew 10 percent (of the caffeine originally present in the dry tea leaves). Although the amount of available caffeine in the dry tea leaves varies depending on the type of tea being brewed, the proportion of caffeine in each infusion should remain consistent with this formula.

Taking into consideration all of these variables, it becomes clear that definitive statements regarding the caffeine content of a cup of brewed tea are almost impossible to make. One must first know a great deal of information about the source of the tea (or have a chemical analysis done on the tea leaf), and then adjust for the brewing technique used. Those who quote definitive caffeine contents or comparisons based on traditional, inaccurate assumptions do a disservice to their readers or customers. That being said, if you have a significant amount of information about the tea in your possession, a learned guess can be made as to whether or not that leaf tea will be in the norm or uniquely different from the above guidelines. Then the brewed tea can be prepared so that the caffeine present in that brewed tea will be as expected.

As interest in tea has increased, much more information is being provided about the source of the tea leaf being purchased, so making an educated guess about caffeine content is becoming more possible. Retailers who specialize in source-specific estate teas from identified seasonal harvests can be helpful in assessing the caffeine content of their teas. Studies that have been done on the caffeine concentration in already-brewed tea (ready-to-drink, bottled tea) show a significant variation in the available caffeine.

The other notable factor is that it is not what one consumes but what one absorbs, and every individual's metabolism and capacity to absorb caffeine and the other components of brewed tea accordingly affects the stimulating and healthful properties of leaf tea. Even what one has or hasn't eaten recently can influence the absorption rate of the components of beverages.

CAFFEINE QUIZ

Which brew probably has more caffeine? The first infusion of a downy bud-set green tea brewed from the plucking of a China bush plant on an early spring morning, or a cup of black tea brewed five minutes from an ortho-dox Assam pluck that was picked in late autumn from a bush that was heavily pruned earlier that spring and fed a hefty dose of organic fertilizer just before monsoon season? The constants are that all the brewing is done with two grams of tea and the same amount of water. The answer: it is impossible to know, as there are several factors involved.

1. If the downy budset green tea has a caffeine content of 4 percent (very high) and 60 percent of the caffeine is extracted during the first infusion: 2000 milligrams × 4 percent × 60 percent = 48 milligrams of caffeine.

2. If the downy budset green tea has a caffeine content of 3 percent (moderate) and 60 percent of the caffeine is extracted during the first

infusion: 2000 milligrams × 3 percent × 60 percent = 36 milligrams of caffeine.

3. If the downy budset green tea has a caffeine content of 2 percent (very low) and 60 percent of the caffcine is extracted during the first infusion: 2000 milligrams × 2 percent × 60 percent = 24 milligrams of caffeinc.

4. Now let's assume that the Assam tea has a caffeine content of 4 percent (very high). After five minutes of brewing, it is safe to assume that at least 80 percent of the caffeine will have been transferred to the brew, so the calculation is: 2000 milligrams × 4 percent × 80 percent = 64 milligrams of caffeine.

5. Now let's assume that the Assam tea has a caffeine content of 3 percent (moderate). After five minutes of brewing, it is safe to assume that at least 80 percent of the caffeine will have been transferred to the brew, so the calculation is: 2000 milligrams × 3 percent × 80 percent = 48 milligrams of caffeine.

6. Now let's assume that the Assam tea has a caffeine content of 2 percent (very low). After five minutes of brewing, it is safe to assume that at least 80 percent of the caffeine will have been transferred to the brew so the calculation is: 2000 milligrams × 2 percent × 80 percent = 32 milligrams of caffeine.

One can see from these analyses that it is possible that the green tea might have 50 percent more caffeine than the black tea, or the black tea might have two and a half times the caffeine of the green tea. There is no practical way of knowing when you sit down to enjoy your cup of tea.

From the believed benefits of ancient times to the demonstrated advantages shown in modern laboratories, drinking tea has proven itself over and over to be a therapeutic life-enhancer. Drink all types of tea, potentially as much as six cups per day. Just remember the advice given by everyone from your mother to Julia Child: eat a varied and balanced diet, with all elements in moderation.

CHAPTER 9

ETHICS IN THE TEA TRADE

I N THIS CHAPTER WE EXPLORE several of the social and political aspects of tea production and marketing. As with dairy, soy, cattle, cacao, and coffee, tea is a labor-intensive crop to bring to market. Dovetailing with similar movements in other food-producing endeavors, many businesses, individuals, and government agencies are involved in efforts to improve both the transparency of tea distribution and the living and working conditions of those involved in the agricultural production of tea at its source. This chapter examines issues in organic production, fair trade, source identification, and sustainability. We also mention several regulatory organizations and certifying agencies.

Organically Grown Tea

Organic tea production falls into two categories: (1) tea that is certified organic by one of several international agencies, and (2) tea that is grown according to traditional methodology that inevitably follows organic principles but has not been validated by a certifying agent. When a tea is "certified organic," it has met the conditions set forth by at least one of the regulatory agencies that has established guidelines for organic food production. Only then can the product affix the proper seal and use the appropriate terminology identifying which level of "certified organic" the product has attained. As a general rule, a fee is paid to the certifying agency for this service, and any inspection required is conducted at the time of certification and then repeated periodically. The countries with the strictest organic certification standards are Germany, the United States, Japan, and the United Kingdom;

*Though I cannot flee
From the world of corruption,
I can prepare tea
With water from a mountain stream
And put my heart to rest.*

—UEDA AKINARI, JAPANESE AUTHOR
(1734–1809)

however, the European Union's Regulation (EEC) No. 2092/91 is the benchmark for the industry.

Organic certification was originally conceived as a way that a farmer or merchant could convey that the tea (or other agricultural product) for sale had been grown under time-honored and desirable conditions. It is a validation that became necessary due to the increase of modern farming procedures worldwide, combined with broader distribution of product and differences in standard from origin to origin. Tea that is certified organic today is often inspected and marketed as such because of the potential for a "value-added" economic advantage. Organic certification in the twenty-first century is increasingly the domain of big business and less that of the dedicated back-to-nature types—the rebellious farmers and merchants of the late 1900s. During the agricultural land consolidation years of the 1970s and 1980s in the United States, small farmers of food crops were encouraged to sell their ordinary land to large corporations. Many farmers and landowners whose land qualified for organic certification at the turn of the twenty-first century came under a similar pressure to sell that land to large multinationals, so that those companies could quickly gain organic market share.

Tea gardens are traditionally not owned by small landowners, but rather by large businesses or venerable tea families that provide housing, crop land, and support infrastructure for the garden's workers. The conversion of the tea gardens to (or the continuation of) organic methodology is thus dictated more by location and the health of the parent company, rather than by the market forces moving most other organic trade. Artisan tea is unique as well, because much of the terrain on which it is produced is at high altitude and remote, and tended by generations of the same families who have been in the same place for decades, even centuries.

In 2000, when we visited the Kai Hua Tea Factory in China's Zhejiang Province, the largest tea factory in the world, tea was available at any price and every quality. While we toured the facility, we encountered German tea buyers shopping for organic, high-quality specialty tea as well as Sudanese tea buyers looking for some of the cheapest tea on the planet. This is not an atypical scenario, so it is difficult for tea growers to know whether the future market will have as its main criteria quality, organic production, price, flavor profile, or a combination of these elements. In general, tea customers in Canada, the United Kingdom, the United States, Western Europe (Germany in particular), and now members of the emerging middle class in Asia are desirous of drinking high-quality tea, organically grown when possible. For most of the tea-drinking world, however, price is the major consideration, so cost-ratio will affect any potential increase in organic production worldwide.

When a tea is grown organically simply because of tradition or commitment, it means that the tea has been grown following agricultural principles that have never changed, so this is the traditional and only method known to the tea grower. Organic principles might also be maintained because of location, purposeful dedication, or economic bravado. In the highly competitive tea trade, when fees are not paid, validation not tendered, and subsequent revenue not increased ("value-added" hypotheses don't always execute), organic practices continue only within the domain of those growers who are committed to organic agricultural doctrine.

Organic tea production is superior for the land, excellent for the grower and processor, and good for the consumer. In the realm of fine tea there are many examples from excellent certified organic production and other superb examples from sourcings that use traditional, centuries-old methodology. A bit of inquisitiveness directed toward your tea supplier should invite discussion about methods used and sourcing of the tea you want to try.

REGULATORY ORGANIZATIONS

The five most visible and highly reputable major regulatory organizations whose logos you will encounter in the marketplace have set standards for organic production (three of these are government agencies and two are private): Regulation No. 2092/91 of the European Union, the National Organic

Program (NOP) of the United States, the Japanese Agriculture Standard (JAS), the Soil Association of England, and Demeter-International e. V. of Germany.

European Union: Regulation No. 2092/91. The European Union, the biggest organic marketplace in the world, was the first to enact governmental legislation regarding organic production and marketing. The original regulation was drafted in 1991 and went into effect in 1992. As a result, this groundbreaking legislation, known as Regulation No. 2092/91, is now the legislative model for the regulation of organic producers and traders in most other countries. The European Union has since modified, clarified, and amended the regulation, so that it is now ninety-five pages long and quite comprehensive.

Regulation No. 2092/91 is the legal basis for the production, processing, and trade of all organic products in the twenty-seven countries of the European Union, as of publication. Products labeled "organic" must be certified according to these guidelines and are then allowed to be identified with the official label of the European Union. Only two categories of "certified organic" are allowed: one for products that contain at least 95 percent organic ingredients, and one for products containing 70 to 95 percent organic ingredients. For a comparison of this regulation and the USDA legislation, see the Organic Trade Association's comparison of standards in this chapter.

One example of the complexity involved in including its diverse membership is that all common terms for "organic" in the different member states are equally protected in their use (for example, *biologisch* in German, *écologico* in Spanish, and *biologique* in French). There are instances in which individual countries within the European Union have standards that differ from those of Regulation No. 2092/91. This is acceptable as long as they are stricter than the basic standards. For complete information regarding Regulation No. 2092/91, visit the website of the Institute for Marketecology at www.imo.ch.

United States: USDA National Organic Program (NOP). During the 1990s the U.S. Department of Agriculture (USDA) developed a set of national organic standards, and activated them in 2002 under the legislation known as the USDA National Organic Program (NOP). This legislation requires that all organic products be certified by an independent agency approved by the USDA. Products labeled "organic" must be certified according to the guidelines of this legislation. Four categories of organic content were established: 100 percent organic, 95 percent or more organic, 70 to 95 percent organic, and less than 70 percent organic. Products are required to be identified with the appropriate official label of the USDA.

For a comparison of the USDA legislation and that of the European Union, see the Organic Trade Association's comparison of standards in this chapter. For more information on the USDA's NOP, visit http://agriculture .senate.gov/Legislation/Compilations/AgMisc/OGFP90.pdf.

Japanese Agricultural Standard (JAS). The certification of organic products sold in the Japanese market is regulated by the JAS. All certified products are identified with the official JAS organic seal of the Japanese government. The JAS law regulates all labeling of agricultural products and is managed by Japan's Ministry of Agriculture, Forestry, and Fisheries (MAFF). The JAS organic standard is presented in various Japanese regulations and notifications (for example, Law No. 175).

JAS certification requires a unique certification procedure, although its requirements can be evaluated during the same inspection as that for another international agency. An example of both international cooperation and peer pressure is that the EU Regulation's Concentration Standard of Residual Agricultural Chemicals (perhaps the strictest in the world) is stricter than Japan's. For many years green tea harvested in Japan could not be exported to the EU. Because of the efforts of the Kyoto Green Tea Cooperative Society and the whole-tea industry in Kyoto (where the premier tea-producing region Uji is located), leaf green tea produced in Kyoto now meets this EU standard. Since 2003, green tea produced in Kyoto may be imported into EU member countries. More information about the JAS can be found at the IMO website (www.imo.ch).

England: The Soil Association. This private agency located in Bristol was founded in 1946 by a group of farmers, scientists, and nutritionists. It is a charity funded solely by members and donations from institutions such as charitable trusts. Today the Soil Association is the primary organic organization in the United Kingdom, and its symbol is the UK's most recognizable and trusted organic mark. Soil Association Certification Ltd. (known as "SA Certification" and established in 1973) is the auxiliary of the Soil Association that supervises organic certification to the Soil Association standards. It is the UK's largest organic certification body, now certifying 80 percent of all organic products sold in the UK.

SA Certification covers both the EU Regulation No. 2092/91 and the Advisory Committee on Organic Standards' (ACOS) compendium (these

COMPARISON OF EUROPEAN UNION AND U.S. ORGANIC STANDARDS

This information comes from the Organic Trade Association.

Cultural and political differences are substantial:

- *Cultural.* While states in the United States use one language and have similar cultures, EU member states have different languages and cultures.

- *Political.* Federal laws supersede state laws in the United States, while the EU consists of twenty-five sovereign state governments, each of which can grant exceptions to established Regulation No. 2092/91 rules and regulations.

Some cropping standards differ.

- *Agriculture conversion period.* Conversion (transition) periods as written in the EU regulations may be interpreted as being shorter than the three-year, no-exceptions rule found in the United States. The European Union generally requires two years for annuals and three years for perennials, with some exceptions.

Labeling requirements are similar.

- *"Organic."* Both agree that at least 95 percent of the ingredients must be organic.

- *"Made with."* Both agree that 70 percent of the ingredients must be organic.

In the EU the remaining 30 percent must be on published lists of "not commercially available ingredients." This list is subject to interpretation by the certifier or member state.

- *"Below 70 percent."* The EU does not allow "organic" to appear anywhere on the label. The USDA allows identification of organic ingredients on the information panel in products containing 50 percent or more organic ingredients.

- Percent organic declarations in the United States are not mandatory, but in some EU situations declaration may be required.

- Under EU regulations, "transition to organic" labeling is allowed. In the United States such labeling is not allowed.

represent modifications made by the Department for the Environment, Food, and Rural Affairs, the government agency that advocates internal UK organic standards). Since the mid-1970s, however, the Soil Association has been developing its own standards; in some areas the Soil Association standards exceed other international requirements, particularly in the area of animal welfare. SA Certification works with consumers, farmers, growers, processors, retailers, and policy makers. The complete Soil Association standards must be ordered from the Soil Association (there is a fee).

Germany: Demeter-International e. V. Located in Darmstadt, Demeter is the international trademark for products certified from Biodynamic Agriculture worldwide, with principal offices in Germany, Belgium, and Singapore. Demeter-International e. V. is a nonprofit organization whose members work together as an international confederation. Membership is contractual, based on adherence to the Biodynamic Agriculture method originated by Dr. Rudolf Steiner in his "agriculture course" in 1924. Biodynamic is the oldest codified form of organic agricultural renewal, as it incorporates the whole farm, including all processing and handling. In 1994, Biodynamic was the first organic system to establish standards for processing. For more information, visit www.demeter.net.

Other national agricultural-control agencies. Many other national agricultural-control agencies have organic regulations. For instance, Argentina, Australia, the Czech Republic, Hungary, Israel, and Switzerland have regulations considered equivalent to or more stringent than the European Union's Regulation No. 2092/91.

CERTIFYING AGENCIES

Depending on the certification desired and the country in which the tea will be retailed, certification may be carried out by that government's regulatory agency, independent certification agents, or both. Some well-known certifying agencies whose logos you will also encounter in the marketplace include Switzerland's Institute for Marketecology, Germany's International Federation of Organic Agriculture Movements, California's Quality Assurance International, and California Certified Organic Farmers.

Switzerland: Institute for Marketecology (IMO). The IMO (headquartered in Weinfelden) is one of the first and most renowned international agencies for inspection, certification, and quality assurance of ecofriendly products. Its worldwide activities are accredited by the Swiss Accreditation Service (SAS) according to EN 45011 (ISO 65), the international standard for certification. The IMO offers certification for organic production and handling according to the European Union's Regulation No. 2092/91. It is also accredited by the USDA for organic certification under the National Organic Program and is licensed to provide JAS certification for the Japanese market. For more information visit the IMO online at www.imo.ch.

Germany: International Federation of Organic Agriculture Movements (IFOAM). IFOAM (based in Bonn) was founded in 1972, when the president of the French farmers organization Nature et Progrès put forward a worldwide call to ensure a future for organic agriculture. Progressive farmers from such diverse locales as Canada, England, France, Germany, and India became active. A decade later participation was initiated by farmers in the United States as well as by African proponents of organic agriculture. IFOAM also works with the Food and Agriculture Organization of the United Nations. Today IFOAM is influential in coordinating activities internationally regarding policy and practicality within the organic movement. One of IFOAM's founders, Eve Balfour, proposed that the characteristics of truly sustainable agriculture might be summed up as "permanence," an agricultural concept the world is once again embracing. For more information, visit IFOAM online at www.ifoam.org.

California: Quality Assurance International (QAI). Since 1989, the independent, third-party QAI certification program of organic food systems has been designed to certify every step of the organic chain: from the land on which the product is grown, to the producers growing the product, to the postharvest facilities preparing the product, to the processing and handling facilities transporting the product. Currently, the QAI (headquartered in San Diego) offers organic certification under the USDA NOP for producers, processors, private labelers, distributors, retailers, restaurants, wild crop harvesters, and food-crop greenhouses. According to the QAI, a nationwide independent shelf study found that two out of three certified organic products on U.S. store shelves use QAI certification services. For more, visit the QAI online at www.qai-inc.com.

California Certified Organic Farmers (CCOF). Headquartered in Santa Cruz, the CCOF primarily certifies to USDA NOP standards, offering its organic certification program throughout North and South America for food processors, farms, livestock operations, retailers, private labelers, and brokers. However, effective February 10, 2006, CCOF upgraded its international division, renaming it CCOF Global Market Access. CCOF offers a variety of services to ensure that products are recognized as organic throughout the world. CCOF is IFOAM-accredited and offers verification to the European Union's Regulation No. 2092/91 standard, Japan's Ministry of Agriculture, Forestry, and Fisheries (MAFF)–USDA export arrangement, and other national requirements in addition to its basis, the USDA certification program. For more information visit CCOF online at www.ccof.org.

Fair Trade

Similar to the origins of the organic movement, the concept of fair trade has at its roots several parallel organizations. These humanitarian and religious agencies desired to increase the economic viability of disadvantaged workers in some of the world's most impoverished regions, assist refugees to reenter society, and help others recover from various natural disasters.

Then, in 1968 the United Nations Conference on Trade and Development in Delhi communicated the message "trade not aid." Since that time fair trade has exploded. In 1973, Fair Trade Organisatie in the Netherlands imported the first fairly traded coffee from cooperatives of small farmers in Guatemala.

The concept of fair-trade coffee accounts for 25 to 50 percent of the turnover of fair-trade merchandise in Europe. Primarily because of the keen interest in fair-trade food items in the UK, the increase in fair-trade food products sold in Europe from the mid-1990s through 2003 and 2004, for example, has been phenomenal, with food items now constituting the bulk of the merchandise sold fair trade in Europe. In the United States coffee sales alone have altered the fair-trade category significantly, so now food sales have changed from being traditionally less than 10 percent to now representing more than 30 percent of the merchandise sold as fair trade. In the Pacific Rim, fair trade's biggest growth market in recent years, jewelry, crafts, and furniture comprise the bulk of sales, with food products still well under 10 percent of the total.

By the late 1980s and early 1990s fair trade had developed into an economic model defined and administered by several organizations, spearheaded by the "founding fathers" of fair trade—Fairtrade Labelling Organisation International (FLO-I), the International Federation for International Trade (IFAT), the Network of European World Shops (NEWS!), and the European Fair Trade Association (EFTA). In an effort to organize and streamline the efforts of the many agencies involved, these four key organizations banded together informally as FINE, an acronym based on the first letter of each group's name. For more information on these agencies, see www.eftafairtrade.org.

FAIR-TRADE STANDARDS

Next we explore what fair trade is and how it is administered, particularly in regard to tea. First and foremost, the core fair-trade food products are generally (but not always) certified, but only those that are certified may be labeled with one of the various official logos (marks). Nonfood merchandise is rarely regulated and never marked. For marked food items, standards needed to be generated, and these are at the core of the fair-trade position in the global grocery market.

Because the problems of agricultural producers and workers differ from product to product, there are two general standards—one for small farmers and one for workers. The first applies to smallholders organized in cooperatives, and the second applies to workers whose employers pay decent wages. Both standards stipulate that buyers must do the following:

- Pay a price to producers that will cover the costs of production and living expenses.

- Pay an additional premium that producers are expected to invest in development.

- Partially pay in advance, acting as creditor, when requested.

- Contract for long-term planning, as possible.

In addition, there are specific fair-trade standards for several products. The vast majority of tea is grown on sizable estates or gardens owned privately or by companies. Workers' concerns on tea plantations focus on fair wages and decent working conditions. For these workers as well as those in factories, there are minimum health, safety, and environmental standards. No child or forced labor is allowed.

For more on the FLO International's standards, go to www.fairtrade .net and search for "Generic Standards for Hired Labour Situations." For

TEA ESTATE WORKERS' WELFARE ISSUES

When the English controlled tea production in their colonies of Ceylon and India in the twentieth century, they created tea estates that often encompassed thousands of acres of land. These estates operated as self-sustaining social units and provided housing, food, schooling, and medical care for the tea workers and their families who lived on the estates. The rural and mountainous location of tea gardens often meant that no other work was available to the tea worker, creating a situation where the tea factory owners had the upper hand over the workers who were dependent on the tea estates for their existence.

Despite the fact that today India and Sri Lanka (Ceylon) have independence from English control, these countries still continue to operate the tea gardens under the English system of providing food and shelter for their workers. Only today, with the return of privatization and national pride, tea estates operate with the ethical awareness of the importance of the workers' lives and welfare as well as the interdependent contribution that each makes to the common good of the other. Social harmony is an important order of the day.

Workers are no longer treated as outsiders, and workers' concerns are addressed with conviction, not compulsion. In India governmental regulations require that the estates pay a living wage and provide workers with their basic needs of food, medical attention, and shelter. The most respected estates do more than that, however. They offer prenatal care, day-care centers, recreation centers, and training centers to provide education and skills that can bring people out of the tea gardens and into higher-paying computer and service jobs. Children are schooled until they are the legal age to work; child labor abuses are not part of the methodology of these tea estates.

For example, in Sri Lanka, the Bogawantalawa Estate is comprised of twenty-three sub-estates, eleven tea-processing factories, forty-five thousand acres of tea gardens, and more than sixteen thousand workers—a population that certainly qualifies as a small town. This estate is proud of the programs that it offers workers—savings and loans programs, libraries, computer learning centers, and mandatory schooling for children. No child labor is used. Scholarship programs are made available to deserving students.

more on their standards for the tea industry, go to www.fairtrade.net and search for "Product Standards for Hired Labour Situations."

FAIR-TRADE CERTIFIERS

Throughout Europe, Japan, North America, Mexico, Australia, and New Zealand, more than twenty national "Labelling Initiatives" have been established to monitor and personalize the general standards, so that unique situations relative to certain crops or working conditions can be included in their national regulations. FLO International is the most recognized fair-trade standard-setting organization. FLO International initially acted as the coordinating association for the Labelling Initiatives but in 2005 the Certification Unit of the FLO International became a limited company, now known as FLO-Cert Ltd.

FLO-Cert Ltd., as the umbrella organization now responsible for inspecting and certifying producers and trade for the twenty national initiatives, has been instrumental in generating the new blue and green common mark and has been phasing out most of the old marks, such as the various well-known national initiative versions of Max Havelaar, the original Fairtrade mark. By the end of 2005, FLO-Cert Ltd. was involved with the certification of more than a million producers, workers, and their dependants in fifty countries. As of the writing of this book, the FLO-Cert Ltd. mark is provided only to commodities, and only to those with origins in the Global South. All products that meet FLO Fairtrade standards must carry the newly designed Fairtrade mark. FLO-Cert Ltd. is also charged with guaranteeing that products sold under this new Fairtrade label conform to FLO International standards.

Due to the autonomy of the other early agencies, there are still several certification agencies around the world that monitor and may certify or grant permission to use one of the many official labels for fair-trade products. Fairtrade Foundation and Rättvisemarkt are two such agencies; Trans-Fair agencies monitor the United States, Canada, and Japan, but only food products. As has happened in the organic industry, organization has had its benefits and problems, but most observers feel that fair trade has benefited those for whom it was established. They believe that in general it is helping to provide better living conditions for some of the world's poorest workers and those suffering from various forms of marginalization. Fair-trade monitoring has been particularly valuable in increasing the awareness of women's value in the marketplace by ensuring equal pay and in protecting children's rights to education and limited work at a defined age requirement.

In the case of tea production many tea-growing countries instituted their own regulations regarding workplace standards and labor policy years ago. In Kenya, for instance, the government of Jomo Kenyatta gave all the land back to the people, and the government is now responsible for all education and the health care of tea workers. Under the Kenya Tea Development Authority money from fair-trade supplements cannot go to workers; rather, it must be reinvested in an estate's infrastructure. In fact, many fair-trade supplements in tea-producing regions are invested in physical operations because they cannot be legally provided to the workers as compensation, so fair-trade regulations don't always reach the goals intended.

One of the reasons that fair trade is able to continue is the commitment of the buying public to support it. The retail consumer has to be charged a premium to purchase the item being sold. The consumer pays directly for the costs of the economic model, by paying a higher fair-trade base price for the goods, plus the fair-trade premium that supports the fair-trade system. This is known as the direct-contribution system; however, fairly traded goods do not all employ this principle.

There is no validation system for nonfood goods; rather, merchandise is traditionally sold through "company stores" (such as Ten Thousand Villages), church groups, trunk sales, and so on. An honor system works for these goods, the majority of which come from village women working alone, in small groups, or from small entrepreneurial businesses that produce limited quantities of an item. According to the *Fair Trade Yearbook*, this works because "the very variety of handcrafted items are their strength . . . unique handcrafted items are not subject to direct comparisons with regard to price and performance." In the marketing of food products, the validation system of the identifying mark is of some assistance in identifying fair-trade goods, but there are many fairly traded food items that do not carry the mark and compete instead in the open market at competitive prices.

Ethical Tea Partnership

The Ethical Tea Partnership (ETP) is a positive example of industry leaders establishing a program by which the methods of tea production and the living conditions of its workers can be monitored and improved upon from within its own industry. Founded in 1997, the ETP is an international, non-commercial alliance based in Europe and North America, whose purpose is to independently monitor the life of tea workers worldwide. Beginning with Kenya, Malawi, northern India, Sri Lanka, Tanzania, Zimbabwe, and Indonesia, ETP monitoring now extends into Argentina, Brazil, China, and southern India. Funded completely by its members (who are leading tea packers), the ETP complements such groups as Fairtrade.

The key elements of ETP monitoring are openness and autonomy. When the independent ETP monitors from PriceWaterhouseCoopers visit a tea garden, they note both current conditions and changes from previous visits. Because they are familiar with local statutes, languages, and customs, these monitors evaluate and report on the conditions in the garden without prejudice. Usually visiting a garden for several days, they interview workers, managers, owners, and members of the community, who interact with those on the tea estate. There is no mandatory economic model, rigid certification standard, or cost to the tea garden, and there is no value-added mark that brings a higher price for the estate's tea production. The tea produced by an ETP estate competes in the marketplace along with the other tea from its region. Any increase in price that it might command is based on its higher quality and the reputation brought to it by having been grown under higher standards.

The goal of ETP is to continually improve the quality of the workplace so that the product's quality will also improve, so that tea buyers and ultimately tea drinkers will prefer to purchase tea from ethically sourced gardens. As there is no identifying logo allowed, the only way that the consumer knows of a tea's affiliation with ETP is that some packers promote the ETP by listing its Web address on a tea's package. Many bulk tea sellers also endorse the goals of the ETP, and in some cases they will identify a garden-specific tea as being monitored.

The tea industry has seen many changes throughout the decades, including adherence to many involuntary and voluntary regulations regarding production, distribution, and marketing, combined with the social and political upheavals of recent generations. As the world's tea drinkers become more familiar with an increased variety of types of tea, and learn about the natural history and methods of production of high-quality teas, improvements in both the quality of life for the workers and the tea itself will certainly continue.

CHAPTER 10

COOKING WITH TEA

IN CHINA TEA IS NOT CONSUMED WITH MEALS; rather, it is embraced as a thirst quencher and refresher before and after meals as well as for an energy boost throughout the day. In Japan, however, some teas, such as Konacha, are praised for their ability to harmonize and pair with strong-tasting or oily foods like raw fish. In India, Sri Lanka, Thailand, and Vietnam tea is consumed whenever the mood strikes, and a cup of spiced chai has been known to quell the fire of mouth-numbing, spicy-hot dishes.

Fragrant and versatile tea leaves are also often used in cooking, where the flavor of a particular style of leaf subtly complements and enhances the flavor of the food with which it is paired. Across Asia each spring, just as the previous year's supply of tea dwindles, a fresh crop of new leaves floods the market, when the annual tea harvest swings into production. In China, when newly emerging bamboo shoots begin to poke their heads above ground, for example, other seasonal greens and vegetables begin to reappear in the markets. This happy coincidence means that it is time to purchase new tea for sipping and to relegate what little remains of last year's tea supply for kitchen use.

Cooking with tea is both fun and easy. Think of tea as an ingredient— use green or oolong tea to create flavorful yet delicate infusions when poaching, steaming, braising, or marinating fish or shellfish. These teas are also useful in creating flavorful big-bowl noodle dishes. For marinating pork, beef, or chicken, use brewed black or oolong tea to add a flavor boost. Pluck the tea leaves from your teapot and finely chop them, then add as you would greens to rice dishes, stir-fries, or savory meat sauces. You might include tea leaves in your savory fillings for homemade dumplings. The flavor of tea never overpowers. It is a versatile seasoning that can also be used for adding a delicate hint of color to sauces, fruit desserts, and breakfast smoothies. Follow the Japanese example and add *matcha* powder for flavor and to bring about a bright, emerald-green color to cakes, cookies, puddings, and ice cream.

Tea is rich in healthful antioxidants as well as in vitamins A, B, E, and K. From these leaves we can obtain a wealth of minerals, such as chlorophyll, copper, fluoride, magnesium, phosphorus, and potassium. Vegetable soups and light broths can benefit from the subtle flavor that tea contributes; use brewed tea instead of water and you are building in flavor as well as adding vitamins and healthful antioxidants.

This chapter highlights some of our favorite recipes for cooking with tea. Enjoy!

SAVORY CHINESE MARBLED EGGS (CHA YE DAN)

MAKES 8 EGGS

8 large eggs

1 teaspoon plus ¹/₂ teaspoon coarse sea salt or kosher salt

18 points of star anise

2 sticks Ceylon cinnamon

2 large pieces dried mandarin orange, tangerine, or orange peel

12 whole black peppercorns

4 tablespoons Assam tea leaves (or other dark-liquoring and flavorful full-leaf tea)

2 tablespoons black soy sauce

1 or 2 slices crystallized ginger

6 Sichuan peppercorns

1 tablespoon sherry vinegar

These marvelous eggs are a staple at tea markets in China. We see them offered at breakfast or lunch or as a snack. The intensity of flavor and depth of color is controlled by the quantity of ingredients added to the steeping liquid, combined with the length of time that the eggs are left to steep. Our classic technique produces beautifully colored eggs and minimizes the green-ring effect that often appears around the yolk of hard-boiled eggs. The eggs must be left uncovered in the fridge for at least one week before use. This airing changes the chemistry of the eggshell lining and allows the shell to be shed without tearing the marbled finish.

These deliciously flavored eggs add a bit of zip to an appetizer plate or provide an exquisite garnish to either a green or composed salad. Although these are often served with beer in China, marbled eggs may also accompany a properly chilled Beaujolais or Provençal rosé or a toasty hot tea such as Longjing.

Place the eggs and 1 teaspoon of the salt in a heavy saucepan, large enough to hold the eggs in one layer. Add cold water to cover the eggs by 2 or 3 inches. Bring the water to a boil over high heat; then decrease the heat to low immediately and simmer uncovered for 20 minutes.

Drain the pan and quickly cool the eggs by either running cold tap water over them or placing them in a bowl of ice water. Let them sit in cold water until well cooled, about 20 minutes. (Quick cooling helps prevent a green ring from forming around the yolk.)

To make the marbling mixture, combine in a small bowl the star anise, cinnamon, orange peel, black peppercorns, tea leaves, soy sauce, remaining ¹/₂ teaspoon salt, ginger, Sichuan peppercorns, and sherry vinegar. Set aside.

One after the other, resting an egg in the palm of your hand, crack the outer shells by carefully tapping them with the back of a wooden spoon or rice paddle. This creates a weblike pattern in the shells that will color during steeping. Try to cover the eggshells with random cracking, but don't worry if there are large portions of solid shell, as these eggs will also look enticing.

Place the eggs in a nonstaining saucepot. Add the marbling mixture and about 3 cups of cold water to cover the eggs completely. Bring to a boil over high heat, then decrease the heat to low. Simmer, covered, for 3 hours, checking them occasionally to rearrange the eggs and spices for even cooking. Add water as necessary to maintain the liquid level.

Turn the heat off and let the eggs steep in the pot, covered, for at least 10 hours or up to 24 hours. Remove the eggs and discard the steeping liquid.

If serving the eggs at room temperature, peel them carefully to reveal the pattern and serve. Mound them up in a bowl, halve, and arrange them attractively yolk-side down on a platter, or quarter them to use as a garnish.

Peeled eggs will keep in the refrigerator in an airtight container for up to 5 days. Unpeeled eggs will keep in the refrigerator in an airtight container for up to 1 week.

CLAMS IN SWEET WHITE MISO AND GREEN TEA BROTH

SERVES 4

24 small to medium-sized Littleneck or Countneck clams

JAPANESE-STYLE RED PEPPER SPICE MIX

1 tablespoon black peppercorns

1 teaspoon coarse sea salt

1 tablespoon black sesame seeds

1 tablespoon brown or white sesame seeds

$^1/_2$ teaspoon cayenne pepper

$^1/_2$ teaspoon smoked Spanish paprika (preferably *agridulce*, or bittersweet)

BROTH

1 quart plus 1 quart water

4 tablespoons green tea leaves or 8 green tea teabags

8 tablespoons sweet white Japanese miso

1 (2-inch) knob gingerroot, peeled and finely grated

This easy-to-make soup is so delicious you will add it to your everyday repertoire. Create your own variations: instead of clams, substitute narrow strips of sweet white fish, or for an elegant flourish, butterfly two dozen shrimp and add them, tails attached, to the miso broth. Add a splash of color with finely shredded spinach or seaweed. Boost the aromatics with crisp, clean slices of fresh lemongrass. For a burst of flavor, finish the dish with a dash of the sassy Japanese-Style Red Pepper Spice Mix.

Wash the clams in a pan of cold, clean water. Scrub the shells and discard any that are cracked or gaping open. Change the water several times and leave the clams to soak for 10 minutes, to disgorge any remaining sand. Rinse the clams well and set aside to drain.

To make the Japanese-Style Red Pepper Spice Mix: Using a mortar and pestle, crush the black peppercorns until you have small, cracked pieces that are not too big but not yet powder. Add the sea salt and crush just a little. Add both types of sesame seeds and crush until they begin to lose their shape. Mix in the cayenne and the smoked paprika and combine well. Set aside.

To make the broth: In a kettle bring 1 quart of the water to a boil over high heat, then remove from the heat and let cool for 3 minutes. Place the loose tea leaves or teabags in a $1^1/_2$-quart saucepan. Pour the water over the tea leaves, cover with a clean kitchen towel, and brew for 2 minutes. If you are using loose tea leaves, strain the brewed tea into a saucepan. If you are using teabags, lift them out and press them gently against the side of the saucepan to drain before adding the brewed tea to the pan.

With the remaining 1 quart water, brew the same tea leaves a second time, using the method just described. Add this second infusion to the brewed tea in the pan. Add the miso to the brewed tea and mix well. The miso will separate. Add the gingerroot to the tea and miso mixture. Mix well and set aside.

Place the clams in a 4- or 6-quart saucepan or Dutch oven and add enough water to cover. Simmer, uncovered, over medium heat, then cover the pan and cook for 10 to 15 minutes, until all the clams have opened.

Using a slotted spoon, remove the clams from the pan. Drain the clams, then divide them among soup plates, being careful to not dislodge them from their shells. Stir the tea broth and ladle a generous amount over the clams. Scatter a sprinkling of red pepper spice over each dish and serve hot.

PINEAPPLE JEWEL RICE WITH SPICY SHRIMP

SERVES 4

- 3 cups uncooked Thai white sticky rice
- 1 cup Japanese rice vinegar
- 4 tablespoons toasted sesame oil
- 3 tablespoons hot chile paste
- 6 tablespoons peeled and chopped gingerroot
- Juice of 1 lime
- 2 pounds shrimp, peeled, deveined, and washed
- 1 can unsweetened coconut milk
- 1/4 cup packed light-brown sugar
- 4 tablespoons coarsely chopped wet pu-erh tea leaves
- 1 ripe pineapple, whole

In Xishuangbanna, the tropical region of southern Yunnan Province, the owner of a local restaurant presented us with one of his specialties—a fresh pineapple filled with fragrant sticky rice. The addition of pu-erh tea is our idea, a nod to the hill tribe people of Xishuangbanna and neighboring Myanmar, who have a history of "eating tea."

Preparing sticky rice requires a different method of cooking than other types of white rice. We find the natural sweetness and chewiness of sticky rice quite appealing. Thai sticky rice must soak for eight hours before cooking (although it may be steamed a day in advance; cover with plastic wrap and refrigerate until needed).

Be sure to read the entire recipe before starting. This recipe requires one whole day and multiple cooking techniques. None of it is difficult, however, and the results are incredibly tasty and beautiful.

Place the rice into a 2-quart saucepan. Cover with lukewarm water to 3 inches above the top of the rice and soak for 8 hours.

Drain the rice and rinse. Line a steamer basket with a double layer of cheesecloth and place the rice in the basket. Fill the bottom of a wok or steamer pan with boiling water and set the steamer basket on top. The rice should be suspended above the boiling water and not come into contact with it. Steam the rice for 45 minutes, or until the rice becomes opaque and sticky. Add more boiling water as needed during steaming to prevent the pan from drying out.

Preheat the oven to 350°F (177°C). In a small bowl, combine the rice vinegar, sesame oil, chile paste, gingerroot, and lime juice. Place the shrimp in a large bowl and add half of the marinade. Mix well to coat the shrimp. Cover with plastic wrap and refrigerate. Reserve the remaining marinade.

Heat the coconut milk to a simmer in a saucepan over medium heat until bubbling. Remove from the heat and add the light-brown sugar. Stir well to dissolve the sugar. Set the mixture aside to cool.

Place the cooked rice in a large bowl. Pour the coconut milk and sugar mixture over the rice and mix well. Add the chopped tea leaves and mix again.

Cut off the top and bottom of the pineapple with smooth, straight cuts, exposing the juicy, inner fruit. Carefully cut the pineapple in half lengthwise. Cut the fruit away from the shell of the pineapple (be careful not to damage the shell), leaving about $^1/_2$ inch of fruit attached to the shell. Set the shells aside. Cut the trimmed pineapple fruit in half again, lengthwise. Cut off the fibrous core and discard it, leaving 4 trimmed pieces of fruit. Finely chop to obtain 2 cups. Save any remaining fruit for garnish and snacking.

Drain the juice from the chopped pineapple, add the fruit to the rice mixture, and mix well. Spoon the rice mixture into the reserved pineapple shells, mounding it slightly. Place the filled pineapple shells in an ovenproof baking dish, cover with aluminum foil, and bake for 45 minutes, or until the rice is thoroughly heated. Remove the pineapple shells from the oven and set aside, covered, while you cook the shrimp.

Now set the oven temperature to broil. Remove the shrimp from the marinade, drain, and place on a lightly oiled broiler pan. Carefully broil the shrimp for 2 to 3 minutes per side, turning once, until evenly browned and slightly charred on both sides.

Place the broiled shrimp in a shallow bowl. Add half of the reserved marinade, mix well, and set aside. Uncover the pineapple shells and place them on a platter. Divide the rice among 4 plates and top with a serving of shrimp. Drizzle the remaining marinade over all and serve warm.

SHRIMP WITH LONGJING TEA

1 tablespoon Longjing tea leaves

1 cup water

2 tablespoons plus 1¹/₂ teaspoons cornstarch

2 teaspoons ground white pepper

1 pound medium shrimp, peeled, deveined, and rinsed

2 tablespoons plus 2 tablespoons peanut oil

2 tablespoons oyster sauce

1 teaspoon soy sauce

1 teaspoon sesame oil

1 tablespoon aged rice vinegar

2 ounces fresh snow peas, strings removed

2 ounces green beans, cut into 1-inch pieces on the diagonal

¹/₄ cup scallions, cut into ¹/₂-inch pieces on the diagonal

SERVES 4 TO 6

This specialty of the city of Hangzhou was created to feature that region's famous Longjing (Dragon Well) tea. The tea's slightly toasty flavor perfectly underscores the sweetness of the shrimp.

Place the tea leaves in a teapot or heatproof measuring cup. Bring the water to a boil over high heat, then remove from the heat and let cool for 3 minutes. Pour the water over the tea leaves and brew for 3 minutes. Strain and reserve the tea leaves and the brewed tea liquor for later use.

Place 2 tablespoons of the cornstarch on a plate and add the white pepper. Mix well. Pat the shrimp dry and roll them in the mixture one at a time. Set aside.

Heat a wok or skillet over medium heat for 1 minute. Add 2 table-spoons of the peanut oil and heat for an additional 30 seconds. Add the shrimp and stir to prevent sticking. Cook the shrimp for 2 minutes, or until they turn pink and opaque. Quickly remove from the pan and drain the shrimp on paper towels.

Mix the oyster sauce, soy sauce, sesame oil, and rice vinegar in a bowl and set aside. Add a few tablespoons of brewed tea to the remaining 1¹/₂ teaspoons cornstarch and stir to make a smooth paste. Add ¹/₂ cup of the brewed tea and stir to dissolve. Set aside.

Add the remaining 2 tablespoons peanut oil to the pan and heat on medium-high for 30 seconds. Add the snow peas and green beans and sauté for 2 minutes. Add the cooked shrimp and scallions and heat for 1 minute. Add the reserved tea leaves and the oyster sauce mixture. Heat for 1 minute. Finally, add the tea and cornstarch mixture and cook for 1 minute, adding a few tablespoons of water to the sauce if it becomes too thick. Serve hot.

INDIAN BLACK TEA, CORN, AND MUSHROOM SOUP

10 teaspoons (or 10 teabags) Assam black tea
leaves

2 tablespoons dry whole
green peppercorns

2 tablespoons whole
green cardamom
pods, crushed

1 (3-inch) knob of
gingerroot, peeled and
cut into thin slices

2 (5-inch) sticks Ceylon
cinnamon, broken
into pieces

4 whole star anise

10 cups water

2 teaspoons salt

3 ears sweet corn,
husked and washed

3 medium-sized
zucchini, washed and
trimmed

1 pound white mush-
rooms, washed and
cut into thin slices

1 large red pepper, cut
into thin 1- to 2-inch
slices

1 pound spinach,
washed, trimmed,
and finely chopped

1 lemon, seeded and
thinly sliced

SERVES 4

This flavorful and fat-free vegetarian soup features an infused tea–broth that is built on the strong, hearty flavor of Assam black tea. This recipe is very flexible, so use your favorite seasonal vegetables or add chunks of chicken or sliced scallops. Accompany with bowls of fragrant rice, which can be added to the soup if desired.

If using teabags, remove the string and tags. Make a cheesecloth bundle with the tea leaves, green peppercorns, cardamom, gingerroot, cinnamon, and star anise. Place the bundle in a stockpot with the water and bring to a boil.

Infuse the bundle for 4 minutes. Use a skimmer or small strainer to remove the cheesecloth bundle and discard. Add the salt and decrease the heat to low to keep the tea mixture warm.

Steam the sweet corn in a steamer or saucepan for 5 minutes. Place the corn on a cutting board and let cool for about 2 minutes. When cool enough to handle, cut each ear of corn into $1^1/_2$-inch-thick rounds and set aside. Cut each zucchini lengthwise into 4 pieces. Cut each quarter into $1^1/_2$-inch lengths using a diagonal cut.

Increase the tea mixture heat to medium and add the corn. Simmer for 5 minutes. Add the mushrooms and simmer for 5 minutes. Add the zucchini and the red pepper and simmer for 2 minutes. Finally, add the chopped spinach and the lemon slices and cook for an additional 2 minutes.

Ladle into bowls and serve hot.

SPICY OOLONG-SMOKED DUCK BREASTS

4 duck breasts

Salt

2 ounces (¹/₂ cup) Hairy Crab or Tieguanyin Fujian oolong tea leaves

3 teaspoons Sichuan peppercorns

1 (5-inch) stick Ceylon cinnamon, broken into small pieces

1 teaspoon white peppercorns, crushed

6 whole star anise

¹/₄ cup light-brown sugar

SERVES 4

These aromatic duck breasts are quite tasty. Leave the fat attached while you hot-smoke the breasts, but remove the fat before slicing. Use as a garnish for composed green salads, wild rice salads, or Asian noodle dishes.

Sprinkle the duck breasts lightly with salt. In a small bowl, combine the tea leaves, Sichuan peppercorns, cinnamon, white peppercorns, star anise, and brown sugar.

Line a wok or Dutch oven with tin foil and spread the tea and spice mixture on the tin foil. Fit the pan with a round rack that will elevate the duck breasts over the tea and spice mixture.

Place the duck breasts on the rack, fat side up, and cover the pan. Turn the heat to medium-high and after 2 or 3 minutes quickly lift the lid. The tea and spice mixture should be starting to smoke; if not, turn the heat up a little bit and check again in 1 or 2 minutes. Regulate the heat so that smoking occurs, but don't let the tea and spice mixture burn.

Smoke the duck breasts for 45 to 90 minutes, depending on the thickness of the meat. (Thick duck breasts, which are similar in size to large bone-in chicken thighs, take twice as long to smoke as thin breasts, which are the size of small boneless chicken breasts.) Fully cooked duck breasts should be ruddy golden-brown in color, glistening on the outside and pinkish in color inside when fully cooked. Use an instant-read cooking thermometer to check the progress of the duck breasts; fully cooked duck breasts should reach an internal temperature of 165°F (74°C) after resting for 4 to 5 minutes.

After the duck breasts have rested, cut them into thin slices, and serve immediately.

GREEN TEA POT DE CRÈME

MAKES 6 (4-OUNCE) PORTIONS

To elicit an Asian mood, bake this delicious dessert in shallow rice bowls or in an assortment of colorful and shapely handle-less Japanese teacups.

2 cups heavy cream

2 teaspoons pure vanilla extract

³/₄ cup sugar

Pinch of salt

1¹/₂ teaspoons matcha powder

6 egg yolks, beaten

Preheat the oven to 325°F (163°C). Bring 1 quart of water to a boil. Remove from the heat and set aside.

Place the cream in a heavy-bottomed saucepan over low heat. Scald the cream until bubbles form around the edges and it is heated through, about 5 minutes. Remove from the heat and stir in the vanilla extract.

In a small bowl, combine the sugar, salt, and matcha powder until well blended. Add this to the egg yolks and mix well. Add ¹/₄ cup of the hot cream to the egg mixture, whisking vigorously. Add another ¹/₄ cup of the cream and whisk again. Carefully pour this mixture and the remaining 1¹/₂ cups hot cream into a double-boiler or saucepan over medium heat and mix well. Cook for about 10 minutes, or until the custard is thick enough to coat the back of a spoon, at about 170°F (77°C). Be careful not to let the custard boil or it will curdle. Remove the custard from the heat and strain through a fine-mesh sieve into a large measuring cup.

Place 6 ramekins (or teacups or rice bowls) in an ovenproof baking dish and fill the ramekins three-quarters full with the custard mixture. Carefully pour the boiled water around the ramekins in the baking dish until the water rises three-quarters of the way up the sides of the ramekins. Cover the baking dish with aluminum foil and bake the custards for 25 to 30 minutes, until the edges of the custards are set and the tip of a knife inserted into the center of the custard comes out clean.

Place the custards on a cooling rack and loosely cover them with aluminum foil. Let them cool to room temperature, about 30 minutes. Refrigerate for 4 to 6 hours. Remove 30 minutes before serving.

GREEN TEA CHIFFON CAKE WITH WALNUTS AND CRYSTALLIZED GINGER

CAKE

2¹/₂ cups all-purpose flour

³/₄ cup plus ³/₄ cup granulated sugar

2 teaspoons double-acting baking powder

3 tablespoons matcha powder

¹/₂ cup chopped walnuts

3 ounces crystallized ginger, finely chopped

8 large eggs, separated

¹/₂ cup grapeseed or canola oil

³/₄ cup water

2 teaspoons lemon extract

Pinch of salt

SERVES 10

This lighter-than-air chiffon cake makes adults giddy with guilty pleasure. Perhaps it's because the impressive cake size makes us all feel like children again. Or maybe it's because the cake's light and delicate texture encourages us to take a larger-than-usual slice. The matcha powder tints the cake a lovely pale green color and the walnuts and crystallized ginger add a crunchy, snappy texture and flavor that is a playful contrast to the sweet, tender cake.

To make the cake: Preheat the oven to 350°F (177°C). Butter the inside of a tube pan and dust with a generous pinch of flour. Sift the flour into a mixing bowl. Measure out 2¹/₂ cups, then sift with ³/₄ cup of the sugar, the baking powder, and the matcha powder. Add the walnuts and crystallized ginger and mix well.

With an electric mixer beat the egg yolks with the oil, water, and lemon extract. Slowly add the flour in three batches and blend well. Place the egg whites in a dry mixing bowl and add the salt. Beat on low speed until frothy, then increase the speed to high until soft peaks form. Add the remaining ³/₄ cup sugar and beat until stiff and glossy peaks form. Gently fold the egg whites into the batter, incorporating just one-third of the egg whites at a time.

Carefully pour the batter into the tube pan. Gently tap the pan on a counter to level the contents and smooth the top of the batter. Place the cake in the oven and bake for about 1 hour, or until a knife inserted into the center of the cake comes out clean. While the cake is baking, make the glaze.

1¹/₂ cups powdered sugar

2 tablespoons freshly
squeezed lemon juice

1 tablespoon freshly
squeezed orange juice

1 teaspoon corn syrup

³/₄ teaspoon ground
ginger

1¹/₂ teaspoons peeled and
grated gingerroot

2 tablespoons finely
chopped crystallized
ginger

To make the glaze: Sift the powdered sugar into a small bowl. Add the lemon and orange juices and mix well using a whisk until it thickens into a glaze. Add the corn syrup and continue to mix. Add the ground ginger and the gingerroot, mixing well after each addition. Set aside and cover to prevent the surface from forming a crust.

When the cake is finished baking, set the pan on a cooling rack for about 20 minutes. Run a thin knife around the edge of the pan to loosen the cake, then turn the cake out onto the cooling rack. Turn it back over to right side up. Let the cake cool completely, about 30 minutes.

Spread the glaze over the top of the cake. Let it drizzle over the edges and down the sides of the cake. Sprinkle finely chopped crystallized ginger over the top. After the glaze has set, carefully place the cake on a platter and serve.

LAPSANG SOUCHONG AND JASMINE TEA ICE CREAM

SERVES 8 TO 10

This exotic combination of flavors appeals to those seeking something out of the ordinary in their ice cream. Fujian Province is the historical home of both smoky Lapsang Souchong tea and elegantly perfumed jasmine teas. We blended the two into a rich custard-based ice cream, and the result was provocative and wonderful. Let the flavors meld for a day before serving, and you will be richly rewarded.

3 tablespoons Fujian Lapsang Souchong tea leaves

3 tablespoons Fujian jasmine tea leaves

3 cups milk

1 cup light-brown sugar

1 cup heavy cream

8 large egg yolks, beaten

$^1/_4$ cup granulated sugar

2 teaspoons pure vanilla extract

Place the tea leaves, milk, light-brown sugar, and heavy cream in a saucepan over low heat. Simmer, uncovered, for 5 minutes, then remove from the heat. Let the tea leaves infuse in the milk and cream for 4 to 6 minutes. Strain the liquid into another saucepan and set aside.

Whisk the egg yolks until well blended. Add the granulated sugar and whisk until incorporated. Add $^1/_4$ cup of the hot tea, milk, and sugar mixture to the eggs, whisking vigorously to keep the eggs from curdling. Repeat this step, adding another $^1/_4$ cup of the mixture to the eggs.

Now add this egg mixture to the pan of remaining hot tea and milk and continue whisking to avoid curdling. When the mixture is well blended, carefully pour the mixture into a double-boiler or return the saucepan to the stove. Cook over low heat for about 10 minutes, stirring continuously, until the mixture is thick enough to coat the back of a spoon. Be careful not to let the custard boil or it will curdle.

Strain the hot mixture into a heatproof bowl and add the vanilla extract. Mix well. Allow the mixture to cool completely, about 20 minutes, then cover. Place in the refrigerator and let cool for at least 5 hours. After cooling, pour the mixture into an ice-cream maker and freeze according to the manufacturer's instructions. Transfer to an airtight container and store in the freezer for up to 4 days. Allow the ice cream to soften before serving.

WHITE TEA SNOW SORBET

1¹/₂ cups plus 2 cups
   cold water

2 cups sugar

¹/₂ ounce (14 grams)
   white tea leaves

Freshly squeezed juice of
  ¹/₂ lemon (or 1 lime)

MAKES ABOUT 1 QUART

This "snow" is excellent as either a dessert or a palate refresher between courses. This recipe is based on water, so if your tap water is not pure and good-tasting, use spring water. If you use a traditional budset white tea, this is a full ¹/₂ cup gently packed; if you use a new-style leaf white tea, this is a heaping, well-packed ¹/₂ cup (see "White Teas" in chapter 3 for information about the different types).

Garnish the sorbet with candied citrus peel, chopped crystallized ginger, a simple crisp cookie such as a crêpe dentelle, or a thin square of dark chocolate.

In a teakettle or saucepan over high heat, bring 1¹/₂ cups of the water to a boil, then remove from the heat and let cool to 165°F (74°C), about 7 minutes. Combine the remaining 2 cups water and the sugar in a heavy saucepan over medium-high heat. Bring to a boil and simmer gently, uncovered, for 1 to 2 minutes, to completely dissolve the sugar. Pour the mixture into a 1-quart measuring cup and set aside to cool.

Steep the tea leaves in the 165°F (74°C) water, covered, for 3 minutes. Pour the brewed tea liquor through a strainer, reserving it and the budsets or leaf tea, and let both rest for 1 to 2 minutes. Recombine the once-brewed tea liquor with the budsets or leaf and steep again, covered, for a full 5 minutes.

Strain the twice-brewed tea liquor into the sugar syrup, and stir in the lemon juice. Cover and let chill in the refrigerator for at least 4 hours or up to overnight. (Chilling longer than 4 hours improves the texture.)

Pour the mixture into an ice-cream maker and freeze according to the manufacturer's instructions. Serve immediately or transfer to an airtight container and store in the freezer for up to 3 days. This snow melts rapidly, so scoop and serve quickly in chilled bowls.

BUYER'S RESOURCES

The following big-league tea companies sell quality leaf and ship their products nationwide. But don't overlook local tea vendors. Search for one who stocks an excellent selection of carefully chosen tea and from whom you can learn about the subtleties of tea. Visit often and purchase a small quantity of every tea they sell. A good relationship with a local tea merchant is a valuable opportunity to taste a wide variety of tea and build tea knowledge, putting you on the fast track to experiencing their best teas as well as seasonal or rare teas when they arrive. For more on purchasing tea, see chapter 6.

Adagio Tea
1500 Main Avenue
Clifton, NJ 07011
www.adagio.com

Assam Tea Company
1829 28th Street North
St. Petersburg, FL 33713
727-327-9991
www.assamtea.biz

Barnes & Watson Fine Teas
270 S. Hanford Street
Seattle, WA 98134
206-625-9435
www.barnesandwatson.com

Cooks Shop Here
65 King Street
Northampton, MA 01060
866-584-5116
www.cooksshophere.com

Den's Tea
2291 W. 205th Street, Unit 101
Torrance, CA 90501
301-328-3336
www.denstea.com

Floating Leaves
2213 NW Market Street
Seattle, WA 98107
206-529-4268
www.floatingleaves.com

Grace Tea Ltd.
175 Fifth Avenue #810
New York, NY 10010
212-255-2935
www.gracetea.com

Harney and Sons Ltd.
PO Box 665
Salisbury, CT 06068
888-427-6398
www.harney.com

Harney and Sons Tasting Room
13 Main Street
Millerton, NY 12546
www.harney.com

The Highland Tea Company LLC
45 N. Fullerton Avenue, Suite 405
Montclair, NJ 07042
973-509-1669
www.highlandteacompany.com

Holy Mountain Trading Company
PO Box 12420
San Francisco, CA 94112–0420
888-832-8008
www.holymt.com

Ito En
822 Madison Avenue
New York, NY 11201
888-697-8003
www.itoen.com

Mark T. Wendell
50 Beharrell Street
PO Box 1312
West Concord, MA 01742
978-369-3709
www.marktwendell.com

Peet's Coffee and Tea
Available in company stores and specialty shops nationwide.
800-999-2132
www.peets.com

Perennial Tea Room
1910 Post Alley
Seattle, WA 98101
888-448-4054
www.perennialtearoom.com

Red & Green Company
1608 Harrison Street
San Francisco, CA 94103
415-626-1375
www.rngco.com

Rishi Tea
Available in specialty stores nationwide.
www.rishi-tea.com

Silk Road Teas
2980 Kerner Boulevard, Suite A
San Rafael, CA 94901
415-458-8624
www.silkroadteas.com

Simson & Vail
PO Box 765
3 Quarry Road
Brookfield, CT 06804
800-282-8327
www.svtea.com

The Stash Tea Company
PO Box 910
Portland, OR 97207
Available in specialty stores nationwide
800-826-4218
www.stashtea.com

Tea Circle
8657 Lancaster Drive
Rohnert Park, CA 94928
707-792-1946
www.tea-circle.com

Tea Trekker
65 King Street
Northampton, MA 01060
413-584-5116
www.teatrekker.com

Ten Ren Tea
Available in company stores nationwide.
800-650-1047
www.tenren.com

Upton Tea Imports
34-A Hayden Rowe Street
Hopkington, MA 01748
800-234-8327
www.uptontea.com

GLOSSARY

There are many descriptive and explanatory terms associated with tea. Starting with the manufactured leaf and moving right on through to the brewed beverage, this glossary takes a look at the terminology used to describe the various attributes of leaf, liquor, overall flavor, and aroma. Enologists have encouraged food enthusiasts to explore the world of vocabulary in the definition of fine wine; tea lovers have no less of a challenge—and an equal amount of fun describing the qualities of their favorite beverage.

CLASSIC LEAF STYLES (SHAPES) OF MANUFACTURED TEA (DRY LEAF)

White Tea
Traditional:
    Sword or bird-tongue (budset)
Modern:
    Sword or bird-tongue (budset)
    Open or leafy
    Flat or flaky

Yellow Tea
Sword or bird-tongue (budset)
Open or leafy

Green Tea
Sword or bird-tongue (budset)
Open or leafy
Flat or flaky
Twist
Spiral or crimped
Needle or wiry
Ball or rolled
Compressed

Oolong Tea
Open or leafy
Flat or flaky
Crimped
Ball-rolled

Black Tea
Twist or curly
Spiral or crimped
Needle or wiry
Ball or rolled
CTC (cut, torn, curled)
Granular
Fannings

Pu-erh Tea
Loose-leaf pu-erh
Twist
Needle or wiry
Compressed or packed pu-erh
Bricked or caked
Bowl or cup

TERMS USED TO DESCRIBE MANUFACTURED TEA (DRY LEAF)

Bloom. A leaf luster indicative of careful sorting and handling.

Clean. Leaf that is free of debris, odd-sized particles, excess dust, and so on.

Crepey. The crumpled appearance of well-made, large, broken-leaf tea.

Even/make/neat. Used interchangeably, these terms refer to tea that is consistent in size and correct to grade; indicates a well-made tea. Example: a properly made Darjeeling TGFOP would be described as "make" or "neat."

Grainy or granular. Properly-made CTC tea.

Musty. Can be a positive attribute in well-made pu-erhs and a few oolongs; more often, however, this is an off-taste that indicates improper drying and potential mildewing.

Nose. Aroma (smell) of the dry leaf; can only indicate smokiness; off-taste (tiredness); the intentional addition of a fragrance (as in flavored or scented teas); or contamination by a foreign smell (usually negative). Unlike the aromatics of brewed tea, which can afford a glimpse of the ultimate flavor profile of the brewed tea, smelling the dry leaf reveals very little.

Ragged/uneven. Uneven sorting or poor manufacture; the opposite of the term *even*, this is never a good attribute.

Tip (tippiness). Consisting of, or inclusion of, the budset during harvest; when appropriate, this is positive and an indication of a fine pluck; however, not all teas should be comprised of or have tip, so tippiness may indicate the inappropriate addition of purchased tips.

TERMS USED TO DESCRIBE THE TASTING QUALITIES OF BREWED TEA

Aroma. The scent released from the leaf as a result of the brewing process; a suggestion or preview of the combination of the brisk flavor components and the taste attributes inherent in the leaf being brewed. There are two types of aroma: the fresh, clean, or dull aspects that show style and quality of manufacture, and the floral, nutty, or grassy descriptors that correspond to the flavors that the palate will amplify.

Astringency. A sensation of drying felt throughout the mouth; similar to what mixologists refer to as "pull" (an essential quality in a great cocktail), this sensation is refreshing and satisfying, thirst quenching and stimulating all at the same time.

Bakey or baked. An overly fired leaf, not a positive toasty or smoky characteristic; a negative dry, overcooked taste.

Biscuity. An aromatic term used most often with black tea made from Assam bush, this is a positive attribute that indicates proper manufacture and the presence of the signature malty taste that Assam bush teas should possess.

Body. The sensation of viscosity on the palate, variously subcategorized as light, medium, or heavy, in reference to the concentration of heft as sensed by the sides of the tongue; also known as fullness; the opposite of the term *thin*.

Bolt, bolted, bolting. The phenomenon, common to modern Darjeelings and several astringent green teas, wherein the brisk flavor components suddenly overwhelm the body characteristics and the cup qualities become unpleasantly assertive and harsh.

Bright. Indicates a clean, clear style that refreshes the palate; the opposite term is *muddy*.

Brisk. Having an appropriate amount of astringency; a palate-stimulating brew that is not heavy and will readily accept the addition of dairy (if desired); brisk teas are of necessity well made; the opposite term is *soft*.

Burnt. Usually considered an off-taste, primarily the result of sloppy manufacture.

Character. A positive term that designates uniqueness of flavor due to *terroir* or style of manufacture; the opposite term is *common*.

Clean. Indicates purity of flavor and an absence of any off-tastes; the opposite term is *harsh*.

Coarse or uneven. An irregular tea, often a blend (mixture of batches) that doesn't unify properly.

Colory or coppery. Specific to black tea, most commonly used with orthodox leaf, a positive indicator of good pigmentation and general high-quality manufacture.

Common. Plain, timid, and not distinguished; could refer to a bad crop year, poor manufacture, or just a simple tea.

Creamy or creamed. Refers to the precipitate that forms when brewed tea cools; some teas cream more readily than others. An important factor in the marketing of liquid tea beverages.

Dull. May refer to a slightly muddy coloration, a flat taste, or both.

Earthy. A positive attribute in several fine varietals of green, oolong, and pu-erh teas, but the term can also indicate improper storage.

Flat. A generally unexciting, tedious brew; this can be caused by poor firing in the manufacture or from a tea's being old.

Fresh. Indicates a new-crop tea or proper storage of any tea; not a positive component of a tea that needs maturing.

Fruity or stone fruit. *Fruity* is a negative term in reference to black tea, as it indicates improper oxidation (firing); *stone fruit* is the customary positive descriptor for the aromatic quality of standard Formosa oolongs, as a familiar and engaging attribute.

Full. References a positive sensation of body and good heft; indicates a well-made tea.

Green. In reference to black tea that is usually a poorly made tea, hurried in the early processing so it tastes raw or underdeveloped; in green tea vernacular, *green* indicates a steamed leaf in the Japanese style and is good for the style.

Harsh. Generally negative, indicates hurried manufacture or poor-quality leaf; also sometimes used as the description for tea that has bolted during brewing; the opposite term is *clean*.

Heavy. The most extreme heft of body.

Light. The most minimal heft of body.

Metallic. Negative in most tea, shows particular soil influence or questionable storage, not usually derived from manufacture; some green teas show a metallic flavor component that can be positive.

Muddy. Showing an excess of particulate in the brew; a generally negative opacity that tends to dullness; may also refer to the cult-brewing style "tea latte" in which CTC tea is brewed "hard" with steam in an espresso machine.

Plain. A brew that is simple and clear but lacks character.

Pointy or point. The extreme of bright, a sharpness and piquancy that may be off-putting; an old-fashioned term used primarily in reference to black tea.

Pungent. References the stronger teas (more usually from the Assam bush) that possess an elevated level of the classic attributes of good black tea.

Raw. Similar to bitter and harsh; generally unpleasant; however, *raw* is also used to describe the most classic method of producing the compressed forms of pu-erh, such as *beeng cha* (in this case *raw* is used interchangeably with *green*).

Smoky or tarry. When intentional (as with Lapsang Souchong), this term refers to leaf that has been traditionally smoked over charcoal or green wood; when the leaf has not been deliberately smoked, a *smoky* taste is generally

the result of a flaw in manufacture (with a few provincial exceptions).

Soft. Smooth, lush, and subsequently often timid in flavor; not a negative term; the opposite term is *brisk*.

Stewed. An unpleasant characteristic usually caused by improper (imprecise) manufacture or the primary leaf being held too long before processing; indicates lackluster tea handling during manufacture; can also refer to leaf that has been steeped far too long.

Strength. That *je ne sais quoi* that references the totality of all the positive attributes of tea in the cup; the sum of the parts.

Tainted. An off-taste introduced to the brewed tea from either improper storage of the leaf adjacent to a strong odor, or water that has a bad taste.

"Tea." Refers to the flavor that one has in one's mind that a particular class of brewed tea should taste of—frequently a taste memory from the past; for Westerners it is often the basic flavor of a classic Ceylon tea, in East Asia it could be either *sencha* (in Japan) or Young Hyson (in Mainland China), and so on.

Thin. A generally negative term that indicates an overly light brew that lacks the expected character of a proper cup of tea; can also be tea that has been brewed incorrectly or intentionally diluted; more negative than mild.

Woody or weedy. A grassy taste that is undesirable in most white, oolong, and black teas but desirable in most green teas, some yellows, and a few raw pu-erhs.

FOOD ADJECTIVES USED TO DESCRIBE THE TASTING QUALITIES OF BREWED TEA

The Master List

Aromatic, Bold, Crisp, Floral, Grassy, Herbaceous, Kelpy, Lingering-finish, Malty, Mineral, Nutty, Piney, Short-finished, Smooth, Spicy, Sweet, Vegetal

DESCRIPTORS BY CLASS OF TEA

Below, for each class of tea, we list the general terms first and then the food adjectives. This list is general but accurate. You may find exceptions to the trends shown here, but so do we and that is the fun of tea!

White Tea Flavor (Taste) Components

White tea is undergoing constant redefinition. As it is described today, there are several flavor profiles that can apply, but in general white tea is smooth and mellow due to its light oxidation while it dries.

General terms
Body—full, Clean, Fresh, Full, Soft

Food adjectives
Floral, Short-finished, Smooth, Sweet

Yellow Tea Flavor (Taste) Components

Yellow tea is processed almost the same as is green tea, but an extra processing step mellows it out and changes its assertiveness. Yellow tea is still very rare and expensive due to a small yield.

General terms
Astringent, Body—medium, Bright, Brisk, Character, Clean, Fresh, Soft

Food adjectives
Aromatic, Short-finished, Smooth

Green Tea Flavor (Taste) Components

Of all the great classes of tea, green tea requires the most creative and descriptive set of terms for describing its flavor components. Because of the subtlety of a brewed cup of green tea, it is especially complex and fun to determine the appropriate adjectives to use. There are so many styles of green tea that this list is long, but because green teas differ in their processing, green teas can be as different one to another as they are from black teas.

General terms
Astringent, Body—varies from light to full, Bright, Brisk, Character, Clean, Earthy, Fresh, Full, Green, Soft, Strength, "Tea," Woody

Food adjectives
Aromatic, Bold, Crisp, Floral, Grassy, Herbaceous, Kelpy, Lingering-finish, Mineral, Nutty, Piney, Short-finished, Smooth, Spicy, Sweet, Vegetal

Oolong Tea Flavor (Taste) Components

With an even greater range of taste profiles than green teas, oolong teas have this potential because their oxidation can vary from 20 to 80 percent, the base leaf can be from so many different subvarieties of *Camellia sinensis*, and oolongs are traditionally infused many times. We limit this list to the classic flavor profiles.

General terms
Body—full, Bright, Brisk, Character, Clean, Earthy, Fresh, Full, Heavy, Light, Soft, Stone fruit, Strength

Food adjectives
Aromatic, Bold, Floral, Herbaceous, Lingering-finish, Mineral, Short-finished, Smooth, Sweet

Black Tea Flavor (Taste) Components

Black tea is the most common tea consumed in the West. It is often drunk with milk or sweetener. The flavors that you elicit from black tea will vary with the method of brewing and the water used. Experiment, experiment, experiment.

General terms
Astringent, Biscuity, Body—varies from light to full, Bright, Brisk, Character, Clean, Colory, Coppery, Full, Point, Pungent, Smoky, Soft, Strength, "Tea"

Food adjectives
Aromatic, Bold, Crisp, Lingering-finish, Malty, Nutty, Short-finished, Smooth, Spicy, Sweet

Pu-erh Tea Flavor (Taste) Components

Pu-erh, the only truly fermented tea, varies incredibly because of the existence of both loose-leaf and compressed styles, and its great variation in age. You will discover your own way with these teas. Pu-erh's flavor components are among the most exotic in the world of tea and are well worth exploring.

General terms
Biscuity, Body—full, Bright, Brisk, Character, Clean, Colory/coppery, Earthy, Fruity, Full, Heavy, Point, Pungent, Soft, Strength, Woody

Food adjectives
Aromatic, Floral, Herbaceous, Lingering-finish, Musty, Nutty, Short-finished, Smooth, Sweet

HUE TERMS USED TO DESCRIBE THE LIQUOR

The color of tea ranges from pale gold to dark purple-black. As one might imagine, dark, thick black and pu-erh teas brew the darkest color. Slender, needle-like black tea leaves produce red-hued coppery colors. Oolong teas from China are golden/greenish/blue, while Taiwanese oolongs tend toward tawny golden brown. Chinese green teas are light yellow or pale green, and Japanese green teas surprise with vivid yellow-green or emerald green colors. White tea has been likened to the clear color of the full moon.

The Master List: Color

Amber, Artichoke, Burnt sienna, Burnt umber, Copper, Forest, Golden, Pine, Russet, Silver, Straw, Wheat, Yellow

The Master List: Clarity

Bright, Clear, Dark, Matte, Medium, Opaque, Pale, Sparkling, Tinged copper, Tinged golden

White, Yellow, or Green Tea Color and Clarity Descriptors

Color

Amber, Artichoke, Forest, Golden, Pine, Russet, Silver, Straw, Wheat, Yellow

Clarity

Bright, Clear, Dark, Matte, Medium, Opaque, Pale, Sparkling, Tinged golden

Oolong Tea Color and Clarity Descriptors

Color

Amber, Burnt umber, Golden, Russet, Silver, Straw, Wheat, Yellow

Clarity

Bright, Clear, Dark, Matte, Medium, Opaque, Pale, Sparkling, Tinged copper, Tinged golden

Black and Pu-erh Tea Color and Clarity Descriptors

Color

Amber, Burnt sienna, Burnt umber, Copper, Golden, Russet

Clarity

Bright, Clear, Dark, Matte, Medium, Opaque, Sparkling, Tinged copper

BIBLIOGRAPHY

Avery, Martha. *The Tea Road: China and Russia Meet Across the Steppe.* Bejing, China: China Intercontinental Press, 2003.

Bliss, Marion. "Brewing Up the Latest Tea Research." *Agricultural Research Magazine,* United States Department of Agriculture, Agricultural Research Service (September 2003).

Blofeld, John. *The Chinese Art of Tea.* Boston: Shambhala Publications, 1997.

Breen, T. H. *The Marketplace of Revolution: How Consumer Politics Shaped American Independence.* New York: Oxford University Press, 2004.

Chen, Ke Lun. *Chinese Porcelain: Art, Elegance and Appreciation* (English edition). San Francisco: Long River Press, 2004.

Chow, Kit, and Ione Kramer. *All the Tea in China.* San Francisco: China Books and Periodicals, 1990.

Chuen, Lam Kam. *The Way of Tea.* Hauppauge, NY: Barron's, 2002.

Dattner, Christine. *The Book of Green Tea.* New York: Universe Publishing, 2002.

Emerson, Julie. *Coffee, Tea, and Chocolate Wares n the Collection of the Seattle Art Museum.* Seattle, WA: Seattle Art Museum, 1991.

Evans, John C. *Tea in China: The History of China's National Drink.* Westport, CT: Greenwood Press, 1992.

Faulkner, Rupert. *Tea East & West.* London: V&A Publications, 2003.

Gardella, Robert. *Harvesting Mountains: Fujian and the China Tea Trade, 1757–1937.* Berkeley, CA: University of California Press, 1994.

Gascoigne, Bamber. *The Dynasties of China.* New York: Carroll & Graf, 2003.

Goodwin, Jason. *The Gunpowder Gardens: Travels through India and China in Search of Tea.* London: Chatto & Windus, 1990.

Graham, Patricia J. *Tea of the Sages: The Art of Sencha.* Honolulu, HI: University of Hawai'i Press, 1998.

Hudgins, Sharon. "Raw Liver, Singed Sheep's Head, and Boiled Stomach Pudding: Encounters with Traditional Buriat Cuisine." *Sibirica,* vol. 3, no. 2 (October 2003): 131–152

Isao, Kumakura, and Marybeth Stock. *Flowers and Wagashi: Traditional Japanese Confections.* Tokyo: Toraya Confectionary Ltd., 1998.

Kuroda, Ryōji, and Takeshi Murayama. *Classic Stoneware of Japan: Shino and Oribe.* Tokyo: Kodansha International Ltd., 2002.

Lange, Amanda. *Chinese Export Art at Historic Deerfield.* Deerfield, MA: Historic Deerfield, 2005.

Lee, Ki Won, and Hyong Joo Lee. "Antioxidant Activity of Black Tea vs. Green Tea." *The Journal of Nutrition* 132 (April 2002): 785.

Leung, Lai Kwok, et al. "Theaflavins in Black Tea and Catechins in Green Tea Are Equally Effective Antioxidants." *The Journal of Nutrition* 131 (September 2001): 2248–2251

MacFarlane, Alan, and Iris MacFarlane. *The Empire of Tea.* Woodstock, NY: Overlook Press, 2004.

Mah, Adeline Yen. *Watching the Tree: A Chinese Daughter Reflects on Happiness, Tradition and Spiritual Wisdom.* New York: Broadway Books, 2001.

Maitland, Derek. *5,000 Years of Tea: A Pictorial Companion.* New York: Gallery Books, 1982.

Manchester, Carole. *Tea in the East.* New York: Hearst Books, 1996.

McKay, Diane L., and Jeffrey B. Blumberg. "The Role of Tea in Human Health: An Update." *Journal of the American College of Nutrition* vol. 21, no. 1 (2002): 1–13.

Mowry, Robert D. *Hare's Fur, Tortoise Shell, and Partridge Feathers: Chinese Brown-and-Black-Glazed Ceramics, 400–1400.* Cambridge, MA: Harvard University Art Museums, 1996.

Mueller, Shirley Maloney. "Seventeenth Century Chinese Export Teapots: Imagination and Diversity." *Orientations: The Magazine for Collectors and Connoisseurs of Asian Art,* October 2005: 59–65.

Okakura, Kakuzo. *The Book of Tea.* Tokyo: Kodansha International Ltd., 2005.

Paludan, Ann. *Chronicle of the Chinese Emperors: The Reign-by-Reign Record of the Rulers of Imperial China.* New York: Thames & Hudson, 1998.

Pan, Chunfang. *Yixing Pottery: The World in Chinese Tea Culture* (English edition). San Francisco: Long River Press, 2004.

Pasqualini, Dominique T., and Bruno Suet. *The Time of Tea.* Paris: Vilo Publishing International, 2002.

Pei, Fang Jing. *Treasures of the Chinese Scholar.* New York and Tokyo: Weatherhill, 1997.

Pos, Tania M. Buckrell. *Tea & Taste: The Visual Language of Tea.* Atglen, PA: Schiffer Publishing, 2004.

Quingzheng, Wang, Rosemary E. Scott, and Jennifer Chen. *Serene Pleasure: The Jinglexuan Collection of Chinese Ceramics.* Seattle, WA: Seattle Art Museum, 2001.

Riccardi, Victoria Abbott. *Untangling My Chopsticks: A Culinary Sojourn in Kyoto.* New York: Broadway, 2003.

Rosen, Diana. *The Book of Green Tea.* North Adams, MA: Storey Books, 1998.

Sadler, A. L. *Cha-No-Yu: The Japanese Tea Ceremony.* Boston: Tuttle Publishing, 2001.

Schapira, Joel, David Schapira, and Karl Shapira. *The Book of Coffee & Tea: A Guide to the Appreciation of Fine Coffees, Teas, and Herbal Beverages.* New York: St. Martin's Press, 1975.

Sensabaugh, David Ake. *The Scholar as Collector: Chinese Art at Yale*. New Haven, CT: Yale University Art Gallery, 2004.

Sheeks, Robert H. "Tea Bowls of the Himalayan and Mongolian Peoples." *Arts of Asia*, March/April 1992: 72–79.

Smith, Paul J. *Taxing Heaven's Storehouse: Horses, Bureaucrats, and the Destruction of the Sichuan Tea Industry, 1074–1224*. Cambridge, MA: Council on East Asian Studies, Harvard University, 1991.

Smith, Robert. "Whence the Samovar? " *Petits Propos Culinaires* 4 (February 1980): 57–72.

Soshitsu XV, Sen. *The Japanese Way of Tea from Its Origins in China to Sen Rikyu*. Honolulu, HI: University of Hawai'i Press, 1998.

Spiller, Gene A. *Caffeine*. Boca Raton, FL: CRC Press, 1998.

Stella, Alain. *Mariage Frères French Tea: Three Centuries of Savoir-Faire*. Paris: Flammarion, 2003.

Stella, Alain, Gilles Brochard, and Catherine Donzel. *The Book of Tea* (revised edition). Paris: Flammarion, 2005.

Stinchecum, Amanda Mayer. "Making Tea." *Saveur*, September/October 1994: 68–78.

———. "Steeped in Tea." *Saveur*, April/May 2003: 25–30.

Tokunaga, Mutsuko. *New Tastes in Green Tea: A Novel Flavor for Familiar Drinks, Dishes, and Desserts*. Tokyo, Japan: Kodansha International, 2004.

Ukers, William H. *All About Tea, Volumes I and II*. New York: Tea and Coffee Trade Journal, 1935.

Vitell, Bettina. *The World in a Bowl of Tea*. New York: HarperCollins, 1997.

Yu, Lu. *The Classic of Tea* (translated by Francis Ross Carpenter). Boston: Little, Brown and Company, 1974.

INDEX

Mozambique, 238

Mushanokojisenke, 323

Mushroom, Indian Black Tea, and Corn Soup, 387

N

Nagatani, Soen, 169

Nagi, Ken, 313

National Japanese Sencha Association, 330

National Organic Program (NOP), 367–68

Nepal, 234–38

Nepal Tea Planters Association (NTPA), 236

Nerchinsky Treaty, 210

NEWS! (Network of European World Shops), 373

New Zealand, 253

Nijiriguchi, 326

Nilgiri Biosphere Reserve, 204

Nilgiri Planters Association, 204, 206–7

Nilgiri tea, 203–7

Nuwara Eliya tea, 225, 266

O

Ogawa School, 330

Okawachi, Japan, 177

Omotesenke, 323

Oolong tea
    antioxidants in, 353–54
    Chinese, 142–49, 152–53, 156
    classic leaf styles of, 396
    color and clarity descriptors for, 402
    defined, 77, 80
    flavor (taste) components of, 401
    manufacture of, 77–83
    multiple infusions for, 81–82, 147, 288
    oxidation in, 82, 145
    South Asian, 83
    Spicy Oolong-Smoked Duck Breasts, 388
    steeping time for, 288
    storing, 280
    styles of, 83–84, 263–64
    Taiwanese, 216–20
    Thai, 250–51
    water temperature for brewing, 285

Opium Wars, 26

Organic tea production
    benefits of, 365–66
    categories of, 364–65
    certifying agencies for, 370–72
    standards for, 366–70

Oribe, Furuta, 314, 315, 316–17, 318

Oribe pottery, 316

Oriental Beauty, 158, 218–19

Orthodox tea
    grades of, 208
    manufacture of, 89–92, 207

Osmanthus-scented tea, 108

Oven-drying, 66–67

Oxidation
    in the body, 352
    in tea, 16, 51, 77, 82, 84, 90–92, 94–95

P

Paklum, 131

Pan-firing, 61–65, 190–91

Pan Long Yin Hao (Curled Dragon Silver Tips), 260

Panyang Congou, 129, 131

Panyaro, 190

Pearl-in-a-Shell, 273

Penn, William, 20

Peradeniya Botanical Gardens, 226, 228

Phoenix Mountain, 154–55, 156

Pi Lo Chun. See Green Snail Spring

Pineapple Jewel Rice with Spicy Shrimp, 384–85

Pingfang tea, 219

Polyphenols, 91, 351–52, 353

Porcelain. See Ceramics

Pot de Crème, Green Tea, 389

Presentation teas, 109, 273

Prices, 278–79, 280

Primary drying, 56–57

Puch'o-cha, 190–91

Pu-erh tea
    aged, 140, 141, 142
    antioxidants in, 353
    beeng cha, 96, 98–100
    classic leaf styles of, 396
    color and clarity descriptors for, 402

Yin Hao Jasmine, 103, 159

Yin Zhen Jasmine (Silver
Needles Jasmine), 102

Yixing teapots, 301, 306–8

Yoshimasa, Ashikaga, 166, 177,
314–15, 324

Yue ware, 188

Yumbu Lagang, 347

Yunnan province, China
black teas of, 136–37, 265
green teas of, 130
pu-erh teas of, 137–42
tea's origins in, 4, 6, 96

Yunomi chawan teacups, 319,
322

Yuto, 333

Z

Zaire, 238

Zambia, 238

Zao bei, 102, 160

Zao Bei Jian (Imperial
Sichuan), 135

Zen Shan Xiao Zhong, 133–35

Zhejiang province, China, 124,
130

Zhong Zi, 9

Zhu Ye Qing. *See* Bamboo Tips

Zimbabwe, 238

Zisha teapots, 302, 305, 306–8